The Way
Things Happen

The Way Things Happen

Ingaret Giffard

*'The art of letting things happen became
the key to me with which I was able to open
the ''Way'' to wholeness'.*

C. G. JUNG

William Morrow and Company Inc.

NEW YORK

Library of Congress Catalog Card Number: 89-62367

ISBN 0-688-09516-X

Printed in Great Britain
First US Edition
1 2 3 4 5 6 7 8 9 10
BOOK DESIGN BY HUMPHREY STONE

TO MY MOTHER,
OF WHOM THIS STORY IS TOLD
'AS A MEMORIAL TO HER'

There shall also this, that this woman
hath done, be told for a memorial of her
ST MATTHEW 26 v.13

Illustrations

Contents

PART I

Myself at the age of 11 or 12 in the woods by the Vicarage at East Farleigh, Kent.

1

By the Back Stairs Only

My mother's family upbringing was by no means unusual in England in
the second half of the nineteenth century. The aristocracy and what were
then called 'the upper classes' appear for the most part to have lived
their lives in complete outward obedience to certain rigid and generally
recognised codes of behaviour. But whereas the norms of social conduct
were everywhere taken for granted, awareness of human sensibility was
sadly lacking. In this respect my grandfather (my mother's father, whom
I can only dimly remember) was no exception. He had a large beard and
a large estate in the south of England, and he married twice. His first
wife bore him four children and then died. His second wife, my mother's
mother, produced twelve children. I remember her face as being very
pretty, lineless, and completely without expression. She always seemed
to be sitting in a large chair in some boudoir or drawing-room, her hands
folded in her lap and a lace cap upon her head. I can never remember
her either in movement or in authority, despite the sixteen young human
beings at large around her. The stepchildren, of course, were older and
so demanded from her only a limited response. But her own brood
surely called for personal attention – although, in fairness, that may
have been too much to expect, for my grandmother's energies must
have been almost totally engaged in the extended bodily processes of
giving birth. For this very reason, perhaps, personal intimacy between
parents and children seems not to have been common practice in those
days, and certainly not in the stratum of society to which my
grandparents belonged.

Accommodation for their many offspring was found in the top floors
of a Gloucestershire manor house, with day nurseries, night nurseries,
several individual bedrooms for the older children, and a bedroom each
for the nursing staff. Access to this other world of the nurseries was by
the back stairs only, which led down to the stone-floored kitchen quarters

3

and also up to the attic rooms in which the servants slept. On the ground floor of the Manor there was a green baize door which separated the kitchen quarters from the main entrance hall, as also from the drawing-rooms, dining-room, study, billiard rooms, gun rooms and so on. Food had to be brought by this route to the front of the house four times a day, but the green baize door worked on a self-shutting spring so that human segregation was complete.

One of the consequences of this segregation was that the upper floors were run entirely by nurses. They alone had complete authority over their charges. In human terms, the nurses were as little known to their employers as their charges were to the nurses. The only real communication in the Manor was between the kitchen staff and the nursing staff, and again only by way of the back stairs. Food for the nursery had to be brought up those well-scrubbed, winding wooden stairs three times a day, and doubtless it was accompanied by an endless stream of gossip. Conversations from the dining-room repeated by the parlourmaids, and certain oddities in the guests' behaviour must have given rise to some healthy gusts of laughter both on the back stairs and in the housekeeper's room below.

All too often, though, the top floors of the Manor did not resound with this healthy laughter. According to my mother, the best of the food brought up the back stairs was eaten by the nurses, and the children were all consistently undernourished. After supper, when baths and washing engaged the energies and attention of those in charge, one or other of the children, feeling both ravenous and reckless, would sometimes volunteer to creep down the back stairs in a secret attempt to raid the larder. Such a venture entailed not only tiptoeing down the creaking stairs but also waiting, crouched and trembling, hidden by the last bend in the stairs, for exactly the right moment before making the final dash to the larder and, with luck, seizing a loaf of bread. Then the return journey, equally fraught with danger, had to be negotiated. Sometimes, my mother told me, a successful snatch was achieved; more often, the hungry child was caught, brought back to the nursery and severely punished.

My mother was the eldest but one of this abandoned and battery-hen-produced family; she was also by far the most high-spirited and courageous and so, inevitably, the chief offender. Her punishment was always the same: confinement in complete darkness in a locked cupboard in one of the more distant bedrooms on the top nursery floor where her cries and bangings were out of earshot. However, when the moment came to count heads and beds, she would be remembered. She would

4

be unlocked, scolded, sometimes even whipped, and put to bed. There she would lie, empty in stomach but filled with a slow-dying and fluttering fear. Vainly she would try to remember the texts scattered round the nursery walls – 'God is love', 'Thou, God, seest me', 'Perfect love casteth out fear' – as she lay tense and sweating, until finally exhaustion triumphed and she slept.

At this period religion seemed to follow the same implacable pattern of remoteness from inner reality as did the life of the family, with its unawareness of the importance of personal communication. Religion meant going to church for Matins punctually at eleven o'clock on Sunday mornings. The village church was not far from the Manor, so my grandfather's copse was carefully cultivated to conceal it from view. This emphasised the sense of privilege and privacy of the Manor and also the remoteness of the one from the other. Nevertheless, as the church bells started pealing at 10.45 am the whole family (including my grandmother, unless she was yet again in an advanced state of pregnancy) would assemble in the main hall, gloved and hatted, and then follow my grandfather's lead as he walked slowly down towards the church along a neatly swept gravel path, bordered by lawns and flowerbeds all beautifully trimmed and weeded. After sedately crossing a small, arched wooden bridge over the stream that marked the borders of the southern end of the estate, the party would proceed along a path which led to a gate (unlocked by my grandfather) giving private access to the public and touching reality of the small country churchyard. Many of the villagers, gathered in the churchyard to await the family from 'the big house', would drop little bobs of respect as the large group passed by on its way to the porch. From there my grandfather led the way to the great front pew with his name on a card attached to it, reserved for him and the rest of the family. Even if none of them had appeared, I am sure no one else would have dared to occupy that pew.

Religion did not end with Sunday attendance at Matins. On every other day of the week the whole household gathered in the dining-room for early-morning prayers. The staff sat solemnly in a row on one side of the large dining table, paying subservient attention. On the other side, facing them, sat the sixteen children. My grandmother sat at one end of the great table and my grandfather at the other end, with the Bible and prayer book open before him. The Lord's Prayer came first, with participation from both the staff and the family. It so happened that my mother's immediate younger brother, Bertram, was afflicted with an appalling stammer. He was a beautiful little boy with fair hair, blue eyes and a highly sensitive and nervous disposition. That his son should have a stammer was both incomprehensible and unacceptable to my grandfather. There were times when, during the repeating of the Lord's Prayer, the sound of the quavering, stammering voice of Bertram was clearly audible, and my grandfather became so incensed by his young son's limping and uncertain contribution that, after the prayers and before the reading of the daily lesson from the Bible, he would give him a good clout on the head with it. Then, opening the Holy Book, he would find his marked place and begin to read. My mother who, because of her innate spirit of independence, had suffered even more cruel punishments in the nursery, never failed to be both disturbed and outraged by such events and their memories.

Whereas some people who have suffered cruelty or lack of love in childhood repeat the pattern of their deprivation with aggressive attitudes or behaviour in adult life, others, such as my mother, react in quite the opposite way. To the end of her days she was a fierce opponent of aggression of all kinds, whether it was a stranger hitting a small child, or a dog, in the street, or one of our nurses trying to lift my young brother into an over-hot bath. But while she was invincible in the defence of others, tragically she was never able to conquer the deeply-rooted and clearly irrational but dominating fears which had their origin in her childhood. With hindsight, I believe that, had there been just one human being in whom she could have confided, the pressures would have been lessened. For, as we know today, such stringent repression only adds to the power of demonic fears. But to whom could she have turned? Obviously not to her parents. Then what about her large family of sisters and brothers?

The eldest and first-born son, Donald, had turned out to be what, in those days, was called 'a bad lot' and was despatched to Canada. My mother's immediate elder sister Susan, with only one year between them, was a quiet and unobtrusive person with no particular claim to anything except a lifelong obsession with religion. Her imagination never extended to anything else, not even, it would seem, when, late in life, she married a parson and had two children. Next on the list came Bertram, the stammerer, who, my mother told me, as a little boy was always dressing up in sheets and playing at 'being a clergyman'. He grew up to be good-looking, popular and witty, and, despite his stammer, he did become a priest. Although Bertram was the member of my mother's family who became closest to her, perhaps his stammer made her shrink from burdening him further with her sorrows. Or perhaps she felt that, being such a convinced and devout believer, Bertram would view her 'irrational fears' either as a result of sin or a demonstration of a lack of true faith. Both are possible.

Following Bertram came Stella. By now my grandfather may have mellowed somewhat, for Stella was unquestionably his favourite daughter. He spoiled her, cosseted her and even dangled her on his knee. In this context, it is interesting to note that she alone of the family made a really happy marriage and, after her husband's death, she became a practising spiritualist. After Stella there were the twin girls, Olive and Violet, who, cocooned before birth by mutual love and dependence, maintained this relationship throughout their lives. Olive had an amusing and natural way with her, but Violet was submissive and quiet. Each was as unselfish as the other and, like the rest of the family, extremely 'religious'. Olive married and had two children, and both her home and her children were shared with an equally charitable love by Violet. By the time three more children were born to my grandparents – Colin, Stephen and Emily – the atmosphere at the Manor must have become much more relaxed and human. Instead of authoritarian nurses, these younger children had elder members of the same family to turn to for assistance. They also had an occasional governess.

Colin grew up to be an amusing and lovable character, enjoying society, gambling and horse-racing. His younger brother, Stephen, could not have been less like him. An intellectual (the only one in the family), highly strung and with strong socialistic leanings, he stuck out like a sore thumb in this ordinary family pattern. During the First World War he was sent to Ireland and had two serious nervous breakdowns which caused him to be posted home. As a very little girl I remember his returns. It was nice having an odd uncle who was only four years older than oneself! I think he was as fond of me as I was of him. Emily, the youngest, was only two years older than I, and although we shared certain adolescent jokes and intimacies, often with regard to 'men' and other such imponderables, Stephen was in fact the only one of my mother's family with whom I shared a close understanding.

Two further children were born to my grandmother. One was a boy called Martin, whom my mother, when a small girl, had seen floating in a pond in the Manor garden, drowned. He had been three years old at the time. The other child had either died at birth or been stillborn.

And then there were 'the steps', the children of my grandfather by his first marriage, who only came occasionally into my young life. The elder son I never knew because he had emigrated. But I do remember three tall, strong-minded women, all of whom had married and had children. They would sometimes 'come and stay' when members of the second family were in trouble. The eldest, Millicent, lived in India, where she was reputed to lead a very 'fast' life. The middle daughter, for some

7

reason, was called 'Auntie Dick'. And then there was Florence, who was less available to the second family. As a child I did not take greatly to 'the steps': they were too big and too bossy; and they were certainly not persons with whom my mother could have shared her inner difficulties.

It is possible that she would have found her disturbed fears easier to bear if she had had the same strong response to religion as most other members of the family. However, she alone of the family had a deep intuitive sense of reality. Like her sisters and stepsisters, she had had virtually no education, yet she would arrive, quite naturally, at the heart of a problem and would reach an individual and practical decision on it. So it may well be that the discrepancy between the early teaching that 'God is Love' and living a life with very little demonstration of that 'love', undermined her religious convictions. Yet religion, in its essence, meant a great deal to her.

The final circumstance that could have helped to alleviate my mother's suffering would, of course, have been a truly happy marriage. But, alas, that was not the way things worked out.

2

The Dream

Of my father's personal background I know very little. He had one brother, Charles, and one sister, Magdalen, both younger than he was. How they were brought up I have no idea beyond the fact that both he and his brother were never sent to school but were tutored at home in Devonshire. Then my father went to Oxford, took his law qualifications, and became a successful barrister. I have in my possession numerous prints of Oxford which he collected, so presumably Oxford was an experience on which he liked to look back. His brother qualified along the same lines, though less well, and then married Maggie his cook, or was she his housekeeper? Very occasionally, in early childhood, my brother and I were sent to stay a few days with them. Aunt Maggie was fat and kind and ignorant. I liked 'Syrup of Figs' and my brother liked Enos Fruit Salts because it fizzed, so every night we were allowed a dose of each as a treat. But we never stayed long enough for either to have very drastic effects! My Aunt Magdalen (who in the future was to play an important part in all our lives) married a clergyman who, at the time of their meeting, was a curate in a London parish. He had blue eyes, curly hair, and had apparently gained quite a reputation for the emotional power and attack of his sermons. My father's uncle was Lord Chancellor at this time, and so occupied the highest position in the British judiciary. Consequently, and perhaps questionably, after Aunt Magdalen's marriage her husband, Bernard, was appointed to one of the more attractive livings within the powers of the Crown.

It was some months after this that my father met my mother. He had come down from London to Gloucestershire to spend the weekend with cousins of his who lived at the Hall in a village a few miles from my mother's family home. One day my father was walking along the country lanes, perhaps for the sake of getting some healthy exercise, when he met my mother walking in the opposite direction. She was wearing a long skirt trimly belted at her slim waist, with her brown hair rolled up under a small white sailor hat. They passed each other without comment. Indeed, although my father was a stranger, it is possible that my mother did not even notice him. Be that as it may, my father, without doubt, fell deeply in love with her at first sight.

So, understandably, it was he who took the initiative. He left a visiting card at the Manor, and this was automatically reciprocated. Then the two parties called on each other and took tea. My father began to press his suit, and my mother's parents began to press for her acceptance of it. After all, she was the eldest but one in a large family and she was very beautiful. And there were four other daughters all of whom, somehow, had to be married off. And it had already been proved that none of them stood much of a chance while my mother was around. Already her natural gaiety, childlike nature and good looks had earned her some recognition in the county. A few male noses were on her scent, though of course from a very discreet distance. But when my father appeared my grandparents at once saw him as a serious proposition. He fulfilled all the conditions that the society of that period demanded. He was successful in an honourable and well-accepted profession, the law. His family was one of the oldest in the land: their name was even in the Domesday Book. They had always been Royalists and had held positions close to the throne; they could even count Sir Richard Grenville as one of their forebears. Further, there was in my father's possession a Bible given by Charles I to another of his ancestors for bravery in services rendered to the Crown. Amid these grandiose, heroic, and somewhat hysterical considerations, what was completely forgotten was that my mother had scarcely left the schoolroom. She was only seventeen years old and receiving no more than a penny a week for pocket-money!

There was no doubt that my father was most desperately in love with her. Having come across many snapshots of him with his direct but rather melancholy blue eyes, and his dolefully drooping walrus moustache, I cannot exactly see him as a powerful emissary of romantic love, but for my mother he had one great personal asset. Quite recently, as he admitted to her, he had been engaged to another girl; but the engagement had been broken by her and he had been jilted. This touched my mother's tender heart much more than all the aristocratic connections which, like coloured balloons, were popping and dipping round her head with every fresh breath of speech. She said to me once, 'He couldn't be let down twice . . . it seemed so unfair.' So they became engaged.

There was one incident of this time that my mother later recounted to me. It had happened after the public announcement of the engagement and when my mother was wearing the beautiful emerald and diamond engagement ring given to her by my father. One day, perhaps sensing her lack of worldly knowledge, my father somewhat diffidently asked her:

'Do you, my darling, know how babies are born?'

She stared at him, perplexed, and shook her head.

He turned away and then said slowly, 'Perhaps you should have a little talk with your mother about it?'

'Very well,' she replied, rather mystified by the whole idea.

But the next day my father had changed his mind. 'Perhaps, on second thoughts, you should not mention what we talked about to your mother,' he said.

Loving her so deeply, he probably hoped that he would have the honour of initiating her successfully into physical love. Or did he fear that through knowledge of the biological facts he might lose her? My own view is that up to this point my father himself had never, physically, known a woman. His cloistered boyhood and adolescence had been an entirely enclosed experience. Then, when he was old enough to go to Oxford, he had not only had to meet the open world for the first time, but had also had to work extremely hard to get a good enough degree to establish himself as a wage-earner and a man of position. This he did. But I suspect that, partly because of his high moral attitudes, his intellectual success at Oxford may have been achieved through the exclusion of many of the more human aspects of a young man's life.

My father and my mother were married from the Manor in Gloucestershire. I have a photograph of my mother in her wedding dress; she is looking directly into the camera with complete simplicity and composure. I think the honeymoon was spent at a resort on the south coast, perhaps Bournemouth, or Hastings, or Eastbourne, all of which were very popular at that time.

After her death I came upon my mother's old diary of this period and I opened it hoping to find something revealing in it. But nothing personal was disclosed. So what had made my mother write a diary at all? It was unlike her. She was not scholarly. Was it perhaps at my father's suggestion? Or did she embark on it feeling that she was beginning a new life and was now an important person? Or perhaps writing a diary was just something to do on her honeymoon.

One small but significant incident should be mentioned here. Much later in life, my elderly mother and I were talking about my going to see the opening performance of a new play. My mother's mind was arrested by the phrase 'first night' and she said, as if to herself, and in a rather

11

My mother on her wedding day.

wandering way, 'Oh, that first night . . . I crouched in a corner . . . clutching my nightgown round me . . . and crying out "Not tonight! Not tonight! Not tonight!" ' It was the only time she ever mentioned this intimate subject either to me or, I am sure, to anyone else.

On returning from their honeymoon, my parents went to the house that my father had taken for them on a long lease. It was a smallish but charming house (which I can dimly remember) standing deeply in the country south of London, but big enough to accommodate a family, together with a nurse, cook, house/parlourmaid, or whatever staff should prove necessary. It took a little time for the whispering to start. 'Whatever's happened to Ellen?' . . . 'She's quite changed' . . . 'So quiet now'. And then, later on, 'No sign of a family yet?' . . . 'Extraordinary' . . . 'Perhaps he?' . . . 'Or she?' And then, 'She's a completely different girl' . . . 'But she's not ill, exactly, is she?'

I think it was the older and more sophisticated 'steps' who started these well-founded rumours. At this period they came down occasionally to stay with my mother in her new home 'for company' when my father was on circuit, or had to spend the night in London. And the rumours were both right and wrong. My mother *was* 'a completely different girl' but she was also very sick – though not in the commonly accepted sense of the word. Sadly, in those days, mental illness was something about which the medical profession knew very little, and ordinary people even less, so states of psychological tension and conflict could only proclaim themselves openly through some 'physical illness'. Consequently, the only means available to my mother of relieving her inner tensions was by giving them physical expression, and she did just that.

Those around her continued to ask themselves – and each other – what could account for this great change in my mother. She seemed to have no energy available, and would spend every afternoon 'resting' on her bed; it was as if she had lost her love of life. My mother herself remained absolutely silent on the subject. She was like a big registered parcel sealed at both ends; and nothing and no one could break the seals. No communication was possible. Her beauty remained, but it too, somehow, was frozen.

But, inevitably, the return home meant a return to the old problems. And, on one occasion, it was a return to a new problem. In her absence, my father had taken to sleeping with a loaded revolver under his pillow. This terrified my mother. She pleaded with my father to get rid of the revolver, but he persisted in the practice as if of necessity. And my mother continued to lie taut and wakeful through the nights of terror.

I once asked my mother, 'Were you afraid you'd shoot him?'

13

She looked first horrified and then very sad. 'Oh no,' she replied quietly, 'I was afraid I would shoot myself.'

So what of this strange ritual of my father's which continued despite my mother's pleadings? My father was not a man who was lacking either in character, courage or physical strength. With hindsight, and with modern knowledge, I have sometimes thought that for him the loaded pistol must have served as a sexual symbol. Even the shape of a revolver is suggestive of this. Was the pistol some form of reassurance to my father of his own masculine sexual prowess? Or a defence against the lack of it? It is impossible to say.

After a few more months of marriage, my mother was still not pregnant. How could this be explained? My father, who longed passionately for a son and heir to his inheritance, must have felt rather desperate. And my mother, without doubt, was caught up in a situation which was driving her into a condition of dangerously controlled irrationality.

So the second round of whispers started. 'Something's gone very wrong' . . . 'What can it be?' . . . 'Why on earth isn't Ellen having a baby?' The problem of possible infertility had come out into the open.

I don't know whether it was my father, with his London connections, or one of 'the steps' who first heard tell of a doctor (a woman, but famous nevertheless) who dealt with such female complications. My mother received this news without interest or understanding. But my father made an appointment for my mother to see this doctor, booked her into the doctor's nursing home in London and no doubt accompanied her there before he himself went off to his Chambers.

Once inside the nursing home the problem was quickly tackled. My mother, trembling with horror, was told that she must have an immediate internal examination. She was laid flat and then her legs were strung up high above her. The reason for her infertility was soon discovered: the hymen had never been broken. So, briskly, with a knife, the skin was cut. What should have naturally surrendered itself to love was crudely but expertly cut by a surgical instrument. Then a greased and shaped thick glass cube was stuck into the opening to the womb to keep the entry free, and the flesh from shrinking. To the doctor it was a very simple minor operation. To my mother, without any understanding or explanation, the examination and its follow-up were horrifying, humiliating, and very painful. A few days later, with the glass cube still in position and the wound scarcely healed, my mother was told to get dressed; then she was put in a cab and sent to the station to bump her way home painfully on the train. No provision had been made for the after-effects of such an operation on a young girl. On arriving home, my mother stumbled up the stairs, got into her dressing-gown and collapsed on her bed. There she spent the rest of a painful afternoon alone.

That evening, when my father arrived back from London, he picked up the letters lying waiting for him on the silver salver in the hall. These included one from his sister Magdalen. It should be explained here that my father's family were greatly given to squabbling. They wrote letter after letter to each other ranting, railing, and complaining and, according to my mother, all about nothing. But the disagreeable family atmosphere had always affected her. On the day of her return from the nursing home the letter from Aunt Magdalen was of such a negative character that my father, after he had opened it, remained standing in the hall reading and rereading it with mounting anger. Hearing the front door open and shut, followed by complete silence, my mother struggled from her bed, pulled her dressing-gown round herself and made her way uncertainly to the top of the stairs. My father, his face red with fury, raised his eyes, saw her, and cried out, 'Listen to this! Just listen to this!' He then proceeded to shout aloud the torrent of abuse that he had just received from his sister by post.

It is difficult to explain exactly what happened to my mother at this moment. In her own words, an overpowering negative force roused by my father's angrily shouting the contents of the letter up to her struck at her inner being like a flash of lightning. Unable to bear any more, she opened her mouth and screamed and kept on screaming, as if unable to tolerate one single further word, or even thought, of hate. Hearing her own involuntary and continuing screams, even she herself did not know what had happened, or realise that she was in a state of shock after the callous proceedings at the nursing home. She thought she was going mad. My father thought she had gone mad. He ran up the stairs to her, but the screaming didn't cease. He picked her up and laid her back on the bed and tried to steady her . . . and at last succeeded as the screams turned to sobbing.

That was the end of my mother's pretence of having any inner freedom. The screams were her final agonised protest against psychological slavery. Fear she had always known: it had been kneaded into her system from birth like great lumps of undigested dough, and it had remained in lumps, sometimes swelling up, sometimes for short periods seeming almost to disappear. But at this dangerous and vulnerable moment after the hymen operation, she had been totally exposed. Terror, instead of being a lump in her inner being, alternating both in size and seriousness, had, in a moment, become a cancerous growth which was never again to leave her mind at peace.

Some months later she became pregnant. Everyone, I suppose, drew a breath of relief: life was continuing its normal course. My father was obviously delighted, hoping for a son. My mother, too, I think was very glad. She had always loved children, namely her young brothers and sisters. To have a child of her own would mean that she would never again be quite alone. But of one thing I am sure there can be no doubt: I was conceived in terror.

I have never forgotten an incident which occurred shortly before my mother's death as a very old lady. During the latter years of her life I spent every possible weekend with her in her house in Surrey. As usual, at breakfast-time, I went into her bedroom. She was sitting propped up on pillows in her bed. She was still beautiful. Her hair was white, as also were her teeth. Her complexion was clear; her eyes very blue. But they were looking puzzled.

'Darling, I had such a strange dream last night,' she said slowly.

I should explain at this point that in her latter years my mother was greatly helped by two Jungian analysts, Dr Godwin Baynes and Dr Alan McGlashan. She also discussed many of her dreams with me, and I had become interested in them. For both of us dreams were of great importance.

So I asked my mother quietly, 'What was the dream about, darling?'

Thinking back, she said slowly, 'I was sitting in a garden and a gardener was working nearby. There was a nest of flying ants quite near us and he was vigorously stamping them all to death. I felt rather distressed by this, so I asked him why he was doing it. He replied, "This lot were neither the creative nor the fertile species, lady, but the next lot that comes will be." '

We had both accepted that 'people' in dreams almost invariably represented aspects of the dreamer. This is why, in interpreting a dream, one asks the dreamer for his associations with the figures in the dream. Accordingly, I asked her, 'How would you describe a gardener, darling?'

'Well, he's a man who grows things, of course. He plants for the coming seasons . . . that's his real job . . . besides tidying up . . . they all belong together,' she replied.

'So the gardener in your dream would seem to be a positive figure?' I suggested.

We agreed on that. However, not feeling fully satisfied, I went to look up 'flying ants' in the dictionary. I discovered, to my amazement, that the generic name for flying ants was 'hymenoptera'.

I went back to my mother and very gently began to question her.

'You've always told me that your obsessive fears became increasingly dominant immediately after you'd had your hymen operation . . . in fact, at the very moment when you stood on the stairs and screamed and screamed – is that correct, darling?'

A shadow passed over her face but she nodded.

I took her hand and said very slowly, 'Let's go back to your dream.' I paused. 'The generic name for flying ants is hymen-opt-era.' I paused, having spaced the words to make the meaning more apparent. Then I continued quietly, 'So you see what the dream is telling you? A strong creative side of yourself, represented by the gardener, is stamping out all the flying ants in a certain nest. When you ask him why he is doing this he says, "I'm doing it because this lot are not the fertile creative species . . . the next lot will be . . . but I must get rid of these first." '

My mother hesitated. 'You mean the next lot will represent the creative aspects in me?'

'That is what the dream would seem to be saying,' I replied.

She was very quiet for a moment and then said, 'Tell me again . . . what was that word?'

'Hymen-opt-era,' I repeated gently.

She lay very still for quite a while with a look of wonder on her face. Then she smiled and with complete acceptance and understanding said, 'How wonderful.'

A few weeks later, very peacefully, she died in her sleep.

It is strange that, even today, there are still those of us who are unaware of, or even deny, the existence of some timeless 'force' available, presumably, to all of us? It is, as I have been made to understand from my own experiences, a force with which we can communicate and which also has the power to communicate with us. I use the word 'force' for the following reason.

Looking back on my life and pondering deeply about this, many years after my mother's death, I was asking myself whether, faced with the curious synchronicity of certain events, one was justified in continuing to call them 'mere coincidences'? I was perplexed in my mind on this point. It was just at this time of deeply felt inquiry that I received a letter from someone who was quite unknown to me, asking if she could come and see me. The writer of the letter turned out to be a famous archaeologist. She came to my house in London, walked into my study and put down a manuscript on my desk entitled 'Notes on a Dialogue'. The title interested me. I leaned over and read the opening sentence: 'There is a force available to man which is inaccessible to man's intellectual capacities.'

17

I was quite amazed: those words seemed to have been plucked straight out of my own mind. I sat down with my visitor and we spent a most interesting morning together. As she was leaving she said, 'We must try to get nearer to this force: make it more specific, give it a name.'

I hesitated, and then disagreed. 'I don't want to give it a name,' I said. 'We can imprison the imponderables when we give them names. Take "God", for instance. I drop a valuable bit of china and break it and I say, "Oh, my God". In that way, in a word, I not only misrepresent God but by doing so I put Him in prison. That is why I like your reference to a force that is unavailable to the intellectuality of man. I don't want to go beyond that point. I just want to be able to recognise that force . . . and honour it. I think that puts us in our place,' I added, 'and it also leaves the imponderables free.'

She said, 'You mean that sometimes by knowing more we can in fact know less?'

'Something like that,' I replied. 'I want to maintain, perhaps increase, my awareness of this force. Beyond that, nothing more.'

I think we parted as friends who had agreed to differ.

3

'Troubled Bricks'

My father died when I was six years old. But three years after my birth my mother had another child, a son, Roger — which gave my father a great personal sense of joy and achievement. Telegrams were despatched to one or two parishes in the neighbourhood of his family home in Devonshire, ordering the church bells to peal proclaiming the important fact that another male descendant of our ancient lineage had been born. I am glad that my father had his lifetime's wish granted before his death. It would appear that, from early childhood, his life had been very confused and unfulfilled. Just before he died he said to my mother, 'I've been a hard husband . . .' Had he? Perhaps. But life had been hard on him, too. I remember nothing personal about him except, occasionally, after his daily return from London, playing 'bears' with him under a big, woolly hearthrug, and being very excited and happy at the fun. I am told, too, that once as a very small child, coming into the dining-room for breakfast, I announced importantly, 'Daddy, last night I had a dream about an angel', to which my father replied gruffly, 'Now, I don't want any of that morbid nonsense down here, please.'

Until I was about ten there was a photograph of my dead father hanging over my bed. I liked having it there. I used to kneel on the bed and stare at it for long periods. I remember coming down one morning in tears and saying, 'Oh, Mummy, I miss my Daddy . . . I miss him.' Then I wept passionately. So it was thought wise to remove the photograph of the moustached gentleman staring straight out at me with direct, sad eyes. Did I miss him? Have I always missed him? Can one miss someone that one knows only from snapshots and snap judgments? I suppose he was a severe man. When I was five or six years old he refused to allow me to go to dancing classes with other children of a similar age. He considered dancing to be immoral! But, despite his refusal, my mother took me to the classes. She told me, often, that she nearly wept because

19

I was the only one in the class who didn't know what a skipping-rope was for and couldn't manage to jump either over it or under it. However, I made up for that in later life! But what sort of 'later life' would I have had if my father had still been alive? Could he ever have understood my passion for personal freedom which would have cut straight across his own conception of how a young girl should behave, just as it cut across that of my contemporaries?

After my father's death, the position of my mother and we two children was discovered to be highly precarious. In the euphoria surrounding my mother's marriage, all practical details for the future seem to have been overlooked. I am told that my father had suggested drawing up a marriage settlement, an idea which my grandfather shrugged off as being totally unnecessary. However, before his marriage my father had taken out a life insurance policy and, consequently, on his death we did come in for a very small, steady income of about £300 per annum. My mother was also left with the long lease of our country home, in which, of course, we could no longer afford to live. The landlord tried to squeeze her both legally and financially, but my mother, unexpectedly, stood firm. She flatly refused to take any financial responsibilities for the lease, telling the landlord to refer any legal difficulties to her uncle by marriage, the then Lord Chancellor. The connection worked like magic, not only in this but in other ways also. My great-uncle was a darling old man. I remember that whenever we met him he gave both Roger and myself a golden sovereign. Had he known of our precarious financial situation and realised that a golden handshake would have been more appropriate, I am sure he would have come to our help.

Immediately after my father's death all the antique furniture and silver was put into store. When my father had been on circuit he had built up a valuable collection of antiques. Among his possessions was a very old family screen which he had searched for and finally unearthed in the stables attached to an ancient farmhouse which had, at one time, belonged to our family. This oak screen not only had peep-holes through which the servants could peer to see whether the roasted boar was cooked; it was decorated with original paintings of all the family marriages in the West Country over the past five hundred years. My father was told by experts in London that there were many church screens of a similar type, but that this was the only manor house screen of which they had any record.

Having disposed of the lease of our house, we were not only homeless but also purposeless. Fortunately, some of my father's relatives came forward, as did some of my mother's old friends, and we were all three 'invited to stay'. So for the next few years no less than three wonderful country houses were open to us as 'home'. The grandest of these was the turreted Court in Gloucestershire, which my mother had known since childhood. The owners, now an elderly couple, were still living in this castellated house and had three grown-up, unmarried daughters who occasionally visited them. Their son was a permanent resident and it was he who ran the estate. Roger and I loved staying there. It was like living in a picture postcard! The house with its grey turrets even looked like a castle, and beyond the gradual slope of the wide lawns there was a lake with a tiny island in it, on which nested moorhens and ducks who were in constant, enthralling movement over the water. There was also an old punt moored to the bank. My mother was very firm about the punt, which was only to be used when she was with us. We always obeyed her without question. She rarely said 'No' and, when she did, always explained to us fully the reasons for it. She spoke to us as if we, too, would see the point. And so naturally we did.

Happily, people seemed to like having us to stay. My mother, outwardly, was young and good company. And, indeed, her newly-found independence had somewhat helped her. She was now responsible for us; and that was worth a fight. Sometimes we would hear our hosts say to her, 'The children are no trouble', which puzzled me a lot. What was there to be troubled about?

True, when staying at the Court there were some little difficulties that I had to get over. For a start, when we came down to breakfast in the vast dining-room I, being a girl, had to climb on to a chair and kiss my elderly host 'good morning' . . . and my host had a very long and speckly grey-and-white beard seemingly all over his lower face. Roger, being a boy, was let off this particular greeting. Then sometimes we were both taken for 'an afternoon drive' with our host and his wife, and once or twice, as a special treat, either my brother or I was hoisted up to sit beside the coachman. And it *was* a treat sitting in such a special place high above the world, but there was a drawback too – the habit which the horse in front of me had of lifting up its tail, making quite a few rude noises in the process, and then dropping its 'Number Two', as it was called in the nursery, on to the road. This, together with the smell, made me feel terribly shy. I didn't know where to look. Certainly not at the coachman. So I would stare away to the left over the hedges until I could be sure that the whole performance was over. Then I would once again turn back and listen to the steady sound of the horse's hooves on the country lane, the jingling of the bits, and watch the quick sensitive pricking of the horse's ears at any new sound or sight in the hedges.

21

There was one real horror within our 'castle' that Roger and I had to live with. We had found out that our hosts also had a daughter who was both deaf and dumb. She was 'hidden' somewhere in the Court but we never quite discovered where. Nor did we want to, for we were terrified by the strange, mad noise that could occasionally be heard coming from the upper bedroom floor. It was neither a shout nor a scream; it was neither a woman's voice nor a man's. It was a very loud animal sound as if someone, or something, was making a furious effort to speak. This noise was often accompanied by the sound of bangings and breakings of various objects on the floor above us.

On these occasions Roger and I would run away as fast as possible, and there were plenty of places to run to. The bracken-covered hill at the back of the Court was our favourite place of refuge. We would scramble up it, panting. As small children we did most things together and I, being the elder, was both leader and protector. However, although our true affection remained unchanged, as we grew older our differences in temperament became much more apparent. Roger was an extravert and at the same time a good deal more conservative than I was. He excelled at every kind of sport. I, on the contrary, was much more introverted and, from an early age, read every book I could lay my hands on. Also I always questioned the accepted 'normalities'. A small incident perhaps illustrates these differences between us. Roger, who had always wanted to go into the Navy, had gone to the Royal Naval College at Osborne on the Isle of Wight at the usual age of eleven or twelve. During his first holiday he told me that he had been made to run, stripped to the waist, between two rows of boys who, armed with wet towels, whipped him as he ran by. Osborne in those days was renowned for its bullying.

When Roger told me about this I was both horrified and outraged.

'But what had you done?' I cried, almost in tears.

Roger shrugged. 'Nothing,' he said. 'It was someone else who'd done it.'

My whole world seemed to collapse. 'But that's so unfair!' I cried. 'It's wicked – '

My brother merely laughed. 'Oh, somebody had to get a wigging,' he said. 'It didn't really matter who'd done it.'

I was completely silenced. I can still remember how, at his words, a totally new concept of life seemed to slip into position. Looking back, I think his attitude was the more mature. At the time, I had been deeply affected by his unjust treatment, whereas he had merely dismissed it with a shrug of his shoulders.

*

The second 'home' that was open to us was my father's cousins' house in Kent, but although we were always welcome we didn't go there often, nor did we stay long. It was a nice house but somehow a feeling of great sadness hung over it. Edwina and Edgar, by now middle-aged, had been deeply in love and had married despite the fact that they were first cousins. Cousin Edwina was very deaf and, probably because of her deafness, she was extremely absent-minded. She and her husband also had a house in London. Rumour had it that, at a rather grand dinner party they were giving in the town house, my cousin Edwina came down to greet her guests clad only in a long petticoat and a camisole! She had great character and individuality, so I don't think the incident would have dismayed her.

But, although she and Edgar adored each other and there was no shortage of money, they longed for only one thing, a child. They must have spent thousands of pounds touring the world trying to find some medical assistance in this matter. But they had no success. I think it was this deep sense of deprivation in both cousins that gave the house its atmosphere of melancholy. Cousin Edgar shouting down the long table to Edwina, and she replying in the oddly accented speech of the almost totally deaf, was disturbing to witness. Nevertheless Edwina maintained her intelligence and her dry sense of humour. Much later in life, when I had 'come out', it was decided that I should be presented at Court and that Cousin Edwina should accompany me. Accordingly I was sent to classes to be taught how to do a Court curtsey, and she and I finally joined the queue of carriages and chauffeured motorcars in the Mall, all waiting for entry to Buckingham Palace.

Once we were gathered together in the Grand Hall, my cousin Edwina looked round the crowded assembly of youthful, white-clad figures, all wearing three nodding feathers attached to their beautifully dressed heads. Leaning towards me she said in what she believed to be a hushed whisper but which was, in fact, a resonant and penetrating utterance: 'This place looks like a cross between a chicken-run and a confirmation service!' The remark echoed loudly through the Grand Hall and there was an instant flutter of hundreds of feathers turning and bobbing in our direction. My cousin, of course, remained sublimely unaware of the reason for this concentration of attention upon us. And I, happily, instead of losing my nerve at the sudden focusing of all eyes upon us, was hard put to it to suppress what, in the circumstances, could only have been described as ribald laughter.

The clergyman husband of my father's sister, Magdalen, now had a living in Kent and, of the three 'homes' at our disposal after my father's death, the Vicarage became our most constant refuge. It stood high on a hill with a fine view over the surrounding hop-fields right down to the river in the lower valley. Beyond the river one could see the uprising of the green fields opposite. We would arrive by train at a station in the valley, to be met by the pony-trap in which we were driven slowly and steeply up from the river level, past an inn and a tiny shop (which was called the village), then up a longer and less steep hill which led directly to the open white gates of the Vicarage. The drive itself was long and winding, with thick undergrowth on either side of it and tall trees locked together above our heads hiding the sky. For us, it was like an exciting secret tunnel. Then we would round a last bend, come out from under the trees, and see the large rambling Vicarage ahead, with a broad gravel sweep before it large enough to facilitate the easy turn of a trap, or a carriage, or in later days, a motorcar.

It was at this point that the whole haphazard beauty of the Vicarage garden was revealed. While far from being a scene from a picture postcard, to us as children this garden became profoundly personal. Immediately facing the entrance to the Vicarage stood a large tulip tree, its curved branches elegantly trailing almost to the ground. Beyond it lay dipping green lawns, each carrying in its curved bosom a buttonhole of many-coloured rosebushes. The garden itself was bordered by a closely-wooded and darkly mysterious copse. It was thickly carpeted with strong and dusty ivy clambering over large stones and disguising hidden dells. One's foothold therefore was uncertain, which made the copse all the more exciting to explore. There were trees of many varieties growing there and marking the borderline between the Vicarage and the lane without.

Aunt Magdalen and Uncle Bernard had had no children, though they had been married shortly before my father married my mother. I remember that Aunt Magdalen slept in the big bed in the largest bedroom while Uncle Bernard slept in the adjoining dressing-room. For some reason there was always a huge Great Dane sleeping outside the two bedroom doors. My mother once told me that Aunt Magdalen had said that 'having no children was not her fault', whatever that meant. She and Aunt Magdalen became very close and easy companions. My aunt was highly intelligent and very humorous. She was tall and rather thin, with a long face, an aquiline nose and very blue eyes, and wore her greying hair screwed up untidily in a knot in her neck. Somehow, even in a dirty old skirt and a rough well-worn cardigan and wellington boots, she managed to look distinguished. Little as Aunt Magdalen cared about her appearance, she did most passionately care about animals. This, of course, was another delight for Roger and me. There were always three large dogs about: the Great Dane that was kept in the stables by day, a collie, and a smaller dog that lived in the house – as well as three cats, curled up here, there and everywhere, purring and rubbing themselves against our legs. There was a parrot in the dining-room, its piercing shrieks and chatter drowning the continual grumbling of my father's mother who lived with Aunt Magdalen and Uncle Bernard. When the parrot was let out of its cage I was always frightened, but invariably it would make straight for Roger and perch on his shoulder, and he didn't seem to mind.

Outside, the stables were our nearest and most enthralling playground. Here there was the pig, Clara Butt, unfailingly grunting and routing in the filth of her sty. There were Dartmoor ponies in the paddock, and a donkey munching at the clover. There was also a goat who was tethered on the lawns by a very long rope, so that we had to take care to be well out of range of a horned attack. Then there was the pump in the stableyard whose function was explained by a notice pinned on the bathroom wall, written in my aunt's hand, saying: 'Please save the water, it all has to be pumped up by hand.'

For every day spent at the Vicarage there was much truly natural life for us to learn to understand, to enjoy, and in which to participate. Looking back, I think these immediate contacts with nature must have been of great and enduring importance for both Roger and me. They must, in measure, have helped to compensate for all that was *not* natural about life at the Vicarage.

My mother never forgot a small incident which occurred on our first arrival there, soon after my father's death. We had all scrambled out of the pony-trap and turned to walk up the three shallow curved steps that led to the large oak front door of the Vicarage. As I mounted the first step I suddenly paused, took my mother's hand and held it tightly.

'Mummy,' I said, 'this house is built of troubled bricks.'

It was, perhaps, an odd remark for a child of six to make. But what was truly strange was that it proved to be an accurate forecast of disturbing events that were to occur at the Vicarage, first to my mother, then to me, and finally to my young brother.

4

The Voice

For the next few years we continued this spasmodic and nomadic existence: 'staying away', as it was called. Sometimes we stayed in lodgings, but always, at the back of our minds, was the knowledge that, in an emergency, a telegram to Aunt Magdalen would secure us a welcome harbourage. I think Aunt Magdalen must have had a pretty lonely existence. Her personality was larger than life-size. It just didn't fit in with village parochial commitments.

Aunt Magdalen was at her best during the hop-picking season. This was in late summer when an odd assortment of people, mainly from the slums of the East End of London, came down into the Kentish fields to pick the hops. They slept in caravans, or weatherproof sacks, and picked from daybreak until daylight faded; or perhaps I should say until the pub opened. We children would then scurry past the lighted windows and the open pub doors where the Cockney crowds were gathered outside, men and women together, all with their glasses of beer raised in their hands and frequently shouting and fighting among themselves, but always accompanied by roars of raucous laughter. Most of the women wore battered old hats on their heads, skewered down by hat-pins, against the sun's heat. Once they had a few pints inside them the hat-pins would come out and some rare old fights would begin.

It was at this point that my Aunt Magdalen used to stroll down the long hill from the Vicarage and first stand and watch, then mingle with the fighting ladies. In her long, well-worn old skirt and shabby jersey she herself looked rather like a hop-picker . . . until she spoke, which resulted in a momentary silence of assessment before the drunken brawling broke out once more. This was Aunt Magdalen's moment. Quietly, and quite fearlessly, she would push her way into the midst of the grappling ladies, give one of them a surprisingly hard smack on the

26

cheek and then, in the subsequent pause of surprise, with an easy grin she would snatch the hat-pin from the aggressor, make some wry remark, and hand the hat-pin back to its astonished owner. In this way she turned herself from an enemy into an accomplice and took the charge out of the aggression. Aunt Magdalen had a very dry sense of humour somewhat similar to that of the Cockneys, and they were quick to spot it and appreciate it. They saw instantly that this odd 'lady' had something going for her and consequently also for them. So, as the hop-picking season progressed, Aunt Magdalen's appearance outside the pub, sometimes with a dog or two, sometimes on her own, would be received with rousing cheers, some drunken and some sober.

Uncle Bernard was rarely at home, except when writing his weekly sermon. He had his own 'interests'. So, at Aunt Magdalen's invitation, we lived more and more at the Vicarage. The nursery suite was always ready for us: up two steps from the main landing and tucked into its own corner in the large Vicarage. It was composed of a large night nursery where my mother and I slept, a large day nursery with a communicating door in which Roger slept, and our own bathroom and lavatory. The beds were kept aired, and the fires laid, in readiness for our arrivals, whether expected or not. The day nursery had a huge brass fender which stood before the crackling wood fire, and in front of it was a hip-bath in which, in the early days, Roger and I, in turns, both took our baths, with my mother in supervision. This we simply loved. Yes, looking back, of all our 'homes' this was the best; and it felt like a real one.

Then, when I was about ten years old, someone called 'Uncle Harry' died. He was a connection of my father's but we had never heard of him until then. In his will he left my 'father's widow' four thousand pounds. He had only seen her once, but my mother must have made a great impression on him. The money came at a timely moment, for the problem of 'education' was rearing its ugly head. We could both of us read and write, climb trees, and were at home with animals, but there was not much else that we could do. So my mother used some of the money to acquire a short lease on a small house within walking distance of central Folkestone.

At about this time my mother's health deteriorated badly. This may have been due to the emotional conflict resulting from the long periods spent either at, or away from, the Vicarage. Or perhaps the responsibility of running a small house and educating two young children, on a minimal income and with a world war looking increasingly likely, became too much for her. I suspect it was the former, but in any event, in our own little semi-detached house standing in a row with other similar semi-detacheds, I became aware as never before of my mother's inner tensions. She had managed to find us a small co-educational school in Folkestone to and from which, with a Miss Byford who was to become our dear friend and domestic help, we would take the one-mile walk in all weathers. Every day before setting off I would slip into my mother's still darkened bedroom, and in one glance I knew whether it was, for her, a 'good' day or a 'bad' day. If it were the latter, I would take off my slippers and creep about the house with my fingers to my lips to warn everyone concerned as to how my mother was feeling.

Matters being thus, and probably on Miss Byford's advice (our friend and helper later became matron of a hospital), my mother found herself a doctor. He attended her quite frequently, always bringing with him a tape-measure. Finally he decided that one of my mother's legs was longer than the other! This, according to the doctor, threw her bodily balance out of true and led to attacks of giddiness and depression. It sounded plausible, and surely a tape-measure could not lie? All too often in those days the symptoms of an illness were looked upon as the illness itself.

So a bathchair was hired and my beautiful young mother was helped into it and we took her, almost every fine weekend, for an outing along The Leas at Folkestone. From there she could both see the sea and sometimes hear the military band playing on the seafront. I can remember the hat that my mother wore on these occasions: it was blue and had two big feathers, one blue and the other mauve, slanting backwards and moving in the sea breezes. It sounds ghastly, but in fact she looked most striking in it, though far too young and beautiful to be confined to a bathchair.

The school in Folkestone that my mother had found for us proved to be a lucky choice. There were about thirty pupils, both boys and girls, and the school was run by two very intelligent and devout sisters, the Misses Hull. The elder sister did most of the household duties, for, when called upon, the Misses Hull also took in a few boarders. And there were occasions when Roger and I went to them as boarders.

The first of these was shortly after we had joined the school, when my mother, exhausted after buying our new house, getting the furniture out of store, measuring up for curtains, and settling us in, with Miss Byford's help, went to the Vicarage for a week's rest.

It felt strange being right in the middle of busy Folkestone, instead of in one of the quieter outlying districts. In fact, on our very first evening as boarders I saw long queues of people waiting in the streets to buy editions of the evening newspaper. 'What's happened?' I asked wonderingly, as I watched these queues lengthening.

'They are waiting to read the casualty lists,' explained the elder Miss Hull. She never lied to anyone. 'We are now at war with Germany . . . and those people want to read the latest news.'

Only now did this new shadow creep over our lives. I went to bed in a sober mood. Then, with the darkness, the shadow deepened . . . for, at about four o'clock in the morning, I was wakened suddenly by the sound of – of what? I scrambled out of bed and went to the window. I had been awakened by the sound of marching feet: hundreds and hundreds of khaki-clad figures, carrying rifles, were marching down our empty residential street towards the sea and the harbour. They were marching in perfect unison, headed by an officer looking directly before him. It was at that moment that the First World War became a living reality to me. From then on, every morning when I heard, or was woken by, those marching feet, I would leave my warm bed and stand watching them. It became a kind of ritual. The linoleum under my feet was cold and I became very cold also; but not until the last khaki-clad soldier had vanished round the bend in the road would I even contemplate turning my back on them and returning to bed.

The reality of war was enhanced when an increasing number of wounded soldiers began to emerge from the hospitals and fill the streets of Folkestone. Some were without a leg, or legs; some had lost an arm, or a hand, or even eyes; and these latter had to be carefully led by a wounded comrade. Others had their heads wrapped in bandages or supported themselves on crutches. But they could, and did, still talk . . . and even occasionally laugh . . . and they were all dressed in the same bright blue uniform which denoted the war-wounded.

These blue-clad figures touched me deeply. History lessons had taught me that countries had 'gone to war' against each other; and then one side or the other had won. But nothing had prepared me for these horrors. Could grown-up people really do things like this to each other? Then suddenly I had a bright idea. I would write a play, perform it at our little school, ask all the parents to come and pay a few pennies for their tickets and then, with the proceeds, I would hire a charabanc and send a group of wounded soldiers in it to spend a whole day in the lily woods. There was a lovely wood near Folkestone where, in the spring, the lilies grew wild and the sight of them was miraculously beautiful – or so I had thought on my one school visit there.

No sooner thought than done. I wrote a play with the leading character (based on my great-uncle) being the Lord Chancellor of England, plus one or two supporting parts. Roger was to play the part of the Lord Chancellor – but Roger's becoming word-perfect was quite another matter! I had to bully him unmercifully to make him concentrate. Eventually a date was fixed, parents were invited and came to see the 'play' which was performed in the school. The proceeds added up to thirty shillings – enough in those days to hire a charabanc and send thirty wounded soldiers to spend a whole day, and I hoped a happy day, in the lily woods!

At this period, new feelings of all kinds were awakening in me. There was a boy at our school, Pat, who was the son of a well-known woman novelist. This made him very glamorous to me; particularly as I had read all his mother's books. He was a year or so older than me, slight, good-looking and high-spirited. And suddenly I found that I could be high-spirited too! Often, before a meal, I would sit close to the fire and burn one of my cheeks a bright pink and then sit next to Pat with the 'pretty' pink cheek on his side. I would even race with him along the rough ground near the beach at Folkestone and fall down on purpose so that Pat would have to come and pull me up! Up to this moment my life had been a rather serious and inwardly solitary affair, so all this was quite a new experience for me.

Both the Misses Hull were dedicated Anglicans. Therefore Roger and I were initiated into a form of worship unlike any that we had previously known. On Sunday the Misses Hull and their boarders walked in crocodile formation down to the beautiful old parish church of Folkestone. There, to my amazement, we were directed into the choir-stalls to be seated in the front row! The choir of men and boys was behind us, maintaining the music and song, but I scarcely noticed them. We were right up close to the altar with its rich brocades and lighted candles. We were enveloped by a mysterious smell and the sound of sacred music. I was completely awed by the magical atmosphere inside the church. I suppose one could call it the marriage of reverence and ritual? Previously, church had been something that one 'did' on Sunday. Now it became something one could also feel; and so, presumably, need never lose? Consequently, after some months of attendance at the Holy Eucharist at Folkestone Parish Church, religion took on a new importance for me. More than anything else I wanted to be confirmed and so be able to go up to the altar and kneel before it as other people did.

But there was much opposition to this idea.

'Confirmed? At eleven years old! Ridiculous!' Aunt Magdalen wrote. I think, looking back, that she had become disillusioned with religion.

Even my mother was uncertain. 'You're very young, darling,' she used to say. 'It's such a serious thing to do.'

That, of course, I knew. That was why I persisted so stubbornly with the idea.

The Misses Hull were entirely on my side, and, with their support, the matter was finally arranged. I could not go to the parish church to take my confirmation classes; it was too far away. So, during termtime, I attended classes given by the Canon in the rather 'low' church nearby. I remember only two things that I was taught in these classes. First, that on the day of my confirmation the Holy Dove would come down to me from Heaven. Secondly, I was told that as I knelt before the Bishop and he put his hand on my head and blessed me I would, miraculously, 'become a changed person'.

The classes were concluded after about three months. Then, all dressed in white, we girls (I was perhaps the youngest) sat, absorbed and motionless, in the nave of the church. My eyes searched for the Holy Dove but I could not see it anywhere, neither up in the roof, nor over the altar, nor even fluttering above our heads. I felt panic rising inside me. Was I the only one who couldn't see the Holy Dove, in which guise the Canon had told us the Holy Spirit would appear to us all? Was I the only wicked one? And, if so, how was I wicked?

At last came the moment when the queue of waiting girls shuffled out into the aisle and knelt, two by two, before the Bishop. I knelt. He put his hand on my head and said some words and I rose and returned to my seat. But I had felt no change within me whatsoever. I felt exactly the same person as I had been all my life. So what was wrong with me? My sense of misery and distress was great.

I realise now that my confirmation could easily have precipitated a profound inner crisis of adolescence. What could have been more natural than for me to see the whole thing as 'just another fairy tale' in which I had been stupid enough to believe? Or as a deliberate lie I had been told by some clergyman in order to get me into 'his' church? The questions were unanswerable, and there was nobody to whom I could turn for help; least of all my mother, to whom my attitude was already protective. I knew that she was somehow overburdened, in a way that I did not fully understand. I told myself that I must keep very quiet about my doubts, then perhaps something would happen and I would be enabled to understand. For, despite my misgivings, I still believed there to be something here in which I could trust. I just had to wait, and continue to wait. Looking back on my emotional confusion at the time of my

31

confirmation, I can see this as an intimation of a new awareness awakening in me.

A week or so after the confirmation service we went down to the Vicarage in Kent for the Easter holidays, as was customary. On Easter Sunday I made my first Communion at the small parish church, and Uncle Bernard was the celebrant. I insisted on going to the Communion service before breakfast because this, the Misses Hull had explained to me, showed a greater reverence: the first food to pass my lips that day would be the Body and Blood of Christ. I remember feeling a bit sick, partly from the emotion of this new experience, and partly because I was never very good at doing active things like walking to church before I had had any breakfast. In Uncle Bernard's church I missed deeply, and with great longing, the music, the reverent rituals, and the whole beauty of Folkestone's old parish church. But I accepted, inarticulately and without understanding, that this, too, could be part of a necessary experience.

One evening, when we had been at the Vicarage less than a week, I was lying in bed watching my mother 'change for dinner' in the old day nursery that she and I shared. She was doing her hair at the dressing-table. Suddenly there was a knock at our bedroom door.

'Come in!' called my mother.

It was Uncle Bernard who entered. 'I thought I'd just come and say goodnight to the children,' he said.

My mother rose. She looked a little flustered, as I had noticed she often did in Uncle Bernard's presence. 'How dear of you,' she said. 'Ingaret is already in bed, as you see. I'll go and see if Roger is yet out of his bath.'

She went out into the passage and Uncle Bernard approached my bed, and sat down beside it. Almost immediately his hand felt its way under the bedclothes, in between the sheets, and then, low down, his fingers began to explore my young body. He began to stroke it. I felt terribly uncomfortable. It was even worse than having to kiss our host's greying and bushy beard every morning before breakfast when we were staying at the Court.

Then, suddenly, we heard my mother coming back from the adjoining day nursery.

Instantly my uncle withdrew his hand and stood up. 'I'll say goodnight to Roger tomorrow night,' he said.

He and my mother looked at each other. Then he turned and left the room.

Slowly my mother sat down by the mirror and began again to put the final touches to her hair.

I was puzzled. 'Mummy, when Uncle Bernard was sitting here he put his hand right under the bedclothes – ' I began.

My mother wheeled round in her chair. Her face was flushed and she stared at me. 'What?' she exclaimed.

I was taken aback. 'He was only trying to stroke me – ' I began.

My mother burst into a passion of tears. 'Oh my God! My God!' she cried. And that was something that I'd never, ever heard her say before. Then, burying her head in her arms on the dressing-table, she went on sobbing.

I was totally confounded. What had I done wrong? What had anybody done wrong? I slipped out of bed and went to her. 'Mummy, I'm sorry . . . I didn't mean to say anything wrong – '

She gathered me to her. 'You didn't, my darling . . .' She held me close. Then, pulling herself together she said, 'Now you must get back to bed, poppet . . . and I must go down to dinner or I'll be late.'

I saw her drying her tears. Then she tucked me up and went towards the door. But at the door she turned suddenly, came back, and took me in her arms. 'I'd never do anything that would hurt you children, never. You do know that, don't you? Don't you, darling?'

Quite mystified, I gave her an enormous hug and, as far as I was concerned, that was the end of the matter.

However, even before this incident occurred I had felt a slight but quite perceptible change in the atmosphere at the Vicarage. I had sensed it first in my mother. She looked strained and uneasy; or was it that my own awareness had deepened? Either way it unsettled me.

Of course now, as a family, we all had new individual problems to deal with. I was too old at eleven to continue at the little co-educational school at Folkestone. And Roger had to be got ready for his first preparatory school, Cheam, which at that time was considered to be the best in the country. My mother had written to the headmaster (whom she and my father had known slightly when they lived in Surrey) and explained to him her precarious financial position. The reply was prompt. 'We would consider it a privilege to have your son at our school for no fee at all.' My mother was very grateful and, after we had all three discussed it, she wrote and thanked him for his offer but insisted on making a token payment. She told me much later that she felt that Roger might otherwise be looked upon as a 'charity child'. What with Roger going to a preparatory school 'all on his own', and me being sent to a school where I would be more fully stretched intellectually, there was no doubt in any of our minds that our 'threesome' was about to undergo a basic change. Was it this that accounted for the difference in the atmosphere at the Vicarage? I think not. Rather it was due to the fact that since our last visit there had been two basic alterations in the Vicarage life.

First, Uncle Bernard had got himself a motorcar. He claimed that his parochial 'duties' were taking up so much of his time that a motorcar was necessary. With it, obviously, he could now cover a much wider area for 'visiting'. Certainly he was out most of the day.

I noticed that this disturbed my mother. One morning shortly before lunch she came to me.

'Darling, you are so good at climbing trees. Would you go and climb that birch at the end of the drive and tell me if you can see Uncle Bernard's new motorcar on the hill on the opposite side of the valley?'

I, of course, was eager to be off. It was like playing a spying game! I shinned up my favourite tree pretending it was the 'crow's-nest' and that I was searching the seas for my ship's safety. I knew quite a bit about ships not only because I loved them but also because, since early childhood, Roger had decided that he was 'going to be a sailor'.

Reaching a good height in the birch tree at the end of the drive, I scanned the opposite side of the valley. Yes, there it was! Uncle Bernard's large yellow motorcar standing glued to the right-hand side of the road like a bee sucking honey.

Delighted, I scrambled down and ran to find my mother.

'Yes, Mummy, it's there!'

'Where?'

'On the road across the valley.'

'Which side of the road?'

'The right-hand side.'

My mother made a funny face. 'Mrs Mason's,' she said, looking suddenly careworn. Then she glanced at her watch. 'And he left after breakfast . . . three hours.' She turned away.

'Perhaps Mrs Mason's ill or something,' I suggested helpfully. Mrs Mason, I knew, was a widow. And surely widows could more easily be ill than other people?

'No, she's not ill,' my mother said flatly. Then she pulled herself together. 'But thank you, darling. That's all right now. I just wanted to know where he was.'

She turned and moved slowly back to the house.

I didn't give the matter much thought at the time. Uncle Bernard's 'interests' had always been an unknown quantity to Roger and me. All we knew was that every Sunday – or was it Saturday? – he went to The Gateways for 'luncheon'. This very large property belonged to a very large elderly lady who obviously had a very large income, and a very large cellar. She also had an elderly but somewhat comely female companion. After these visits to The Gateways Uncle Bernard always returned home late in the afternoon, looking flushed and in an unusually 'joky' mood.

'Had a good lunch?' Aunt Magdalen would invariably inquire in her dry and somewhat sarcastic voice.

'Thank you, yes,' came the reply.

'I trust you found your hostess interesting?' Aunt Magdalen might continue. It was a phrase she often used. That is how we children came to talk of Uncle Bernard's 'interests'.

'Delightful, yes,' Uncle Bernard would reply, quite unmoved. 'I think I'll go to my study now and have a nap to sleep off my excellent lunch.'

Uncle Bernard's study should have been a wonderful place. He had rows and rows of books behind glass doors all along one side of the room. Two large windows looked out on to the garden where it was bordered by high trees. A large desk stood in front of one window; and a comfortable chair before the other. A fire burnt in the grate; and above the mantelshelf were two long crossed oars showing that Uncle Bernard had won a prize for rowing at some time. But the glass doors looked as if they had never been opened, and the books as if they had never been touched. And the trees outside made the study very dark. So we children, who were under strict orders 'never to disturb Uncle Bernard', hardly ever went near the study; nor did we want to.

The other thing that had changed since our previous visit to the Vicarage was that Aunt Magdalen had found herself a friend – the wife of the vicar in the adjoining parish. They saw each other every day either in one vicarage or the other. They also wrote to each other every day, and I would sometimes come across Aunt Magdalen reading and rereading these very long daily letters. This friendship, of course, cut into the time my aunt and my mother would normally have spent together and resulted in my mother feeling very lonely and at a loose end. It was company that she needed. Unlike me, solitude to her was never a friend but always a threat.

Uncle Bernard certainly should not have found it difficult to pursue his parochial 'interests'. There were the Willoughbys, a widowed and retired admiral who lived in a large house about a mile away with his two daughters. The elder daughter was always 'ill' and, in consequence, she had a friend, a woman somewhat her junior, who 'attended to her'. They shared two rooms in the large house, into which no outsider was ever allowed to go – not even the doctor except in an emergency. That left the pretty younger sister very much at large. Then there were the Misses Kennedy who lived not far from the Vicarage, along the lane to the left and beyond the hop-fields. I think Uncle Bernard's 'interests' must have been scattered far and wide.

One afternoon, near the end of this Easter holiday, Aunt Magdalen asked my mother to accompany her on a visit to her friend in the neighbouring parish. My mother was glad to go, and suddenly Roger made a great to-do about wanting to go too. We both loved being driven in the pony-trap but it was not really big enough to take four people comfortably, so I suggested I should stay behind. They all knew that I was happy up a tree reading a book, or playing with the animals in the garden or the stables. As I stood at the front of the house watching them drive off, I remember that it was a lovely spring-like day. Roger stood by the back door of the trap waving to me until finally they turned a bend in the drive and were out of sight.

I turned back into the Vicarage which suddenly felt very quiet and empty. It was a large house, with an enormous yawning black 'cavern' under the stairs where all the unneeded objects of other seasons were stored. There was the big cradle which held the logs for the downstairs winter fires; the croquet box with balls and mallets packed inside it; the rolled-up tennis net pushed into a far corner; and baskets for the walnuts, currants, apples and other fruits, all of which we enjoyed picking when in season.

I walked slowly up the stairs towards our quarters to get my book. As I mounted I examined again all the pagan idols and images which covered the high wall on one side of the stairs. I did this often because, to me, their hideousness simply couldn't be explained. They repelled me. Uncle Bernard had picked them up in early life, when, as a young clergyman, he had been appointed to foreign parts. But the reason for bringing them back and then hanging them up on show had always been obscure to me. These idols were most of them carved in wood, and those grinning, twisted effigies gave me the creeps.

Upstairs I looked everywhere for my book but could not find it. I was reading bits of it aloud to my mother. I can even remember its title: *Life of the Princess de Lambelle*. Was it possible that my mother had left it downstairs somewhere? I searched the drawing-room and the dining-room but with no success. Then surely it must be in Uncle Bernard's study? My mother spent ages with him in his study. She must have forgotten and left it there.

Very hesitantly I came past the 'cavern' under the stairs and turned to the right down the little private corridor which led to Uncle Bernard's study. Surely asking for a book couldn't be a 'disturbance', could it? After a moment's pause I knocked on the door.

'Come in,' called Uncle Bernard's voice.

I opened the door quietly and went in. 'I'm sorry, Uncle Bernard, I'm just looking for Mummy's book that I'm reading to her . . . it must be here, I think.'

I looked round the room for it.

Uncle Bernard rose from his large armchair. 'Shut the door, Ingaret,' he said. I did so.

Then Uncle Bernard said very, very softly, 'Come here, Ingaret . . . I've something to show you.'

The book, of course! I approached him happily.

Suddenly his strong arms were round me, pulling me, crushing me against him. His tongue was all over my face and in my mouth. His hands were all over my body, up my gym skirt, then down into my school blouse . . . tearing, searching, crushing me, and trying to force me back into the big armchair that he had just vacated.

I could have become paralysed by the terror that seized me. Instead I became strong in my desperation to escape. I fought him like a wildcat. I bit his face and his hands. I kicked his legs with my heavy garden boots. With my nails I scratched and clawed at his close and dreadful face. I squirmed, I twisted, I jammed my knee up between his legs (the place where Roger had told me that it hurt most). I even remembered not to call out or scream, for there was no one to hear and I didn't want to waste my breath. All the agility and childish strength that had been developed in the climbing of trees and riding bareback on the ponies in the paddock came to my aid.

Even a strong man cannot satisfactorily hold a wildcat. So, as I squirmed and kicked and bit and scratched, Uncle Bernard was forced slightly to shift his grip. At that moment I ducked away, ran to the door, opened it, rushed out and up the private corridor which led from his study and into the main body of the house. I knew he wouldn't follow me there: the green baize door leading to the kitchen quarters was too close; anyone could come through at any moment. I stumbled my way through the hall towards the front door. Air . . . fresh air . . . fresh air. I opened the first glass door and slammed it behind me. Then, fumbling, I opened the big oak door and pulled that, too, shut behind me. I was outside: my knees were weak and my whole body trembling. But I managed to stumble down the three stone steps and then I leaned against the brick wall of the house for support. I looked round me, seeking the reassurance of the familiar garden scene . . . but I could not find it! The graceful tulip tree with its elegant trailing branches was now dipping up and down, up and down, in some hideously macabre and mocking dance. I shifted my terrified glance from it to the undulating lawns only to find them, too, caught up in the tight grip of some frenetic and corrugated movement, endlessly rolling and shifting. I could not see or focus . . . I would fall. I tried to tighten my grip on the brick wall, feeling that, if I did fall, I too might become a part of the mad scene.

It was then that I heard the Voice. It spoke calmly, clearly and with great authority. It said:

'This is man: it has nothing whatsoever to do with God.'

Slowly I looked up and around me.

As the words were spoken everything visual seemed to drop back into its natural stance. The tulip tree in front of me regained its still grace. The lawns, too, as I turned my eyes towards them were once again their gentle, flowing selves. It was almost as if the whole of nature had heard the Voice too, acclaimed it, and immediately stood to attention because of it.

I remember nothing after that. Not because I fainted or anything of that sort. I think that perhaps, comparatively speaking, there was just nothing else to remember . . . except the Voice.

This was the only occasion in my life when what I will call this 'force' became audible to me. Perhaps it was the only occasion when my need of it had been an immediate and dire necessity?

I made no mention of the incident to my mother. And I think my instinct was right. Of course, at the time, words like 'attempted rape' or 'sexual assault' were completely unknown to me. All I had felt was terror. But terror of what? I was too young even to know that. Nor did I feel any particular astonishment in relation to the Voice. After all, in the Bible, God had been speaking to people all over the place – Jacob and Moses and Noah – and He'd always been very direct and practical in what He had said. And He had always spoken the truth. So why, in an off-moment, shouldn't He have spoken to me, particularly as He had said that He liked little children? Or had that been Jesus? It didn't really matter because in some funny way they all managed to be the same person . . .

I was only eleven at this time but the memory of the Voice has always remained with me; and as I grew older this sense of protection became a part of living reality. Man was one aspect of this reality; God was another. They had to be separate, otherwise communication between the two would be impossible. What was almost unbelievable to me was that this communication seemed to be as important to God as it was to man; I think it was this realisation that, in the future, prevented me from feeling any discomfort whatsoever when I encountered Uncle Bernard in the hall, or the garden, or at mealtimes.

Shortly after this we returned to our little house in Folkestone. It was nice being home again, even if, for a lawn, we only had a patch of green that was about as big as the billiard table at the Court!

5

Last Memories of Childhood

The next time we visited the Vicarage we found that yet another change
had taken place. Uncle Bernard, again complaining that his 'parochial
duties' had become too far-flung, had engaged a young curate to help
him. When we arrived for the school holidays we found that the Reverend Haywell was already installed. He even had his own study, which
fact greatly impressed me. Its window faced the front drive but was
hidden behind a thick growth of laurel bushes. The Reverend Haywell
had only just been ordained, so I suppose he must have been some ten
years older than I. He was clearly too young to be a companion for my
mother; nor was he the type. He was an extremely tall, gangling young
man, who looked down at one from a great height, but his blue eyes
were those of a child. Sometimes he had to wear spectacles, particularly
when he was in the drawing-room trying to play Bach by the piano's
candlelight. Bach was his passion. With his long legs tucked away
somewhere, his shoulders bent forward, and his tongue hanging out
because of the effort of concentration, he would spend hours struggling
with the intricacies and the profundities of Bach.

At the start, with the cruelty of childhood, I used to imitate him, with
my slender shoulders hunched forward and my tongue hanging out (I
was rather a good mimic). But that soon stopped. Gradually, without
much being said, Mr Haywell and I realised that, somehow, we had a
lot in common. In consequence, and quite naturally, I got into the habit
of creeping through the laurel bushes and tapping gently on his study
window. Instantly he would rise and open the bottom window so that
I could scramble up and sit on the sill. In this way, and in hushed voices,
we would talk for hours on end. This was a tremendous experience for
me. Except for my relations, I had never before talked either to, or with,
a man. I cannot remember what we talked about, but in quite a short
time a close understanding developed between us. I can even remember

wondering whether I might discuss with him my puzzlement regarding that elusive Holy Dove. But I decided against it. After all, he was a clergyman, so perhaps it wouldn't have been quite fair. Besides, my doubts now seemed to be bothering me scarcely at all.

I still remember vividly one particular conversation that we had. I was perched on his windowsill as usual, wearing my old gym skirt and a child's corduroy hat pulled down over my head, with my long fair hair hanging down my back.

Suddenly, looking up at me from his desk, Mr Haywell said, very seriously, 'Ingaret, if I wait five years for you, will you marry me?'

I looked at him with astonishment. 'Why five years?' I asked practically.

'Well, when you are seventeen we could be legally married,' he replied.

I thought about it. 'But s'pose I don't want to get married?' I said.

He looked at me and said quietly, 'Then I'd wait till you did.'

'I might never.'

'That would be sad,' he replied.

'Would it?' I thought about that, too.

'Anyway, just remember I'll wait for you.' He gave me a very gentle smile and we dropped the subject.

It was shortly after this that the changes in our lives – my mother's, my brother's and mine – began to take practical shape. We had very little money, as my mother records in her old scribbled exercise book:

I have put aside £100 for the proper education of each child. That only leaves me £100 a year. So, somehow, I must work. And in order to work I *must* get well.

I find it extraordinarily interesting that, at this period in time, my mother should have thought the 'proper education' of her daughter to be as important as that of her son, and so had arranged her finances accordingly. Perhaps, at heart, she had always been a spirited and even emancipated woman?

Accordingly, new plans were put into action. The house in Folkestone was sold and with the proceeds my mother rented a small, white, 'pebbled' house (as we children called it) out in the country. It was about a mile from the nearest village, and although the views from it were not spectacular, at least it looked out over green pastureland. This house had a lawn that would have been big enough for a tennis court if we had had enough money to buy a mower to cut the grass, and to pay for a tennis net and rackets and balls. That, of course, was out of the question, but our landlord and neighbour, protesting only very slightly, agreed to keep our lawn in trim with his mower. Perhaps it was no accident that our new home was only fifteen or so miles from the Vicarage?

The first practicality was to buy Roger's school uniform, and my mother sold some valuable books of my father's to pay for this. I too was to go to a new girls' school in Folkestone, also as a boarder. It looked more like a large private house than a school, with a pleasant garden approach, and was run by a Frenchwoman, whom we called 'Mademoiselle'. This delighted me because, for some reason, I had always wanted to be able to speak other languages.

At this new school we all had to wear green, but not as a set uniform, which meant that my mother's outlay for my school clothes was considerably less than for Roger's uniform. She could therefore afford to make me a white silk blouse to wear with my green Sunday coat and skirt, although it had to have short sleeves because she was unable to run to the extra half-yard of silk for long ones. However, unfortunately for me, short sleeves were the very height of fashion at that time. So on my first Sunday at the new school I came in for a number of jeering and sarcastic comments from the other girls, who looked upon my blouse as being 'over-posh'. The fact that we wore no uniform apparently did not alter the fact that uniformity of thought prevailed. My mother and I decided I had better conform, so we changed blouses by post! For the very first time it struck me that perhaps men were easier to 'get on with' than were those of my own sex!

Now that Roger and I were settled in our new schools, my mother concentrated her efforts on 'getting well', as these further passages from her old 'diary' record:

I am tired of seeing so many doctors. The last one told me that he was quite certain that with massage and electric treatment my leg would get quite well. He also recommended that I should go and see a psychologist, Dr Crichton-Miller, who is well-known for his successful treatment of shell-shocked soldiers.

At our first interview Dr C-M asked me two questions: 'Are you in love?' and 'Why aren't you married?' as if to infer that if I had been able to give a satisfactory answer to these two questions I need not have been there! He then alluded to my obsession. But that I can *never* talk about. I then went to his nursing home: a large country house packed with patients who all looked very queer. I had to do some funny things. I was given a tray filled with objects: I could look at them for half a minute and then I had to write down as many of them as I could remember. Dr C-M would also call out words and I would have to give my immediate association with them. It all struck me as very odd. I did not see how it could possibly affect my leg!

42

Every day Dr C-M said that I should walk a little further. One day he suggested I should walk to the station about half a mile away. I said, 'Oh, that will be much too far.' As I finished speaking I noted a faint glimmer of a smile on his very attractive face. I jumped off my chair and ran to him. 'Am I suffering from hysteria?' I cried. He answered, 'I wouldn't say that. But the pain is here,' he touched his head, 'and not here.' He touched his leg. I sprang round the room. 'Then I can leave here tomorrow!' I cried. 'Well, perhaps not as quickly as that,' he replied. Next morning when the nurse came in with my breakfast I hugged her with delight. I said, 'I can walk! I was suffering from hysteria!' I dressed hurriedly, walked to the village, hired a bicycle, and rode for miles on it. As I came peddling back up the drive Dr C-M saw me from his study window and we gave each other a delighted wave. Later he said he wished he had a few more patients like me! Then I left for home and no one can imagine the delight of my children when they met me!

I remember her homecoming very clearly. It was the day after Roger and I had returned to the little 'pebbled' house for the school holidays. The morning was fine and sunny and we were waiting anxiously with Miss Byford on the front doorstep for my mother's arrival. At last a taxi turned into our tiny driveway, drew up, and my mother got out of it. Directly she had paid the taxi-driver she hugged us and then, leaving her suitcase just inside the front door, led us round to the back garden. There, without saying a word, she picked up her long skirt and petticoat and ran, at high speed, all round the still-born tennis court, jumped over an ancient ancestral cannon acquired by my father which stood at one end of it, and then she ended up once again beside us, breathless but triumphant.

We were speechless with amazement. We had known my mother in a bathchair: we had known her occasionally riding in the pony-trap. But my mother running and jumping was something that we had never been able to imagine. I was quite overcome with excitement. Mummy was well! She'd never be ill again! The illness was all over!

How can this seemingly miraculous cure be explained? Let us start with the truism that 'nature abhors a vacuum'. Into the vacuum created by the absence of warm, personal love in my mother's early life had crept love's opposite, fear. This had undoubtedly contributed to her total incapacity to understand my father's passionate desire for her. After his death, life itself gave my mother's fear ample nourishment: extreme poverty; two children to support; and her own physical 'ill-health' – which was like a cancerous growth in her inner being – with which to come to terms. But the physical symptoms were merely the shoot above ground; the main plant was an extended rhizome underground, holding together her inner repressions and the secret psychological conflicts which gave rise to her fears. It is significant that the 'obsession' which my mother touches on in her diary was that she actually had cancer; this was exacerbated by her total incapacity to speak about it, even to her doctors, because, as she once told me, she was 'afraid of being thought mad'. She dared not bring her sickness of mind into the spectrum of 'consciousness'. Consequently the enemy within gathered in strength, expressing itself in 'dark clouds of depression' and also 'threatening voices in her mind'. There were intermittent periods of 'peace' but these, paradoxically, were even more alarming to my mother because they emphasised that she could never take for granted even an hour's respite from her anxieties.

The enlightened Dr Crichton-Miller was on the right lines when he had immediately questioned my mother about her love-life, using the word-association tests. Clearly her infatuation for Uncle Bernard – which was becoming increasingly obvious to me, despite the pains she took to hide it from us children – was seriously affecting her emotional well-being. I now realise that she must have had to pay a heavy additional price for this illicit relationship: guilt. Guilt regarding her religion; guilt regarding her children; and guilt regarding her own personal integrity. So guilt, in its turn, became yet another repression which added fuel to my mother's secret fears.

In a clinical situation today one should be able, through dream analysis and with the patient's associative assistance, to work a possibly painful but certainly fruitful way back to childhood, so exposing the initiation and birth of this inner negative force, fear. In the process the power of this force would lessen as the patient's recognition of it, and personal identification with it, gradually increased. In my mother's case, with psychiatric help, the problem might even have been totally resolved; indeed, with Dr Crichton-Miller's assistance, she had already taken a huge step forward in recognising the unreality of her 'physical symptoms'. In a flash she had realised that these were symbolic outer expressions of her inner emotional difficulties; that her seeming inability to 'stand on her own feet', which her anxieties gave rise to, was not consistent with the practical and efficient person she knew herself to be in ordinary-life terms.

There are only two dramas that I remember in connection with the little 'pebbled' house in the country which was briefly our home. Miss Byford was only able to stay for a few days following my mother's return from the nursing home, so my mother had engaged a young maid to help with the cooking and cleaning, little expecting that she would have acquired a new lease of life by the time we arrived home for the school holidays.

The first incident was set in motion by the maid, whose name was Geneva. One night, at bath-time, she asked me casually, 'D'yer know 'ow babies come?'

I looked up at her, puzzled, and shook my head.

She pushed her soapy hand in between my legs and said, 'They come out o' yer there.'

I was astounded.

That night, when my mother came to tuck us in, first Roger in his smaller room and then me in mine, I said in an urgent and astonished voice, 'Mummy, I know how babies come . . . they come from here!' I patted my stomach proudly.

There was a moment's silence. Then my mother said quietly, 'Who told you that, darling?'

'Geneva!' I replied excitedly.

My mother didn't say any more. She sat on the bed and read to me, and then, when I was feeling sleepy, quietly left me.

It was not usual for her to call us in the morning, as she did the following day.

'Where's Geneva?' I asked, blinking my eyes sleepily.

'Come and see,' said my mother.

I scrambled to the end of the bed and we both looked out of the window. It was pouring with rain. It was rather early and nothing seemed to be in motion in the surrounding countryside except for something bobbing up and down between the uneven hedgerows that bordered the road leading to the village. I stared at the moving object.

'What's that?' I asked.

'That's Geneva's umbrella,' said my mother quietly.

'What's she doing?' I asked, bewildered.

'I've sent her away,' my mother answered in the same unemotional voice. 'I don't think she was the right sort of person to look after young children.'

I was surprised. We'd all seemed to like Geneva. 'But what'll we do now?' I asked.

'Do for ourselves.' My mother smiled. 'We won't find another maid in a hurry.'

In this my mother was right. Geneva had walked to the village and told the story of her disgraceful treatment to everyone she met, and the news of her dismissal spread like wildfire through the neighbourhood. I am only surprised that goods ordered in the village were still delivered to us. It had, of course, been high-handed treatment on my mother's part, but all my mother cared about was to protect her children. Possibly her very limited knowledge of all matters sexual, and her subsequent fear and withdrawal from them, had influenced her behaviour. It is an extraordinary anomaly that a woman who was so dominated by inner fears could be totally fearless in the defence of those whom she loved.

The second incident also proved this point. It happened on my birthday. I woke up very excited and possibly rather cold, for there was no such thing as central heating in our little house. There were fireplaces everywhere, but it was both expensive and troublesome to use them, particularly without a maid. I dressed hurriedly, as always, to get down to a welcome fire in the living-room and also to see what birthday presents were piled up by my plate. But before I could reach the table I collapsed. Somehow I was carried up to my bedroom. My mother took my temperature, which was 103 degrees. My breathing, too, was laboured and unnatural. We had some beautiful and very old lace curtains in the sitting-room which were of some value, but without pause my mother tore them into shreds, made two hot bread poultices (I suppose she learned this treatment from the nurses of her childhood) and bound them round me, both back and front, with stockings. Telling Roger to sit beside me, she then took her bicycle from the shed and started to ride and also to push it along the snow-covered road which led to the village. There, from the chemist's, she rang for a recommended doctor, who said he would come at once. So my mother, as quickly as possible, half-rode and half-pushed her bicycle home again along the winter road.

Finally a doctor arrived. He sounded my chest. He looked at the home-made poultices.

'Your little girl is very ill,' he said. 'She has pneumonia. These poultices have probably saved her life. They may just have stopped her from getting double pneumonia. But she must be kept in the warm. Can you make up a fire?'.

'In my room, yes.'

My mother went and made up such a huge fire in her bedroom that a long mirror hanging near the fire cracked in two. (Not a lucky sign, as she told herself, and me later.) Then I was carried on my mattress along the narrow corridor, finally to be laid on the floor in my mother's bedroom.

I was kept there for quite some time, with the fire alight both day and night, and my mother, helped by Roger, doing everything in the house. Eventually I made a complete recovery, but I think my mother's sense of shock had been severe. Even when I was better, somehow the little white 'pebbled' house never felt like home again for any of us. My mother became overconscious of its remoteness and the consequent vulnerability of our situation, which had been accentuated by my illness and by the long stretches of time she had spent alone there while Roger and I were away at school. Uncle Bernard came over quite often by car to see my mother in the holidays, so I imagined he must be a frequent visitor in term-time too. On such occasions we were always 'sent out into the garden to play'. It must have been very hard for my mother to bring herself to give up the house because, in consequence, she would finally have to wrench herself free of the 'hypnotic power' which bound her to my uncle. However, she bravely made the decision, and so another change in our lifestyle took place.

Roger returned to Cheam, and I went back to my school in Folkestone. There my mother unbelievably found herself a job. She started as a VAD in one of the military hospitals in Folkestone, but this she soon found to be emotionally too great a strain. She had had no nursing training whatsoever, and although she badly wanted to help the war effort, the physical agonies and horrors with which she was confronted, combined with the long hours of work, proved too much for her. Then, quite by chance, she saw an advertisement in the local paper, answered it, and got herself a job as hostess in a small private hotel in Folkestone. She was not paid but she lived in the establishment rent-free, which was a very important asset to our exchequer. Her duties were light: supervision of the staff; supervision, too, of the dining-room arrangements; and a certain mingling with the guests after dinner in the drawing-room. Her beauty and ease of manner would have been an asset to the little hotel. On one occasion my great-uncle, the then Lord Chancellor, came down from London with his wife for some sea air. They drew up outside the hotel in their crested and chauffeured Rolls-Royce to take my mother out to lunch. This, my mother told me later, created quite a stir in the hotel.

The loss of our latest home had created a change in all our attitudes. Roger had now left Cheam and was to go to the Royal Naval College at Osborne. He had had a most successful time at preparatory school, being popular both with the masters and with his contemporaries, yet every report seemed to reach the same conclusion: 'Could have done better if he had tried.' In the examination results he always came between the middle and the bottom of the class, but his natural, easy-going and agreeable temperament, combined with his success at all forms of sport, made up for his academic laziness. (At the age of sixteen, he was chosen to play rugger for the Navy – the youngest player ever to have achieved that honour.)

The exciting day came when we three went to London to buy Roger's naval uniform. And, of course, it had to be bought at Gieves. Nowhere else was permitted. It was not until many years later that my mother let it be known to us that Roger had gone to the Royal Naval College as one of the three chosen 'King's Scholars'; in other words, free of charge. In fact, the Admiral had replied to her letter of application saying that they had never before had a request for a place at the college from a parent who had so little money; but, they added, they would be proud to take Roger. So, at Gieves, he was measured up first for this and then for that. The cost of a naval uniform, together with the accessories, appeared to be staggering. My father had given my mother many precious gifts of jewellery, some of which I'm sure she had to sell in order to pay for Roger's naval outfit. We were all breathless with the importance of this event.

A day in the West End of London was thrilling enough, but especially so since my mother was going to take us to have tea at the Piccadilly Hotel. As children, we had never really seen London, except with suitcases in our hands, scrambling from one platform to another, or driving in a cab from one station to another en route for our various country 'homes', so the Piccadilly Hotel seemed almost like a palace. Tea was brought by a waiter. We wondered whether we could afford to order muffins? Yes, my mother nodded, we could, and these were followed by some gorgeous cakes. I can still remember how new and strange it all felt and how much we laughed at ourselves, munching muffins at one end of the foyer with the orchestra at the other end playing tunes that made me want to get up and dance and sing! I think my mother enjoyed our pleasure enormously. Looking back, I can see that with the loss of our most recent home, and Roger's entry into the great outside world, the curtain finally came down on the scene of our childhood.

6

Growing Up

No doubt the importance of Roger's being 'in uniform' when only eleven years old helped to bring some of my own simmering ideas to the surface. I enjoyed being at The Larches, the school which I was now attending in Folkestone, and seeing my mother every weekend. But I didn't enjoy the schoolwork. I had done quite a lot of looking about, and listening, and even reading. So finally I came out with my request.

'Mummy, please, can I go to a proper school too?'

'A proper school?'

'Yes!' I was all eagerness.

'But what's wrong with The Larches?'

It was difficult to explain. 'Well, you know, if I've finished my lessons before the others, all the mistress does is to send me out into the garden to weed the flowerbeds, or the drive or something. There's no point in trying.'

'I see.' My mother was thoughtful.

'But I know where I want to go!' I said quickly. 'I've been reading about it . . . if it wouldn't be too expensive . . .' I faltered, realising that it would also mean separation from my mother.

'Well, where is it?'

'Bedford High School,' I whispered.

'A High School!' My mother was almost shocked.

I nodded. 'It's got the highest academic successes of any school in the country – '

'But a High School – '

'Oh, don't you see, Mummy, all the girls going there will be wanting to work – '

I broke off. There was a pause.

'And do you want to work?' My mother sounded surprised.

I nodded.

It was a new concept for my mother. Young girls in her day 'came out' and then got married. So strong had been her love for me that, while she had wanted me to have the best possible education, she had assumed that her daughter would nevertheless go on to make a 'good marriage' and live happily ever after.

I sensed her hesitation. 'Besides, p'raps I'll have to earn my living,' I said practically. 'It isn't as if we're rich or anything.' I paused. 'But it's mostly because I really want to,' I added.

At my previous school, which I had called my 'Mademoiselle' school, I had been greatly attracted to a half-English, half-Greek girl called Ruria. She was dark-skinned, with strongly-marked features and dark brown eyes. She was the only foreigner in the school and the only one to whom I had ever spoken. This fact alone I found to be extraordinarily fascinating. But as she was two years older than I our relationship, even in that small, intimate school, was severely limited. Occasionally, however, when going out for a walk along The Leas we were allowed, despite the difference in our ages, to walk together in crocodile. On these walks I learned a few facts about my friend. Ruria was an orphan; Ruria lived alone with an elderly aunt; Ruria was flamboyant both in appearance and temperament. I was particularly enthralled by this because I had been used to people who kept their feelings under cover and did not bring them out in eruptive explosions. But I think it was the fact that Ruria was an orphan that touched me most deeply. I couldn't even imagine what life would be like without my own mother. Then, suddenly, with no warning, the 'Mademoiselle' school collapsed. All we girls were given a term's notice with no reason offered. We discovered later that the school had been in financial straits for some time.

'The Larches', to which I then moved, was a bigger but quite pleasant private school with a large garden. This enabled my mother still to earn her keep as 'hostess' in the private hotel in Folkestone and, at the same time, to keep in touch with me.

Then, to my delight, after my first term at The Larches, Ruria's aunt allowed her to join me there; something we had both been very eager to bring about. We and another girl all shared a bedroom, and during this period our friendship developed. Ruria and I, as far as was possible, became inseparable. Our attachment was highlighted by one incident. The Larches was considered to be in a 'safe' part of town, being some distance from the harbour, but as it was midway between central Folkestone and Shorncliffe camp, the troops still marched past my new school and down to the sea for embarkation to France (and I still stood sadly watching till they were out of sight). Also, the school had a 'dugout', which was to be our refuge in the event of attack by the enemy.

One day, towards lunch-time, the alarms sounded all over Folkestone. We girls had been 'rehearsed', so we knew exactly what to do: we all ran out of the house, together with the mistresses, to reach our dugout in time. Only when we were all squashed inside did I see that Ruria was missing. I pushed and burrowed my way back through the crush of schoolgirls and mistresses, and because I was both nimble and strong, no one really noticed what I was up to. I knew where she would be: on her bed fast asleep. I shook her awake. 'Quick! You must come! The alarm's gone!' Bemused, she rose and stumbled along beside me until we reached our dugout and scrambled inside. I saw that the headmistress, who detested me, was looking very angry. Later, when the scare was over, she wrote what I am sure was an unwilling letter of appreciation to my mother, saying that her daughter had 'behaved with great bravery'. But after that episode, to our astonishment and dismay, Ruria and I were no longer allowed to share a bedroom. Perhaps our headmistress knew more of the facts of life than we did?

It was towards the end of this term that two important events in both our lives synchronised. Firstly, Ruria, two years older than I, had now reached school-leaving age. And secondly, my mother, faithful to her word, had started investigating the possibilities of Bedford High School. This second event mercifully helped to compensate for the painful farewell that Ruria and I had to bid each other at the end of the term. We made promises to meet in the holidays. But, knowing my holiday position, I did not see much chance of Ruria ever coming to stay at the Vicarage. Nor did I see much chance of my ever being able, or even wanting, to leave my mother and Roger during our precious holidays together. So it came as a shock when, not long after Ruria and I had parted, I received a telegram saying 'Please come at once'. And the signature at the bottom of the telegram was that of Ruria's aunt!

Instantly I felt that something dreadful must have happened to Ruria. An accident? An illness? She might even be dying . . . she must be dying . . . otherwise her aunt would never have summoned me. In those days, household telephones were not facilities that could be taken for granted, so I talked to my mother, consulted the railway timetable, and then went off to send a telegram to the given address: 'Coming today. Love Ingaret'. That was both clear and cheap. Meanwhile my mother had, rather unwillingly, packed my night-things in a small case, and she then came with me to the station. I had never travelled by train on my own before, but I think my mother's main concern about letting me go was because I had been so deeply disturbed since receiving the telegram.

After a short journey I arrived at Ruria's nearest station. I must have taken a taxi, for I was in desperate haste and I remember arriving, quite quickly, at a medium-sized house with a medium-sized garden standing in a row of similar houses. I also remember that the front door was opened to me promptly by a lady of outsize proportions. I could tell at a glance that she was Ruria's aunt, for they both had the same dark look.

'Are you Ingaret?' the outsize lady asked.

I nodded.

She let me in to the hall. 'Ruria's bedroom is the door immediately facing you at the top of the stairs,' she said. Then she vanished along some ground-floor corridor.

Feeling both mystified and apprehensive, I ran up the stairs. Quietly I opened the door to see a tear-blotched Ruria sobbing on her bed. She clutched at me and began mumbling out her thanks and her distress so that it was almost impossible to disentangle the two. However, at last I was able to discover the truth. Two nights previously, Ruria's 'aunt' had confessed to Ruria that she was not her 'aunt' at all; she was her mother. But, as she had never been married, that made Ruria her illegitimate daughter. This news had so shattered Ruria that she had swallowed what remained of a bottle of sleeping tablets belonging to her 'aunt' in an effort to commit suicide. And she had very nearly succeeded. But a doctor had been summoned in time and had been able to deal satisfactorily with the physical situation. Only the human problem now remained. For Ruria, sobbing in my arms, kept on repeating, 'And if I have to live like that I'll do it again . . . I'll do it again. I don't want to live like that, I don't . . . I'll try to kill myself again.'

Ruria's distress amazed me. I simply couldn't understand it. 'But you've found your real mother,' I said immediately. 'She's not your aunt at all. She's your real mother.' I put my arms round Ruria, trying to check her sobs. 'And that's important. She's your real mother.'

'But I – I'm illegitimate . . .'

I hesitated. I knew very little about 'illegitimacy' except for what I'd read in books and from history. And, of course, in history it *was* terrible. Kings and queens were beheaded in front of enormous crowds of people, or they were put in the Tower of London for life, or were secretly poisoned. But for ordinary people like us . . .

I hesitated. 'Does being illegitimate really matter?' I asked, feeling extremely ineffectual.

Ruria's sobs increased with such intensity that I realised I wasn't helping at all.

Then suddenly an idea came to me. 'Anyway they must have loved each other like anything to do all — all that together . . . mustn't they . . . they must have — '

Ruria drew breath. 'They did love each other . . . she said so . . .'

So I was on the right track. 'Well, isn't that the most important thing?' I said quickly. 'I mean, lots and lots of people just don't love each other . . . and — and that's illegitimate too . . . in a sort of way . . .' I stumbled to a halt.

'Illegitimate too?' Ruria repeated dully. She turned towards me, her poor puzzled face blotched red from her passionate sobs.

I nodded and then said firmly, 'Anyway, if I had to choose, I'd choose to have things your way, instead of mine . . .' I paused, and then added with difficulty, 'I . . . I don't think mine ever did much . . . love each other, I mean.'

However Ruria's sobs, which had lessened, now started again. 'But what about the stigma?'

There was a silence. I sensed that Ruria was moving towards another compulsive weep. So I spoke quickly.

'Stigma?' I repeated uncertainly. That was something I had never really thought about. Nor did I think much of it now. So I just stuck to my point. 'They really loved each other,' I repeated. 'And that's the only important thing . . . and she's your real mother and not just any old aunt.'

Eventually, through never shifting ground on this point, I was able to persuade Ruria of its truth. I even managed to introduce the word 'love-child' into the argument. It was a word I had never used before and, hearing it, Ruria started to cry again, insisting that I had made the word up. So, with difficulty, I found a dictionary, looked up 'love-child' (trembling somewhat in case it wasn't there) and then pointed it out to her in print. This did seem to have a reassuring effect.

I stayed with Ruria for two days, and the simple statement that, unlike me, she was a child of love seemed not only to stick but to stabilise my poor friend. On the third day I took a train back to my mother, having previously phoned her at the hotel from a call box. I had not seen much of the outsize lady, Ruria's 'aunt', because our food had been sent up to the bedroom. However, she came to the front door to see me off and, with a certain dignity, thanked me for helping Ruria, which cannot have been easy for her.

At the station I was lucky enough to find an empty carriage in the train. So, drumming my heels against the floor, to the rhythm of the steady chug-chug-chug of the smoking engine as the train pulled out of the platform, I thought back to Ruria and her distress. In my mind I went slowly over the whole episode. Of one thing I was sure: I was sick and tired of the word 'illegitimate'. And then, for the first time, I became acutely aware that it was both a word and a situation that most people seemed to find shocking. So why hadn't it shocked me? Wasn't it very wrong of me not to have been shocked? Ever since going to school I had been told that I didn't pay enough attention to 'proper' behaviour. My schoolmates thought of me as 'affected' or 'putting on airs'; the mistresses found me difficult. So obviously there were two kinds of people: those who kept the rules, and those who didn't. Or was this an over-simplification? Suppose each person really was two people? This thought rather excited me because that was exactly how I sometimes felt. 'Ingaret' was someone who did things and to whom things happened. But 'I' was a rather different person, someone who was aware of something 'other', not only in people, but in almost everything. I had grown up with remarks like 'Ingaret's dreaming again!' or 'What are you thinking about now?' and, admittedly, even as a little girl, I could sit quite still for long periods, either with or without a book. I could never explain that I was not exactly 'thinking'; it was more that I was allowing my mind to remain in a certain state of openness and readiness so that a void which had been 'nothing' could, if it were in the mood, turn into 'something' – as if of its own accord!

As the train pulled slowly away from the little country station, I stared at the emerging countryside with pleasure: cornfields, green fields, some lying flat beneath the sky and others running up to meet it in a rollicking frolic of fun; hedges of tangled undergrowth, or neatly built wooden fences to contain the cattle browsing undisturbed; trees, some grouped together, others standing solitary and alone – trees that years back I had so loved to climb. A large oak standing in a field close to the railway track suddenly caught my eye and I leaned forward imagining that I could almost feel its gnarled bark under my hands. In the past, I had always thought of oak trees as the wisest of all the trees growing in the copse at the bottom of the Vicarage garden. But this particular oak had had a hard time, for I could see that some of its branches were blackened and leafless where it had been struck by lightning in some violent storm. Nevertheless, despite the damage, the oak stood steady and upright, its roots sunk deeply into the earth which gave it life.

The train pulled slowly round a corner, and as the oak tree disappeared from view my thoughts switched back to Ruria, who had also had a hard time. I had read somewhere that growing-up was painful, yet I had not found it to be so. To me, it had felt rather like playing a game of Blind

Man's Buff: one's eyes were bandaged, but one could still retain a sense of light, even if only a gleam at times; and with outstretched hand one could get one's bearings and hope to make human contact. It had been a game which I had enjoyed greatly, even though I had frequently stumbled and even fallen.

Suddenly I realised that I was thinking of the climbing of trees and the playing of nursery games as though they were things of the past, which seemed to indicate that I, too, must be growing up. Surely being able to look back must also mean that one was going forward? Momentarily my mind switched back to the old oak tree. Surely that oak tree, from the time it was an acorn, must have known that 'growing up' must also be 'growing-down'? That it was only by sinking its roots ever more deeply into the earth that it could maintain its hold on life? Perhaps this was also true for human beings? The idea caught my interest with a surprising intensity, yet it didn't feel new; it felt rather like something that had, at long last, erupted into recognition.

On returning to Folkestone my mother told me that her inquiries about Bedford High School had proved satisfactory. Consequently she had already completed the entry form, and there was a good chance that I would go as a boarder the very next term.

'But can you really afford it, Mummy?' I asked. It was an automatic reaction.

My mother nodded. It was only then that I allowed myself to begin to feel excited. I was also very touched, for I knew that this would put more than a financial burden on my mother: it would deprive her of her only confidante. So long as I was at school in Folkestone we could see each other most weekends, but once I went to Bedford we would no longer be in easy contact; and I was perhaps the only person who intuitively understood her 'secret illness', as I called it to myself. She had been much better since her treatment with Dr Crichton-Miller, but the shadow was still deeply within her.

At about this time my mother told me of a conversation she had had with one of the guests at the hotel where she worked. The guest had been an American woman who had noticed some strain on my mother's beautiful face and had remarked that she 'looked tired'. My mother had very evasively mentioned her 'ill-health'. The American woman had looked at her and said quietly, 'The sickness is not in your body; it's in your soul.' My mother had repeated this remark to me with awe and added, 'And, darling, I believe she was right.' At the time it had made a kind of sense to me, but nothing of course that I could really understand.

The day before term started my mother told me that she was accompanying me to Bedford; so we travelled up together. As we were saying goodbye I made a hesitant suggestion. 'Mummy, couldn't you find us a new place for the holidays? Somewhere more exciting for all of us?'

'Exciting?'

I nodded. 'Don't you remember when some lady at the hotel took you to a *thé dansant*? You loved it.'

'But I couldn't dance,' my mother replied truthfully. 'So nobody asked me twice.'

'You could learn.'

'At my age!'

'Why not?' I asked stoutly. 'You don't look like anybody's mother.'

My mother laughed at that; but I knew she was feeling depressed at leaving me.

'Well, we'll see,' she said.

Then she left me at the front door of my school-house and went off to catch the train back to London.

I discovered that of the six houses for boarders mine was the only one that had a married woman, Mrs Burton, as its housemistress. This, for some reason, pleased me.

Having unpacked, I found my way downstairs and into the study where I mingled rather self-consciously among my housemates but kept both my eyes and my ears open. Here I found no foreigners amongst the girls and seemingly no flamboyance. Everyone and everything, it seemed, was both concentrated and conforming. However, this was what I had chosen; and if I, too, worked hard for the next couple of years, hopefully I would pass all the examinations that would enable me to go up (or was it down?) to Oxford and study law. To be a barrister, like my father, was still my dedicated but entirely secret ambition.

For the next two years, I did work extremely hard. Unfortunately, for some reason I was put on the Modern side of the school. The Classical side included languages, history and other subjects which I enjoyed, but on the Modern side I was taught algebra, botany, geometry, etc., none of which greatly interested me. Hockey was the game we played in winter and it proved to be one of the few games that I really detested, so I always volunteered to be goal-keeper which meant that I got extremely cold but was left, in measure, to my own thoughts. In the summer we played tennis, but the rather effective overhand serve I had developed both at the Vicarage and at our other 'homes' was instantly condemned as being 'unladylike', so I had to conform and serve underhand. Happily, my individualism did not prevent me from becoming ordinarily friendly both with my classmates and with the other boarders in Mrs Burton's house.

One incident in particular stands out from this period. A very close friendship suddenly sprang up between two other girls in Mrs Burton's house, one dark, one fair, and both some two years younger than I. Olive, the older girl, was the daughter of a ballet dancer, or so it was rumoured with a certain envy; Katherine, the younger, fair-haired girl, seemed to be a fairly typical schoolgirl from an apparently ordinary family. But this relationship brought about a change in Katherine that was, to me, markedly apparent. The whole expression of her face seemed to alter, and sometimes a look of terror would flash across it. She grew to be increasingly reticent until, finally, she seemed to retreat into an almost paralysed and speechless anonymity. The fact that nobody else in the house appeared to notice this change in Katherine puzzled me greatly. Could I be imagining the whole situation? Yet 'imagining' was the wrong word, for I didn't know what to imagine. Then one day I found Katherine secretly crying with deep and desperate sobs. It was no good speaking to her: she would have been too terrified to answer. Nor could I speak to anyone else, for 'splitting' was the one unforgivable sin in our girlhood concept of honour. Finally, after much painful self-argument, I asked Mrs Burton if I could see her privately.

Consequently our housemistress summoned me to her private sitting-room.

'Well?' she asked as I stood before her.

'I don't really know anything . . .' I started hesitantly. Then I finished in a rush, 'Katherine and Olive are great friends . . . but it is doing something terribly bad to Katherine.'

There was a pause.

'What?' asked Mrs Burton quietly.

I stumbled with my words. 'I – I don't know. She's become quite different. I think she's frightened of something – ' I said, and then took refuge in silence. Then I added, 'Perhaps Olive bullies her or some-thing?'

'Thank you for telling me,' Mrs Burton replied. She paused. 'I'll have a word with Katherine.'

'But you won't say who – ?' For a moment it was I who was deeply alarmed.

'Of course I shall never mention your name,' Mrs Burton replied firmly.

Feeling weak at the knees I left the room. What on earth had I been talking about? Despite Mrs Burton's reassurance I felt I had done something wicked. If it got out I'd probably be sent to Coventry and no one would ever speak to me again . . .

This interview had taken place in the early afternoon. That evening when we were doing prep in our studies, a great commotion suddenly broke out in the house. It sounded as though trunks were being carried or bumped down the stairs and into the hall; then we heard raised voices and, we thought, tears. I trembled: the whole situation seemed to be building up into an explosion. Then finally, through our net-curtained windows, we caught a glimpse of a gardener, or perhaps a taxi-driver, carrying trunks and boxes out to the street, followed by Olive, a hat on her head and a small bag in her hand, walking beside someone who was presumably her mother. Then, as if by magic, they all disappeared through the garden gate. It had been a very swift and effective operation. I drew a breath of relief.

All the girls in my study instantly went into a huddle whispering and questioning. I stood apart, wondering what would happen if they ever found out what I had done.

Then the study door opened and Mrs Burton stood in the entrance. 'Olive has had some very bad news,' she said quietly. 'She has had to go home at once. She won't ever come back here.' Then she turned and left the room.

All the fizz went out of the girls' curiosity. I gave a quick glance at Katherine who was immediately being questioned. Looking genuinely bewildered she just kept repeating, 'Quite honestly I don't know any-thing about it . . . I don't truly . . .' So interest quickly died. Prep was resumed. And, was it my imagination or did Katherine already look more relaxed?

That night, as we were going up to bed, Mrs Burton was standing in the hall. As we passed her to say goodnight, she drew me aside and said very quietly, 'Thank you, Ingaret. You've done us a great service, but your name was never mentioned.'

After that I felt safe; and so, I fancied, did Katherine. Gradually the furtive look left her face and the colour came back into her cheeks. The normal school routine continued. But I could never explain to myself why it was that I was the only one who seemed to have noticed the negative change in Katherine. Could it have been because the expression of repressed terror on Katherine's face reminded me of the look I had so often seen on my mother's face, the look that since childhood had told me that it was one of her 'bad' days? Had Katherine, too, been 'ill', and if so, what was this 'illness'? I couldn't find answers to the last two questions but at least I had managed to answer the first to my reasonable satisfaction.

Three school terms passed, during which I and my schoolmates were pressing forward towards matriculation, and I swotted with the best of them. Then I received a letter from my mother which, temporarily, took my mind off my work. At the hotel in Folkestone where she worked, my mother had met a very nice woman called Lady Knowles, who had suggested that she should take a week's holiday and go with her, as her guest, to a small, sea-facing hotel in Southsea. Now I knew that this, no matter what were my mother's wishes, would be a great hurdle for her. New faces, new places, and a new and quite unknown venture would always alarm, if not terrify, her. However, she wrote, 'I remembered that you said you wanted somewhere more "exciting" than the Vicarage. So, as Lady K is such a nice person I have accepted.'

I was thrilled. Suddenly I had visions of us all going to the seaside for the summer holidays, which would make both a timely and perhaps needed change. Of course there had been the sea at Folkestone, but it had always seemed so far away, when viewed from where we walked in crocodile along The Leas, that it had never really felt like the sea. And when we were taken to swim it was always to a swimming-pool with no one to teach us how to swim. Perhaps at Southsea we would be nearer to the real sea and at least able to paddle! I wrote back delightedly to my mother.

During her week in Southsea with Lady Knowles my mother sent me a letter which made me feel even more excited. She wrote: 'Lady Knowles, like you, has insisted that I take dancing lessons! There are plenty of tea-dances here and she thinks I should go, so I am having dancing lessons at the Grand Hotel! As a matter of fact, at the first lesson I met a very nice man, a major in the Indian Army. He is no better a dancer than I am, so we had some good laughs together about that! I'll tell you about it in the holidays.'

This all sounded quite a new note to which I was keenly alert. I began dreaming of days by the sea, and dips into the ocean. Then, to my dismay, my mother wrote to say that she had actually booked rooms for the coming holiday but something had gone wrong. There had been a double-booking. All the rooms and boarding-houses in Southsea appeared to be booked, and of course she could not afford a hotel for us, so the visit would have to be postponed. In consequence we were to spend the summer holidays at the ever-ready Vicarage. I felt utterly downcast.

Even there a new difficulty had arisen. Aunt Magdalen wrote that

Winifred, the parlourmaid, had measles. Of course she was in quarantine but Aunt Magdalen thought it would be inadvisable for Roger and me to come to what might be an infected house, so she had made arrangements for us to stay in the gardener's cottage down in the village.

Looking back, I can see now that this holiday must have been a near-disastrous experience for my mother. No longer could she be in daily touch with Uncle Bernard. Whereas Roger and I, once we had walked up the long hill, could still play in the woods, gardens and stables of the Vicarage, my mother, without even the possibility of telephone communication, had to sit alone for hour after hour in the cottage waiting for Uncle Bernard to arrive, or not arrive. And when occasionally he did pop in, there was no opportunity for anything but furtive and low-spoken intimacies between him and my mother. Also, whereas before she had known whether Uncle Bernard was in the Vicarage or out visiting his parishioners, now she had no knowledge whatsoever of his movements. In the past, when he had been out, she had been able to imagine both the worst and the best. Now she could only imagine the worst. Before, there had at least been the privacy of Uncle Bernard's study for them to get up to whatever they did together; but now, for my mother, there was nothing but the tormented longings of both body and being.

Day by day I noticed that my mother grew paler and thinner. I think she scarcely slept at all. The strong erotic emotion aroused by Uncle Bernard – perhaps the only one she had ever known – held her captive in its unlimited yet thwarted power. Then, one Sunday night, the situation came to a climax. It was towards the end of the holidays and Roger had already returned to Osborne. Outwardly my mother still maintained herself, though the inner wreckage was visible to me. On this particular Sunday she and I went to Evensong on our own. Together with the rest of the congregation we listened to Uncle Bernard's impassioned and, to me, somewhat theatrical sermon. After the service Uncle Bernard came, as usual, to exchange greetings with his parishioners in the church porch. He whispered a few hurried words to my mother after which, I noticed, she turned very pale. Without speaking, we two returned slowly to the cottage, which was only a few hundred yards from the church. My mother went straight up to her bedroom and I went into the sitting-room where a cold supper had already been laid for us by the gardener's wife. Cold chicken and salad for two was on the table; biscuits and cheese and some apples.

At that moment I heard my mother's gasping sobs. In the little bedroom above she was sobbing her heart out and the sound came right through

60

the plastered ceiling. I ran up but the door was locked. I shook the door but the sobbing continued. I went on shaking but it was no good. She did not want me there: there was nothing I could do. Slowly I went back down the narrow wooden stairs and as I did so I could hear Uncle Bernard's car drawing up outside the cottage. I watched him as he walked up the tiny garden path and into the cottage. He opened the sitting-room door and we faced each other across the supper table.

'Where's your mother?'

I looked at him steadily. 'Upstairs . . . listen!'

We could both hear quite clearly the desperate sobbing coming from the room above us. Uncle Bernard turned and went hesitantly up the wooden stairway. I heard him call out very quietly, 'Bernard here.' Then he knocked at the door and called out more loudly, 'Bernard here!' Then the creaking of the floorboards above my head and the diminishing sobbing told me that my mother had unlocked the door and that Uncle Bernard was with her in the bedroom. Finally the sobbing ceased completely. I suppose this silence lasted for about ten minutes. Then, unbelievably, Uncle Bernard's footsteps could be heard coming slowly down the stairs. I also heard my mother's renewed and impassioned weeping. It seemed almost to shake the cottage ceiling.

Uncle Bernard opened the sitting-room door and again we stared at each other across the room.

'What have you done to her?' I asked harshly.

He glanced at me for a brief moment, his blue eyes totally blank. Then, carelessly, he shrugged his shoulders. It was only then, during the tense silence that followed, that I knew that I wanted, more than anything else in the world, to kill him. He was destroying my mother, so I would destroy him. In the instant that the thought turned into words, so the words became for me an absolute reality. A burning and furious resolve came over me. I would kill him! Never had I felt such an upsurge of sheer physical strength combined with an icy and implacable coldness of intention. Without hesitation, I darted to the supper table, picked up the carving knife that was lying beside the cold chicken, gripped it tight and, raising my arm, rushed across the little room to plunge the knife deeply into his heartless heart.

But, of course, it was comparatively easy for him, a grown man, to grab hold of my wrist, which he then twisted so violently that the knife fell with a clatter on to the linoleum. Uncle Bernard kicked it away across the room and loosened his grip on me. Just for an instant we faced each other; then he crossed the room, turned and, with a half-smile on his lips (his eyes never smiled), he left the room.

I heard the front door shut, followed by the garden gate; and I heard the sound of the engine as his car moved off. Then, and only then, did I realise that I was shaking from head to foot. I put out my hand to find a chair, but even that effort was too great. I thought I would fall . . . so I sank back on to the windowsill. Now the room began to spin round me. I concentrated my gaze on the supper table: cold chicken was there with a carving fork beside it; two plates were there; a salad in a bowl was there; a loaf of bread on a board was there; some cheese on a plate and some butter in a dish were also on the table . . .

Somehow this concentrated and repeated listing helped my inner balance. Slowly I stood up, but my knees almost buckled beneath me, so I gripped a nearby chair and sat down again. I stayed motionless for quite a while even though I could still hear my mother's intermittent sobbing. I knew that before I could manage the stairs I must be steadier on my legs; and that before I could face my mother I had to be in complete control of myself, or else, instantly, she would notice my condition.

By now my mother's crying had somewhat quietened. I sat very still for a few moments longer, then rose to my feet, went to the sitting-room door, opened it and crept slowly up the stairs. Quietly I opened the bedroom door, crossed the room to the bed on which my mother lay, and took her gently in my arms. Two things were clear in my mind: I would *never* tell my mother what had just happened; and Uncle Bernard, I knew, would never *dare* to do so.

7

Ambiguities

The following spring, having booked our rooms well in advance, we succeeded in spending our holidays at Southsea. Lady Knowles was already installed in her small private hotel which was quite close to us, so my mother had a friendly presence to whom she could turn for company. For me, however, our arrival was a disappointment. Vividly, I had imagined watching the sea heaving and gathering together its mountainous powers in order to crash down jubilantly and triumphantly upon the docile sands of the tranquil beach; and the sound of the sea, too, if not the sight of it, would be with me all through the night, possessing me even in my dreams. But although our sitting-room had big bow windows, I found that, between our lodgings and the sea, there was a vast expanse of green grass, common land open to all. And this common was crowded with children playing games, grown-ups strolling about, and dogs chasing and smelling each other in free and curious recognition.

For Roger, already accustomed to Dartmouth, the absence of the sea meant little, so he was happy to make new friends on the common, kicking a ball about with them or wielding a cricket bat against a bowled assault. For me, too, there were compensations. One or two of the people on the green were flying kites, and these kites seemed on occasion to be difficult to manage. There was one tall and solitary young man trying to manipulate his king of all kites. He was dark and good-looking, and somehow I felt very attracted to him, although he himself was totally engrossed in manoeuvring his enormous eagle of the sky. Not receiving any recognition from him I moved closer, also watching the kite with fascinated absorption but hoping, with an even deeper concentration, that one day he would talk to me. He could scarcely avoid it! After we had chatted a bit, I discovered that his name was Bill and that he was a midshipman in the Navy. He was also, I realised, the first 'grown-up' man with whom I had ever had a conversation (apart from the curate, Mr Haywell, at the Vicarage, and my mother's youngest brother, Stephen, who was only four years older than I). Bill explained to me how one should manoeuvre a kite, and he allowed me to have a try. Seizing hold of the long strong cord, I found this such an ecstatic moment that I quite forgot to miss the sound of the sea.

As a result of these varied activities the normal pattern of our holidays took on a completely different form. My mother spent most of the mornings 'having coffee' with Lady Knowles at her private hotel. Then, as usual, she would take her daily rest after her lunch with us in our lodgings. One afternoon a week she had her dancing lesson, combined with *thé dansant*, at the Grand Hotel, and on the other afternoons she usually went for a walk with her dancing partner, the aforementioned major in the Indian Army. Roger, who was always a popular and gregarious figure, spent most of his time with his new friends on the common.

Suddenly, during this first proper seaside holiday, it struck me that we all seemed to have grown into a new independence in relation to one another. And this, in a rather exciting way, was matched by a new sense of personal independence alive in all three of us.

One day Roger suggested that he and I should secretly follow the major and our mother on their regular afternoon walk. 'Let's stalk them,' he suggested, grinning, 'then we can see what they're really up to.'

I took to the idea, and so, keeping a good distance between us and them, we set out behind them. But they walked so slowly that stalking them proved rather dull. They must have talked as they went along, but they never turned their heads towards each other except when they were about to cross a road. Then the major, after looking both ways, would take my mother's arm and guide her across to the opposite pavement. At such moments, giggling, we would dart behind someone's drive gates, or into a shop porch, or behind a pillar box if one were handy. And then, when the coast was clear, we would continue to 'stalk' them, as Roger insisted on calling it. I noticed that the major always walked on the side of the pavement that was closest to the road. He would even change sides on the pavement to do this. I wondered why.

''Cos he's got decent manners, I suppose,' Roger grumbled. Looking back, I think he felt somewhat displaced by the appearance of another man in our small family unit.

From behind, the major looked rather nice. He was of middle height, straight-backed, sometimes wearing a grey flannel suit and sometimes 'bags' and a tweed jacket. And always, like my mother, he wore gloves.

This irritated Roger. 'What the dickens does he want to wear gloves for?' he asked. 'He's not in uniform.'

'But men do wear gloves, don't they?' I inquired.

'Not unless they're in uniform,' Roger persisted. He could be very stubborn when he felt like it. He paused. 'Unless, of course, he's terribly posh,' he added unwillingly.

'Well, p'raps he is terribly posh,' I suggested hopefully. That would add a further element of excitement to this already momentous holiday.

Sometimes the two strollers left the busier shop-filled streets and turned into wider and quieter roads. Here an occasional garage had sprung up, and these enchanted Roger. His overriding ambition at that time was to possess his own motorbike. He knew, of course, that he would have to wait years and years before he would either be old enough or, more important, rich enough to be able to own one. But that did not stop him from lingering lovingly at every garage which housed a motorbike. Sometimes, so intent was he that we would almost lose our strollers.

Then one morning, after breakfast, my mother announced that she had invited the major back to our lodgings for tea.

'When?' asked Roger.

'This afternoon,' my mother replied.

A long silence followed this announcement.

'What's his name?' Roger asked finally.

'John D'Oyley,' my mother answered quietly. 'Major John D'Oyley.' She paused. 'He is anxious to meet you both . . . to meet both my children,' she added.

I suppose we could have guessed something from that, but neither of us did.

'D'Oyley,' Roger made a wry face. 'A frog . . . a Frenchie.'

'Not at all,' said my mother quickly. 'He happens to be descended from one of the oldest families in this country . . . possibly even older than your father's because his family dates back to Saxon times.'

I was aware that this statement, among members of the Giffard family, would have been regarded as close to heresy. Instantly I sprang to my father's defence.

'How could he be?' I asked. 'William the Conqueror was the beginning of everything – in this country, I mean – wasn't he?'

There was a pause. 'I don't really know,' my mother answered wearily. She must have heard many such arguments down the years.

Lately I had noticed that when she returned from her afternoon walks she often looked rather tired, so I interpreted her present look of slight strain as being due to this unaccustomed daily exercise.

She shifted in her chair. 'Anyway, he's coming to tea this afternoon,' she repeated. 'He'll be here at about four o'clock and he'll come in his motorcar.'

'He's got a motorcar?' Roger brightened visibly.

'Of course he has,' replied my mother. 'He's a major in the Army.'

There was no obvious connection between these two sentences but Roger and I, who knew almost as little about the Army as my mother, could not help being impressed.

My mother rose to her feet. 'Well, I shall go out this morning and buy a few nice cakes.' She paused. 'And perhaps I had better have some scones too . . . men don't always like sweet things.' Then she turned to me and added, 'Would you like to come, darling?' I knew from her voice that she wanted me, perhaps even needed me, to accompany her. I thought of Bill flying his enormous kite on the common but swiftly decided that this was not an ordinary sort of day; so the choice was not really mine.

I nodded my head. 'I'd like to come,' I answered.

With seeming irrelevance I suddenly remembered my romantic pre-conceptions of this holiday by the sea. I would paddle, and then lie down on the sands where the shallow, frothing waves could cuddle up to me, and then perhaps I might jump up and cautiously approach the turbulent incoming tide. For my mother had firmly impressed upon me that never, never was I to go too far out into the water because, as I could not swim, I could easily be pulled out of my depth by a strong wave or current. Now, staring out of the window across the common whilst waiting for my mother to get ready, it struck me, fancifully, that something of this nature was already happening to all three of us. The moon had changed: new tides of experience were about to break down upon us – and all because a major in the Indian Army was coming to have tea with us.

My mother returned with her hat and coat on, and together she and I took a rather constrained walk towards the shopping area. My mother seemed preoccupied. She hardly spoke. Preoccupation, of course, was a natural part of all shopping expeditions because comparing prices was routine. One went to the first shop, then, uncommitted, one went on to the second shop, always asking the same question: 'Are you sure you haven't got anything a little cheaper?' Shopping was quite a concentrated exercise, yet my mother's present preoccupation seemed to be of a different nature. But, as I reminded myself again, this was clearly not an ordinary sort of day.

As if to confirm this, I suddenly heard my mother saying to the man behind the counter, 'And a small packet of China tea, too, please.'

I was amazed. Of course, if the major came from India he might be glad of a change in tea. But equally he might have grown quite attached to Indian tea, which we always bought because it was cheaper. In any case, if he was in the British Army and had a motorcar, what was he doing in India? This was the main question that nagged me.

Finally, laden with small parcels, my mother and I left the shop. Then suddenly, outside on the pavement, my mother said, 'We won't go back the way we came, darling . . . we'll go back by the church.'

Every Sunday my mother and I went to an Anglican church for the celebration of the Holy Eucharist. It was a beautiful church with a good choir and a forceful preacher. But I very rarely listened to the sermons. I had got so used to Uncle Bernard's 'put on' orations that I preferred my own wandering thoughts. They led me to all sorts of places, places that I didn't otherwise have very much chance to explore. So we set off towards the church and, instead of passing it, my mother paused to look at the noticeboard in the churchyard where the times of the church services were posted. She studied them for quite a long time, then she said quietly, 'I think, darling, I shall go to Confession . . . now.'

I was completely taken aback. Of course I knew all about Confession. I had been to Anglican churches since I was ten years old, first at both my early schools and then sometimes with my mother during those holidays that were not spent at the Vicarage. It seemed that I had stared at those little black confessional boxes scattered round churches ever since I could remember, except in Uncle Bernard's church and the one I attended in Bedford. And now my mother was actually going into one. I felt totally confused. I had often wondered how wicked one had to be, how great a 'sinner', before you had to go behind that black curtain into one of the little black boxes and confess to the priest in order to have your sin, or sins, forgiven. Privately I had concluded, in my childish way, that murder might be the only thing really bad enough to drive one into a confessional box. But even there surely another difficulty could arise, or so I thought. For I knew that whatever you confessed had to be held as a sacred secret between the priest and God Himself. Only on those terms could the priest grant you forgiveness for your sins. But what if the whole country was looking for a murderer and only the priest and God Himself knew who the murderer really was? That, surely, could put the priest in a terrible fix? And as my mother most certainly was not a murderer, why was she going into one of those little black boxes?

Perhaps my mother sensed my confusion and dismay, for as we stood in the churchyard she turned to me and said quietly, 'I shan't be long, darling. So wait for me here, please . . . and don't squash the cakes!' She forced a smile, then turned and walked up the short path to the church and finally disappeared into the darkness of its great porch.

I hung about by the bench on which she had placed the shopping for what seemed ages, then I moved away and read some of the headstones above the graves. Then I went over to the noticeboard and studied the days and times of all the church services. I read them over and over again, until at long last I saw my mother emerge from the darkness of the church porch. She was holding a handkerchief to her face and sobbing as if her heart would break. I picked up the shopping and ran to her, leading her back to the noticeboard which shielded us from the occasional passers-by. We stood there together while the tears streamed down my mother's pale cheeks despite the handkerchief that she held to her eyes while she tried to check her great gasping sobs.

'Darling, whatever's happened? What is it?' I asked in deep alarm, and I put my arm round her, for I felt that she might collapse from the sheer torment of her sorrow.

In time, and in jerks, the words came out through the sobs. 'He said adultery . . . was such a dirty sin.' Her sobs broke out anew as if the very sound of the words brought with them a violent reaction.

Dropping the parcels, I put both my arms tightly round my mother, the better to support her. As always when she was distressed, my immediate pain was for my mother, but this time my concern for her was equalled by the intensity of my hatred for the priest. How could a man of God, who was there 'to grant forgiveness' to all those who 'repented of their sins', speak so to any suffering human being? I could find no answer to this question, and by that I was profoundly shaken. Consequently, inside myself, I made an immediate and implacable resolve: never, under any circumstances whatsoever, would I go into one of those little black boxes and 'confess my sins'. If I were wicked and a sinner, then I would choose to go to the proper Hell which (or so I had been taught) awaited all sinners. At least there I would be subject to, and dependent upon, God's judgment only and upon nothing else. After making this secret resolve I added to myself the words, 'For ever and ever, Amen.'

My arms were still round my mother and I was trying to check her sobs. 'Listen, darling,' I said, 'he doesn't know what he's talking about . . . he's only a clergyman . . . how can he know? He can't . . . he simply can't.'

The words tumbled out of me seemingly of their own accord, and they presented themselves to me not as an argument, but as a rightful arrangement of priorities that was both invisible and yet invincible. Of course I knew what 'adultery' was: it was a word that came into the Bible and history. But it was not a word that had a place in the life of my mother and so it seemed to fly right out of my mind, over my head and far away. Only later was I able, unemotionally, to question it. At this moment all I could do was to repeat, 'He can't know anything about it . . . he can't . . . he just can't.'

Eventually my mother, her eyes swollen with tears, was able to contain her shock and so regain something of her self-possession. I retrieved the cakes in their paperbags from the ground, took my mother's arm, and very slowly we left the churchyard and headed back to our lodgings. We moved like sleepwalkers, and I was glad not to have to talk. My own inner disturbances from the past had been brought abruptly to the surface by this event. I thought to myself, with some surprise, how my own uncertainties over my childish 'faith' at the time of my confirmation had seemed, almost magically, to resolve themselves; or perhaps it was simply a question of acceptance being more important than understanding. But the problem that my mother now had to come to terms with seemed to be on quite a different scale.

When we arrived back at our lodgings my mother went straight to her bedroom. In the sitting-room I found Roger 'making things ship-shape'. Not only was he a genial extravert, he was also gifted in dealing with the practicalities of life, so I was not surprised to find the table already laid for our cold lunch. All Roger's magazines about electronics and motorcars and motorbikes had disappeared from sight. It was all as tidy as a cabin at sea — or so Roger claimed. And Roger himself had put on a clean pair of grey flannel trousers.

'Where's Mum?'

'She's gone to her room.' I hesitated. 'I think she's a bit tired,' I added.

'What about lunch?'

'We'll take it in to her on a tray.'

'Getting ready to go into the attack on the army major?' Roger grinned.

I said no more, and when I took my mother's lunch into her room I was relieved to see that, although she was lying on the bed, her eyes were no longer red and swollen and her expression was less distraught.

'Thank you, darling.' She raised herself into a sitting position.

'Roger's tidied up the sitting-room,' I said, 'so all I've got to do is lay the table and put out the scones and cakes. So have a good rest when you've finished your lunch.'

'I . . . I'll be all right quite soon,' my mother said. 'It was just the shock – '

I returned to the sitting-room to find that Roger had already swallowed his lunch and disappeared to join his friends on the common. I cleared and relaid the table, got the tea ready, and then sat down by the window, looking across the stretch of green grass that was alive with scuttling human ants to where the sea, a thin blue-grey line against the sky, gave evidence of its existence.

I pondered deeply. How could the word 'adultery' ever have cropped up in my mother's confession to the priest? I rose and looked up the word in the small dictionary that I always carried around with me. Yes, the word was there. 'Adultery. Unfaithfulness in marriage.' I put down the dictionary and went back to my chair. But my mother was no longer married. Of course, she had been once. But now she was a widow, so presumably she no longer had anyone to whom she had to be 'faithful' – except herself. I also knew that 'adultery' involved something that was called 'physical intercourse'. At this point in my life I had had no enlightened information on the subject of 'sex'; indeed, the very word 'sex' seemed to be excluded from what was considered polite conversation. However, Roger and I had often shared both baths and bedrooms, and in consequence I knew exactly how my young brother's body was formed and what it looked like. 'Physical intercourse', I supposed, was when the man's body got into the woman's body through the same little hole between one's legs from which 'the curse' – as it was called at school – emerged?

I returned to the perplexing question of 'adultery'. My mother, I reassured myself, could not commit 'unfaithfulness in marriage' because she was *not* still married. But then the thought struck me that she might have participated in this physical act (willingly or otherwise) with a man who *was* married. Would that make her guilty of 'adultery', too? Suddenly I remembered my mother's dancing partner, the unknown visitor, the major! He seemed to be the obvious and, indeed, the only possible candidate. We didn't know any other men outside the family. But would he fit the bill? Somehow I had to find out how, when and where this event had taken place. Certainly not on their walks together, for, as Roger and I had witnessed, the major did not even take my mother's arm except to cross the road. But could not that all have been 'camouflage', just in case someone the major knew in Southsea had seen them together? Also, of course, Roger and I had not followed the strollers every single day, so the major could have taken my mother to his house to commit 'adultery'; or he could have driven her far out into the countryside . . . At this point I felt rather triumphant. I was carefully building up a 'case for the prosecution', as I would one day be doing in court when I was a barrister! Consequently all I had to do now was to prove that the major was a married man; and that fact I would confirm at the coming tea-party.

My thoughts were interrupted by the sound of a car drawing up outside the house. My mother hurried into the sitting-room. She looked rather nervous but I noticed that she had put a little rouge on her pale cheeks which seemed, somehow, to strengthen my case.

'I hope Roger won't be late,' she said. 'It'd look so rude.'

Glancing out of the window I saw him already racing across the common towards our lodgings.

'He's seen the motorcar . . . he's coming now,' I said.

We heard the doorbell ring. 'Shall I go down and let the major in?' I asked eagerly. I'd never met an adulterer before.

'Oh no,' said my mother quickly. 'I've told Mrs Watkins that we've got a friend for tea. She'll open the door and bring him up.'

We heard voices coming up the stairs, then the door opened, and Mrs Watkins said, 'Here's the major, Ma'am,' and disappeared. She probably couldn't make head or tail of his name.

The slight, medium-sized figure of the major entered. When seen face to face he had a quiet, direct look; calm grey eyes, a small moustache, neatly combed hair, together with a rather dapper appearance.

'This is my daughter Ingaret, John.'

I noticed that they were on Christian-name terms. The major held out his hand to shake mine.

Then my mother added, 'And that is my son Roger running up the stairs!'

We all turned and Roger rushed in. 'Sorry, sir.'

'Oh, that's all right. I was a bit early.'

Breathlessly Roger gasped, 'You've got a smashing motorcar outside, sir. Armstrong-Siddeley, isn't it?'

'Yes. They're good cars, aren't they?'

'Spiffing, sir.'

'And a car is useful when one's on leave in England.'

Very useful, I thought to myself.

'I hope I'll be able to have a motorbike one day,' Roger continued eagerly. Then he paused. 'But I daresay in the Navy it might not be necessary.'

There had always been an automatic division in our minds as to what was 'longed for' and what was 'necessary'.

The major smiled. 'Things turn up trumps sometimes,' he said quietly. Then he paused. 'When I was your age I wanted to get into the Navy – but I'm afraid somehow I couldn't get through those exams.'

'Were you disappointed, sir?'

'Very . . . but happily I've learned to love India.'

He and Roger grinned and exchanged a friendly sort of man-to-man look.

'Bad luck, sir.'

The queerest thing of all to me was hearing Roger calling someone 'sir'.

My mother stepped forward. 'Well, shall we all sit down and have some tea?'

We all settled at the round table near the bay window.

The major looked out. 'Nice view . . . though the sea's a bit far off, isn't it?'

'That's what I think.' I spoke up with difficulty. My thoughts were all tangled up with motorcars and adultery and the Army in India and Roger suddenly seeming to be so grown-up. 'But isn't India a long way away for the British Army to get to?' I asked hesitantly.

'When you're there it certainly feels like it sometimes!' The major looked at me quite seriously across the table while he was buttering his scone. I watched his hands: they were the most beautiful hands that I had ever seen on a man, long-fingered, sensitive, and deft. He could have been an artist!

I drew a deep breath. I was about to ask the carefully prepared question in the case for the prosecution. 'But if you've got your own family with you, I s'pose it helps a lot, doesn't it?' I asked in a deliberately casual voice.

'My family?' The major stopped buttering his scone and looked across at me. 'I'm afraid I have no family – ' he paused, 'except, of course, my grandparents. They live here, in Southsea, and they brought me up. That's why I always spend my leave here, at home with them. They are my only living family.'

My 'adultery' theory was shattered: the major wasn't married! So how had the word 'adultery' ever come into my mother's confession to the priest? Suddenly I felt profoundly depressed. The whole thing instantly moved beyond my comprehension. However, I pulled myself together sufficiently for it to be an amiable and relaxed tea-party.

At the appropriate moment the major looked at his watch and rose to say goodbye to us. Of course, we all insisted politely on escorting him down the stairs and out to where his motorcar stood beside the pavement.

Roger examined it with delight. It looked very smart and well-kept and was what was called 'a four-seater'. The yellow paint was spotless. Yellow! Uncle Bernard also had a yellow motorcar; not such a bright yellow – but bright enough to be spotted right across the valley from my viewpoint in the birch tree, standing outside Mrs Mason's cottage where it had stayed, seemingly, for hours on end. Suddenly I recalled the whole episode, and for a moment I was so shaken that I could scarcely wave goodbye as the major drove off.

'Decent chap,' said Roger. 'I like him.' He grinned. 'You must make up to him, Mum, and then one day he might even teach me to drive his car!'

Rather desperately I turned to them both. 'I feel like going for a long, long walk – will it be all right about the washing-up?'

'Of course,' said my mother. She looked relieved, almost happy. 'Mrs Watkins is going to do it for us. I arranged that, too . . . she's such a nice person.' But she spoke abstractedly because she was watching the yellow motorcar drive slowly out of sight. Then she turned and went back into the house with Roger chattering beside her.

I walked resolutely away from the common and along to where a crooked path ran right down to the shore. Once on the deserted beach, I drew a deep breath and flopped down on the sand. For a time I sat motionless, staring ahead of me and scarcely noticing the sea. Then the steady rhythm of the waves helped to activate a corresponding rhythm in my own being. As I watched the waves gathering, mounting, and then breaking down to embrace the receiving sand, darkening the colour of the sand but never changing the mutual exchange of their partnership, so my emotional confusion gradually gave way to a growing capacity for thought.

The major wasn't married . . . so seemingly the 'adulterer' had to be Uncle Bernard . . . not because he, too, had a yellow motorcar, but because of the sobering fact that, as far as I knew, he was the only married man that any of us had known at all intimately. But Uncle Bernard was a clergyman! I almost flinched at the thought. That was why I had not immediately thought of him. But it was even more difficult to imagine how my mother could have managed to commit 'adultery' with Uncle Bernard than it had been with the major. The more I thought about it, the more sure I was that it could not have happened at night, which, I presumed, was the normal time for such a thing to occur between two people who lived under the same roof – for at the Vicarage my mother and I always shared a bedroom; and when she had a dream or a nightmare, even the slightest sound from her would awaken me.

Nor could I possibly imagine that she would have dared to creep across
the top landing of the Vicarage and up the three little steps that led to
where Uncle Bernard and Aunt Magdalen slept, in separate rooms and
with the Great Dane positioned outside their doors. So where else? The
only other place in the Vicarage was Uncle Bernard's study. But what
with Aunt Magdalen wandering about the house and grounds with her
animals, and the maids flitting up and down stairs, not to mention
certain parishioners trailing up the hill 'to see the Vicar', I could not see
that as a possibility either.

I paused, and dismissed the Vicarage. Then I remembered Uncle
Bernard's yellow motorcar. Like the major's, it was a 'four-seater', so
presumably 'adultery' could have taken place inside it. But even this
seemed unlikely, for Uncle Bernard's motorcar must be known to everyone in the district and would have aroused the suspicions of anyone
who came upon it parked in a country lane. No, that wasn't on,
either.

Staring out at the sea, so immediate and yet so infinite, I made an
ugly face at it, and then another ugly face; and I knew that I did so out
of a profound sense of frustration which had brought me close to tears.
I caught my breath to stop the tears and instead gave a deep, deep sigh
– and suddenly I heard the sea sighing with me, one deep sigh after
another. And then, because the tide was coming in, one wave, bolder
than the rest, ventured close to me, splashing right over my shoes and
feet. I gave a little squeak, partly of pleasure and partly of surprise at the
coldness of it, and was suddenly reminded of a christening that we had
stumbled upon in a church not so very long ago: as the priest had dipped
his hand into cold water and then touched the baby's forehead, the baby
had squeaked and kicked out its feet as I had just done.

Glancing round to see that no one was looking, I pulled off my garters,
stockings and gym shoes and held my bare feet straight out in front of
me. The sea took the offering with delight. I continued to watch the
baby waves creeping up over the sand and feeling my feet. Then, in
retreat, they started to play Tom Tiddler's Ground (as Roger and I had
so often done in the past). I watched the wavelets as they withdrew
slowly, slowly, away from me and tried to approach the Tom Tiddler
wave himself without being caught in movement. But they never succeeded. There were large splashes and loud chuckles of delight as the
retreating baby waves joined the advancing wave and together they
moved swiftly and forcefully towards me, demanding my recognition.
And I gave it to them. I joined in. I waited until they had reached my
knees . . . then, regretfully, I drew back, pulled on my stockings over

my wet legs, then my shoes, and ran panting up the cliff path towards our lodgings. But my mood had changed. I felt quite light-hearted. I told myself that I must never forget that I had been christened by the sea.

8

Life Turns a Somersault

At the end of the holidays, feeling rather nervous, I went back to Bedford High School. I was now just seventeen and my matriculation examinations were looming ahead. Although I had been educated on the 'wrong' side of the school, with the emphasis on the Modern subjects rather than the Classical, I was determined to matriculate. But feeling 'out of position' made me more apprehensive than, perhaps, I needed to have been.

The holiday in Southsea had been folded up neatly, like a pack of cards, shuffled, and put back into place. We had seen no more of the major, nor indeed had there been very much time for that. Holidays always flashed by and this one had gone even more quickly than usual. My mother had made no further mention of the major, although their walks continued. In the short time left after the tea-party, Bill, the kite-flyer, reclaimed my interest.

The summer term seemed to flash by, too. Then, unexpectedly, came a letter from my mother. Although it was quite near the end of term she wrote that she was coming up to see me the following weekend. She wanted to see how I was getting on. Not working too hard, she hoped? She suggested that we should have lunch together if my housemistress would permit it. I asked Mrs Burton and permission was given. And when my mother arrived I was glad to see her, and glad of the break, for I had been working very hard. My mother was looking quite perky. She wore a new dress too, which brought out the vivid blue of her eyes. She had always chosen her clothes, and mine, with good taste – in so far as our meagre resources permitted. But on this occasion she looked almost fashionable.

We had lunch together at a cheap little restaurant in Bedford and chatted away happily. Then my mother said rather seriously, 'I want to talk to you, darling.' She paused. 'Could we go back to your house and walk about the garden?'

'Of course we can,' I said instantly. Mrs Burton's house had a large garden which we were only allowed to go into on special occasions, but I was sure that my mother, looking so stylish and beautiful, would be allowed to do anything. And I was right. Mrs Burton joined us briefly and then went back to the house, and we were left to stroll round the garden until finally my mother, finding a wooden seat under a tree, sat down upon it and I sat beside her.

There was a short silence, then my mother reached out and took my hand. 'Darling . . . Major D'Oyley – John – has asked me to marry him.'

Momentarily I was struck dumb. Marriage . . . my mother's remarriage . . . I had never even thought of such a thing – even since discovering that the major was not a married man and might, therefore, be looking for a wife.

'So what are you going to do?' I asked after a short silence.

'I've said I will marry him,' my mother answered quietly. She paused. 'He's the kindest man I've ever met,' she added.

There was a long silence. Then my mother said, very hesitantly, 'But of course it means I will have to go out to India with him.'

'India!'

For the first time my mother's voice broke. 'Yes, darling.' She took both my hands. 'But I couldn't go without you . . . I couldn't . . . couldn't!'

I can still remember the way my heart seemed to drop into my boots. No point now in matriculating; no possibility of going to the Bar; no white wig and wary but conclusive arguments; nothing –

'I couldn't . . . I couldn't travel all that way . . . all that way without you, darling . . . I just couldn't.'

I understood instantly that she was right. And I tried to pay attention.

'No, darling, I see that. You couldn't possibly go without me – to begin with anyway . . .'

'And you wouldn't mind?'

Mind? Mind seeing my mother happy, and looking fashionable and coming into her own, and with a kind man to look after her?

'No, darling,' I said quietly. 'Of course I wouldn't mind. How could I?'

'And you might even like it . . . India, I mean,' she suggested hopefully.

'Of course I might . . . it might be wonderful,' I said, trying to keep the lack of conviction out of my voice.

'So it might be rather wonderful for both of us all round?' my mother suggested.

'I'm sure it will be,' I said firmly. I could feel her insecurity.

She squeezed my hand. Then there was a silence. I looked at her sideways. Her face had suddenly tightened: I could see the strain in the muscles and the well-known dilation of the pupils in her eyes. Of what was she now afraid?

'There . . . there's one other thing – ' she said, as if in answer to my inner question.

I waited. It was sometimes a great effort for her to speak, even to me, about herself.

'One other thing – ' I prompted gently.

The words burst out of her. 'I – I'll have to ask Uncle Bernard to marry us – ' She clenched her hands together so that the bones stood out white and stiff. 'I'll have to ask him, I'll have to. And I – I don't see how I can go through with that, darling . . . I just don't think I could . . . I couldn't!'

So somehow she was still under his spell.

'But why do you have to ask him?' I asked.

She turned to face me. 'Just look at the hospitality we've received. For years and years now the Vicarage has been our home . . . for all three of us. I couldn't not ask him . . . I just couldn't. It'd look dreadful, so mean . . . and ungrateful . . .' She sounded distraught.

Suddenly a bright idea struck me. 'I not only think that you don't have to ask Uncle Bernard to marry you,' I said quietly. 'I don't think you can even consider it.' I took her hand. 'What about Uncle Bertram? He's your favourite brother, and he's a priest . . . a vicar . . . he's got his own parish . . . and his own church in London. He's the person that you can't possibly not ask.'

Instantly my mother became transformed. 'Bertram! Of course! Why on earth did I never think of him before?'

Because you're still under his spell, I thought to myself. And I sighed.

Aloud I said lightly, 'Perhaps one does take one's own brother a bit for granted! I must ask Roger!' I could even smile.

And so we moved into calmer waters.

My mother had already decided that the wedding was to be in London: 'So much easier for everybody to get to.' And I was to be her only bridesmaid. It sounded so funny, the idea of being a bridesmaid to one's own mother! Then the honeymoon was to be spent in France.

'John loves France. In fact, he's always reading French books . . . classics, I mean,' my mother added hastily.

'What else does he like?' I asked with curiosity.

'Oh, Milton, of course,' my mother answered at once. 'He seems to know Milton off by heart. And chess . . . . he'll work out chess problems for hours on end by himself, or so he says!' My mother laughed. 'And bridge too . . . he's very good at bridge, and he says he'll teach me to play as well.'

To me it sounded like life on another planet.

'And what about India?' I asked.

'Oh, yes,' my mother replied. 'We can't go out till October because apparently that is when India starts to get cool. Before October it's much too hot, or so John says. And anyway he's on six months' leave.'

'So when will you get married?'

'We thought early September. People will be back from their holidays by then, so most of our friends and relations should be able to come.' My mother's words seemed to come straight out of her youthful past.

'So will you stay on in Southsea?' I asked.

'Just till the end of your term.'

I felt an enormous sense of relief. I had feared that she might suggest our returning to the Vicarage.

'And then?'

'Well, I thought to start with we might all go to the Court,' my mother continued. 'Then I shall have to spend some time in London planning the wedding . . . you and I will both be very busy.'

'How?'

'We'll have to buy heaps and heaps of summer clothes. You see, John says it is always hot in India . . . and sometimes very hot indeed. And I'll have to think about my wedding dress, and your bridesmaid's dress and hat.' She smiled at me.

I could scarcely believe the enormous switch in outlook, or the fact that my mother really looked happy.

'From the Court we'll have to go miles into Gloucester in the carriage to shop,' I reminded her.

'Well, I shall do most of my shopping either in London or Southsea,' my mother said, and paused. 'Do you remember that splendid dressmaker in the village quite near the Court?'

I nodded. 'Well, I thought you might like to design four evening dresses for yourself and get her to fit them and make them up for you. Once you've designed them she can tell you how much material to get and you'll be able to go into Gloucester to buy what is necessary.'

Four evening dresses! The implications were magical. And to design them myself, too!

'I'd love that,' I breathed. 'I'd love designing them!'

Suddenly life seemed to turn a somersault and show me a new and totally unexpected face. It spoke in a new voice, too. Previously it had presented itself to me in long, involved sentences, with no sort of punctuation whatsoever. Consequently, one had had to turn them over and over in one's mind in order to understand their meaning. But now all that was changed. Life was unfolding in short, sharp sentences like the headlines in a newspaper. There was a full-stop at the end of each just in order to give one time to draw breath.

So Roger and I stayed at the Court for the summer holidays and my mother came down occasionally to visit us. She divided her time between staying at our old lodgings in Southsea in order to see Major John, and visiting Uncle Bertram and his wife Theresa in London where she was deeply engaged in making all the arrangements for the coming wedding. There were the invitations to be sent out, the church arrangements to be made, and plans to be finalised for the reception which was to be given at a nice hotel within easy walking distance of Uncle Bertram's church. In all these matters Uncle Bertram was very knowledgeable and helpful. Finally, there was shopping to be done for both of us: underwear, tennis dresses, cotton afternoon dresses for wearing at something that was called the 'Club'. My mother certainly had her hands full and I got the impression that she enjoyed being so busy. At the Court, I had my head full of the latest fashion trends. I can still remember the four evening dresses that I designed with great excitement. One was in white satin of mid-calf length, with no sleeves and some rather intricate ruching round its square neck. The second was in a sparkling jet-black material on a silk foundation, with a deep V in front, a tight waist and a flared skirt. Then there was an orange chiffon dress with floating square sleeves, and this also was just longer than mid-calf.

Mrs Denning, the village dressmaker, was ecstatic over making what she insisted on calling my trousseau. She was a clever and dedicated seamstress and, more important, she was a good fitter. The only thing that worried her was that she wanted the dresses to be shorter.

'You've got such pretty legs, Miss.'

'Have I?'

I looked down at them. In woollen or cotton stockings they had never struck me as being pretty.

'And such a figure.' Mrs Denning smacked her lips. 'Tiny waist . . . and a nice little lot up here.' She patted her own full bosom.

'A bit too much?'

'They show you off fine!' she answered.

The fourth dress really had to be shorter because it had to serve first as my bridesmaid's dress. Mrs Denning got over that difficulty by giving it a very deep hem which could be let down if necessary.

One weekend when my mother came down to see us she carried something in a huge paperbag, which turned out to be my bridesmaid's hat. It was a large, floppy, corn-coloured straw hat with a pale blue chiffon lining under the brim.

'If it suits you, darling, it will match both your hair and your eyes,' my mother said. 'And if it doesn't suit you, they'll change it for you.'

I saw from the name on the bag that 'they' meant Harrods! Gingerly I put on the hat and it did fit me; in fact, it was extremely becoming. And my mother was delighted. Suddenly, after I had taken off the hat, she came and put her arms around me and kissed me, holding me very closely to her. 'You do know I miss you, my darling, don't you? I miss you very much indeed. And I'm so proud of you . . .'

I heard the emotion in her voice and correspondingly my own throat tightened. I had just received a letter telling me that I had matriculated. The news had given me a certain satisfaction, but not as much as it would have done if events had taken a different course. Now the only real future seemed to be my mother's wedding. For both of us this represented a parting of the ways, but the fact that my mother felt as I did about it made it much easier for me to accept.

By now, of course, I had 'put my hair up'. It was fair and very long, reaching below my waist, so there wasn't a great deal of choice as to what to do with it. It had a natural wave in front, so I just combed it back from my forehead and twisted it into a large 'bun' in the nape of my neck. Occasionally, too, I did my hair in two long plaits and wound them round and over my head like a crown and skewered them into position with long bronze hairpins. But my mother didn't like that so well. 'It makes you look rather foreign, darling,' she said, puzzled. 'German, or Dutch perhaps.' This idea, of course, greatly thrilled me, but as the plaits were much more difficult to keep in place than the bun I went back to the easy way.

Roger had no such decisions to make as to what he should wear on the wedding day: naval uniform, of course. 'And a clean white shirt,' my mother reminded him. Consequently, during these holidays at the Court, he had no shopping problems. He spent most of the time playing cricket on the village green with the village lads; or else accompanying our friendly host as he tramped the woods and fields of his estate in order to 'keep an eye on things' in preparation for the coming shooting season.

And so the days slipped by until finally the wedding day drew close.

Aunt Magdalen and Uncle Bernard of course had been invited, but I was told that they had not accepted. The rest of my mother's immediate family, together with mutual friends and distant relations, had all sent joyful letters of acceptance. Uncle Bertram's vicarage was very spacious, so he was able to put all three of us up for the night before the wedding, together with two of his other sisters.

On arrival from the country Roger and I found that the vicarage was quite close to the church. All we had to do was to walk there through the graveyard. On the wedding morning, as I was standing in my bedroom before the mirror and putting on my large, floppy hat, suddenly the church bells began to ring. I had not slept very well: the noise of the London streets had been new to me; so was the throbbing of my heart and the uneasy wandering of my mind regarding the totally unknown future that now lay before both my mother and me. The joyful sound of the pealing church bells brought my carefully restrained emotions to the surface. I grew apprehensive. Supposing we all went over to the church and Major John (as Roger and I now called him) wasn't there . . . or supposing my mother wanted to change her mind, when it was too late . . . or supposing –

My bedroom door opened suddenly and Aunt Theresa stood there. 'Are you ready, Ingaret? Your mother is.'

I nodded. But ready for what? . . . Supposing –

'Your hat is very pretty, Ingaret. It suits you.'

'Yes . . . Mummy bought it – ' Why on earth was I suddenly calling her 'Mummy'? I tried to pull myself together. 'Shall I come now?'

'Yes, dear. Your mother is ready.'

I followed Aunt Theresa down the corridor and then suddenly my mother appeared in her bedroom doorway. She looked calm and very beautiful. She wore a plain blue-grey silk dress and a small toque.

'Is it time for us to walk over to the church, do you think?' she asked quietly.

Some more bells suddenly joined in the jingle-jangle and seemed to give us the answer to her question.

'I expect it is,' Aunt Theresa replied.

So we walked quietly out of the vicarage, across the graveyard, and into the church while the bells pealed out ever more joyously, or so it seemed.

The church was fairly full. Major John was already standing in position in the nave. He watched my mother as she walked down the aisle towards him just as I, behind my mother, watched him. The same calm, direct regard was turned towards both of us: he wore a frock coat and a white carnation in his buttonhole. Then the church music started; the choir entered; the vows were taken and there was an address by Uncle Bertram, and finally more music and hymns as the newly-wedded couple turned to leave the church.

The reception that followed was, I suppose, like all other receptions: champagne and chatter. Roger was in his element as he wandered round filling up the glasses, talking and laughing with everyone. I mixed in, too, but inside myself I felt quite lost. Looking back now, I can see that these must have been the very first moments of my complete emancipation from my mother. Paradoxically, although I belonged to her in terms of life, yet she had belonged more to me than to herself in terms of being, so dominated was she by her persistent inner fears. But now all that was over. My mother was no longer the Hon. Mrs Giffard; she was Mrs John D'Oyley . . . and that was that.

PART II

One of my sketches of our Indian bearer.

9

Struck by Lightning

My mother's letters were frequent during her month's honeymoon and they gave me the impression that she was happy. I was glad of this because, whilst staying on at the Court after Roger had returned to Dartmouth, the solitary adjustment that I had to make to our new existence had been quite difficult. Previously, for both of us, life had been an endless round of activities: ceaseless mental and physical activities at school; ceaseless everyday activities in the holidays; ceaseless financial adjustments of all sorts to be made at all times. Nor could even the certainty of the following day be taken for granted, for there were always the vagaries of my mother's health to be taken into account. But now, neither health nor money was ever mentioned.

My mother and Major John returned to England at the beginning of October. Living by the new rules, we all three moved up to London; a double room and a single room at a nice hotel. There was still a lot of shopping to be done; also medical advice to be given and injections to be received against the perils of unknown India. There were, too, things called 'topees' to be bought as a protection against the sun. Sometimes it almost felt as if we were going into battle instead of to India. However, Major John, despite his introversion, was a calm and steadying influence throughout our preparations.

The sailing date grew nearer and nearer: we were departing in a troopship from Tilbury. Roger, of course, got leave from Dartmouth to come and see us off. That was the worst moment of the whole enterprise – feeling the trembling movement of the enormous troopship drawing away from the quay on which Roger was standing trimly to attention, slowly growing smaller and smaller before our eyes. My mother took Major John's arm, and I felt the tears creep down my cheeks – my beloved younger brother for whom I had battled and with whom I had never argued; who was my opposite in temperament but nevertheless a close inhabitant of my heart. I could only remember one idiotic occasion when I had censured him, and that was when we were both at the same school in Folkestone where, for a brief period, we had been boarders. Suddenly, one day in the playground, a girl of about my own age had pulled up her gym skirt and displayed her knickers for all the pupils to behold. Roger had burst out laughing . . . whereas I was most truly shocked and had seen fit to report the event to my mother.

Irrationally, this incident returned to me when Roger's uniformed figure on the quayside was almost out of sight. What a little prig I must have been! I watched the quay fading into the distance, empty now of everything but tall concrete buildings which were blurred through my tears.

I had never been in a ship before, except for one brief holiday when as children we had been to stay with my grandmother in Jersey. Then I had been sick both going and coming back. And even in this large troopship, as we went through the Bay of Biscay, I had to spend the first two days in my cabin, which, as I loved the sea so much, greatly depressed me. However, life on board ship looked more promising when I tottered up on deck to find it swarming with men. I had never seen so many all together before, except perhaps at a county cricket match. However, as the sea calmed, more women joined the men on deck and soon the dining-room was full. In the evenings everyone changed for dinner, so my creations came out on show. The men too changed into something called 'mess kit'. They looked so glamorous and glittering that I couldn't imagine why it should be given this apparently derogatory title until it was explained to me! Then, blissfully, after dinner a band played out on deck, inviting us to dance. Dancing was the one thing in the world that I knew I could do beautifully. While still at school I had been asked to give a performance at a charity ball in aid of Queen Charlotte's Hospital in London; I had been partnered by a man who was a professional and I hadn't even been nervous! So now I prayed, as I sat on deck beside my mother and my stepfather, that some man would come over and ask me to dance with him. But no one came. Did I look too young? Was I over-chaperoned?

In childhood, behind the green baize door of the Manor, I had often heard the phrase 'giving the glad eye' to someone. But I didn't know what this meant or, therefore, how to do it. Nor did I feel particularly 'glad' at that moment. Finally my stepfather got up, and with my mother on his arm, they did a few decorous and awkward dancing steps. I sat alone . . . but not for long. Almost at once a tall, elegant, Air Force officer came over and asked me to dance. He had an Irish voice and a double-barrelled name and I was in luck, for he danced divinely. We started with a waltz. At that time, it was fashionable to introduce a dip in the turn of the waltz. Of course, Paddy knew all about that, but I didn't. However I followed his dip as deeply and dramatically as he performed it, and with a similar ease. We danced together the whole evening and my partner invented steps so that we whirled, and turned, and swung and dipped until, suddenly coming out of my dream of delight, I saw my mother advancing along the deck towards me.

She looked at her watch. 'Darling, John and I are going down to our cabin now, but I don't want you to stay up later than ten o'clock.'

I looked at my watch. Only another half-hour's dancing . . . I started to protest. But my mother was firm. 'Ten o'clock, darling.' She turned and left.

And so, at ten o'clock sharp, I left Paddy and went down to my cabin. Walking slowly along the deck, I saw various couples sitting closely together under the shadow of the lifeboats or leaning on the railings in the moonlight with their arms around each other. What a waste of time, I thought to myself, because I could hear that the band was still playing. Inexplicably, the sound of the distant music made me dissolve into tears as I made my way down to the lower deck.

I was sharing a cabin with a dull-looking, middle-aged lady who, as I opened the door, was sitting on the bottom bunk pulling the stockings off her rather fat and very white legs. She looked up when I came in and saw that I had been crying.

'What's the matter?'

'I've got to come to bed at ten,' I gulped. 'And I – I so want to go on dancing.'

There was a pause. 'It's better to have to stop when you want to go on,' she said quietly, 'than having to go on when you want to stop.'

My tears stopped abruptly. I had not expected a philosophical reply from my cabin companion. She was wiser and more interesting than she looked, and I knew her words would stay with me.

Once we had left the bumpy, sick-making Bay of Biscay and moved into the Mediterranean the days became as colourful as the evenings. Our great ship trembled across the blue water like a violin bow across its strings. There were games that one could play on deck if one wanted to, and if one got up early, as I did, one could watch the sun rise in a magnificent show of ever-moving colour. This foreign world that I had so often read about really had its own enchantment, although gradually it did grow hotter and hotter.

Eventually we left the champagne sparkle of the Mediterranean and edged our way slowly and almost painfully into and along the Suez Canal. And as we left the sea breezes behind so the dead heat of the arid desertland, now visible beyond both banks of the Canal, increasingly pressed down upon us as if to possess our very humanity.

Finally, our troopship, after edging and squeezing its gradual way forward, reached Port Said and moored alongside the quay, thus cutting off even the faint movement of air created by its slow passage. The heat now bore down upon us with fierce intensity.

Looking over the side, I saw various activities going on below: young boys were diving deeply into the still and filthy water of the Canal, emerging with something in their hands and triumphantly waving to us.

'They're diving for pennies,' Major John explained, and, putting his hand in his pocket, he threw a penny into the water which provoked a further flurry of activity among the boys. Men in boats, too, were clustering round our ship with fruit for sale. They threw ropes attached to baskets up and over the ship's railings, and those who wanted to pulled on the rope, took out the fruit and returned the basket with the money inside it. The din both from the shouting 'bumboat men' and the divers' cries of 'Sahib!' and 'Baksheesh!' was terrific.

Finally, once the gangway was fixed, Major John led us across and on to the quayside.

'We'll go to "Simon Artz",' he said.

'What's that?' I asked, hoping that it might turn out to be an art gallery.

'It's an enormous emporium,' my stepfather answered, 'full of things both good and bad.'

So we stepped into the street, Major John holding my mother's arm and me walking on his other side. He insisted on that. 'Keep close to me,' he told me repeatedly. Now that we were really in the East the heat didn't only hit us from above; it hit us in the face from the crowded streets around us. So crowded indeed was this narrow track that it was quite difficult for us to keep close together. Beggars were squatting on both sides of the track and flies buzzed around them as, in croaking and persistent voices, they pressed their wares upon us. 'Sahib, Sahib . . . Memsahib . . . Missi-Sahib . . .' they importuned us. But we never paused until, under Major John's guidance, we finally reached the doors of Simon Artz and entered.

Once inside, despite the immediate proximity of the jostling crowds in the street, all was absolutely silent. It was certainly an immense store, with a number of huge arched departments all leading into one another, and all silently serviced by gliding, white-clad figures with turbans on their heads. It was somewhat cooler in here because overhead things called *punkahs* were being pulled leisurely to and fro by other men in turbans, sitting silent and cross-legged on the floor, in order to generate some slight movement in the heavy atmosphere.

Major John wanted to give my mother a memento of her first visit to the East, so we make our way to the jewellery department. As I was not interested in trinkets, I strolled through an archway into an enormous carpet department. There seemed to be carpets and rugs everywhere! Seeing some magnificent Persian rugs ahead of me I moved forward to admire them. This particular department was quite empty of Europeans, presumably because tourists and travellers bought trinkets and not carpets. As I stood admiring these rugs, two white-coated and turbaned assistants hurried up to me.

'Missi-Sahib like rugs?'

'Yes – when they are beautiful . . . like these,' I answered politely.

'Most beautiful rugs over that way, Missi-Sahib.' Both natives pointed to the far end of the department.

They seemed to speak with a certain urgency, and made way for me with obsequious movements. So the three of us proceeded across the enormous department until finally we arrived at the far end of the store, quite alone. One of the two Egyptians bent down and pulled away a rug, and then another rug beneath it, and exposed quite a large door in the floor . . . leading, as I thought, to a sort of basement. As he opened the door to this basement I caught a glimpse of another dark face staring up at us from below.

'Best carpets down there, Missi-Sahib,' one of the two salesmen said. His voice was very soft but still had a sense of urgency in it.

I put my foot out in order to descend through the trapdoor into the 'basement' when suddenly, as it were, I was struck by lightning. Something flashed through me in one second from my head to my toes . . . and in that one second I had turned and fled. So unexpected, so instant and so swift was my flight that neither of the men had even a moment to put out a hand to stop me. Nor did they try to follow me, presumably because if they had done so my screams would have echoed through the vast department into the next one. Panting, I finally reached the entrance to the jewellery department. I paused, gasping for breath. My mother and Major John were still bending over the trinket stall . . . the sight of them was almost unbelievable. I was shaking in a way that I could not understand, but eventually I steadied myself and went to join them.

My mother looked up. 'Ah, there you are, darling.' She turned to my stepfather. 'Well, shall we go, John?' We all three turned to leave the store, but as we reached the door to the crowded street my stepfather said to me, 'Keep close to us, Ingaret. I'm told the white-slave traffic is pretty rife these days. Better take my arm.'

I did so. But such was my innocence and my ignorance that I had no idea what his remark really meant. Surely slavery had come to an end aeons ago? However, I did take his arm. It felt quite strange but oddly comforting struggling through the crowds and hanging on to a man's arm. Suddenly I realised that this was something that I had never done before.

Without linking arms it would have been impossible for the three of us not to get separated, so crowded was the pot-holed track along which we were edging our way. Naked children, wearing nothing but loincloths, scrambled, pushed and clung to us, all with hands outstretched, crying, 'Baksheesh! Baksheesh! Missi-Sahib!' Again there were beggars on both sides of the track, some blind, some without legs, all beating their begging bowls with the same cry of 'Baksheesh!' Clusters of flies swarmed round the open sores on their faces and bodies before moving away to buzz around us. There were also the local people jostling down the same track, some of the women with half-covered faces and all wearing saris and long dresses. And just as the so-called 'road' was thick with bodies, so the air was as thick as treacle, while the sun in an oddly white sky sucked away my energies as if it were devouring them.

At long last we reached our ship and, once up the gangway, I was able to draw breath. I found a shady corner on deck where I could escape from the sun and think about my first impressions of the East. Again and again my thoughts returned to the incident in the department store. What had prompted my instant flight? I could still feel 'the flash of lightning' passing through me. Looking back on it, I realised that there had been an unnatural sense of urgency in the two natives as they accompanied me to where the 'most beautiful rugs' were stored. At the time, their urgency was understandable. They wanted to show me the best of their wares, as did shopkeepers everywhere; and they hoped to persuade me to buy something. But however many times I went over the incident in my mind, I could not explain the even greater urgency of my lightning dash across the empty department before either of the men had had time to put out a hand to stop me.

It was not until many years later, when I was idly reading a book called *White-Slave Traffic in the East*, that I realised how narrowly I had escaped abduction. If I had shown even a moment's hesitation before turning away from that open trapdoor, one of the natives would have put his hand over my mouth, the other would have pinioned my hands behind me, and together they would have slid me swiftly down into the open arms of the man waiting below, and then immediately shut and re-covered the trapdoor with the two rugs which had originally concealed it. The whole procedure would have taken seconds. And later, when my mother and stepfather came in search of me, the man would have pointed to the jostling crowds in the street, saying 'Missi-Sahib go out there,' and so, of course, I would have been lost for ever. Even as a grown woman, so strong was my reaction to this book that I could not go on reading it; and the immediacy of my flight from the turbaned shop assistants continued to puzzle and amaze me.

Pondering in my corner on the deck, I suddenly realised that our ship was once again in motion. We were leaving Port Said, with its arid deserts and impoverished humanity, and beginning to ease our way cautiously through the Suez Canal. I rose to my feet. Before long we would be reaching the Indian Ocean, a prospect which both excited and alarmed me. The boisterous masculine activities of the Bay of Biscay had reduced me to a violent condition of seasickness, so what effect would an ocean have on me? But when we finally made our entry into the Indian Ocean I was enchanted. This was a delicate and shimmering sea, and to be surrounded by it was, for me, exquisite. It had the sparkle of champagne, and so soaked was it by sunlight that at moments it appeared to be almost white. It was smooth and friendly and played childish games with the flying fish which lent their own diamond-dropping idiom to the glittering waters.

I sat on deck either by myself with a book, or with my mother and stepfather, and this interlude gave me time to think about the relation-ship between them which appeared to be so quiet and effortless. Major John's care of my mother seemed to be as profound as was his interest in classical literature. He admired her beauty, both in appearance and in spirit. He took an interest in her clothes; and very much later I learned that she had even been able to speak to him of her 'irrational' fears. It was perhaps in consequence of all these factors that a new relaxation became evident in my mother's being. For my stepfather, too, it seemed that life had suddenly acquired a new meaning. I did not know at the time that Major John had only once before in his life loved a woman, a married woman to whom he had for years remained constant, despite the usual necessary marital evasions. Then one day he had learned that she had betrayed him: she had taken a second lover. Helped perhaps by his inherent good breeding, without making a scene he had turned and walked straight out of her life. He had asked for a transfer to his regiment in India and there had continued his normal bachelor army life until that fateful afternoon when, on leave in Folkestone, he had seen my mother across the room in the Grand Hotel where they had both been 'taking dancing lessons'. Major John was the second man who had fallen in love with my mother at first sight, and to the end of his days he was to find in her perfection; as she was to find in him a gentle and steady support.

We arrived in Bombay when the sun was beginning to lose its fevered midday concentration. That very same night we were to travel by train to Jhansi, where my stepfather was to receive his posting orders. Meanwhile Major John suggested that we should all go to the Bombay Yacht Club for tea, so we took the taxi on there after depositing our luggage at the railway station. A spacious green lawn lay beyond the clubhouse and close to the sea, and upon the lawn was a collection of small tables and chairs which were nearly all occupied, as the British were taking tea. We joined them, and tea was brought to us by spotlessly white-garbed and turbaned Indian servants. There was the clatter of china, and voices and laughter all around us, but we managed to find a table to ourselves.

Suddenly, out of the clubhouse and across the green lawn advanced two figures: one was a tall, broad-shouldered Indian in a long white coat with jewelled buttons and wearing a white turban fastened in the front by an enormous jewelled brooch. By his side walked a slender and most beautiful Indian woman: a magnificent sari draped her elegant form, and jewels flickered and shone from her elegantly dressed black hair. These two persons walked, side by side, up and down the length of the green lawn, then turned and retraced their steps. They repeated this pattern for a considerable time, up and down, up and down, exchanging only an occasional comment which was accompanied by a turning of their heads. Nobody except me seemed to notice them.

Finally, with restrained but excited curiosity, I asked my stepfather who these two people were.

Major John gave them a glance over his shoulder. 'Box-wallahs,' he replied. 'I believe they're the only two Indians allowed into this club.'

'Why?' I asked.

He misunderstood my question. 'Because they are exceptionally rich, I suppose,' he replied, and filled my mother's teacup.

For all the years that have passed, I can still remember that scene vividly. All those English people sitting at their little tables along the sea-wall, wearing shady hats and cotton dresses and chatting together to the tinkle of cups and occasional bursts of laughter, seemingly quite oblivious of the two dignified figures silently pacing up and down the lawn. I would have rejoiced at being able to talk to them, but of course there was no chance of my doing so in those days.

A little later the sun, as if from sheer exhaustion, sank below the distant sea-line and we rose to continue our journey.

10

Arrival in India

We took a rather battered taxi to Bombay station and, on arrival, Indian porters rushed forward to take our luggage. My stepfather replied to their appeals in their own language, Hindustani, and we began to follow the porters who were wheeling our piled-up luggage towards the platform where our train was waiting. But it was slow going. Every so-called platform was parked with bodies, some stretched full-length on the ground asleep, others awake, others cooking on small braziers, and little children skipping about all over the bodies or around the sari-clad women. And the air was as full of the noise of voices as the platform was full of the densely-wedged bodies. How would we ever get through?

'Follow the porters,' my stepfather said; and sure enough, the porters, shouting their heads off, were slowly making headway through the recumbent bodies.

'What's happened?' I asked, amazed.

'Oh, it's always like this,' my stepfather answered casually. 'These people could live here for a week . . . or more . . . before their train arrives.'

'A week!' my mother gasped.

My stepfather turned to her, smiling. 'An irrational country,' he said, 'therefore no sense of time in our dimension.' He paused. 'I daresay they may find it a bit of a change, too . . . a sort of holiday. What baffles me is how they ever catch the right train from the right platform and arrive at the right station!'

So we followed our porters, picking our way and taking infinite care not to step on any of the Indians under our feet. But the crowd seemed scarcely to notice us: they were so busy shouting, cooking and sleeping. At last we arrived at the correct platform and the luggage was piled into our carriages. Two sleepers had been booked: a double one for my mother and stepfather and a single one for me. To my amazement a huge block of ice stood in each, while a small fan whirled overhead. But the windows of both compartments were locked.

'Keep your window locked,' my stepfather told me. 'It keeps it cooler and it's safer.'

I looked along the length of the train and understood his meaning. There were Indians covering every inch of the train, some on the roof, many in the corridors or standing or sitting on the outside steps. We all three went to our sleepers, and not long afterwards the train began to move forward in a series of jerks. Once out of the station it chugged along at a very slow, comfortable pace which made me understand why all those Indians travelling on the roof of the train, or squatting on the steps, were able to keep their position. I imagine that none of them could sleep. But neither could I. I did not even bother to undress. I turned off the light in my compartment and for the whole night sat by my window staring out into the darkness.

Once we had left Bombay and its outskirts we moved into a land of complete blackness. Just occasionally we stopped at stations where the same congested scrambling of bodies took place, some Indians laden with packages leaving the train and others boarding it. But the stations seemed to be few and far between, and when we moved from their flickering lamp-lights we passed again into total darkness. Through the whole night, I saw nothing except three campfires. Somewhere, in what presumably was hilly country, for the fires were at higher levels, some Indian was either cooking, working, or perhaps sending up a signal of identity into the black night. I noticed that even the stars were like pinpricks in the invisible heaven. I was totally hypnotised by the whole experience, stirring only occasionally to wipe the sweat off my face, for despite the ice the carriage was extremely hot.

The train eventually arrived at Jhansi, and we proceeded to a private bungalow where friends of my stepfather were to put us up for a night or two. But I remember nothing of this because I fell prey to an attack of 'heatstroke'. I was unconscious for about three days, during which time I lay in bed either in my bedroom or, at night, on the verandah. When I recovered, I was told that I had succumbed to this tropical hazard because I was so very fair-skinned and fair-haired.

Meanwhile my stepfather had acquired his posting from headquarters in Jhansi. We were all to proceed to a place called Ahmadnagar.

'A small cantonment,' Major John explained, 'but quite agreeable, and not too far away.'

His last remark was meant as a consolation to me, for I was still 'a bit groggy on my pins', as he remarked.

I don't remember how we got to Ahmadnagar. But I do remember Ahmadnagar itself. It was my first real entry into a dimension of which I knew absolutely nothing but which could be summed up very briefly by one word, 'Men'.

For the first week or two after our arrival, I tottered around and, together with my mother, tried to come to terms with life in India. India itself was very present; but life seemed somewhat absent. My stepfather disappeared early every morning to go to his military headquarters; and we were advised to stay in the bungalow out of the heat. Our Indian cook, who had been in my stepfather's service for some years, went to the bazaar and bought the food for the day. Our houseboy, or 'bearer' as he was called, bore all the responsibility for the bungalow itself and for our needs, including the laundry. A *chokidah*, sitting outside on the verandah, pulled the *punkah* to and fro all day long, sometimes with his hands and sometimes with his feet, in order to produce some movement of the hot air. So what on earth were my mother and I to do either with our hands or with our feet, not to mention our minds? I loved reading, but where were the books? I hated sewing, but now with gratitude I began to mend my own clothes, putting on a button where needed, or darning a hole in my tennis sock. I wrote to Roger but knew he was working hard for his exams, so an immediate reply was unlikely. Only a matter of months ago I too had been working hard for exams, but here all I had to do was wage war against the heat. For my mother, life was somewhat easier. She had always liked doing tapestry work and had brought all the necessary materials with her; also, on their honeymoon, my stepfather had started to teach her bridge, so she had her bridge hands to study as well. Then, in the afternoons, we both rested for an hour or so . . . from the fatigue of doing absolutely nothing.

Possibly my stepfather sensed something of the emptiness of our long hot days, for suddenly one morning he said, 'I've asked rather a nice chap to come along this afternoon. He's in the ICS – the Indian Civil Service. I want a word with him later – but I thought you two might give him a cup of tea first.' Then he turned to me, 'And quite soon, you know, you'll feel like going to the Club for a spot of tennis and some dancing.'

These words cheered me up enormously. My stepfather frequently talked about 'the Club', yet the English connotation did not raise a particularly exciting picture in my mind. But in India, visiting the Club seemed to be *the* great event in everybody's day; in fact, such were its attractions that it was apparently worth waiting until four o'clock in the afternoon for the day to begin.

First, however, we had to entertain Mr Cox for tea in the bungalow, and this turned out to be more of an ordeal than I had expected. I suppose Mr Cox was about thirty years old; he was good-looking, easy and rather personal in his approach – or so I felt. My mother and Mr Cox conversed together while our bearer poured out the tea, but I couldn't help noticing that his gaze kept coming back to me, initially with a question attached to it and later with undisguised amusement, as if we were sharing a private joke. But it was no joke to me and I became almost tongue-tied with shyness.

Then, horror upon horror, when tea was over my mother said, 'My husband won't be long, Mr Cox.' She paused and turned to me. 'So why don't you show Mr Cox round the garden, darling?'

I was aghast. To start with, we didn't have a garden. We had one big tree in the middle of our dusty circular drive, surrounded by a few scanty bushes totally devoid of leaves, whose names I didn't even know. Under the tree was a wooden bench.

Mr Cox jumped at the suggestion. 'How nice,' he said, his eyes on my face. 'I'd like that.'

'I'll go and get your hat, darling,' my mother said. She turned to Mr Cox. 'My daughter had heatstroke on arrival,' she explained, 'so she must be careful.' She turned and left the room. I neither spoke to nor looked at Mr Cox but instead took up an attitude of appearing to listen intently for my mother's return. Mr Cox stood facing me, never taking his eyes off me, nor the faint smile off his face; somehow I could tell this without looking. I realised I had exactly the same 'butterflies in my tummy' as I had had just before my matriculation exam.

My mother returned with my big floppy bridesmaid's hat in her hand. 'There you are, darling.'

I put it on carelessly, thankful that in some measure it hid my face.

'Well, shall we go?' said Mr Cox pleasantly.

I rose and we left the room, crossed the verandah and walked down the steps into the drive.

'There's a bench there, I see,' said Mr Cox, 'under that tree. It'll be in the shade. Shall we go and sit down?'

I nodded. I was so shy that I was speechless. I had never before been alone with a strange man. Suddenly I remembered Mr Haywell at the Vicarage. We had sat together talking for hours on end, quietly so that no one would hear us, and we had never run out of things to say. But, of course, then I had been a child . . . and Mr Haywell had been a clergyman, which made him quite different from an ordinary man.

Mr Cox and I reached the bench and we sat down. I was more than ever grateful for my big floppy hat.

Then, to my despair, I heard his voice saying very gently, 'Look up, little blue eyes . . .'

My discomfort was acute but I knew I had to respond: he was my stepfather's guest, and to do nothing would be terribly, terribly rude. So I raised my head and looked at him, and I think he saw and perhaps understood the embarrassment, even powerlessness, in my face.

He smiled and said very gently, 'I'm not going to eat you, you know.'

The phrase suddenly reminded me of the conversation between Little Red Riding Hood and the Big Bad Wolf. The words from my childhood came vividly to mind and I smiled.

'Why are you smiling?' asked Mr Cox.

I told him, and we both laughed.

'Well, if I'm to be called Mr Wolf,' Mr Cox said lightly, 'what am I to call you?'

'My name is Ingaret.' And for a moment I felt quite at ease.

Then, looking at me again, Mr Cox said, 'Well, Ingaret, tell me how you are enjoying India.'

I thought of the long days. 'Oh, I expect it'll be all right.'

'All right?' He sounded surprised. 'D'you know that India is packed with British troops? God only knows how many battalions are stationed about the place, not to mention Indian Army regiments. And rumour has it that there are only three unmarried English girls in the whole of India!'

'But I don't want to get married,' I said firmly.

Suddenly the memory of my matriculation certificate, which my mother had had framed when I received it, flashed into my mind. At home it must be hanging on some wall . . . but we hadn't got a home . . . so it could be anywhere or nowhere. Suddenly I felt desperately lonely. Was it the result of the heatstroke which made me switch from mood to mood?

'But surely you'll enjoy having a good time, won't you?' Mr Cox was insisting.

A good time. What was a good time? . . . when one was grown up?

I nodded. 'Of course,' I said vaguely, then I looked at my watch. Good manners had been served. 'P'haps we'd better go in now,' I suggested. 'I expect my stepfather will be back.'

So we strolled back to the bungalow and I felt that my initiation rite into the 'world of men' had passed off quite satisfactorily.

*

After a period of 'settling in' at Ahmadnagar we paid our first visit to the Club, and I felt I could endure my empty days with this to look forward to as evening drew near. There were tennis courts; there was a shady garden with tall trees beneath which an Indian regimental band, all dressed in khaki, played popular tunes whilst we were drinking our cups of tea. There was also a small dance room, which overjoyed me . . . perhaps someone would ask me to dance? My stepfather, my mother and I stood watching one or two couples gyrating round and round the small dance floor. Then a man still dressed in tennis clothes strolled along from the men's end of the Club. My stepfather spoke to him by name. 'Want to dance?' he asked. 'If so, let me introduce my stepdaughter. But I warn you that she is an expert!' And so I was launched into the Club world.

Of all the men I met and danced with, I still have vivid memories of one man in particular. He would emerge from the billiard room every evening to stand at the door of the dance room for half an hour or so, his huge Airedale dog beside him. Tall, grizzled, in his late thirties perhaps, blue-eyed, strongly featured, and with hair almost the same colour as his dog's, the man would stand motionless, watching . . . well, just watching me. Directly I admitted this to myself it seemed to create a bond between us. He was the first man I had met in India who had interested me – and perhaps attracted me. It was quite an exciting feeling.

'Who is that man?' I asked my partner, as I saw the watcher turn on his heel and leave the room, followed by his Airedale.

My partner replied, 'His name is Hamilton-Temple-Blackwood. He's in the Green Howards.' Then he added, 'He's an odd chap; a loner; lives in his bungalow quite alone with his dog. Sticks to the men's end of the Club too . . . scarcely ever see him down this end.'

Yet every evening this man came and watched. I couldn't help knowing that his eyes never left me, but I took care never to meet his gaze as we danced past him. From the other end of the room, yes, but never when we were close. In this way we seemed to establish an understanding of something that I didn't understand at all, but which existed in its own right.

Then I discovered something else, namely that the Indian day could prolong itself into the night by adventures that were called 'moonlight picnics'. I didn't enjoy them greatly. My mother and stepfather never came with me, so I was picked up by someone in a *tonga*, or a car, or even on a motorbike, and so conveyed to the scene.

These picnics always took place on open ground, for there were no woods or rivers around Ahmadnagar. Tablecloths were spread out and bottles and baskets opened, and above us a full moon lit up the whole scene with astounding brilliance. I never drank any alcohol for the simple reason that most alcoholic drinks seemed to have a depressing effect on me; instead of becoming gay and voluble, as other people did, I merely felt tired and empty of words. So when the 'loving-cup' of whisky, wine or whatever was handed round to the seated picnickers, I hung on to my lemonade, and drank it out of the bottle just to show that I wasn't a prude!

The people I met at the Club were mainly men and a few married women; some younger, some what were called 'senior'. The women seemed to be as much a part of army life as were the men and would frequently allude to 'my' regiment. There seemed to be a positive disease of snobbery with regard to these regiments. The British Army, of course, took first place on the snobbery list, with the Cavalry regiments enjoying social precedence over the Infantry. The Indian Army noticeably came last, despite the fact (as I discovered later) that it was only those with the highest grades in their exams at Sandhurst who were allowed to choose whether they wanted to go into the British or the Indian Army.

My mother, who was unaware of the social snobbery in army circles, once made an amusing 'gaffe'. She had been brought up, as were my brother and I, in what can only be called well-bred surroundings, where eccentricity, as with Aunt Magdalen, was a commonplace and snobbery was taboo. Playing bridge one day with three other women, and listening to their chatter about the '60th', the '11th' and the '7th' regiments while she dealt the cards, my mother looked up and said innocently, 'I think it's so clever of you to remember all those numbers.' An indignant silence followed, for the social standing of all three ladies depended on those very numbers.

Many years later, at a dinner in London, I found myself sitting next to General Auchinleck. We were discussing India and he said, 'I wonder what went wrong there?'

'The women,' I answered instantly.

This strikes me today as a very brash judgment. Now, with a more mature outlook, I think that the women of India (of whom I knew very few) must have had an almost unbearably difficult life. They were separated from their husbands for the whole of the 'hot weather', which lasted from four to five months, and, if they had families, the chances were that they were also separated from their children in England. If 'social snobbery' helped to fill some of the empty gaps in their lives then that, too, may have been a much-needed comfort.

11

Poona

After we had spent a few months at Ahmadnagar I suddenly received an invitation to go and stay with the family of an old friend of my stepfather's in Poona. This friend was a professor with quite a high position in the medical world; and he also had a daughter. Girls in India were very few and far between; so, 'Would these two girls like to meet each other?' wrote Professor Chatham. My stepfather assured me that to go and stay with people you had never met was quite common practice in India. 'If you ever hear of a girl anywhere, catch her quick!' he added with a smile.

Consequently I made the journey to Poona and was the guest for several weeks in the home of a very nice family of three. The daughter, Jean, was dark in colour and some four years older than I. She was a most amenable and responsible person, the sort of girl who made me feel that I had been at school with her.

The first time Jean and I visited the Club in Poona I was staggered. This enormous glittering palace made our little Club in Ahmadnagar look like a railway-siding. The Poona Club had a huge ballroom with a high ceiling ablaze with lights and a raised stage at one end where the band played by day and night. The bandsmen were presumably garnered from the British regiments stationed there, and they looked most impressive in their fine regimental uniforms. There were crowds of men strolling around with glasses in their hands, or gathered together in groups, laughing: men in polo-kit, men in tennis shorts, men in plus-fours, and quite a few in kilts. I could easily tell at which end of the Club was the bar, and the men's changing room, because of the noise emerging from both!

The Poona Club was the first highlight of my life in India, and I was quite breathless at the spectacle. Jean, of course, was known to everyone and, with an extra girl to hand, she became a double attraction. As daylight faded, the men crowded round us. Then the band began to play dance music and we were both whirled off on to the large dance floor. As I danced I wondered about the men wearing kilts. Did they wear anything under them? Were they stationed here? Or were they just on a course? (I had already picked up some of the local jargon.) I was suddenly very much aware of the searching gaze of a man who stood in his kilt at the entrance to the ballroom with a glass of whisky in his hand. He was watching the dancing intently and yet, at the same time, he seemed to be looking at, or for, something else. He had a noticeable if enigmatic face: his very presence seemed to present a question and also to demand an answer.

'Who is that man standing there in a kilt watching us?' I asked my partner with curiosity.

My partner turned his head. 'Oh, a chap in the Black Watch, here on a course, I believe.'

The Black Watch, I thought wryly as I was whirled off. What a perfect description for this particular man!

At the end of the dance my partner and I sat down and he called for a drink. Then, to my amazement, I saw the Black Watch man crossing the floor towards us.

'Hello, Acland!' he said to my partner. 'May I be introduced?'

'Of course, old chap, sit down. This is Miss Giffard and this is Captain Davidson. What'll you have?'

'Thanks, I've got my whisky,' the Highlander answered. But as he spoke he never took his eyes off my face, and his eyes were green. 'May I have the next dance?' he asked.

'Yes . . . yes, of course.' For some reason I felt confused.

'Didn't know you were a dancer, old chap,' my partner said lightly. 'Never even see you except on the squash courts or the golf course, or in the bar.'

The man in the kilt smiled. ' "The time has come, the Walrus said, to talk of many things . . ." '

Quickly I interrupted, ' " – of ships, and shoes, and sealing wax – " '

'Not to mention girls,' Captain Davidson answered quickly, but the enigmatic expression on his face scarcely changed.

Then the band started to play a waltz. Captain Davidson rose to his feet and held out his arms. 'I'm a bloody awful dancer,' he said. 'D'you mind?'

His arms were already round me and his cheek was very close to mine. 'No,' I said. So we stumbled off round the room. It wasn't so much a dance as an intimacy.

'I just had to meet you,' he murmured, as uncertainly we twisted and turned. 'What's your other name? Mine's David.'

'Ingaret,' I answered. I didn't bother to tell him how to spell it. He knew too much already.

The waltz came to an end. Instantly he led me out to the darkened terrace and we sat at a table in the garden.

'What are you doing in Poona?' he asked me.

I told him that my family was based at Ahmadnagar and that I was staying in Poona with a friend of my stepfather's.

'Ahmadnagar is not too far away,' he answered. 'I've got a motorbike and I could come over and see you.'

I hadn't even the capacity to catch my breath, so I merely nodded.

'How old are you?'

'Eighteen . . . just.'

'God!' he said. 'How marvellous.' He leaned forward, took my hand and kissed it. 'But we understood each other, didn't we? Even before we met.'

Again I nodded. I still couldn't swim, yet all the same I felt as if I were swimming, not against the current but being carried along by a strong tide that was keeping me afloat while at the same time sweeping me out to sea . . . out, out, into a wider ocean.

He was still holding my hand and now he kissed it again.

'D'you mind my doing that?'

I shook my head.

He rose quickly to his feet, pulled me up into his arms, and then at first gently, later passionately, probingly, he kissed me on the lips.

I felt as if my whole body had received an electric shock. I trembled . . . then clung to him . . . clung to him . . .

He felt me trembling. 'It's all right,' he said. 'Are you frightened?'

I nodded. 'I – I've never been kissed before,' I whispered. 'I mean, not on the mouth like that.'

There was a short silence and then he said, 'I'm a lucky chap. You're even more marvellous than I thought – ' Then he said gently, 'Much, much more marvellous.' He paused. 'Now, don't be frightened.'

Very, very gently he began to kiss my neck, my cheeks – then equally gently he bit my ear.

I responded violently in an involuntary spasm of my whole body.

'My God!' he murmured. 'You're an innocent – and yet you react like a professional . . . it's unbelievable. I'm in luck.' Suddenly he drew back and there, in the shadows of the half-lit garden, he faced me. 'But I –

I'll protect you,' he said, 'even against myself – provided I've got the bloody guts to do so.'

I'd never heard so many swear words before in all my life. At that moment we heard the band beginning to play 'God Save the King' and, almost involuntarily, David stood up straight to attention.

At the end he said, 'I'll take you home.'

'But I'm staying with the Chathams. We'll all have to go home together.'

'Oh, hell,' he said. Then he added quickly, 'Never mind . . . just hold out your arms and come to me.' Trembling, I obeyed him. 'Now look up at me.' I did so. I could scarcely breathe from the beating of my heart. 'Now you kiss me as I kissed you.' I put my arms round his shoulders and pressed my parted lips to his. We clung together, I could feel the whole strength of his body pressed against me. What was this tremendous force that was dominating us and yet uniting us?

Gently he disengaged himself. 'We must go and find the others,' he said.

Somehow we reached the ballroom and joined our friends. After a few words David said, 'Goodnight all,' and then he roared off on his motorbike.

Jean and I returned to the bungalow in her father's car. 'Enjoy the evening?' she asked.

'Very much.'

'You made quite a hit with David Davidson,' she smiled.

I felt my hands begin to tremble but I answered steadily, 'Well, he wasn't much of a dancer, was he?'

'No!' laughed Jean. 'I saw you left the ballroom pretty quick.' I knew then that she had accepted that my absence from the ballroom had been due to the fact that David wasn't much of a dancer.

Once back in the bungalow we went very quietly to our separate rooms; but I couldn't sleep. My whole body felt as if it had a live battery inside it charging me to remember – to remember. Only finally did I sleep.

The next morning when my breakfast tray was brought into my bedroom by the bearer there was an envelope on the tray addressed to me. The note inside was brief and it read:

When you get this I shall already be on my way to England. I've got three months' compassionate leave as my father has been, and still is, pretty ill, and so there are things to see to. I didn't say anything last night because I couldn't bear to spoil things. You know, I've been a bit of a rogue with women all my life, starting at the age of sixteen when I seduced a hospital nurse who was

temporarily in our home looking after my father. But last night, with you, everything was rather different. Have I said that dozens of times before to dozens of other women? Yes, of course I have . . . but last night the *difference* was different, and I mean that, which means that I'll be back. I don't know when, I don't know where from, and I don't know why. *But I'll be back.*
David.

P.S. D'you know, you've got quite a marvellous body? I could even enjoy watching you dance in another man's arms, and for me to be able to say that means something!

I read the note over and over again. He'd gone already . . . I took longer than usual eating my breakfast. Then I picked up the note, put it in my suitcase, and locked it away. I kept it for many years before finally losing it — but by that time I could remember every word of it by heart.

After breakfast Mrs Chatham said smilingly, 'I've just heard from your mother. She's asking whether we aren't tired of having our guest for so long?'

I had only been there for about three weeks and Jean was as good company as the Poona Club was enchantment.

Jean interrupted, 'Oh, don't let her go yet, Mum . . . unless she wants to.' She turned to me. 'People stay with each other for ages and ages in India, you know. It's not like England where perhaps you can't get servants. Do stay, Ingaret.'

'I'd like to,' I said quietly. 'If you're sure . . .'

'That's settled then.' Mrs Chatham smiled at me, and so did Professor Chatham.

'Hooray!' said Jean. 'Come on, Ingaret, we've got to get your tennis racket re-strung, remember?' She turned. 'Can we have the car this morning, Daddy?'

Professor Chatham nodded over the top of his newspaper, so immediately after breakfast Jean and I, in order to avoid the heat of midday, went off in the car driven by an Indian uniformed chauffeur and were taken to a sports shop in the bazaar. My old school racket certainly needed repair: the three sagging strings reminded me of this; and inside me I felt as if I were sagging, too. Three months' compassionate leave . . . I could hardly stay with the Chathams all that time. So when David did come back, would I ever see him again? Would I? He had said he was 'a rogue'. He had made no secret of it. I didn't even know his address; and even if I had, I would never have written.

Suddenly I felt rather desperate. Jean was talking Hindustani to the shop man as we waited for the strings to be mended, so I could allow myself to feel desperate . . . just for once . . . there was nobody there to notice . . . tears were very near.

'Ingaret!' When I turned, my face was in position again, and Jean was handing me my newly-strung racket. It was now so strong that I could run up to the net and volley every ball I could reach. That was my favourite way of playing the game, but in those days women were supposed to stand back in the court and let the men do the volleying. At that moment I felt like smashing something, if only to ease, and in some way come to terms with, my frustrated emotions.

Instead, I threw myself into the communal club life like a diver off a rock into a rough sea. Headfirst I plunged into the social life of Poona. I watched polo-matches; I played tennis, and took part in tennis tournaments; I went to cocktail parties but drank no alcohol; I went to fancy-dress balls where everyone wore masks; I even borrowed Jean's jodhpurs and took part in hilarious cross-country chases before breakfast. I was glad on those occasions that I was able to ride astride. And, of course, I danced whenever I could, both at the Club and at private parties.

As a result, I found the most perfect dancing partner. Geoffrey was fair and slight, he wore a monocle and was in an Indian Cavalry regiment. But I could not forget David. My new partner was very gentle and considerate, and quite soon he was deeply in love with me, but I was unaware of his feelings. I just thought that dancing with him was lovely and that he felt the same way about it as I did.

Then, one day it all came out; at a prosaic moment, too. We were having tea together in the gardens of the Club after several games of tennis. Suddenly, as I was pouring out the tea, Geoffrey said, 'Ingaret, if I proposed to you, would you consider accepting me?'

'Propose!' I nearly dropped the teapot. 'What d'you mean, propose?' I stammered.

'I would like us to be engaged,' he said simply.

I stared at him, slightly aghast. 'Engaged?'

'I – I'm sorry,' he said. 'I've been too blunt about it. I thought you knew how I felt about you.'

I shook my head. 'No . . . no . . . I didn't.' I stared at him. He looked so downcast and awkward that I felt desperately sorry for him, and also very touched that, feeling as he did, he had treated me so decently – so gently – so honourably.

'Are you sure?' I asked.

He looked up, opening his eyes. 'Of course I am!' he replied. 'I've been sure for quite a time.'

Engaged? Well, why not? I liked him awfully; and if we were 'engaged' I need never dance with anyone else again except him, and everyone would understand. 'All right,' I said, and I smiled at him. 'Let's be engaged.'

His delight was almost painful; at the same time it filled some sort of gap in me. And now suddenly I heard the band playing my favourite waltz. I jumped up. 'Come on, don't let's bother to change. Let's go and dance as a celebration!' We were still in our tennis clothes and dancing in one's tennis clothes was something that was not done at the Club.

When Jean and I got back that evening I announced the news at dinner. 'I'm engaged to Geoffrey Cholmondley,' I said brightly. 'He proposed to me this evening, and I accepted him.'

There was a brief silence. Jean gasped slightly and Mrs Chatham said quietly, 'You've thought it all out, dear, I'm sure?'

'Well, not exactly,' I said. 'But I think it'll be all right. In fact, I feel rather excited . . .'

'What will your mother say?' Professor Chatham asked from the far end of the table.

'Oh, if I'm happy, she'll be happy too,' I replied. Happy? Momentarily I wondered. I turned quickly to Jean. 'And he is a decent sort, isn't he, Jean?'

'Oh, I think he's awfully nice,' she said. 'And he's a "sahib", too.' In Indian terms this meant that he was a gentleman.

'Well, dear,' Mrs Chatham rose, 'I hope you'll be very, very happy.' She stooped and kissed me on the forehead.

The next morning, at midday, a package was delivered from a jewellery shop. It was from Geoffrey, and contained a note saying, 'With all my love, to celebrate our engagement.' Inside was a beautiful little ring with one lovely diamond in the centre. I pushed it on to the third finger of my left hand, feeling rather proud that I knew which finger to put it on. Then I flashed it about and ran on to the verandah where Jean was sitting and showed it to her.

'Oh, how lovely,' she said. 'He must be rich . . . it's a big diamond.'

Rich? Rich? I'd never even thought of that. It might be rather nice to be rich for once.

At the Club that evening I thanked Geoffrey for my beautiful ring and we danced together ecstatically, and no one came over to ask me for a dance because gossip spread like wildfire in Anglo-Indian society. By now our engagement was common knowledge. I drew a deep breath of relief.

The next morning another little parcel arrived, bearing a card which

110

said 'With all my love'. It was a small but beautiful gold wristwatch. I was quite startled. However, I put it on and showed it to the Chatham family at lunch-time.

'The fellow must be besotted!' Professor Chatham said to me with a twinkle. Jean was the only one who, I felt, had some reservations. 'Don't you like him?' I asked her.

'Oh, very much,' she replied. 'But it all seems – a bit quick.'

And for the next few weeks the speed of events continued. It was a hectic time during which I deliberately threw myself into every kind of activity; and Geoffrey, of course, played an important part in all of them. And, because he was so happy, that seemed to make everything all right.

Then two significant things happened. First, Geoffrey was despatched on some military duty to a place south of Poona; he would only be away for a month, but he left me his address. 'Write to me every day, won't you?' he pleaded.

'Of course,' I agreed. After all, I liked writing. I might even try him out with a few of the poems that I had written in the past – the not so distant past when I had had time truly to be able to think, and the determination to learn.

Then, going with Jean to the Club as usual on the day after Geoffrey's departure, an elderly woman, whom I knew only by sight, came up to me and said very nicely, 'Congratulations, Miss Giffard. I hear you're engaged to that nice Captain Cholmondley. When are you going to be married?'

I stared at her in amazement, for the word 'marriage' had never entered my head, nor had Geoffrey and I ever discussed it. When we had met at the end of the day at the Club, the pleasure of being together was a full-time occupation.

'I – I don't really know,' I mumbled.

'Well, I hope you'll both be very happy,' the lady said, and left with a smile.

Marriage . . . not a state for which I had ever yearned . . . but, of course, I was 'engaged to be married'! The days and weeks had passed so swiftly that I had had no time to look ahead. Now I felt overcome by this sudden vision of the future. I sought Jean out and said, 'Would you mind if I went back early this evening, now, in fact? I've got a bit of a headache.'

'The sun,' Jean said quickly. The Indian sun was a monster for all of us and dominated our movements.

'Could be,' I lied. 'But I'll take an aspirin when I get home.'

So I took a tonga back to the bungalow. It bumped its way over the uneven road accompanied by the driver's repeated cry of *'Joldi jau! Joldi jau!'* I knew that meant 'Go quickly'. Then I saw him cracking his whip over the back of the little pony whose ribs were sticking out on either side like rows of false teeth. However, I didn't try to stop him. Nor could I even think properly: I had got out of the habit of thinking. In the last few weeks, since David's departure, I could see that I had doused myself in wave after wave of extraverted activities. Words began to come back to me. David's very name disturbed me ... which perhaps suggested that I was on the right track. I felt somehow that a price, or a penalty, had to be paid – but for what and to whom I didn't know. Myself perhaps?

On arrival at the bungalow, Mrs Chatham gave me some aspirin and took my temperature, which was normal; yet I had never felt more abnormal in my life. She told me to have a good sleep, which, thanks to the aspirin, I did. But when I woke the next morning I was a changed person. For once David never came into my mind at all; but Geoffrey did. And I thought of him without any kind of feeling whatever. It seemed to me that I was utterly emptied of all human emotion in relation to him. I have never forgotten the horror of that experience. I saw myself as incapable of human love, of human fidelity, even of honour. I threw myself, shuddering with tears, on the mercy of my kind friends the Chathams. I got dressed but wept intermittently throughout the morning. My tears came in bursts of horrified self-knowledge: I couldn't be emotionally faithful to anyone, even for a week. I hated both myself and poor Geoffrey – my tears would start again at the mere thought of him.

Then I asked the bearer for a small box, which he brought me. I took the ring off my finger and the watch off my wrist, and scribbled a short note.

Geoffrey, I'm terribly sorry. I just don't feel the same any more. I must call it off. I am returning your lovely presents with much gratitude for all the trust and care you have given me. I'm so sorry. I can't write any more. There's no one else, but it's all over. It's just a fact. Please forgive me. Ingaret.

P.S. I don't even know why or how it happened.

I asked Jean if she would register the parcel and send it to Geoffrey's address, which I gave her. Then I said to Mrs Chatham, 'I think p'raps I'd better go home, don't you? Mother really ought to know.' I felt literally as if I'd committed a crime. The kind Chathams helped me to pack and sent a telegram to my mother saying I would be returning the following day. So I went 'home' to Ahmadnagar and, in due course, I received a painfully distressed letter from Geoffrey but I never answered it. It wasn't a matter for argument or even explanation, for neither of us could understand what had happened.

At this time, of course, I had never heard of the word 'projection'; namely, that an unused or unacknowledged emotion within the human psyche both can and does project the strength of its unrecognised reality into any other available area of life, or on to any other available person. The reality of this projection is always powerful; and never entirely real. Just as a blown-up balloon can float magnificently in its own right but, with the prick of a pin, becomes deflated and shrinks to nothing, so, when the human psyche can no longer carry the weight of its own unrecognised emotion, the 'projection' can collapse and be withdrawn. At the age of eighteen, all I could see was that David's sudden departure had deeply disturbed me. In the words of my childhood, 'the cupboard was left bare', and so I had stuffed that cupboard full, not with real food but with tinned goods. Consequently my newly-awakened feelings had 'projected' themselves, without my realising it, on to another man. Suddenly, as I stood at my bedroom window staring out at the empty sun-baked garden, I was amazed to find myself thinking like this for the first time since I had been in India.

Curiously, I said nothing of all this to my mother. If she heard of it through the normal gossip channels, then I would explain the matter to her in simple terms. It felt as if the fire inside me, which had flared up briefly and dangerously with David, had now gone out and there was no point in poking through the ashes for warmth. So I was glad to be back in Ahmadnagar and away from the scene of my conflicting and imperfectly understood emotions.

12

Ups and Downs

Meanwhile life at Ahmadnagar continued effortlessly and aimlessly. My mother and stepfather were now constant bridge players at the Club. As for me, I felt as if I were looking down the wrong end of a pair of binoculars: everything seemed to be smaller rather than larger. The only thing that pleased me, because it was in continual growth, was the relationship between my mother and Major John. Now it was my stepfather who had become my mother's confidant and support. And surely he, as a man, would be a better support than I, as a child, could ever have been? For me, however, the days were empty. I bought a paintbox and some brushes, but to my inexpert eye there seemed nothing much to paint: always the same flat, arid landscape, and the same sky burnt white with heat.

Suddenly, I decided to try painting our bearer, who was such a dear old man. But I wasn't altogether surprised, when I handed him the finished portrait, that he just held it up before him, first one way, then the other, then sideways. Clearly he could make neither head nor tail of it! Feeling somewhat discouraged, I took a photograph of him, a good clear photograph. But when I handed this to him he treated it in a similar fashion. He stared at it but it conveyed nothing to him, upside-down or down-side-up. I felt rather relieved, deciding that his bafflement was no reflection on my attempted painting or photographic skills, but was perhaps an interesting example of the difference between the Indian and the British outlook. For an Indian, trying to see life from the British point of view simply turned everything upside-down. Equally, I suspected, the British, no matter how devoted they were to their staff, frequently failed to perceive the Indian priorities. The outer eye alone was not sufficient for either race.

Another thing that greatly puzzled me was that the emotion of religion seemed to have deserted me completely. I no longer felt any need, still less any desire, to go to church. Sunday, for me, became just a day when the regimental band did not play in the evening at the Club. My mother and I must have gone to 'early service' now and again but I can remember neither the church nor the priest, which suggests that I had no religious leanings whatsoever at this time.

The next thing to disturb our long, heavy days was talk of the approaching 'hot weather'. Apparently during the hot season all the women 'fled to the hills', which presumably meant that my mother and I would be separated from Major John. I wondered how we would get by on our own? I had learned a few of the commonly used Hindustani words but not enough to give orders.

'Oh, that'll be all right,' my stepfather said. 'I've rented a bungalow for you up in Kashmir. But you won't be leaving yet awhile.'

Yet, although it was only mid-April, the days grew hotter and hotter. Previously we had sometimes felt a little movement in the air – it could scarcely be called a wind – and at such moments the pressure was lightened and one could even draw a deep breath of momentary but real refreshment. But now the sun was beginning to beat its drums more loudly in order to summon its troops, glittering and fully armed, for an even more ferocious assault. A further test of endurance was the emergence of more mosquitoes, more snakes, more scorpions. Now, we all three had to sleep on the verandah, tucked in under our mosquito nets, instead of in our bedrooms. But even outside it was completely airless and therefore extremely difficult to sleep. Directly the sun ventured over the horizon we fled from its brazen presence back into the bungalow which was still as full of the previous day's used-up air as we were full of the desire to sleep. Some days, after a night of tossing and turning, frequently woken by the *chokidah* walking round the bungalow and swinging his *buttee* or lantern, I felt too weary and too indifferent even to go to the Club.

It was on one of these occasions, while I was sitting outside on the verandah waiting impatiently for the shades of evening to revive me, that I suddenly heard the noise of a motorbike coming up the drive. Surely I recognised that sound? I stood up. Yes, it was David Davidson on his powerful Harley-Davidson!

I ran down the verandah steps to meet him. 'David!'

Getting slowly off his machine he came towards me but didn't take me in his arms as I had expected.

'The family are out,' I said quickly.

'Then let's go and sit there in the shade,' he said evenly, pointing to the bench standing under the only tree in our 'garden', where Mr Cox and I had sat a hundred years ago . . . or so it seemed.

Suddenly I remembered why David had had to leave India so unexpectedly. 'How is your father?' I asked tentatively.

'Oh, Dad's all right now . . . in fact, directly I got back he seemed to take a turn for the better.' Suddenly he took hold of me and kissed me; a different sort of kiss, gentle and yet caring. It made me feel as if I'd come home.

I drew back. 'So what were you doing all that time?'

'Oh, there were family things to settle,' he said, watching me. 'Then after the nurse had settled my father in for the night, I used to make a bolt for London.'

'What did you do there?' I asked.

'Went to Murray's Club.'

'What's that?'

'A night club,' David answered easily. 'Filled with beautiful and wicked young women . . . and quite a few of them were glad to see me back, which was nice.'

I had heard of 'night clubs' but I had never yet met anyone who had been to one. 'What is a night club? Does one dance?'

'Possibly.' He paused. 'Or possibly there are better interests to pursue.'

Suddenly I knew that neither David nor I would ever deceive each other. 'You mean girls?' I asked quietly.

He nodded. 'Tarts would perhaps be a better word,' he suggested.

I thought for a moment. I had never heard the word 'tarts' used in this way, so my mind went back to the girls. 'But having so many girls, isn't it like reading a book for the umpteenth time? If you know how it's going to end it's no surprise.'

'But suppose it's always a happy ending . . .' David said quietly. 'Besides, if you take enough trouble you can always find surprises.' Suddenly he turned and looked very directly at me. 'You're one . . . in your way.'

The personal switch rather disconcerted me. Then I heard him saying, 'But you – what have you been up to in my absence?'

I hesitated. Then I said awkwardly, 'I – I got engaged.'

'In what?'

'I got engaged to be married,' I explained with difficulty.

'Good heavens! So directly my back's turned – ' he began with great amusement. But I put out my hand to stop him and told him the whole story, even the fact that once I'd cried so much that I'd run out of handkerchiefs and had had to use facecloths to dry my tears.

'You poor little creature you.' Now his voice was very gentle. 'But why did you cry? It was the other chap who ought to have cried, surely?'

I shook my head. 'No. He was the nice one . . . it was me who was awful.'

'Come here . . .' In the gloaming I groped my way nearer to him on the bench. 'I must keep my eye on you, mustn't I?'

Gently he put his hand on my breast. 'And your heart's beating like a racehorse – it needn't, you know.' Gently he fondled my body and pang after pang of delight flashed through me. Then he removed his hand and kissed me very lightly on the lips. But I knew that he knew that I was longing to be crushed once again in his arms, as at our first meeting. Yet for some reason he desisted. 'Tell me . . . tell me . . .' he said, 'when I was away did you miss me?'

I could not find the words to describe my turbulent feelings on reading his farewell note, so I just nodded.

'And did you think of us? And if so, what did you think?'

That was an easier question to answer, for I had thought of 'us' a lot. I said slowly, 'I thought that before you came along I – I had been like an unused piano that had stood for years with the lid tightly shut . . . and then suddenly, with you, the lid had been opened and the piano itself had begun to play music.'

'But what sort of music?' David asked quietly. It was typical of him that he should ask the one essential question.

I thought swiftly. I didn't know much about music. I thought of Mr Haywell and his Bach – but no . . . 'Chopin,' I said, 'or Mendelssohn . . . melodies. I – I can play some of them myself.'

'And perhaps there will be other melodies to learn,' David said even more quietly. Then he paused and added slowly: 'Perhaps you and I might even learn to play a duet together . . . one day?'

A light flashed in our garden, bobbing up and down in the swift Indian twilight. But it was only our *chokidah* walking round the bungalow keeping watch, and waving his *buttee* up and down against the unwelcome presence of some lurking night-reptile.

'Well, now I must be off,' David said, rising. 'Back to Poona . . . got to report for duty tomorrow.'

I was amazed. 'But why did you come here this evening?' I had supposed it was for some military reason.

'To see you, of course,' he answered simply. 'Spent the night with a pal of mine in the Green Howards who is stationed here.' He paused. 'But now I really must be off.'

A vision of David whirling through the black Indian night on his powerful machine disturbed me. 'You won't fall asleep . . . or have an accident, will you?' I asked anxiously.

117

'Not a hope!' he answered. Then he added wryly, 'Don't forget . . . I'm used to sleepless nights!' Then, with a kick of his foot, he started up the heavy motorbike, turned on his lights, jumped on to the machine, and disappeared into the darkness.

Flashing on my torch I walked slowly back to the bungalow. There our bearer had already lit the lamps. I sat down. Would I ever see him again? He was at the same time too frank and yet too enigmatic a human being for me ever to be able to find rational answers to all the questions that his presence stirred up in me.

13

Kashmir

The hot weather was now upon us and all the women were making for
the coolness of the hills. So my mother and I packed our trunks and
my stepfather escorted us to Ahmadnagar railway station from where,
together with our bearer, we would catch a train up to Gulmarg. But on
arriving at the platform, Major John told us that we would have to travel
the second part of the journey in a *dhooli*. 'They'll carry you up the steep
part of the mountain to Gulmarg,' he said. 'And our bearer already
knows his way around up there. He's been to Gulmarg before with me.'

So we chugged away in the train with our bearer checking up on us
at every station. Finally we arrived and made our acquaintance with a
dhooli, which consisted of two poles supporting a kind of bed which was
hoisted on to the shoulders of four Indians. One was supposed to lie
down in this, but I could not resist sitting up as we were slowly carried
up the steep fir-clad hills of Kashmir. My stepfather had told us that
John Corfield, of the ICS, would be waiting to meet us at the top, which
was reassuring because neither my mother nor I could speak more than
a few words of Hindustani.

At last we came to a clearing from where we could see Gulmarg lying
below us in a kind of bowl surrounded by hills. I could clearly make out
the clubhouse with a tennis court or two and a polo-ground but little
else. And the cool air came to greet us and not to beat us as did the hot
air in the plains.

By now Mr Corfield had arrived and we introduced ourselves. 'These
chaps will take all your trunks up to the bungalow,' he said, pointing to
a steepish path going upwards for about a quarter of a mile before
disappearing into the surrounding forests. 'Would you like to go up on
foot or by pony?'

'On foot,' my mother said. 'I got quite cramped travelling in that train.'

The Indians went before us carrying our luggage and, after half an hour's climb up the steep and narrow track, we reached a forest of fir trees, on the outskirts of which we found our bungalow. It was made of stout wood, and looked straight down through an immense clearing in the forest on to the central plain below.

'Oh, what a lovely little place!' my mother cried. 'It looks just like a Swiss chalet.'

I didn't know, nor did I know how my mother knew, what a Swiss chalet really looked like! But since her remarriage she frequently made remarks of that sort which, presumably, she had picked up from my stepfather.

'It is very like one,' agreed Mr Corfield. He looked at me. 'There are plenty of other bungalows quite near but hidden in the trees,' he explained. 'Would you like me to come along tomorrow and take you down to the Club?'

'Oh, don't bother to come all the way up here again,' my mother said, 'We'll find our way. But of course it would be nice to meet you at the Club. Thank you very much indeed.'

So Mr Corfield departed and our bearer, as usual, took over. As Mr Corfield paused at the wooden garden gate, he turned and waved to us. He was to become a dull but faithful friend.

Suddenly I did not care tuppence about the Club. It was the cool air that was exciting. I drew in great lungfuls of it. Then I ran down the narrow pathway to the wooden gate and looked upwards. Behind the bungalow, high above the surrounding firs, was a mountain-top and, as if in defiance of the plains below, there was snow on its peak! I was quite breathless. It was the first mountain I had ever seen in my life. I wondered whether anyone had ever climbed it? It stood aloof and powerful under the pink light of the sinking sun – the very same sun that had obsessed and possessed all of us in the plains below – and seemed to maintain within its massive impassivity the whole secret of being. It touched (or seemed to touch) the sky; yet it was deeply belonging both to us and to the earth. Suddenly a strange, almost mystical sense of oneness overcame me. This was what belonging was all about: it was as much a mystery as it was a solid fact. And then quite suddenly I didn't want to climb the mountain. I just wanted to know how to belong to it. That would be enough.

It took us all that late afternoon and evening to unpack and 'settle in'. Happily our bearer, as was customary, knew all the ropes and, by now, even a little of the English language. Then, as the sun set, we went into the sitting-room to find a wood fire burning in the grate! That was wonderful, 'almost like being in England', as my mother said . . . except, as I told myself, in England we wouldn't have had a mountain behind us for our protection.

We went to bed early and I slept well. But, despite Mr Corfield's assurance that there were other bungalows nearby, that first night felt as if the two of us were quite alone, halfway up the mountain and deeply hidden in a forest of firs, with no one within call. Yet, somehow, I felt at peace.

The next day, having got the bungalow ship-shape and eaten food most miraculously supplied by our bearer, we walked down the steepish path for the half-mile that separated us from the Club. Having reached our goal I saw that four people were playing tennis; however, the polo-ground was empty and there was no suggestion of a regimental band playing music in the Club – for, of course, there were no regiments here.

We sat in the large, rather bleak clubroom, had tea with Mr Corfield, and then someone turned on a gramophone. It played rather creaking songs in the background, but no dance music. The reason for that became plain to me later: this place had plenty of women, dozens and dozens of them all chattering and crowded together, but there were very few men. They, poor devils, were still working below in the sweating plains. Leaving the Club that evening with my mother, the whole dreary situation presented itself clearly to me: no dancing; no moonlight picnics; no music; no men; no intellectual stimuli. In fact, physical fitness seemed to be all that Gulmarg had to offer.

In order to escape from the depression which had followed my introduction to the Club, I suddenly decided not to walk home by the path that led up to our bungalow. So, instead of escorting my mother, I hired a pony for a few *annas* and we stumbled and clambered our way up the mountain path. That at least had a hint of adventure in it, for the drop on one side was steep.

After several days had passed in this bewildering vacuum, desperation prompted a bright idea. On that first boring visit to the Gulmarg Club, with the gramophone groaning in a corner, I had met a Mrs Watkins. She was telling me of the difficulty she had in India with her eleven-year-old daughter.

'There are so few children here,' she had complained, 'and no good schools around. And Rosie is rather bright. We couldn't bear to leave her in a boarding school in England; she is too young to be parted from her father and me . . . but neither of us know what to do with her up here.'

I understood only too well! So I said suddenly, 'I'll take over her

121

school-teaching every morning if you like. I have just matriculated. I'd like to teach her' – I paused – 'provided that Rosie, too, likes the idea.'

Mrs Watkins gasped. 'Would you really?' she asked. I nodded. 'Well, I insist on paying you for it. And my husband would agree.'

But I refused payment. 'I shall be only too glad to do it,' I said. 'I rather enjoy working. And I cannot think of anything else to do here – except walk to keep fit . . . which is important, I know . . . but not terribly interesting.' I paused. 'But before we decide I'd like to meet Rosie. I'd like to know what she feels about it.' I paused again. 'I've got a brother who is three years younger than me, so I'm quite used to having a younger person around!'

And so it was arranged. I met Rosie, who was dark-haired, tall for her eleven years and very bright. We got on well together. I found quite a lot of exercise books and maps among her possessions, and quite a few school books too. So, every day (except Sundays) Rosie came to our bungalow and we worked together out on the verandah in the fresh air from nine-thirty to twelve. I enjoyed every moment of it.

'What do you want to do when you grow up, Rosie?' I asked her once.

'Oh,' she replied, 'I want to be a married lady like Mummy with lots and lots of children like Mummy's sister.' It was our only point of difference.

My mother, too, was very pleased with this arrangement. After all, she had her tapestry work and a daily letter to write to Major John, as well as halting conversations with our bearer, so it fitted in splendidly.

Then suddenly one morning, when Rosie and I were working happily on the verandah, a whistle from the garden distracted me. I looked up. David was leaning over our garden gate!

'Wait a minute, Rosie,' I said. 'Just go on with what you're doing . . . I'll be back in a moment.'

I ran down the garden path. 'What on earth are you doing here, David?' I asked. To my surprise, I suddenly felt annoyed at the interruption.

'Well, I've got a week's leave,' he replied. 'So I thought I'd come and have a look at Gulmarg – and you.'

I looked at him. He seemed paler and thinner, and those green-hazel eyes had a new darkness in them. Was it a shadow from the mountain and the fir trees? Or perhaps his father had died?

'Have you been ill?' I asked.

'I am never ill,' he replied quickly. 'But for a Highlander that bloody heat in the plains is difficult – though it's the troops I'm really sorry for; they have no perks whatsoever.'

I looked at my watch. It was ten o'clock. 'I am teaching this little kid every morning until midday,' I explained. It wasn't exactly a warm welcome. I saw the expression on his face change, so I added, 'Well, I'm free at midday, so come back then, will you?'

'Well, maybe,' David said quietly. He paused and then turned to walk away down the valley.

I went back to Rosie – and suddenly I stopped being a 'governess'. I turned in my tracks and ran back to the garden gate. 'David!' I called. He had only gone a few steps so he turned and came back. 'David!' I stretched out my hand and put it on his shoulder. 'I'm sorry . . . I was sort of preoccupied . . . but you will come back, won't you? Gulmarg's a dreadful place – it'll be lovely to have someone to talk to. Oh – ' suddenly I remembered, 'and I can show you my mountain!' I cried. 'I'd love to do that. You will come back, won't you?'

He looked at me, smiled, and then said gently, 'You haven't changed after all . . . good! I won't hang around now, but I'll see you at midday tomorrow.'

He turned to leave but again I called him back. 'David.' When he returned I said mischievously, 'The Club's absolutely jammed full with women! You'll find it a perfect place for "poodle-faking"!'

David burst out laughing. He came towards me. 'Where on earth did you learn that word?' he asked. 'I'll be calling you an old *koi-hai* soon if you don't look out!'

'You'll have to call me a young *koi-hai*, otherwise it'll be a contradiction in terms,' I added gaily.

'I reckon I'd better come early and join your lessons in the morning,' David replied. 'Perhaps you really could teach me a thing or two . . .' There was a pause and then suddenly he looked at me rather oddly and said slowly, 'I wonder . . . could you?'

There was quite a long silence between us, then finally he turned and left, calling over his shoulder: 'I'll tell you all my news tomorrow.'

David turned up at the bungalow at noon the next day. I introduced him to my mother who, I could see, instantly liked him. When he spoke he looked at her straightly; and he was incredibly handsome.

'Ingaret is determined to show you her mountain,' she said lightly. 'So I've had sandwiches made up for you both, some fruit, and a flask of coffee. Will that be all right?'

'Splendid,' David said. 'Thank you. It's nice to feel one can sit in the sun for a change, isn't it?'

So we set off to scramble up the mountain. David carried the food basket, and I suppose we climbed about two hundred feet, leaving the firs behind us. Then, turning, I gasped in amazement as I saw the whole range of Himalayan mountains exposed before us, and beyond us, on the horizon. Some were half-hidden by the heat mist of morning but most were clear in their full magnificence and timeless participation in the living scene.

'Oh David, look!' I flopped to the ground in a mixture of delight and exhaustion and David sat down beside me. We sat and stared at the surrounding magic of the Himalayas, which seemed to dominate not only us but all the life in the valley below. We heard the singing of the birds mingling with the sound of water coming from little streams, and it was like listening to an orchestra of nature.

I stretched out and lay staring up at the hot white sky. 'It is like feeling oneself to be lying on history . . . Indian history . . . isn't it?' I said.

Suddenly David put his hand on mine. 'Yes,' he said quietly. 'But we ourselves must also make history. And we can, can't we?'

I felt he meant something that I didn't quite understand. Suddenly we seemed to be able to meet as persons and not only as a man and a girl. The open and magnificent countryside seemed to affect our relationship. Up in this cool open mountain air perhaps we felt ourselves to be a part of the majestic and yet human reality of the Indian natural world. David made no further comment but I knew that we were sharing the same feelings.

The next day we again climbed the mountain and David told me what I hadn't known, namely that the Indians themselves looked upon the Himalayas as having a mystical power. It was during this second expedition that we had an argument which I can still remember. We were eating our picnic lunch when suddenly I said, 'It's extraordinary to think that I'm here at all, you know; really I should be at Oxford studying law.'

'Not a very good idea,' David said.

'Why not?' I asked, feeling rather indignant.

'Well, my father is a judge . . . and as a judge you've got to follow the legal rulings and official legislations. Somehow I don't see you taking easily to official judgments.'

'Why not?' I asked.

'I think you're rather a law unto yourself.'

This was something I had never thought of before and I didn't think much of it now. 'But I've matriculated,' I said. 'I'm not stupid.'

'But not suited either,' David answered quietly.

'You think I'm stupid – '

'I think you're something rather special,' David said. Then his tone lightened. 'So let's put it this way. What would you do with all that long yellow hair of yours? I don't want to see it all tucked away and hidden under a judge's wig of false white hair!' The picture that his words brought to my mind amused me and we both laughed.

It was only at the end of that day that he mentioned his native Scotland. Pouring himself a glass of beer, and staring at the vast mountain before him, David said, 'You know, I'll be sad to leave all this somehow. It's not the same but it reminds me of the Highlands. They're mysterious too. Not high like these are, of course, but colourful . . . and very beautiful.' His voice changed. 'And we've got moors as well, miles and miles and miles of thick orange bracken and purple heather.' He looked at me suddenly. 'I must take you there one day. And there you can climb the mountains to the top, at least most of them.'

'And walk through the heather?'

'Of course. But it's hard walking . . . especially if you've got a gun.'

'A gun?' I asked stupidly.

'Of course. For shooting.'

'Shooting?'

'The deer.'

'Shooting the deer?'

'My darling' (it was the first time he'd ever called me that) and he drew me gently to him because he could see that I was suddenly near to tears. 'We've got to cull them, we have to.'

'But why?'

'If we don't cull the deer, they go down from the hills and destroy all the farmers' crops. The farmers in the Highlands simply couldn't live if we didn't keep the deer down to size.'

'Well, I don't want to think of it,' I said chokingly. 'I can't bear to think of culling those beautiful animals.'

'Then don't think of it,' he said. 'Just think of me doing this.'

Gently he lifted my hand and kissed it. He told me a few years later that this was the first time that he'd ever kissed a woman's hand. 'Everywhere else,' he had said with what I called his wicked grin. 'But never a hand!'

At the time this simple gesture gave me a feeling of great peace; I felt we both really did belong to the mountains. And the thought comforted me, for I knew that he was leaving for the plains the following day.

14

The 'Strike'

Life at Gulmarg dragged on for another month or so. The days were routine: Rosie, the Club, back on a pony to the bungalow. My mother preferred to walk both ways but I always insisted on riding up the steep, uneven path on my sturdy little pony because at least it provided a certain thrill. This was a frustrating period for both of us, although we kept on reminding ourselves that we were escaping from the baking plains.

At last my stepfather wrote to say: 'The rains have broken. It doesn't make the heat easier to bear. In fact, rather the contrary. It's now just humid heat instead of dry heat. Some people dislike it more; certainly mosquitoes, snakes, cockroaches, beetles and greenfly come out in their thousands to have a spree in the drenching downpours. But the real news is that I am due to go on a Staff Course at Belgaum in a few weeks' time. I think the best thing for you to do is to stay on in Gulmarg for the moment and then come straight down to join me there.' The letter ended with the usual loving messages, and I noticed that the slight tension and unease which I had been aware of in my mother since her separation from my stepfather now seemed to diminish.

We had no idea what a 'Staff Course' was but thankfully we started to get ready to go down to the plains and rejoin my stepfather. Finally, after spending more than two months in Gulmarg we were escorted down to the station by the kind Mr Corfield. And not before time. Apart from the dramatic mountain ranges, the only positive memory I have of Gulmarg is that we always had a wood fire in the evenings – which made it feel a bit like home.

Our arrival in Belgaum was uneventful but we were, of course, delighted to be with my stepfather again. He seemed quite calm and almost indifferent to the prospect of three months' 'swotting' through the Staff Course. And when we asked him what advantages it would bring he seemed to be vague. 'Oh, I think it's always a good idea, if you've been recommended for a Staff Course, to go and sit it out. Might bring in a bit more pay one day!' He smiled and seemed to forget the matter.

So we all three went through the military routine of the next three months; or was it three years? It certainly felt like it. We had breakfast together in our rooms, which were situated in what looked like lines of empty barracks; then my stepfather left to 'swot it out' in some outlying but similar building. For lunch we met up at a huge out-house in which there was a 'restaurant' where all the officers on the course and their families foregathered. Each family sat at separate tables, to which their food was brought by their own individual bearer. After 'brunch' (as it was called) the men left to continue 'swotting' and the women returned to their bedrooms for a rest in the so-called cool.

I remember only one incident of significance during this period. One morning, while at breakfast in our rooms, the rumour spread from one block of barracks to another that there had been a 'strike' among the bearers; and as each representative had a bearer, that meant that all the Indian servants were on strike! We heard from the whispers that were passed around the barracks that the 'strike' had arisen because a Colonel Courthold had lost his temper with his bearer and had struck him! This, so my mother and I were informed by those who were spreading the news, was strictly against military orders. No officer in the Army was ever allowed to hit one of his servants. 'Strikes' in those days were not only unheard of, but quite unimaginable to the British, so the incident was considered to be very serious; indeed, it was viewed by the authorities as such a grave offence that it carried a 'demoting' penalty with it.

We also heard that the restaurant where we should have had our daily 'brunch' had been completely shut down because of the 'strike'.

'But shouldn't we try to get some food from somewhere?' asked my mother. 'Otherwise the three of us may not get any "brunch".'

'Don't believe a word of it,' said my stepfather. 'It's just a rumour! Courthold wouldn't be such a damn fool as to do a thing like that!' He finished his coffee. 'See you at lunch-time,' he smiled. 'Usual place.' And he left for the office.

So at the usual hour for lunch, very uncertainly, my mother and I set off for the restaurant, which was situated quite near our rooms. We stepped inside. Major John had been wrong. The restaurant was completely empty. The food was there, the tables were laid (probably having been arranged so the night before) but there was not a bearer in sight except one – our own bearer! He came forward, saluted us, pulled out our chairs and then went to fetch our food. We sat down.

'Well, I'll be damned,' said my stepfather.

Our bearer returned with his hands laden. He then put down three plates in front of us.

When he had finished, my stepfather stood up. *'Ap-mai ma-bah hai,'* he said, and held out his hand.

Our dear old bearer beamed and they both shook hands. The old man's face was illuminated with joy. Then he took up his proper place behind his Sahib's chair. So we sat alone eating our 'brunch' in that enormous building attended by our solitary bearer, and as we left, of course, my mother and I thanked him also.

When we were back in our rooms I asked my stepfather, 'What did you say to him?'

'I gave him an honorific form of address in his own language,' Major John replied. 'I said "You are my mother and my father" . . . that is the highest possible praise in Hindustani.'

When the Staff Course ended we returned to Ahmadnagar. It seemed odd to be down in the plains again; as if one were a piece of washing left out on the line to be baked dry by the sun. And there were still a few unwelcome reminders of the 'rains'. Krait, a small and poisonous snake, could be observed occasionally in our bathtubs, which were sunk into the ground. Swarms of mosquitoes were still spasmodically on the attack; greenfly settled, like a coat of paint, over certain chosen places. 'Prickly-heat' we escaped with thankfulness for, as the saying went in India, 'You can be ill one day and dead the next.' What was missing, of course, was the wonderful lightness and freshness of the air up among the Himalayan ranges.

Then my stepfather received a letter from the War Office. His recommendation from the Staff Course had been high; and he was now offered command of the 119th Rajputana Infantry in Kohat.

'Where's that?' asked my mother.

'It's a good post,' my stepfather said. He seemed, for such a cool, calm person, to be almost pleased. 'It's in northern India, right on the border between India and Afghanistan.' He smiled. 'Almost like going on active service.'

'When do we go?' asked my mother.

My stepfather referred to the official letter: ' "As soon as possible",' he quoted.

Over the next few days our plans for moving to Kohat took shape. The three of us would go up as far as Lahore together: Major John would install us in a hotel there for a few nights and then return to Ahmadnagar to settle all his regimental and domestic affairs. He would then rejoin us in Lahore and take us on to another hotel in Peshawar. Again he would leave us while he went on up to Kohat to find out about his military commitments, look for a bungalow and finally arrange for us to join him there. Living in India, I thought, was rather like camping out: I'd seen young people in the countryside in England walking along, or climbing hills, with packs and folded-up tents on their backs, and I had envied these wanderers their freedom. Now I wasn't so certain.

On the evening after Major John had left us at the hotel in Lahore, my mother was taken ill. We always had at least two thermometers with us and I found, to my horror, that her temperature was 102 degrees. I hurried to find the hotel manager. He was British, as was his wife. Under the circumstances I would have preferred the manager to have been an Indian, for all this man did was to look up the name of some unknown doctor in his book, and send a bearer with a chit to summon him. I went back to my mother, held her hot hand and waited, it seemed, interminably. The doctor who finally arrived was British and very drunk. He could hardly hold or read the thermometer. Suddenly, both out of fear and fury, I lost my temper. I ordered him out of the room and went and gave the hotel manager a very irate telling-off. I even resorted to the Anglo-Indian habit of using social precedence to give full vent to my anger. 'My stepfather happens to be on the Viceroy's staff,' I lied emphatically. 'If your negligence ever becomes known to him your hotel will be off the list as a reputable three-star hotel!'

This worked. 'I will go myself,' the manager said, 'and fetch the best doctor in Lahore.' He departed, post-haste.

I returned to my poor fevered mother. Soon the second doctor arrived: he, too, was British and not drunk but very efficient. He did all the necessary tests.

'It's not serious. An attack of sandfly fever. Not much to be done but sweat it out.' He gave me a few medications and some advice and then disappeared into the darkness. 'Send a chit if her temperature doesn't come down. But I think it will,' he said as he left me.

I sat down, relieved and somewhat shattered, having ordered a cold supper to be sent to our room. It took a long time coming. Then, suddenly, I felt a violent movement under my feet; glass and china were both rattling and falling. The pictures on the wall were tilting in every direction: the whole room seemed to be in movement. It must be an earthquake! It had to be an earthquake: there was no other explanation.

129

I rushed out of the room thankful, for the first time, that my mother was lying in bed under her mosquito net with a high temperature and totally unaware of what was happening.

I raced round to the front of the hotel. 'What's happening?' I cried. 'Is it an earthquake?'

The hotel manager barely looked up. 'Earth-tremor,' he said. 'That's all. We get them here sometimes.' He returned to his books. Again I wished he had been an Indian: an Indian might have been less articulate but certainly he would have been less indifferent. Trembling, I went back to our room. How could one know that an earth-tremor wouldn't turn into an earthquake?

I returned to find the pictures still sliding about on the walls, and the china rattling around on the uncarpeted floor. My mother, fortunately, slept on. I felt her hand: it was still hot but perhaps not quite so hot. I climbed into my own bed, but I couldn't sleep until the earth-tremor had passed.

Three days later Major John arrived to take us on the next stage of our journey, up to Peshawar. By that time my mother had got over her attack of sandfly fever. She was a bit shaky, but fit to travel. I didn't say anything about the earth-tremor to my stepfather. I could sense that he had enough on his hands, both officially and domestically. So we left Lahore in comparative tranquillity; and I hoped never to see it again.

15

Peshawar

Peshawar, although we only stayed there briefly, seemed to be an attractive place. It was an oddly divided town, one half being occupied by British troops and with its own fort flying the British flag; the other half was in Afghanistan and consequently belonged to the Pathans. The Pathans walked quite freely through the 'British half' of the town, but I do not think we could have done the same in the other half. We were booked into a comfortable hotel, and on the day after our arrival Major John took me down to the Club and introduced me to a few people. Then he went back to my mother, who was still convalescing after her recent illness.

The Peshawar Club was large and reminded me of the Club in Poona. Regimental bands played dance music, and also, perhaps because it was so much further north, the air seemed to have the same kind of freshness. While I was talking to some friends of my stepfather's, a tall young man came across the room towards us. As he approached, one of the women in our group said, 'Whoever is that good-looking young man? He looks rather like a Greek god!'

So, of course, I was introduced to this distinguished-looking young man and we moved out on to the dance floor. I was lucky again. George Tamworth was a magnificent dancer. We didn't speak while we danced, for which I was thankful. Having to carry on a conversation while dancing was, to me, like being spoken to while I was absorbed in a book.

The waltz ended. The tall young man looked down at me. 'Thank you,' he said. 'I'm in luck.'

'Me too!' I replied lightly.

'I suppose now we've got to go back to the Fenshaws,' he said. 'But can I have the next dance?'

I nodded.

We danced together the whole evening and, while sitting out with the

131

Fenshaws between dances, we learned of an extraordinary coincidence.

'How long are you in Peshawar?' someone asked me.

'Only a day or two,' I answered. 'Then I'm going up to somewhere called Kohat. My stepfather has been posted there and my mother and I will join him.'

'Kohat!' exclaimed George. 'That's where I'm stationed.' He looked at me. 'So we'll probably dance together again.'

I spent the next two evenings making many new acquaintances, and the following day my stepfather, my mother and I left for Kohat.

On the journey, Major John explained to us something of the situation in Kohat. 'It's rather different from other stations,' he said. 'It's small and very near the frontier with Afghanistan, as I said . . . the Khyber Pass and all that . . . and the Pathans are a fierce and fearless people. We have to keep our eyes open.'

It sounded exciting. 'What could they do?' I asked.

He told us of an incident that had taken place some years previously. At night the Pathans had made a cautious but swift descent from the mountains, through the Khyber Pass, and then noiselessly and secretly had infiltrated into the British cantonment. They had obviously studied their terrain thoroughly because they made straight for a certain outlying bungalow in which some people called Ellis lived, together with their young daughter Molly. The Pathans had seized and gagged the *chokidah* who regularly patrolled the bungalow by night. They were then able to seize Molly Ellis from her bed on the verandah and, having silenced her effectively, had made off with her back into the mountains.

What was to be done? The British Government and the Indian Civil Service were equally distraught. To send military forces into Afghanistan to rescue Molly Ellis could have resulted in her being murdered by the Pathans, and the subsequent escape of the murderers. It could also have led to war with Afghanistan, which was exactly what both governments were at pains to avoid. While the British Government and its representatives in India were desperately trying to work out a solution, a missionary called Miss Starr, who spoke several of the local Indian patois, had taken matters into her own hands. Without hesitation she had taken her horse and her bearer and ridden up through the Khyber Pass and on into Afghanistan. There she had greeted the Pathans, to whom she was not a stranger, and after lengthy but friendly talks with them, she had managed to bring a terrified but wholly unhurt Molly Ellis home.

'So,' Major John concluded, 'as I said, conditions in Kohat will be rather different from any other station. But I don't want you to be alarmed. That all happened some years ago, and those in command have learned their lesson.'

'How?' I asked.

He hesitated. 'Well, the bungalow allotted to us is actually the original Ellis bungalow and it is a bit remote from the main cantonment. But I've already applied for half a dozen armed sepoys to sleep and keep watch outside the bungalow at night. You'll find that all the women who go out riding early, before breakfast, always have a couple of armed sepoys with them. And at night, when there is a dance, we always see that the Club is surrounded by armed sepoys. Little things like that. But it won't make any difference to your normal daily routine.'

So once again we were all three settled in a crowded train bound for yet another unknown destination, this time a seemingly rather perilous one. I stared out of the window: just mile upon mile of dusty plains. They, at least, one could take for granted, unlike British life in India, which seemed to be disconcertingly spasmodic and at the mercy of hazards like earth-tremors, heatstroke and sandfly fever. Yet people from England kept on saying in their letters: 'You must be having a wonderful time . . .'

Well, I *was* having a wonderful time. I was seeing a new country and I was surrounded by men (which seemed to be every woman's ambition). But there never seemed enough time to get to know anyone intimately, so one learned little about people as individuals, or even about humanity, and this made me feel hungry and underfed. The impact of the mystical Himalayan ranges had been a revelation that would always remain with me, as also my physical responses to David's first kisses; but that didn't seem to amount to much after nearly a year of so-called 'active' living.

I turned to look at my mother and stepfather at the opposite end of the carriage: my stepfather, as always, was reading, and my mother was nodding off. What were they getting out of it all? My stepfather, presumably, professional satisfaction; my mother, security. Then my wandering eyes suddenly caught sight of my side-saddle perched on the rack in front of me. It had been an expensive gift, yet now it looked like an old hunchback, covered with labels carrying the names of the various stations that I had visited but had never really been able to get to know. It was the perfect symbolic expression of all that I had been thinking about! But strong though my feelings and frustrations were, I realised that it was no good thinking ungrateful thoughts, for this only made me feel guilty. I had to face up to certain hard facts. Obviously my intended professional life-to-be had been brought to an abrupt end by my coming to India and, in consequence, the natural urge for emancipation that had always been so strong in me was in danger of being stifled. So how should I compensate for this? I knew that if I were not to become 'a spoilt Missi-Sahib' I had to try to forget my past inner preoccupations and turn more appreciatively to the outer aspects of life in the present. For men, presumably, this was no problem. There were polo matches, hunting, pig-sticking, tiger-shooting, but even though all these sports were open to women, except for polo, I couldn't see myself enjoying any of them. Instead I made a firm resolve that in future I would always have an early-morning ride (even though in Kohat I would need an escort) and that I would pursue as many other sports as possible in the interests not only of physical but also of inner health. I looked up at my old hunchback friend, the side-saddle, with a new determination in my eyes. I was going to be a willing, not a reluctant, extravert.

Kohat turned out to be a good place to put my resolutions into practice. One could look along the range of mountains and see the Khyber Pass quite clearly, and it was down that very pass that the Pathans would, or could, come. The Khyber Pass itself looked like a big cut in the surrounding rock: it was irregular and usually in shadow, and although it was a road it managed to look both empty and threatening. I got into the habit of glancing up at it throughout the day because the vision of those picturesque Pathans mounted on their ponies never left me.

I immediately arranged with George Tamworth that I would go riding with him before breakfast, before the sun grew hot. George was an attractive and likeable man of about twenty-five. He was engaged to be married to a girl in England whom he had known since childhood, and he talked about her a lot. Being in the British Cavalry, George had the customary snobbish hang-ups, and I have never forgotten a remark that he made on our first morning out riding together. It was beautiful in Kohat just after sunrise. There was an innocence in the freshness of the early-morning air; a mystery in the pink of the maturing sky above the jagged rocky mountains. But this innocence was somewhat belied by the presence of the two armed sepoys who rode behind us.

Just as George was bending down to adjust one of my stirrups he looked up at me and said, 'You're lucky, you know, to have me here. I'm in the British Cavalry . . . but your stepfather's only in the Indian Army.'

I was horrified. I knew that women could say things like that . . . but a young man, an officer too, and a gentleman . . . I was tempted to tell him that my ancestor had been asked by William the Conqueror to compile the Domesday Book, but instead I replied gently, 'George, I think I'm very lucky to have an expert horseman like you taking me out riding.'

There was soon to be yet another domestic upheaval. Major John arrived home from the office one evening with a grave look on his face.

'I've been ordered to go to Thal for a month,' he said, and sat down on the verandah to talk to us. Thal, he explained, was a fortress standing on the border between India and Afghanistan. It was occupied by an Indian regiment to maintain and reinforce authority there, and my stepfather was to be in overall command. Apparently the Pathans were getting restive and needed careful watching. 'I can take your mother with me if she wants to go,' he said, looking at me, 'but I'm afraid that she's the only woman allowed in the fort.'

There was a silence. 'If I come, what would happen to Ingaret?' my mother asked.

'Of course she can't be left alone in this bungalow,' my stepfather replied at once. 'But I have plenty of responsible friends with bungalows situated more deeply in the cantonment with whom she could stay.'

'Then, if Ingaret doesn't mind, I'd like to come with you,' my mother said.

'You won't see very much of me,' my stepfather said. 'I'll be very occupied. We all will be . . . military alert and all that.'

'I'd like to come,' my mother repeated quietly. And they both turned to me.

I was amazed at the ease with which my mother had made her decision. My mother, alone most of the day, shut up in a fortress, and literally on the border of enemy territory! I couldn't get over it; and then I began to remember that, together with her irrational fears, she possessed an indomitable courage, deeply hidden but always ready when the occasion demanded, and most particularly with regard to us children.

'Of course I'll be all right,' I said.

And so, in two days' time, they left for the frontier and I moved in with a Professor and Mrs Arundel, who were friends of Major John's and seemed glad to help in this arrangement. After the departure of my mother and stepfather I was increasingly aware of new military tensions everywhere. I could still go for my morning rides with George but now, instead of two armed sepoys, we had to have four; and our terrain also was more limited. We still had an evening dance at the Club once a week but on one occasion the alarm had sounded, bringing the dance music to an abrupt end. The Club was quickly surrounded by Indian Army troops, for Pathans were suspected to be lurking in the shadowy garden. Consequently we were not allowed to go home until dawn had broken, and even then only under armed escort. I found it all rather exciting, but then I was rarely afraid of real happenings. It was the things that didn't happen, or that might happen, that caused me more concern. I wondered, but only idly, whether I might not have inherited this from my mother.

The Arundels were not only very welcoming but also most congenial company. Mrs Arundel had once been a schoolteacher, and Professor Arundel, temporarily attached to the British Command, was writing an historical thesis on the countries to the north of India, including Afghanistan. He was a man of intelligence and spirit, and had acquired both knowledge and understanding of the situation. He explained that between India and Afghanistan there were two sorts of territories. There was an 'administered territory', which was the responsibility of the British; and beyond that there was a neutral tribal territory, a kind of no-man's-land, which separated India from Afghanistan and was not administered by the British. Professor Arundel also explained that the tribes from Afghanistan were a fearsome problem. The Pathans, as could be seen at a glance, were a courageous and picturesque people: tall, fine-looking men, untidy, long-haired, wearing baggy trousers and sheepskin coats, with a rifle invariably slung across their shoulders. Professor Arundel had made a study of the North-West Frontier and he had grown to like the Pathans.

'They're tough,' he told me, 'and splendid marksmen.' He paused. 'But they've got a streak of cold-blooded cruelty in them that defies description – ' Then, perhaps thinking he had said the wrong thing, he added, 'But oddly enough all our troops like 'em. Unlike the Indians, they look you straight in the eye.'

'And which territory is my stepfather in?' I asked.

'Oh, in the administered area undoubtedly, otherwise he would never have been allowed to take your mother with him. Gurkhas are up in Thal at the moment, I believe, and they're the best mountain troops that the Indian Army has ever had.'

'I wonder why they sent my stepfather?'

'Well, he had a pretty high rating on the Belgaum Staff Course,' Professor Arundel told me. 'He's probably been sent up to have a look-see. Get the feel of things. You can't govern the Pathans,' he added, 'but you can get to like them.'

'And what's the country like on the other side of the Pass?' I asked.

'Well, the country between, like a lot of India, can at times be a luxuriant dream. In places the landscape is breathtakingly beautiful, but mostly it's just plain dust-covered anonymity . . . and so, of course, perfect cover for the war-like Pathans!'

'But my mother will be safe in the fortress, won't she?' I asked anxiously.

'Perfectly safe.'

'But supposing something dangerous really did happen there?' I asked. 'Supposing they needed help? How could my stepfather communicate with us?'

'No difficulty,' Professor Arundel answered firmly. 'With the Gurkhas up there, you could send a signal back here any time you wanted, day or night. Those little men seem to dissolve into the very earth itself: they are the world's natural stalkers.' He paused. 'The Pathans are a magnificent charade of flamboyant manhood: the Gurkhas are manhood in being.' He paused again and smiled at me. 'And if I sound prejudiced it's because my brother was in command of the Gurkhas for fifteen years . . . and they were the happiest years of his life . . . or so he always said.'

The month I spent with the Arundels passed quickly, despite my occasional anxieties. Early-morning rides with George; a rest after lunch; an evening visit to the Club and a dance there once a week. George always saw me home at about midnight. It was quite an eerie business getting home: torches in our hands against the snakes on the ground; a few feeble cantonment lights supposedly for illumination. And every night, by the garden gate, George kissed me goodnight – very gently on both cheeks, and doubtless thinking of his fiancée in England. When we were out riding or on other occasions when we were alone together, he invariably talked about his fiancée; it was clear that he was deeply in love with her.

One night, on returning from the Club, I couldn't see the sepoy who was on guard on my side of the bungalow. Supposing Pathans were hidden in any of the thick bushes of the surrounding garden? Suddenly I felt nervous.

'George . . .' I said hesitantly, 'my bed is on the verandah round that far corner of the bungalow. Come and kiss me goodnight there, will you?'

Quite clearly he misunderstood my awkward phrase. 'I'll kiss you here like I always do,' he said quietly, and he did so, on both cheeks.

I couldn't understand this. Was he frightened too? So I advanced hurriedly to my end of the bungalow and, despite my panicky feelings, there was no trouble. Several years were to pass before I understood why George had reacted in the way that he did.

It must have been about eight years later, by which time I was living in London, that I received a letter from the West Country; it was signed 'George' and in brackets was added 'Tamworth'. Of course I knew who George was. But how had he known where to find me? Anyway, the letter asked me, very simply, whether I would have lunch with him at the Berkeley Hotel on a certain date. I wrote and accepted with great pleasure. George! What a lot we would have to talk about!

So we met. He did not look any older, and neither, I hoped, did I. But during lunch the conversation didn't flow, as in the old days in Kohat. I asked him about his much-loved fiancée to whom he was now married, but his responses were brief and somewhat enigmatic. He had an enormous saddle with him which he was taking to be repaired. He seemed to be more interested in that than in me.

Then, while we were still on the first course, he said almost urgently, 'I want to ask you a question.' I looked at him inquiringly and waited for the question, for he was obviously ill at ease. 'D'you – d'you remember that night in Kohat . . . when the Pathan scare was on . . . and I took you home from the Club, and you – you asked me to come along with you to the other side of the bungalow where your bedroom was? Did you mean anything more than what you said?'

Of course I remembered the incident clearly, but how could I answer so as not to hurt him? I put my hand on his. 'Dear George. No . . . I didn't mean anything more than what I said. I was just frightened in case some Pathans were hidden in the bushes . . . and I couldn't see the *chokidah* . . . which made me rather nervous.'

'I see,' he said tersely. 'Sorry to have mentioned it.' There was a pause. Then he looked at his watch. 'Well, I'd better get going. Got to take this saddle to Jermyn Street, and then get the early train back home.'

'Oh George, must you go so soon?'

''Fraid so. Can't afford to miss my train home.'

'Then couldn't I come to Jermyn Street?' I asked.

For the first time he looked at me. 'Not much point, is there?' he asked flatly.

Dismayed, I shook my head. We hadn't even finished lunch. George paid the bill, then picked up his saddle and we made our way to the entrance of the hotel where he asked the porter to find a taxi.

In the hotel doorway I held up my face. 'Let's pretend we're still at the garden gate in Kohat,' I said gently. Quietly he kissed me on both cheeks, as in the past, and we parted.

As I walked slowly back down Piccadilly to catch a bus home, I was very close to tears. Suddenly I seemed to be able to understand George's whole situation. He had managed those two difficult years of separation from his fiancée gallantly and successfully. Now, after eight years of marriage, the intensity of his desire had become blunted and needed to be sharpened by some new experience. So what about that young girl who had seemed to be interested in him in India? Despite my involuntary tears I could see the whole thing so very clearly. I didn't feel insulted. I didn't sit in judgment. But, God, life could be hard on us all, couldn't it? Yet I was glad I had not lied to him. I had always found it quite impossible to lie to somebody that I cared about.

16

The Ambiguous Box-wallahs

Shortly before my mother and stepfather were due back from Thal I received a chit from Military Headquarters telling me that Major John's return would be delayed for two or three days. There was no reason for me to be alarmed – both my parents were well – but certain military details had taken longer than expected.

I was disappointed but the Arundels assured me they were happy for me to stay on with them. However, during my stepfather's absence on the Afghanistan border I had met some new people at the Club, a Mr and Mrs Rhys, who had made very warm and friendly advances to me. Eventually they had asked me to come and stay with them for a few days. I gathered that they lived about twenty miles from Kohat.

'You will see India away from the military,' Mrs Rhys had said, smiling. 'We're right in the middle of the real India.' Put that way it sounded attractive.

So when I heard the news that my stepfather's return was to be delayed I told the Arundels that I had received an invitation to stay with other friends and, if this was still open, I would no longer presume on their hospitality. It appeared that the offer *was* still open. Mrs Rhys said that she and her husband would be delighted to see me . . . so, as I could not stay long, why not come the following day? She told me the time that the train left Kohat and also the name of the tiny station where I should get off. She and her husband would meet me there in the car.

The warmth of her invitation quite touched me. I wrote down the name of the station and time of departure, and went back to the Arundels to tell them of my plans. The following day I packed my suitcase and sent the bearer for a tonga to take me to the station, and it was on my way there that I remembered I had forgotten to give my change of address to Military Headquarters, which was my only contact with my mother and stepfather in Thal. So I called in at Military Headquarters,

140

left a chit with the name of my new host and hostess and of the nearest station, and then continued on my way to catch the train.

The journey was soon over and, on arrival at the tiny station, both Mr and Mrs Rhys were very welcoming. We scrambled into their rather old car, and then we seemed to drive miles and miles along a jagged, open road into nowhere. At last I could see the outline of a bungalow standing entirely by itself on the horizon in the middle of a large area of what appeared to be cultivated green beans. When we reached the lonely bungalow we all got out of the car and, as I walked up the steps to the verandah, a slight tremor of apprehension passed through me. I noticed, for some reason, that there were no telephone wires to the bungalow. This, of course, was quite usual in the cantonment, but not, surely, in such a godforsaken place?

I was shown to my room, where I unpacked my suitcase. From my corner of the verandah I could see nothing but miles and miles of apparently flat yet cultivated green acres. It was mid-afternoon but when I went to the front verandah, where I expected to find my host and hostess, I was surprised to see that they were both hard at work among the beans. Bent double, and wearing large floppy hats against the heat of the sun blazing down on them, they were apparently 'weeding' . . . and they continued to do so for two whole hours! I went back to my room and sat there to rest and to think. But I didn't know what to think – except that they were behaving like Indians and not Europeans: only the Indians could bear to work out in that tremendous heat all through the day. What was so important about these so-called beans? And what were those little white flags doing, dotted about in irregular formation over the extensive growth of greenery surrounding the bungalow? Perhaps for protection against the birds? That was all I could think of. But were beans so very important in India?

By the time I had pulled myself together I reckoned it might be tea-time, so I returned to the front verandah where I found the Rhyses drinking champagne from a newly-opened bottle!

They offered me a glass, which I refused. 'Thank you,' I said. 'I never drink . . . it always depresses me.'

'Oh, nonsense.' Mrs Rhys's voice was quite sharp. 'Don't sip it – drink it straight down.'

Suddenly I felt extremely puzzled . . . but puzzled in a way that I understood. I knew now that, beyond doubt, I had to keep my wits about me.

'If I did drink that I'd be sick all over your floor!' I lied, laughing. 'I've got an allergy or something.' Then with sudden inspiration, remembering their eager welcome, I added, 'And then you'd never ask me here again.'

I happened to have struck just the right note. They both relaxed slightly, though not with approval. I sipped my lemonade and looked out again over the flat green vegetation which stretched to the horizon. 'What are you growing?' I asked.

'Beans . . . can't you see?'

Yes, I could see, and they were beans. But why beans?

'Quite a job,' I said, with what I hoped sounded like admiration. Then, looking round, I asked casually, 'How far is the Club from here?'

It was, after all, the first question that everyone asked in India.

'I've no idea,' said Mrs Rhys coldly. 'We rarely go near it.' She pointed along the open and exposed road that ran through this 'bean' plantation and apparently continued endlessly until it disappeared in distance and dust. 'I suppose the cantonment's about twenty miles along that road,' she said. 'Too far to bother about,' she added with meaning, looking very directly at me.

It was only then that my heart started to bump rather unpleasantly inside me. Twenty miles or so on an open road would be a long way to walk.

I rose. 'I'll go and have a bath, if I may. It was rather a hot journey,' I said as calmly as was possible.

'Of course. But we don't change for dinner,' answered Mrs Rhys.

Yet I remembered that at Kohat she had worn quite a variety of pretty dresses.

'Oh good,' I replied. 'I didn't bring anything much.'

I was glad to leave the verandah.

Alone in my room I sat down. I was extremely troubled. The friendly visitor at the Kohat club had vanished. In her place was a cold business-like woman. But what was her business? I had no idea. The simple fact remained that I was completely trapped. It would be madness to attempt the twenty-mile walk to the station under a blazing sun as there was nowhere to shelter or hide on that long stretch of open road, not even a hedgerow. Nor would a night escape be possible, for even under a full moon in India one had to carry a powerful torch to safeguard against the reptiles that came out in the dark; and a torch would instantly be spotted from the bungalow. So, with my suitcase unpacked, and my hands sweating with fear, I realised that I was a prisoner and not a guest. But for what reason? I couldn't even imagine. It was a terrifying feeling, knowing that there was no possible means of communication with the outside world: none at all. I felt my hands beginning to shake. The whole thing didn't make sense. But why was I so afraid? Why?

I had my bath. I didn't change my clothes as ordered. I joined the Rhyses for dinner and again determinedly gave every appearance of being in high spirits. I knew that that *must* be my role. They must never for a moment be allowed to suspect that I found anything untoward either in them or in their behaviour, and I kept it up all the way through dinner and afterwards. We didn't stay up late and I was glad. Once alone in my room I could think. But as I undressed and then got into my bed on the verandah I realised that I was being watched by the *chokidah* making round after round of the bungalow with his *buttee* which, rather surprisingly, gave out an exceptionally strong light. If I sat up to adjust the sheet, or mosquito net, this light was instantly flashed straight on to my bed. I could feel the sinister atmosphere building up, building up, as I lay there tensely in the darkness.

However, the next morning at breakfast I was again careful to maintain a cheerful front. To my amazement another bottle of champagne was produced and finished by the end of the meal. Dear heavens, I thought, I'm in the hands of a couple of maniacs! My suspicions were confirmed when, after breakfast, Mr and Mrs Rhys had put on large floppy hats against the sun, picked up gardening bags, and gone out yet again to weed among the beans.

'You'll forgive us, won't you, dear?' Mrs Rhys said with artificial sweetness. 'But there's such a lot of weeding to be done with all these beans . . . we're at it most of the day.'

'Can I give you a hand?' I suggested.

'Oh no, dear, thank you very much, certainly not,' said Mrs Rhys hurriedly. Too hurriedly, I thought to myself.

I was glad to see them go. Alone, I tried to think, but I had no idea what to think. I concluded that clearly I had not been asked here for the pleasure of my company. So for what other reason? No matter how deeply I thought, I could not come up with any reason for my being here. Nor could I see any possibility of escape, or even of making contact with the outside world.

After lunch I said that I would like to have a rest. I thought that perhaps when the Rhyses were out I could search the bungalow and find a clue. But when they left to resume their weeding I had no chance to look around because their bearer, obviously under instructions, never for a moment let me out of his sight. Suddenly I felt absolutely terrified at the thought of spending another night in this sinister place.

Then, unexpectedly, just before tea, when after toiling all day under the ferocious sun the Rhyses had gone to have baths, I saw a small blur of rising dust in the distance along that endless stretch of open road.

What was it? An Indian driving his cattle before him? Or a bullock-waggon? But quite quickly it presented itself to me as a large motorcar driven by a chauffeur, with an armed soldier in uniform by his side.

The Rolls-Royce drew up in front of the bungalow. The soldier got out, saluted, and presented me with a chit addressed to Miss Giffard. I tore it open – just as Mrs Rhys in her bathrobe came hurrying into the room, followed by Mr Rhys with only a bathtowel round his loins.

'What's happened? Whatever's happened?' cried Mrs Rhys, obviously in a desperate panic.

'I don't know,' I said. I read the chit.

From Lieut General Sir A. Runciman K C B , D S O

Dear Miss Giffard,

As you may know, your stepfather is an old friend of mine. I have just received a signal from Thal saying that your mother is very ill and that you should be sent for. If you will pack your bags my chauffeur will drive you straight back to Kohat. It is the quickest way as the trains here are few and far between. I should like you to call in here on your way so that you can see the official communication I have received from your stepfather.

Yours very sincerely
Archibald Runciman

I handed the chit to Mrs Rhys and then turned and ran to my room. I bundled everything into my suitcase. But Mrs Rhys followed me. She had read the chit and she was furious.

'Do you know this Archibald Runciman?' she asked.

'Of course I don't . . . I don't know anybody in India – but my stepfather seems to know everyone.'

'Then I don't think you ought to go,' she said. 'I don't trust this man Runciman. It could be a trap.'

I picked up my suitcase. Now I had a Rolls-Royce, a chauffeur, and an armed soldier at my back.

'Of course I'm going,' I said, allowing my agonised concern to sound in my voice. 'My mother needs me . . . she's ill. Don't you understand? She's ill. Of course I'm going – '

I ran past her, suitcase in hand. Directly I appeared the soldier took my case and opened the back door of the Rolls. I clambered in. I didn't say goodbye or thank-you to the Rhyses . . . I didn't even wave. I merely said to the chauffeur, 'Quickly, please. Please go quickly.'

Instantly we moved forward, for the chauffeur had already turned the Rolls-Royce ready for departure. It took us quite a while to cover the long miles to the small adjacent cantonment. I never even thought of the Rhyses: it was my mother I thought of – my mother . . .

After about ten miles or so of journeying we turned in at a wide driveway with an open gate and a large, stout lady was standing awaiting me on the verandah of a large bungalow.

She held out her arms as she came to meet me. 'It's all right, my dear, it's all right, your mother is perfectly well — but we just had to find a valid excuse to get you out of that place.'

'You mean my mother's not ill?'

'No. In fact she and your stepfather should be back in Kohat by now. But my husband had to invent an urgent reason to get you away from those people . . . I don't expect you to understand.'

I nodded. 'But I think I do . . . only of course I don't understand *why*.'

We moved into a large drawing-room but I hardly noticed it. 'How did you know I was there?'

There was a pause, and then Lady Runciman, for it was she, replied very quietly, 'MI5.'

I repeated her words, 'MI5?' staring at her blankly.

'Military Headquarters,' she said. 'You left them your new address . . . but not until you were on your way to catch the train.'

Suddenly I flung myself into her arms and burst into tears. She held me against her large firm breasts and never spoke, but allowed me to cry myself dry.

'Thank you . . .' I gasped at last. 'Thank you.' Then suddenly I found that I could think. 'Does your husband really know my stepfather?'

'Never met him in his life.' Lady Runciman smiled. 'But it made the note more convincing.'

'Oh, you will thank him from me, won't you, please?'

'Of course I will,' Lady Runciman said.

And I believed her. And because I believed her I tried to explain something to her.

'From the moment I arrived,' I said, 'I could feel something . . . something evil.'

'I think we must always try to be able to recognise evil when it occurs,' Lady Runciman said quietly. Then she added, 'And keep it at a distance — with God's help.'

I was arrested by the phrase. In childhood God had seemed such a constant companion, but somehow, out here in India, God had gone to sleep . . . or perhaps it was a part of me that had gone to sleep? I hugged Lady Runciman as I left. She had done more than save me; she had given me food for inner thought.

So, with a packed lunch in my hand, and with my heart no longer in my boots, I got back into the Rolls. I waved and blew kisses as we purred off on the long drive back to Kohat.

I thought a lot during the journey and decided that I would not tell my mother the truth either about my experience or about my rescue. I would just tell her that I had been out in the middle of nowhere, staying with people who never even went to their local Club, and I had been bored. That was an easy lie and one that I thought would be justified. I would, of course, tell my stepfather the whole truth; or as much as I knew of it.

On arrival at our bungalow I rushed up to my mother, who was sitting on the verandah, and kissed her.

'Oh, darling, it's lovely to have you back,' she said. 'But why did you want to leave?'

I told her the already prepared untruth about 'being bored', and it sounded convincing.

Major John picked up my suitcase. 'I'll carry this along for you.' He gave me a look which indicated that he wanted a word with me. 'Won't be a moment, darling,' he said, and kissed the top of my mother's head. 'I want to hear about the Rhyses too.'

Once in my bedroom he shut the door and sat down, and he and I had a very different kind of conversation. 'Tell me about it,' he said. So I gave him a detailed account of my brief and horrifying stay with the Rhyses.

Then he said, 'Now I must give you my side of the story. Here in Kohat we are living in very close proximity to the Pathans. Consequently MI5 have got to keep tabs on everybody, including the British.' My stepfather paused. 'The Rhyses came to the North-West Frontier some years ago. They built their bungalow in the middle of nowhere, as you have seen, then developed acres of "beans" which MI5, like you, suspect. But MI5 are treating *that* as a minor issue in order to ensure that for the moment the Rhyses should not feel themselves to be under suspicion. But young European girls are *not* a minor issue as they discovered when Molly Ellis was abducted. Without the intervention of that miraculous woman, Miss Starr, God knows what would have happened. War? Murder? Or a colossal payment of hostage money by the British Government? None of which would have helped the British in their colonial responsibilities. So MI5 were wise to the fact that, immediately after our arrival, the Rhyses began to visit the Club again.'

'But for what – '

'Presumably to discover *your* way of life. They wanted to know if and when you were ever alone. They also wanted to know where the sepoys, when on guard at night, were positioned . . . and whether our *chokidah* could either be tricked or bribed away from his patrol duties. MI5 were keeping a close watch on the Rhyses because they realised that should the Pathans be planning the abduction of another young girl, it could much more easily be carried out from their very remote bungalow than from ours which is in the cantonment. So when Military Headquarters passed them your chit they immediately contacted Runciman and then arrived at a solution. It was rather drastic action . . . but the only way of getting you away without arousing the Rhyses' suspicions.'

There was a long silence. I could not speak because of the horror of this explanation. Then I asked quietly: 'What about those beans?'

My stepfather shrugged. 'Exactly. That extensive bean growth could conceal within it certain areas of illegal drug growth, cannabis, for example. Equally, those little white flags could, through arrangement and rearrangement, be used to convey messages to the Pathans . . .' He paused, 'But thank God, and also MI5, that you, my dear, are safe.' He took my hand. 'And you were a very brave young lady.'

I thought back. 'I think I was just a jolly good actress.' I replied quietly, then added, 'but we must never tell Mother, must we?'

'Never,' answered my stepfather.

I paused. 'And what will happen to the Rhyses?' I asked.

My stepfather paused. 'Nothing, probably . . . we've no hard evidence. They'll just be kept under surveillance.'

What Is a 'Cad'?

In Kohat we could all feel the approach of the 'hot weather' which was once more moving into the attack. I had expected it to be less hot in northern India than it had been in the south. But this was not so. Overnight the sun seemed to burn deeper and deeper and the glare to become more unendurable. It pierced one's eyeballs as if with a sharp knife. Whenever possible I got into the habit of going about with my eyes half-closed; and, of course, now we all slept out on the verandah closely tucked in under a sheet against mosquitoes, and with torches under our pillows against the advent of snakes and scorpions. There were strange sounds, too, heralding the approach of what I thought of as this 'Hades of heat'. The harsh notes of what were called 'fever birds' croaked in ascending and descending scales all through the dark hours. Jackals howled in accompaniment and pariah dogs whined and moaned from adjoining Indian huts. My stepfather warned me: 'Never touch a dog now that the hot weather has started: a lot of dogs get rabies.'

'Rabies?' I asked.

'They go mad,' my stepfather explained simply.

I must confess I was not surprised.

But we didn't have to endure the hot weather for more than a few weeks, for Major John had already made plans for my mother and me to escape up to Kashmir again and to stay there until the end of the hot season.

'You'll stay in Srinagar first,' he said. 'I've booked you a houseboat . . . but it's not free for the whole season. So I've booked you rooms in Naini Tal for the latter half of the hot weather. Naini Tal is higher up in the hills and has a very nice hotel. And I hope to be able to join you later on for a bit. But I want you to take our bearer with you. Down here in the plains I can easily move in with another chap: half the bungalows will be pretty empty with most of the women gone!'

And so, once more, we were on the move, up to the hills. Srinagar sounded more romantic than the other hill stations; and the thought of living in a houseboat excited me. A train with the usual block of ice in the carriage took us the first part of the journey. Then, on leaving the train, *dhoolies* or *dandies* were ready to carry my mother and me up the difficult mountain paths. The paths along which we wound our way were not unduly steep, so the hills all round us were clearly visible. When we arrived at Srinagar we were met by another friend of my stepfather's. Our luggage was given over to our faithful old bearer who, even here, knew all the ropes, and my mother and I were then conducted to our houseboat.

Many houseboats were moored in the canal but a very reasonable space was left between each. Resting on the tranquil water, they looked rather like great brooding birds sitting in contemplation of the peaceful scene. I saw that there was a pathway along the bank of the canal, from which a small wooden bridge or plank led to each houseboat. Our houseboat when we entered it, we found to be furnished in conventional cretonned comfort, and the silence all around was sublime. Above us on both sides of the canal rose the friendly hills, luxuriant with growth, and the scent of flowers in the air was a welcome relief after the dust of the plains. My mother said she would like to unpack. But when our kind escort, who was secretary of the Srinagar Club, suggested that I might like to see where the Club was situated, I agreed. We walked back along the footpath and I noticed that many, but not all, of the houseboats were occupied.

The Club was only a few hundred yards away. It had a reasonable-sized dance-room with the usual arrangement of tables and chairs both inside and out; and, of course, somewhere offstage was the muted murmur from the bar, for men, in the hills, were not numerous.

'We use this hall not only for dancing,' my escort told me, 'but occasionally also for concerts; and sometimes even for lectures, and the odd amateur theatrical performance.' He looked at me and smiled. 'Just depends what talents we've got up here.'

It sounded almost civilised and I felt expectant.

'Like to have a look at the noticeboard?' the secretary suggested. 'Here are all the Club's arrangements and the corresponding dates for the next few months.'

I looked at the board. There were talks to be given; two concerts, one by a violinist and the other by a pianist; and then, at the end of the month, there was to be a performance of a play called *Tilly of Bloomsbury*.

'We're having a bit of trouble with the casting of the play,' said my companion. 'Just as some man has learned his part his leave is up, and he has to go back to the plains!'

I felt thrilled with the whole idea. 'I'd like to meet whoever's producing it,' I said. I had the sudden thought that perhaps I could get a small part – as a maid or something.

'Rather! Let's all meet at the Club tomorrow.' He looked at his watch. ''Fraid I've got an appointment with the District Officer. Will you be able to find your way back?'

'Of course!' I laughed. 'It's only a few hundred yards.'

It was good to feel that one could walk quickly and easily in the refreshing air. But out in this open valley I chose to walk slowly because I wanted to watch and take in the whole natural scene around me. On either side there were colourful trees and shrubs, orange, red and green, covering the gently curving hills. There was love in the way they clung to the hills like babies to their mother's breast. And a sense of mystery was conveyed by the silence which seemed to fill the whole valley; for it was the silence of growth. In my slow walk I passed a few occupied houseboats but their inmates were quite invisible and inaudible. Bits of washing were hanging out in some; a child's pushchair stood on the deck of another; and in the rear of a third houseboat squatted an Indian servant in his spotless white coat and with a turban on his head. After every few steps I stood still just to drink in the peacefulness of my surroundings. And I sighed with contentment, for Srinagar was so totally different from any other place that we had visited on our travels in India.

The following day I went to the Club to find out about the play. Could there really be a chance for me? A small part of some sort? I was introduced to the producer who was resident in Kashmir and who had started the Amateur Dramatic Society. He looked at me. 'Have you any experience?'

I shook my head. Then I remembered Miss Fogarty, the top elocutionist in the country, who, when I was at The Larches in Folkestone, had given me first prize for Elocution. Tentatively I mentioned this.

'Well, that makes one heck of a difference. If the audience can hear what is being said, it rather helps!' the producer said at once. 'That's the trouble with amateurs . . . they don't know how to speak out.' He looked at me. 'I think perhaps you might play Tilly.'

I was speechless. Tilly was the leading part.

'You've got quite a good opposite number, too . . . Dickie Bramble. Apart from being able to act he plays champion tennis at Wimbledon and is a minus one at golf.' He looked at me. 'I'll introduce you to him tomorrow if you're coming to the Club.'

All I could do was nod my head, and ask, 'When will we start rehearsing?'

'We start next week.'

Tilly! I couldn't even say thank you. I just wanted to rush home to the houseboat and tell my mother the news. So the next day I met Dickie Bramble and it was decided that rehearsals should take place every afternoon when most people were having a nap. Dickie was fair-haired, blue-eyed, and in his way quite a likeable person. From the start he made what might be called a 'dead set' at me. After rehearsals he gave me tea at the Club and then, when the band started to play, we danced together for the rest of the evening. Before I fully realised what was happening, Dickie had entirely monopolised me.

I worked very hard at Tilly and although it was the leading part I found learning the words very easy. My mother used to give me the 'cues' and then I would say my lines – very often more than once, if their inflexions were not to my liking. With Dickie I practised the entrances and the exits, paying particular attention to an imaginary audience. The producer was overjoyed. 'You're a natural,' he told me.

There were two things about the play that were a particular novelty to me: the first was the make-up; the second, being intimate on stage, with Dickie Bramble. He was unduly enthusiastic about the love scenes. 'We're only pretending,' I used to whisper to him. 'You needn't go on about it so.'

'But I like it,' he said.

Then when he had to kiss me, he started trying to put his tongue into my mouth. And although he was an attractive man I simply couldn't stand it.

'If you ever do that again I'll kick you,' I said. 'Yes, right here on the stage and in front of everybody I'll kick you . . . and I'll tell them why.'

I meant it. He knew that I meant it. And he never did it again.

On the night of the first performance I was in my dressing-room trembling with excitement, and hearing the hum of voices from the packed audience behind the dropped curtain. In a few minutes the curtain would go up, and I would go on stage! I was just putting the finishing touches to my make-up when one of the cast, a woman, put her head round the door and said, 'Ingaret, you do know that Dickie Bramble is married, don't you?'

I laughed. 'Of course he's not.' Then we both heard the bell ringing for 'curtain up'.

After the performance was over and we'd all taken a number of curtain calls, I suddenly remembered this woman's remark.

'Dickie, are you married?' I asked.

'Of course not,' he said, and he too laughed.

I thought no more about it until a young man in the Queen's Regiment, whom I had met in the ship on the way out to India, came to me in genuine concern.

'Ingaret,' he said, 'I had a hell of a row about you in the bar the other night. The chaps are dead certain Bramble's a married man . . . and in consequence they were saying some pretty beastly things about you . . . calling you "a tart" and things like that. I gave them hell; but it is a fact that you two are always together.'

'But I've asked him,' I said. 'He's *not* married.'

The young man looked at me, sighed, shrugged his shoulders and left; and I went on dancing with Dickie every evening at the Club.

Finally, the 'scandal' reached my mother's ears. A woman visited her in the houseboat and put my mother fully in the picture. Captain Bramble was a married man, in fact this woman knew his wife because they came from the same village. She ended by saying, 'Your daughter is getting herself a very bad name because she's seen with him every evening at the Club and dances with no one else.'

My mother thanked her. By this time it was late in the evening and she was expecting me back at any moment. However, she left the houseboat and went to the hotel where Captain Bramble was staying. She asked if he was in: and on receiving an answer in the affirmative she marched up to his bedroom and knocked at the door. When it was opened she entered and gave Dickie a 'dressing-down' which apparently was totally explosive. 'And if I hear that you are ever talking to my daughter again I will report you to your Commanding Officer!' she shouted as she swept from the room. At least she had learned one sentence from military phraseology!

As she slammed the door behind her, the adjoining bedroom door opened and an army general came out. 'The wooden walls of these hotels are very thin,' he said. 'I am afraid I couldn't help hearing practically everything you said. I just wanted to tell you that I wish we had more women like you in India.' Then with a slight bow he retreated back into his bedroom.

On returning to the houseboat my mother told me the whole story. I didn't really mind about Dickie but I was bothered by the thought that, if I went to the Club the following evening, there would be absolutely no one to dance with . . . or talk to! No other man would come near me because when I went and sat at 'our' tea-table they would all think I was waiting for Dickie. And, of course, no woman would talk to me either, because of the scandal that was spreading like wildfire through our little community. Had I, or had I not, the courage to walk into the Club by myself, sit down at 'our' table and order myself a solitary cup of tea? All day long the question fidgeted me. It was only at the last moment that I knew the answer. Just as the sun was discreetly lowering itself behind the hilltops I got up and left for the Club.

I walked into the small but crowded clubroom and sat down where 'our' table stood empty but already set for two. I signed to the *abdar* (or head-waiter) and asked him to bring tea for one. I sat for some moments just staring down at the tea-table. Then, to my surprise, I thought I heard footsteps coming across the dance-floor towards me. Looking up, I saw to my amazement that it was the same tall man who, with his Airedale dog, had stood watching me each evening as I danced at the Ahmadnagar Club, years and years ago, or so it now seemed!

'Can I join you?' he asked me quietly.

'Of course . . .'

I almost heard a hush descend in the clubroom as he sat down.

'And what about two teas?' He signed to the *abdar*. Seen closely, he had the same grizzled look and colouring that I remembered, and his eyes were so piercingly blue that they looked as if they had electric lights behind them.

'How nice of you to come over.' This was the first time we had spoken to each other and there was a tremble in my voice. Suddenly I realised what a strain the whole Dickie Bramble affair had been for me.

This nice man, whose name was Major Hamilton-Temple-Blackwood, smiled at me. 'Well, I've waited a long time . . . it must be at least three years since I first saw you dancing at Ahmadnagar.'

'But do you know – '

'Of course I know,' he replied quietly. 'I also know that India is not only a hot-bed of heat but also of gossip.' He paused. 'So let's forget about it, shall we? Besides, that chap Bramble was a cad, you know.'

'A cad?' I had heard the word before, of course, but without quite knowing what it meant. Now I did know. Dickie *was* a cad. But I hadn't spotted it. That was what really alarmed me. I drew a deep breath.

Then I suddenly remembered this nice man's dog. 'Where's your Airedale?' I asked. 'Didn't you bring him up to the hills with you?'

I waited. But Major Hamilton-Temple-Blackwood sat very still, just staring at nothing. Finally he replied quietly, 'Poor chap . . . he got rabies . . . I had to shoot him. I – I insisted on doing it myself. Someone else might have missed him first time.' Then he added with difficulty, 'He was my best friend.'

By this time the *abdar* had arrived with the tea, been paid and tipped . . . but I made no attempt to pour out the tea. We sat in companionable silence until the dance music started again. It was the Blue Danube waltz.

'Shall we dance?' Major Hamilton-Temple-Blackwood asked.

'We needn't,' I answered gently. It wasn't a moment for dancing. Intuitively I sensed that he understood my predicament, just as I understood his grief at the loss of his dog. We were both quite unknown to each other and yet we were close enough not to need explanations. Momentarily he reminded me of David . . . David wrote to me with regular irregularity, in his enigmatic but easily-read handwriting. But no, there was a real difference as well as a real similarity between these two men. David, I feared, exploited – or rather was exploited by – his sensations: this man had them centrally positioned so that he and they were naturally united.

Suddenly Major Hamilton-Temple-Blackwood rose to his feet. 'Come on,' he said. 'After all these years of waiting, just one dance, please.'

So in a guarded and somewhat uncertain manner we turned and slowly revolved to the romance of the Blue Danube waltz. At the end of the evening we parted. 'Goodbye,' he said. 'I hope we meet again.' But I thought to myself that we never would. It came to me that life in India was rather like a game that we used to play as children. 'How many eggs in the bush?' we would say, rattling marbles, or stones, in our closed hands. Somehow we never got the answer right . . . but perhaps that was why we kept on playing it.

The following day my stepfather was due to join us. He had short leave and was going to take us higher up to Naini Tal, where we were booked into a hotel for the remainder of our stay in the hills. He wanted us to see as much of India as possible because at the start of the next 'hot weather' season he was due to retire. So in our *dhoolies* and our *dandies* we were transferred up to Naini Tal.

Srinagar had been an open and feminine resort. The canals, despite the houseboats, were so still that their untroubled surfaces even reflected the cloudless sky above them. The surrounding hills were resplendent in their multicoloured adornment of trees and shrubs; and the gentle breath of the whole terrain was almost audible, so scented and reassuring was it. Naini Tal, however, had quite a different feel to it. The station was situated on three levels: above was a kind of natural open place with hills all around and a confusion of fir trees scattered among them; below lay the hotel, and a little further down was a polo-ground and a number of tennis courts. I decided immediately on arrival that there was no romance here. Nevertheless, the air itself had a fresh vitality to which the gently-breathing Srinagar had no real claim. The hotel had various outlying quarters built on to it, and our two rooms were in one of these long, barrack-like extensions. The main part of the hotel was very welcoming, with a large dining-room, a card room and a ballroom, and it was extremely comfortable, but, for me, it had no charm.

It had been arranged that Major John should spend only the first week of his three-week leave with us up in Naini Tal: after that he would return to the plains and then, towards the end of the 'hot season', he would come up again to visit us in Naini. But personal plans in India rarely come to fruition. Before my stepfather's first week was over, my mother became seriously ill. A doctor was summoned. He confirmed that the illness was enteric. 'Wasn't she inoculated against it in England?' he asked.

Major John turned to me. 'Wasn't she?' he asked.

'We both went together to be inoculated,' I remembered, 'and I was done . . . but she said she wouldn't bother. I don't think she knew what it was all about,' I added. 'We'd neither of us ever heard of enteric.'

The doctor did what he could. A day nurse and a night nurse were provided. My stepfather's leave was extended as 'emergency' leave. Everything possible was done for her, but for two whole weeks my mother lay between life and death. I don't think I have ever suffered such anxiety or such terrible loneliness. Of course, I was not allowed to see her. And whenever I asked my stepfather for news, the answer was always the same: 'Unchanged'. So I struggled through the first two weeks. I didn't know what to do with the mornings; I didn't know what to do with the afternoons; I didn't know what to do with the evenings. Luckily the Club had some sort of library, so thankfully I crept into bed with a book and tried to forget. I devoured words, words, words, without even being able to digest their meaning . . . and then, finally, I slept from sheer exhaustion. And always, the next morning, my mother's condition remained 'unchanged'.

I had my meals as usual in the hotel dining-room, often alone as my stepfather rarely left my mother's bedside. Everyone knew that Mrs D'Oyley had enteric, but all the same, nobody ever came up to me or made inquiries. It may, of course, have been discretion, or possibly indifference? I didn't particularly mind which. At meals I always had a book with me for company.

Then one day, glancing round the dining-room, who should I see but Paddy, my Irish dancing partner on the voyage out to India! He was sitting at a table with two other men.

Suddenly he too saw me, rose and came over. 'I'm so sorry to hear about your mother,' he said. 'Anything I can do?'

I shook my head. I hadn't the heart to dance . . . but perhaps – 'Could we have a chat sometime after dinner? I find the evenings so long.'

'Of course,' he said. 'We'll take care of you after dinner. Those are two pals of mine and we always play backgammon afterwards in my room. It's a gambling game, you know . . . you might like to learn.'

'I'd like to watch,' I said. At that moment the only gamble I was concerned with was the one between life and death . . . but at least down in Paddy's room there would be company.

So I told my stepfather that I was going to watch a card game (as I thought it would be) in the room of a friend of mine, so if I was a bit late back he was not to worry. He nodded: I think the poor man scarcely heard my words. Then, after dinner, I went down to Paddy's room and met his two friends. In a moment they had installed me in a huge comfortable armchair which they pushed up close to the gambling table. I did feel somewhat relaxed by their presence . . . but it wasn't a card-game they were playing. Almost at once, reassured and somewhat hypnotised by the sound of the dice being shaken over and over again, punctuated only by voices and laughter, I fell fast asleep in my comfortable chair. I didn't even wake when, in the early hours of the morning, Paddy picked me up, carried me to my bedroom and, quietly opening the door, laid me down on my bed. When I awoke later the next morning, I was fully dressed!

Later still, Paddy appeared at my bedroom door. He said a polite 'Good morning, sir . . . so sorry to hear about your wife,' to Major John, then he beckoned me outside.

'Ingaret,' he said. 'You may be in for a bit of trouble. I carried you back to your room last night because you were dead-beat. You didn't even wake up when I put you down on the bed. But carrying you along the passage I met some old harridan who gave me such a scathing look that she obviously thought the worst.'

'The worst?'

'Well, either she thought that you were too drunk to walk . . . or that I'd been seducing you!' Paddy said lightly. 'So I thought I'd better warn you as there may be a bit of a freeze-up all round.' He paused. 'So possibly, in your own interests, dearest young lady, you'd better not come again.'

'All right,' I said listlessly. I was getting used to freeze-ups. First Srinagar, and now here. I didn't care about anyone or anything – except my mother.

And Paddy was right. Lady Hatchett, who was a judge's wife, cut me dead, as the phrase went, whenever or wherever she met me: in the dining-room, the passage, the garden; and, as if this 'cutting' were a contagious disease, it spread quickly amongst the other women in the hotel, all of whom knew that my mother was dangerously ill. However, at the time I did no more than vaguely register their behaviour. I had never really cared about what people 'thought'.

As the days went by my mother made a slow recovery, and my stepfather was able to go back to his regiment in the plains. I then took over as her constant companion. It was almost like the old days. Eventually she found her way back to the bridge-table in the afternoons but by then the 'hot weather' in the plains was teetering to an end, or so Major John informed us. 'Any day now the rains could break,' he wrote. 'The monsoons will be welcome, but the humidity of the atmosphere, once the clouds have built up and broken down in huge waterfalls of rain, is for some people more difficult to bear even than the dry, burning heat. I'm more or less used to it. But I want you two to stay up in the hills until I come and fetch you. One thing you will be surprised to see is that the garden is green!'

So we waited, rather austerely and uncertainly, in Naini Tal. Most of the men had drifted back to the plains, but as always in the hills, there were plenty of women around. I could occasionally make up a 'women's four' at tennis, just as my mother could occasionally make up a 'women's four' at bridge, but it was painstakingly dull. Even the band had stopped playing dance tunes and droned out the same dreary musical comedy favourites over and over again.

To our relief, in the middle of October, Major John came up to take us back to Kohat. It was only ninety degrees in the shade there, so the cool weather had really started! Quite soon we would all three be going back to England and, although I had spent nearly four years in this amazing country, I felt I had no real knowledge or understanding of what I was leaving behind me. Yet, at the same time, I knew that I would never forget the living reality of the whole experience. The Indian people themselves made sure of this. The quality of the Indian Army, although largely maintained and directed by the British, could not be overlooked. It was a disciplined and meaningful force, and ready to give support to outside demands without hesitation. I can still remember being impressed with the way my stepfather addressed his troops. Very clearly, his pride was for them as military men, rather than for his authority. And this, in turn, elicited a faithful response. Even I felt affection for these hundreds of khaki-clad figures . . . as I also did for the children who surrounded me, if I ever strolled into one of their colourful little villages, crying 'Baksheesh! Baksheesh! Baksheesh!' And as they crowded round me in the dust, the repeated word became something like a song. I, of course, would already have filled my purse with very small change and as I scattered the coins on the dirty paths and among the flowers, the children would snaffle and shuffle and shout as they ran around searching for them in the dust. Then, while the children were still searching the ground, even though the treasure had all been salvaged, I would raise my eyes from the dusty path and see, towering in the distance, mountains crowned with snow! For a moment this seemed an impossibility. Snow-capped mountains in a country where heatstroke could be fatal: this, I thought, reflected India's supreme paradox. As I stared at the distant beauty of the Himalayas, I told myself that these majestic mountains were there to proclaim the possibility of the impossible; a lesson that perhaps we all, in time, should learn.

PART III

A portrait of myself taken soon after my training at RADA, 1928–29.

18

David

And so we all began to adjust to the idea that we were returning to England; and to Roger. A rather exciting thing happened shortly before we were due to depart, in that David, in one of his letters, mentioned that he was going back to England, on leave, at almost exactly the same time as we were. He was sailing on a different line – BI (British India) instead of P&O – 'but we will meet in England,' he wrote.

Consequently, in May, almost unbelievably my mother, my stepfather and I started to pack our trunks in preparation for our return journey. But we only had summer clothes to pack. 'They'll come in handy,' my mother said. 'It'll be summer in England when we arrive.' After such a long absence, I could scarcely remember what summer in England felt like.

Finally, the train journey to Bombay completed, we drove to the docks, boarded our ship, and installed ourselves in our cabins. Then, slowly, the P&O liner pulled away from the dockside and we began a tranquil voyage back across the Indian Ocean.

On arrival at Port Said, I was both delighted and surprised to see that David's ship was still in harbour. 'Oh, can't I change ships and do the rest of the journey in David's ship?' I asked my mother.

'Yes, if there's a spare bunk, darling, and you'd like to,' said my mother easily. She was in so many ways a very extraordinary woman. 'Let's ask John,' she added.

And so it was arranged. Grabbing a small suitcase, I was making my way towards the gangway of the BI liner with my stepfather when we met David coming across to our ship.

'I was just coming to call on you,' he said.

'Well, I've switched to a cabin in your ship,' I said. 'Our ship's as dull as ditchwater, isn't it, Major John?' Roger and I kept on calling our stepfather 'Major' even though he was by now a colonel.

'Yes, it is a bit antiquated; lots of old *koi-hais* going back to England.'

So David and I went aboard the BI ship. I was shown to a cabin which I was to share with an even older lady than on the outward voyage. And then each ship in turn, first the BI and then the P&O vessel, moved off slowly from the quayside at Port Said and inched its way through the narrow Suez Canal and out into the Mediterranean.

We only had a few days together in which to enjoy our close, knife-edged, ambiguous relationship. But they were important days, for I noticed a slight change in David. To begin with, instead of taking me for granted, he seemed to be watching me both carefully and yet absently.

'I believe you're in love with someone,' I told him finally, in what I hoped was a casual tone.

There was a brief pause, and then he said, 'I'm not quite sure. I've never contemplated "being in love" . . . but perhaps it's "being in love" that contemplates one?'

But our laughter and talks and walks up and down the decks were abruptly curtailed when we reached the Bay of Biscay. Our ship ran into a terrific storm: so ferocious was it that, for a short period, the captain had to change tactics, turn about and go back with the storm instead of sailing against it. He told us afterwards that it was the first time in his career that he had had to do this.

As things calmed down I staggered up on deck and sank into a deck-chair. Throughout the storm David had kept in daily touch with me. He was enjoying the rough seas, he kept saying in his messages. When he saw me lying, white-faced, in the deck-chair, he stopped short and stared down at me. 'Put a lily in your hand,' he said, 'and you'd look like the Madonna.' I could just manage a smile. But later on I thought that it was an odd remark for David, of all people, to have made.

However, we did have a couple of days left in which to enjoy the turbulent seas and watch the mounting waves as they reared towards us. Riding to meet their enormous charged heights was rather like jumping some of the irrigation ditches which I'd had to cross during my early-morning rides in Kohat. But already that felt like another world.

By now I had discovered that David's parents' home was only about fifteen miles away from Blackwater in Surrey, where Major John had rented a furnished house for us. The reason he chose Surrey for our temporary home was because his future work with the Army would entail consultations with the Staff College at Camberley. David seemed genuinely pleased about this. 'Once we get ashore I'll take you round a bit,' he said. 'Show you a few things. Ever been to the Derby?'

I shook my head. 'Only local point-to-points,' I answered. 'I don't know anything about serious horse-racing.'

'Lucky for me,' David answered. 'I'll introduce you to Gipsy Lee,' he explained further. 'I've got a car, you see. It's a Bentley. But it's stood up well to all sorts of adventures.'

It hardly seemed possible that David and I had known each other for almost four years, for they had been years without any chance of developing a real relationship. Here, in the vast loneliness which was England, we suddenly found ourselves with unlimited freedom to get to know each other, and David used it, and me, and his Bentley to the full. He took me to the Derby. We couldn't afford seats, so he drove the Bentley into the crowded car-park at Epsom racecourse and we stood on the seats and watched the horses we had backed trail in towards the end of the race. We enjoyed our own company: we laughed a lot at, and with, each other; and we could also keep silent for quite long periods. Once I put on a new dress which David immediately noticed and admired. He still had his wicked smile, and made his usual ambiguous comments. Could one take him seriously . . . or could one not? Had he run out of girls, and was he just making do with me? As we grew to know and understand each other better, this question remained unanswered in my mind.

Then, on one of our hell-bent journeys across country in the open Bentley, David suddenly said, 'Ingaret, will you come and spend the weekend with us? My parents long to meet you. They've never known me so well-behaved since I was in the nursery.'

'Oh, David, I'd love to meet them.' I'd often wondered what his parents were like. And the fact that his father was a judge greatly interested me.

So David fetched me from Blackwater on a Saturday morning and I was to return home on the following Monday. I was introduced to his parents: his mother was a charming woman with greying hair and a soft voice, and his father, the judge, was tall and strong-featured. Suddenly, as one of the family, I felt inordinately happy. Our lunch, all four of us together, was a pleasant and easy meal. Of course I was aware that I was under some scrutiny, but I also felt that perhaps I had passed the test.

Out in the drive that afternoon, while David was polishing his Bentley, as he always did after a journey, he suddenly looked across the bonnet at me and asked very quietly, 'Ingaret, will you marry me?'

For a moment I was speechless. Was he serious? He looked extremely serious. Slowly I nodded. 'Yes, David, I will,' I said. But I had to put my hand on the handle of the car door to prevent myself from falling. I felt giddy with – with – something . . . but I didn't know what. Everything round me seemed to be out of focus.

David came round and took my arm. 'Let's go and tell the parents,' he said gently. He didn't kiss me.

So we went in and told them, and they were very warm and genuine, and behaved as if they had almost expected something of this sort to happen; whereas I had not given it a thought. The reality of my relationship with David was all that mattered.

Then suddenly his mother left the room and came back with a wonderful emerald and diamond ring.

'I've been keeping this for the day when you get married, David,' she said. 'And I'm so glad to be able to give it to Ingaret as an engagement ring.' She came forward and kissed me and handed me the ring with a warm smile of welcome.

For a moment, after thanking her, I felt so confused that this time I couldn't remember which finger to put it on.

David, with his customary speed in understanding my hesitation, came forward. 'Hey! I want to put it on your finger,' he said. And he slipped it on to the fourth finger of my left hand. 'Fine,' he said.

I nodded. It was lovely, and I was engaged to be married and that was lovely too, especially with David looking so delighted. The whole thing had been so quick that I myself had not been able properly to identify with the occasion; whereas everyone else behaved as if they had been expecting it, even David.

We had a jolly evening, with champagne for dinner, and numerous toasts were drunk. And then we went to our separate bedrooms. But I couldn't sleep. I still couldn't believe what had happened. I was engaged to be married . . . and marriage was something I'd never really thought about – since breaking off my impulsive engagement to Geoffrey Cholmondley three years ago. But to be married to David, to live with him for ever and ever . . . it was quite beyond my wildest dreams of delight. Of all the 'admirers' who had circled round me in India, for want of something better to do, I told myself, David had meant the most to me. Together, we had both been 'faithful' to something, though neither of us, I thought, could have said what this was. I knew that we shared something, something important, and something that was at a deeper level than was customary. I knew that I valued this not only because it came to me through David, but because it opened up in me a reality of feeling that I had never experienced before. I was convinced that it was the same for David, despite his undifferentiated attachments to various girlfriends. And it was presumably because of this feeling that people got married? And marriage meant for ever and ever . . . I fell asleep from sheer happiness.

I was awakened in the middle of the night by hearing my door very quietly opened and then shut. Startled, I sat up in bed but there was darkness everywhere.

'Ssh!' It was David's voice. He groped his way towards me and put out his hands. They were ice-cold: both the fingers and palms of his hands were frozen! 'I've waited outside your door for two hours,' he said, in a hoarse voice which trembled, as I thought, with the cold. 'Two bloody hours I've waited,' he repeated.

I was horrified. 'Oh, my darling,' I whispered. 'But why?' The implication did not strike me. 'Come over here . . . come into my bed . . .' I threw back the bedclothes. 'Quick! Get in!'

He did; and I felt him. His feet were frozen as well. I put my own feet against them and took his stiff hands in mine and began to rub them to get the circulation going. 'Two hours . . .' he kept on muttering, trying to keep his teeth from chattering. 'Two . . . bloody . . . hours.' I sensed conflict and confusion in him – but what about? What had kept him standing there on the linoleum outside my door for two hours on a chilly night?

I suppose we spent about ten minutes or more in my bed whilst I chafed his hands with mine and kept my own warm feet pressed against his. Finally his teeth did stop chattering . . . and a terrible stillness fell over the room.

'You are warmer, darling?' I asked anxiously.

'I'd better be off, now,' he said, and his voice was remote and husky.

Quickly he got out of my bed and stumbled towards the door. I heard it click behind him. Poor David, what could have gone wrong that he should have stood for two hours in the middle of the night outside my bedroom door? Anyway, he was all right now, I told myself, thanks to my resuscitating efforts. In the morning I would ask him what had been troubling him . . . we were going to be together for ever and ever . . . and this would be a part of it . . . me being able to help him. Finally I dropped off to sleep again.

I woke to a sense of overwhelming happiness and fulfilment. The first thing I did was to look at my engagement ring. It trembled in the morning light and looked beautiful. But the real source of my joy was that I had been able to help David during the night when he'd come, frozen stiff, into my bed to get warm. I felt so glad that I'd been able to look after him for once, when it was generally he who looked after me.

I dressed quickly and went downstairs welcoming the beautiful new autumn day. In the study David was sitting alone with his back to the window reading the *Sunday Times*. I walked towards him and then stood staring out at the brilliant sky, flecked with the blues and gold of morning. It corresponded so completely to my own radiant mood.

'Oh, darling,' I said. 'Do look at the sky: it is so romantic!'

There was a slight shuffling of the newspaper pages, then a voice, colder even than his hands and feet had been during the night, said bitterly, 'What is romance?'

Without warning, the sense of new life within fell from me like a worn-out garment. I just felt it drop to pieces at my feet. I stood quite still for an instant. Everything was dead.

But death, in its own right, has a certain dignity, so I heard what must have been my own voice saying very quietly, 'Then David, if you don't know what romance is, I think you had better take this back, hadn't you?' Somehow I managed to pull the engagement ring off my finger and hand it to him.

Still without dropping the newspaper, David took it from me and put it in his top waistcoat pocket. Suddenly the horror of what was actually happening almost overcame me. But I managed to steady my voice. 'I'll go upstairs and pack my suitcase . . . and perhaps you will look up the Sunday trains and take me to the station in the car.' I couldn't help knowing that it was Sunday because I could hear the church bells ringing in the small country town nearby.

David nodded. 'Very well,' he said. Even then he didn't put down the newspaper. I turned with difficulty and left the room.

Unimaginably, we did all four have breakfast together. I think at that point David's parents suspected nothing. They didn't even notice that my ring was missing. Then, after breakfast, without even saying goodbye to my host and hostess, I went to put my night-things into my suitcase and came back downstairs to find that David had the Bentley ready and waiting. He drove me to the station. We never spoke. He carried my suitcase to the right platform and I got into the right train. The station was empty save for the sound of church bells pealing out across the town. Then the engine hooted: David stood stiffly, almost as if to attention, and watched me move out of sight. The train jerked slowly through the valley. The joyful, chiming church bells seemed to fill the whole countryside. But to me they weren't joyful bells, they were funeral bells.

Although I had the railway carriage to myself I didn't cry. I knew I had to hold myself together, otherwise the collapse would have been total. I couldn't even begin to understand what had changed David overnight. I took a bus from the station to Blackwater, surprising my mother by my early return. I kissed her, then looking down at my suitcase I said, 'I'll just take this up to my room.'

I scrambled up the stairs, opened my bedroom door, and the first thing I saw was a large photograph of David staring straight at me across the room. I collapsed on to my bed and burst into a passion of tears, smothering my face in the pillows. Something enormous, something that I'd never felt before, had come to an end and left me empty – and I didn't even know why.

After my continued absence, my mother came up to my room. She was horrified by my condition and took me in her arms. I just told her, briefly, in between storms of tears, 'David and I got engaged to be married. And then this morning he . . . we . . . changed our minds.' Most particularly I did not want to put the blame on David, so I said nothing about his visit to my room. I knew, somehow, that that held the answer to the whole change in David's feelings. Then my tears stopped and I told her I would unpack and join her downstairs. Actually all I wanted was to be alone. The torrent of tears had robbed me of all feeling. I was without life . . . all that ticked over in me was my mind, like a clock . . . ticking away the passing seconds. Why had David come to my room? Why had he waited outside for two hours before coming in? Perhaps he was not fascinated by me at all, but merely by my innocence? Perhaps he thought the challenge of initiating a young girl into the varied practices of making love would give him a thrill that he had not known before? And that a proposal of marriage was the necessary preliminary to this? The sheer, dark cynicism of my ticking mind appalled me, and perhaps the worst agony of all was that David and I had always spoken the truth to each other; or so I had believed. Oh, those dreadful words that seemingly of themselves formed sentences in one's mind, and then like sharpshooters hit one in the belly, the head, the bowels, and the heart. In so doing they could even kill the spirit. As they did mine.

As the weeks passed, this fact became apparent to my mother. Every time I went into my bedroom and saw David's photograph looking at me I could hardly refrain from bursting into tears. I concealed my tears and eventually had the strength to put the photograph away in a drawer. But my inner grief could not be hidden. It stultified my whole being. I felt like a prisoner shut away in darkness. I didn't even believe in the light.

Then one day my mother came to me. 'Darling,' she said, and she spoke with gentle firmness, 'you remember the Brooks?'

I nodded. They were a middle-aged couple who lived down the road with a young widowed daughter, a few years older than I, whose husband had been killed. He had been in the Navy, in submarines, and his submarine had suffered an accident and sunk with the loss of all hands. In consequence his young wife had been, and still was, broken-hearted. 'The Brooks are going to Malta,' my mother continued. 'And of course they are taking Anne with them. They would be very happy for you to join them: it would be company for Anne and they feel that would help her. Would you like to go?'

'Like' was a word of which I no longer knew the meaning. But I would go, if only because I knew most clearly what Anne must be going through. Yes, if I could help anyone who was feeling as I was feeling, I could not possibly refuse to go.

I nodded my head. 'All right,' I said. 'I'll go.' In some ways, perhaps, the further away I was from past memories the better; or so I hoped.

19

Malta

Malta seemed to be divided into two parts; Valletta, which had shops and a club and crowded streets, and stood high above the sea, and Sliema, a mainly residential area, where we were staying in a bungalow belonging to some friends of the Brooks, on a level with the sea. Whether Anne and I shared a bedroom I cannot remember; but we did share a profound and almost unendurable grief. The only difference in our situations was that she could talk to me about her husband's life and death; strangely, the fact that he had been accidentally drowned seemed more difficult for her to accept even than the fact that he was dead. Of my own grief I never spoke. David was not dead: it was I who felt dead. And that could not be talked about. The only occasions when I was stirred slightly into life were when Anne sobbed in my arms and poured out her grief; and then I would do what I could to comfort her.

I remember very little about Malta although I was there for nearly three months. I remember that the sun shone; and that the savage surge and splash of the Mediterranean was audible from our bungalow. In the afternoons we rested, and occasionally in the evenings we were asked to a dance or drinks party that was to be held on the deck of some ship or other. To me it was a near parody of being back at school; or even in India. But whereas school was leading to the adventure of a new and independent life, this mechanical, social routine was a dead end in itself, or so I felt. Oh, we met a few naval lieutenants and a commander or two, but within myself I could find no reactions. I reminded myself of a wind-up doll that I had had as a little girl. My delight at the doll's stiff movements had been ecstatic; my dismay at the present mechanisms of my own behaviour was exactly the opposite.

The sea was the only thing that could momentarily arouse my interest. Very noticeably there were no tides here because we were in the middle

169

of an ocean. But the waves made enraged assaults both daily and nightly against the great roaring rock which was Malta. There were also deep narrow inlets in the rocky defences of this island into which the waves would hurl themselves, swirling and racing forward, surging and breaking in rage, frustration, and white foam. Then they would swirl back in deep and dark intent to gather themselves for the next onslaught. The rocky sides of such inlets rose perhaps twenty to forty feet above the water, and I often stood on those heights staring down at these demonstrations of the ocean's deadly power and strength.

One day, Anne and I were standing looking out to sea with a few naval officers, on our way back from a picnic. I drew apart from the little group and stood gazing down in fascination at the determined advance of the mounting waves, followed by the breaking of their will in foam and fury, and then the sucking back of their flattened but not defeated retreat. Just then, two midshipmen came to join me. 'Wouldn't like to fall down into that lot!' one of them said.

'Why not?' I asked indifferently. 'I'd rather like to jump in!'

He turned to me astonished. 'Bet you wouldn't!'

'Bet you I would.'

'What for?'

'For twelve pairs of silk stockings,' I said calmly. And, although I wasn't interested either in the stockings or in the bet, I did mean what I said.

'OK! Then we'll jump in to save you.'

The two midshipmen laughed with complete disbelief.

I moved a few steps towards the top of the rocky inlet. Then, as I did so, I felt a hand on my shoulder. 'No, Ingaret, you won't.' It was the voice of a tall, fair-haired, blue-eyed Commander, the senior member in our little group. We had never really talked together but, instinctively, he had assumed the role of being my protector.

But the near fury and fatality of the sea continued to attract me. It was better, and safer, than having my thoughts forever wandering back to David; or so I felt.

In consequence, one morning I walked down alone to the swimming-pool which adjoined the sea; under my clothes I wore my bathing-suit. I would have a dip, I decided – anything to pass the tedious, unflagging passage of time. I knew I couldn't swim, but surely swimming-pools were made for people who couldn't swim? However, this swimming-pool was built with access both to and from the open sea: there was a wall between the two, which, in calm weather, isolated the pool from the sea. But on this particular morning the weather was far from calm. The black cone was up, warning against bathing, but I didn't notice it, or, if I did, it failed to convey its message to me. I looked round and there was no one in sight, so I took off my clothes and started to climb down the steps into the pool. I was still on the ladder when an incoming roller swept me off and into the pool, covered me and carried me inexorably towards the inner rocks. Only momentarily could I breathe, and I struggled to catch hold of these rocks . . . but in that very instant the same wave again submerged me, drawing me under and back, with relentless power, towards the ocean itself. I knew I was going to drown – in fact, I was already drowning – for there was no part of the swimming-pool which was not by now deeply submerged by the wild, invading seas. Once again, I was choking and defenceless, and helpless as the waves broke over me.

Suddenly, as the water temporarily receded, I saw a man appear on the high rock above the pool; I saw him put his hands to his mouth and shout . . . but of course no sound reached me, and meanwhile the surging, racing waters covered me yet again. Then, somehow, with all his clothes on, this man was in the water beside me. Clearly he was a strong swimmer: he seized me, spluttering and speechless, and dragged me towards the ladder. Then he clambered up, pulling me after him . . . and, finally, we both sat, gasping, on the dry rocks.

'Didn't you see the cone?' he asked.

I nodded. I had seen it but its implications had not reached me.

'Thank you,' I gasped, and put out my hand.

He helped me up but I was so giddy both with shock and submersion that I could scarcely stand. He led me back up to the dry land above the pool. And finally I picked up my clothes and departed.

I never mentioned this incident to anyone, but I had learned something from it: that, no matter how arid was my inner state of being, I did not want to be drowned. The inner vulnerability of grief persisted. But now I could see it in relation not only to so-called life, but also to near-missed death. And that, somehow, was a valid event.

There is only one other incident of any importance that I can remember from my visit to Malta. I was out shopping with a friend of the Brooks, who lived permanently in Malta, and as we were making our way through the packed streets of Valletta, I noticed for the first time more children than I would have believed possible. They either tumbled helter-skelter over the pavements where we, too, were trying to walk; or they were under our feet, crying or shouting as they crawled around searching for treasures in the gutters.

'I've never noticed so many small children about in the streets before,'

I remarked casually to my companion as we picked our way carefully around them.

'Oh,' she said instantly. 'In this island the people are all Roman Catholics . . . so the fourth son of every family has to become a priest. And all these kids are their illegitimate children.'

I was quite speechless. Being young, I never questioned the veracity of this woman's remark. She obviously knew more about the situation than I did. But it had caught me at a bad moment. I was going through a period of profound disillusionment and disbelief. I was also beginning to realise that, unwittingly, David and I had strayed into an area of being that was unknown, unimaginable – because unexplored – to both of us. And the sudden withdrawal of David from this area had left me empty of everything save the backwash of pain: in consequence I was vulnerable in a way which was quite incomprehensible to me. My companion's reference to the illegitimate children of Roman Catholic priests therefore hit me dead on target. It seemed that I no longer had my old youthful capacity to reason, to force my mind into some sort of understanding of my problems. I merely accepted this piece of information as the truth, and so let it sow its own seeds of disbelief and disillusionment.

My return to England seemed as unreal as my departure from it. On arriving in London I caught a train from Paddington to Plymouth. Roger was now stationed there in the Naval Barracks, and my mother and stepfather had taken a furnished house in Plymouth for six months so that we could see more of him after our long separation.

I was met at Plymouth station by my mother and Roger, and I was truly overjoyed to see them again. Roger looked so much taller and more grown-up in his naval uniform that I could scarcely believe he was my younger brother. Major John was temporarily away in Surrey seeing to the alterations to a house he had bought near Guildford and in which he and my mother would live on his retirement.

The rented house in Plymouth was one in a terrace of tall houses that overlooked the bay. It was quite a capacious affair. 'Which bedroom would you like, darling?' my mother asked, as she was showing me over the place.

'The top bedroom,' I replied without hesitation. On the fifth floor there was a large room remote from the rest of the house, and it also had a large window looking out over Plymouth Sound. I felt I could almost put out my hand and touch Drake's Island situated there in the centre of the bay. There was a desk, too, in front of the window. I would spend my time there.

And passing the time was now my main occupation. Every day 'time' started in the morning when I woke. Then, without comment or change of tempo, 'time' ticked on for the next fifteen hours. Then, with luck, I slept soundly from the sheer exhaustion of the inner nothingness that seemed to surround me. Of course, 'time' hung less heavily at weekends when Roger was off-duty, and my heart warmed to him in the old way. He was amusing too, and could even make me laugh at his funny stories of naval experiences. His days were full of incident, hard work, and comradeship; and I envied him.

One thing Roger told me upset me more than he knew. We had been reminiscing about the past and our various holiday 'homes'.

'Have you been back often to the Vicarage?' I asked. 'I mean, when you were on leave?'

'Good God, no!' Roger replied. 'I just went once, directly after you three had left for India . . . and once was quite enough.'

'Why?' I asked.

'Well, the very first thing that happened was that that bastard tried to bugger me.'

'Bastard? Who?' I asked, bewildered. Then suddenly the penny dropped. 'You don't mean Uncle Bernard?'

'I do indeed.' Suddenly Roger's voice broke: then he asked bitterly, 'How could you leave me alone with that bugger?'

'Oh, Roger, we didn't know – ' I was nearly in tears. 'We had no idea . . . please understand – '

My soft-hearted brother took me in his arms. 'Of course you didn't . . .' He grinned. 'But that's the answer to your question. I went back to the Vicarage once . . . and that very night he came to my room . . . and, God, could I get rid of him! There was no lock on my bedroom door . . . but I kicked him out somehow . . . and kept on kicking him out . . . and in the end I won.' He drew a deep breath. 'So next morning I packed my trunk, dragged it down the back stairs, and told Aunt Magdalen that I was going to stay with the Wimbornes. She asked Uncle Bernard to take me there in the car as they only live about ten miles away. But he just turned a deaf ear . . . you know the way he does.'

'So what did you do?'

'Well, I had to carry my trunk all the way down to the village. I could just manage it, in fits and starts. Then from the post office I rang the Wimbornes and asked them if they'd put me up. So they came to fetch me in their car, and I spent most of my holidays with them after that.'

'Did you ever tell them?' I ventured to ask.

Roger shook his head. 'In my view the chap's just a sex maniac,' he said.

It would have given too much away if I had agreed with him.

When Roger's weekend 'leaves' were over I went back to my old routine. I stayed in my bedroom every morning on the pretext that I was trying to write poetry. Then, after lunch, I would either go for a short walk with my mother, or take a long one by myself. The only thing that I did respond to with enthusiasm was the English climate; it was, after all, an old friend, and it held the only surprises of the week. Wearing a mackintosh, cap and galoshes, I would walk for miles, enjoying the feeling of the rain beating against my face and hands. And then perhaps the human sun of Britain might break out above me and give me a wink of warmth and understanding. Or the heavens might grow thick with cloud and then suddenly, out of the inky skies, would come a flash of zigzag lightning, to be followed by a crash of thunder from the impassioned ordainer of such events. I revelled in these walks because, every afternoon at least, there was something real for me to share in.

I spent most of the mornings staring out across the bay and thinking, thinking hard. Life in India had often seemed meaningless, but at least it had had its active side, as well as an abundance of men, both of which had helped to compensate for, if not conceal, my inner emptiness. But life in England seemed to be an endless oasis, empty both of men and of meaning, and this emptiness had its mouth so wide open that I could even see down into its gullet; and I didn't like what I saw.

What was missing? I thought back a long way and realised that, since childhood, life had been a continual battle. First a battle to help my mother to live with her 'secret' illness; then battles against poverty, which had been dodgy but sometimes fun; then Roger and I had had our joyful battles outside in the open air; then had come my battle to gain a 'serious' education; and latterly I had been fighting a losing battle within myself – to reach an understanding of something that was called 'religion'. But what was there to battle for now, I asked myself, as I sat at my bedroom window staring across at Drake's Island. I became almost identified with that little piece of land in the middle of a great bay and seemingly isolated from all present-day meaning, save through its past history.

Then one morning, as I sat gazing out of the window as usual, my wandering thoughts finally presented me with the answer to this question. I was alone in the house at the time, and I went and got my trunk from the attic, together with a small suitcase. I packed the trunk

174

carefully with my everyday clothes and a favourite book or two; then I packed my small suitcase with my night-things. Somehow I managed to drag my trunk downstairs to the hall and then I sat down and wrote a short note to my mother:

Darling, I've taken my things and I'm going to London. I realise that I absolutely must have some work to do: it's part of my nature. I'd love to go on the stage but I expect that's every young girl's dream! *Don't worry!* Will give you an address directly I've found one from the adverts in the newspapers. I'm convinced that this is absolutely necessary for me. But it doesn't mean that I don't love you very, very much. Lots of kisses, Ingaret.

For the first time in my life I picked up the telephone and ordered myself a taxi. I had to get to Plymouth station somehow. I had already decided that I would leave my trunk in the left luggage office at Paddington, and then, with only my small suitcase to carry, I would go in search of a room. I could also travel about on the tops of open buses – something I had always longed to do – and in this way I would be able to see the sights of this almost totally unknown city. Apart from the night before my mother's wedding, there had only been one occasion when we had been obliged to stay in London, on our way from Kent to Gloucestershire, and a very dramatic night it had proved to be. It was during the First World War, so Roger and I were both very young at the time, and we were woken in our boarding-house by enormous bangs, seemingly breaking out all over London. While my mother, Roger and I stood staring out of the window at the blazing city, all the other occupants were rushing downstairs, calling out, 'Get into a cupboard! Hurry!' We somehow managed to find one which was big enough to take the three of us, although it was a tight squeeze. Then, suddenly, to my relief, there was an ear-splitting bang and the cupboard door was blown into small pieces. Poor Roger was terrified and burst into tears. But I had realised that I was much more frightened of waiting for something to happen than when something actually did happen . . . So now, travelling to London with only four pounds and a return ticket to Plymouth in my pocket, I found the experience to be an exciting and not at all a frightening one. At least I was no longer shut up in a cupboard!

20

The Princess

On arrival at Paddington, which I knew to be on the north side of London, I booked in my trunk as planned and put the receipt carefully away in my purse. Then I went in search of a bus, one that was heading south. I knew that the wind was northerly, so, watching the movement of the clouds, I walked to a bus-stop where I could catch a bus going in the same direction. Eventually I scrambled on to the top of an open bus and asked the conductor for a ticket 'to the middle of London'. He hesitated a moment, then gave me a ticket. 'Piccadilly,' he said. My heart leapt for joy! Piccadilly was exactly right. It was at the Piccadilly Hotel that the three of us had had our delightful tea-party with the band playing after Roger had been to Gieves to be fitted up with his naval uniform for Osborne.

I sat back to feel the refreshing air on my face and also to study the extraordinary phenomenon of the traffic in the busy streets below. Finally, hearing the conductor calling out 'Piccadilly', I descended nimbly and stood looking around. In Piccadilly there seemed to be rows and rows of traffic going in all directions! I bought a newspaper, found a tiny café in a small side-street, sat down and ordered a cup of tea. Then I looked through the advertisements for accommodation and saw that a basement room, in Maddox Street, 'off Bond Street' was advertised for 7s 6d a night.

'Where's Bond Street?' I asked the waitress hesitantly.

She stared at me. 'Not far,' she said. 'Turn left when you go out of here, cross the road, and it's along on your right.'

I followed her directions as best I could, along the crowded pavements and over the busy roads, and eventually came to Bond Street. As I walked up it I stared in amazement at the shop windows. It was like turning the pages of a fashion magazine – furs, jewels, extraordinary hats, and dresses of unimaginable beauty at unbelievable prices. I was almost giddy from gazing when I finally reached Maddox Street. It was a small, rather dark little street and seemed to be filled with garages. When I had found the right number I knocked on the door, which was opened abruptly to reveal a narrow interior and a dark-featured woman.

'I believe you have a room to let?' I asked politely.

The woman gave me a critical glance and shrugged. 'Yer can 'ave a look if yer like,' she replied. So we descended a narrow twisting staircase to the basement which, although the day was quite sunny, was very dark. Then the woman opened a door on to a tiny room lit by one small window. The room had a small camp-bed with no cover on it, just as there was no carpet on the floor. A tin basin stood on a wooden chair; and a tin chamber-pot stood beneath the bed. There was a small table by the bed with a candle on it.

'Water jug and tap out on the landing,' the woman said.

'Thank you,' I replied. I refrained from asking if the water from the tap would be hot or cold, and made my decision. 'I would like to take this room.'

'Payment in advance,' she announced instantly.

'I'll take it for a week,' I answered, and did the sum quickly in my head: £2 12s 6d. I opened my purse and handed her the exact amount. I think she was rather impressed by my accurate arithmetic.

'Key in yer door,' she replied, almost helpfully.

'Thank you,' I said again. 'I'm going out now but I shall never be out late.'

We scrambled up the dark curving stairs and parted. But I took my small suitcase with me.

Outside I found my way back into Bond Street and to a post office. From there I sent a telegram to my mother: 'Got room in W.I. and looking for job. Fondest love. Writing.' I didn't even sign it because it was expensive enough as it was! Then I went to look for a newspaper shop in order to find out what jobs might be available. I had to get a job within the week, or else use my return ticket to Plymouth.

However, walking slowly back down Bond Street I saw something better than a newspaper shop. It was a notice hanging above a small dress shop and it read: 'Wanted. Mannequin'. I stared at the notice; and then I stared at my reflection in the shop window. Could I ever pass as a mannequin? I was slight. I had on a neat, rather short black-and-white suit, a white blouse beneath it and a black tammy on my head. My legs and ankles I knew to be reasonable because people often commented on them, and now they certainly looked their best in my one and only pair of black silk stockings. My black shoes had high heels and I had polished them well. I pondered . . . then drew a deep breath, opened the shop door and walked in. The interior of the shop was carpeted and not very large, and a good-looking, fair-haired woman was sitting at a desk writing.

The woman looked up as I entered, called out, 'Jeanne!' and went back to her account books.

A door at the back of the shop opened and a dark-skinned youngish woman came out as if on cue.

'Madam?' she asked, advancing towards me with a hopeful smile.

'I've come in answer to the advertisement outside,' I replied.

At this the fair-haired woman looked up from her accounts.

'References?' she asked briefly.

My heart sank. Then I suddenly had a brainwave. What about all my 'handled' relations; perhaps now their handles might really come in handy? 'I've never had a job before,' I said honestly. 'In fact, I've led a purely social life . . . and I'm a bit fed up with it.'

The fair-haired woman, who was obviously the owner of the shop, looked me over. 'So you must know people who might come to this establishment if you were employed here?' she asked.

Dishonestly I nodded, although the very thought of dear, sad, deaf Cousin Edwina and unfashionable Aunt Magdalen coming to be dressed in Bond Street almost made me burst out laughing.

The owner looked at Jeanne, and Jeanne looked at her, and they both nodded.

Then she looked me over again. 'You've rather a nice figure,' she said. 'We'll give you a try. My name is Princess S—. I own this establishment. But I'll hand you over to Madame Jeanne for instruction.'

'And – and my salary?' I ventured to ask.

'Five pounds weekly,' Princess S— replied, without looking up. I did the sum quickly in my head. Twenty pounds a month. I felt like a millionaire!

It was arranged that I should start in three days' time and then Jeanne took me into a back room and told me the routine. 'Eight hours' work a day, nine to six with an hour's break for lunch.' I replied in schoolgirl French, to the amusement of us both. But when I laughed aloud Jeanne quickly put her finger to her lips and gave a warning glance to where Princess S— was doing her accounts.

'*Elle est gentille?*' I whispered.

Jeanne shrugged her shoulders, and then nodded her head; but she told me nothing.

It was a Friday and I was to start work the following Monday. Over the weekend I hoped I would have time to find a better room and send my address to my mother. So, back in my gloomy basement, I scoured the 'Rooms to Let' columns by the light of a candle. There was only one that I could possibly afford, in a place called Sussex Gardens, Bayswater – which presumably was still in London, although it sounded like the country. I comforted myself with the thought that I would have the whole of the following day in which to find it.

Although I was able to lock the door of my room, and the water from the tap on the landing turned out to be almost warm, I didn't sleep well that night. Not only was there the continuous rumble of traffic which seemed to be passing right over my head, but also the ceaseless scuffle of mice, or rats, for most of the night. Eventually I fell asleep and woke eagerly to the new day, or was it not yet day? I got up and stared out of my tiny window. Everything was obscured by a thick yellow fog! However, I was determined, fog or no, to find my way to Bayswater.

To my surprise, at about seven o'clock, my landlady brought me a small pot of tea, milk, and three slices of bread and butter. 'Breakfast,' she said briefly, and then departed.

I lit my candle and ate, then I got dressed and looked again at the address that I had to find: 128 Sussex Gardens. It was the word 'Gardens' that had attracted me. So, again carrying my suitcase, I set out. The fog was as deadly as it had appeared – thick, yellow and choking – making it difficult even to see the pavement. My landlady had briefly directed me towards Bayswater: 'Turn right out of 'ere, then left and yer in Oxford Street, then keep on and foller yer nose.'

I 'followed my nose' for what seemed like miles and miles. There were very few people about to ask for further directions and the information, if given, would have conveyed little to me in this yellow darkness, broken only by the occasional glimmer of gas-lit streetlamps. Then I came to a great open silence on my left and I could see the faint outline of near and reassuring trees. Were these the 'Gardens' of which I was in search? I decided to carry on walking until I could find someone to ask. After another half-mile or so I came to a row of small shops, almost like country shops, and I went into one and asked the way to my destination. To my relief, I was told that I was quite close to Sussex Gardens and I was directed accordingly. A gas lamp was placed immediately opposite Number 128, so I was able to find it without too much difficulty. Wearily I made my way up to the front door and rang the bell. After a moment the door was opened very slowly and two dwarf-like figures appeared before me. From their similarity I took them to be sisters. They both wore glasses and blinked at me from behind them with owl-like attention. 'I've come about the room,' I muttered, prepared to hear that it was no longer available.

'Come in . . . come in,' they said in chorus.

I stumbled in to the welcome light and warmth of a spacious entrance hall and on a wall I saw shadows dancing, so there must be a fire somewhere.

'How on earth did you get here?' one of them asked.

'I walked from Bond Street,' I replied.

Their faces expressed mutual horror. 'But in this fog!' Then they added with concern, 'Come on in beside the fire . . . you must have something to eat and drink.'

Thankfully I followed them into a large sitting-room with a wood fire blazing and we exchanged information while we drank cups of tea and ate biscuits. I told them about Plymouth and about my new job in London, and the sisters explained that they were both nurses and had recently retired from working in a London hospital. 'Which is why we want to let one of our rooms,' they said, smiling. 'To help the exchequer!'

I took to them immediately. The room to let, on the third floor, was small but civilised, with a gas fire on a meter. The rent was reasonable, and now that I had a job I could afford to lose the week's rent I had already paid for the dark little room in Maddox Street.

'I'd love to be here,' I said. 'I'll take it.' I paused and then added, 'And now I'd better be getting back to Bond Street.'

The sisters exchanged glances and then one of them spoke while the other nodded agreement. 'Why not stop here for tonight – as our guest? Then tomorrow you can go to Paddington, collect your trunk and bring it back here. And then on Monday, when your new job starts, you can start being our lodger.'

I was so tired, and so touched by this sudden reversal of the Fates, that I had a struggle to stop myself from crying. 'Thank you,' I said. They both rose. 'And now we're going to send you up to your room for a good sleep.'

We all went up to my room, a shilling was put in the meter, and taking off my shoes I flung myself on the clean, tidy bed and almost immediately fell asleep. Later that day I sent a telegram to my mother with my address, and spent most of the evening writing to her.

On Sunday morning I woke to hear church bells ringing. Why had I not heard church bells ringing in India? Was it because the cantonments were so widely distributed? Or because the churches had no bells to ring? Or maybe because my mind had not been able to hear them? I hadn't bothered to try and find out. These church bells, ringing out so joyfully, suddenly transported me back to childhood . . . and also, alas, back to that Sunday with David and his family. Suddenly I knew that I needed the hope that these ringing bells were conveying, the hope that had been extinguished by my parting from David. I needed it badly. Independence might, one day, prove to be both important and even necessary; but it could never be enough. I needed hope as well. I ran downstairs to my new friends. 'Is there a nice church near?' I asked.

They hesitated. 'Well, dear, we go to chapel. But I believe there is a nice church at the bottom of the road. But what about your trunk?'

'I'll fetch it this afternoon,' I said, and departed quickly because I was anxious not to be late: I needed those bells. They ceased ringing just as I walked into the church. It was half empty, with no scent of incense, and the service was just plain Matins with familiar hymns and a not very impressive sermon. But what mattered most to me was that, somehow, I had momentarily renewed a relationship with an area within myself that was an old friend.

On Monday the fog had lifted and I made my way to the little shop in Bond Street. Only two customers came in during the whole morning. Jeanne made a face when I mentioned it, and I saw my job collapsing. However, as the week matured, so did the interest of customers and I was quite busy, walking up and down and showing off the latest models.

Then, when Princess S— arrived to do the accounts on the Friday, she asked me to have dinner with her the following day. 'Just the two of us,' she said. I accepted with a certain surprise. She had popped into the shop during the week but I had thought that her rather intense interest in me and my mannequin performances had been purely professional.

Princess S— lived in a tiny but richly tasteful house, and the door was opened by a butler. I left my coat in the hall, we mounted a few stairs, and the butler showed me into a room where my hostess lay fully stretched on a divan, apparently fast asleep: she was also, very apparently, almost naked. She wore nothing but a most delicately coloured chiffon negligée! When the door closed she gave what was, or so I thought, a somewhat false start, opened wide her great blue eyes, and sat up.

'Oh, how lovely!' she said. 'Forgive my being in my negligée, I just fell fast asleep.'

That statement aroused in me a not very clearly recognised feeling of doubt. Then the Princess sat up, picked up an already opened bottle of champagne, and made as if to pour me out a glass.

'Not for me, thanks,' I said easily. 'I never drink.'

'Oh, but to our new friendship – just one glass, please!' she persisted. As she had only spoken to me twice in the shop, despite her interest in my mannequin performances, I thought this to be rather an overstatement of the word 'friendship'. However, she insisted on pouring out a glass of champagne which, very politely, I refused again. She swallowed the second glass herself and then rose quite steadily to her feet. I was glad to see that beneath her short negligée she wore a small pair of chiffon pants. It was only her breasts (and they were very beautifully formed) that remained almost naked. In fact, when we had helped ourselves to soup from a silver tureen on the table and she bent over to drink the soup, her breasts were practically in the plate! This amused me so much that I had great difficulty in not allowing a smile to appear on my face.

Throughout the evening the butler never appeared again. We helped ourselves from the silver dishes on the sideboard, and when we returned to continue the meal my hostess replenished her glass from the rapidly emptying bottle of champagne, and her blue eyes rarely left me. Once or twice, when putting out my hand for the salt and pepper, her hand immediately found mine and her fingers would caress the palm of my hand with a gentle movement. It was at this point that I began to feel extremely uncomfortable. There was something unaccountably creepy in the atmosphere of this house. I knew I had to escape from it . . . but how? . . . and also keep my job?

My hostess was speaking to me. 'If you're lonely in London at the weekends, Ingaret, why not come and stay here?' She paused and looked at me again with those horridly intent and vivid blue eyes. 'I've got a marvellous bedroom,' she added. 'It's nearly as big as the whole house!' She paused, and then she added suggestively, 'I believe I could make you very, very happy there.'

Now I really could recognise the smell of something alien, possibly even evil. I felt profoundly alarmed. However, instantly, without even thinking, I said quite calmly, 'How very sweet of you. But these first weekends in London I'm going to do a round of churches which will take up most of my time. I want to find a church which really appeals to me.' I paused. Instinctively, even as I spoke the word 'church' I knew that that, by itself, would not be enough. I had to go further. So, despite my thumping heart, I continued, 'I mean, I want to find a church that corresponds to my own feelings about Christ. After all, "Christian" does mean "of Christ", doesn't it? And I suppose we all try to be Christians somehow, don't we?'

But that question was never answered. For even as I said the word

'Christ' I could feel the atmosphere start to freeze. It remained frozen for quite a few minutes, then, without even putting her hand to her mouth, my hostess gave an enormous yawn, looked at her watch, and rose to her feet.

'I'm afraid I don't go in for churches much,' she said. 'But it's quite late. I expect you want to get back to your lodgings before it gets too late, don't you?'

With a suitable hesitation I agreed that perhaps that was a good idea. So we went to the tiny hall and I put on my coat. She saw me out, and, my knees shaking slightly, I thanked her profusely for the delicious dinner and then, running down the steps, I turned to wave to her before disappearing in the direction of Bayswater.

My job in Bond Street continued for quite a time, even though my employer, Princess S——, seemed to have lost interest in me and I was prepared to be sacked at any moment. 'Is she really Russian?' I asked Jeanne on one occasion.

Jeanne shook her head. *'Une Anglaise,'* she said. *'Epouse avec un Russe* . . . but no person ever see him,' she replied, and shrugged.

Then came a bank holiday weekend and I was able to use my return ticket to Plymouth to spend the weekend with my family. Roger, too, had what he called 'a spot of leave', and so for a very brief spell we were all together again. They wanted to know what I did with myself in London. I admitted that there was neither time nor money to do much, though on a Saturday afternoon I was sometimes successful in getting a seat 'in the gods', in order to see a matinee. In fact, Saturday afternoon was the highlight of my week.

Surprisingly, it was my quiet stepfather who took up the subject. 'You've always been interested in the theatre, haven't you?' he asked. 'I've noticed that the first thing you read in the newspapers are the theatrical reviews.' He paused. 'Would you like to go on the stage?'

I remembered *Tilly of Bloomsbury* and my amateurish success.

'Of course!' I replied. 'I'd love it, but first I'd have to be trained professionally, which makes it impossible.'

There was a pause. 'If I paid for your training, would you entertain the idea?' Major John asked quietly. While I was catching my breath he added, 'I think you're quite wasted as a mannequin, or whatever they are called.'

The whole weekend passed in flights of fancy, cogitation and discussion, and it was finally decided that I should return to London, find out which was the best drama school and apply for a place there. Then, if I were accepted, Major John would pay the fees and my mother would make a contribution towards my board and lodging. On that Sunday evening when I caught the train back to London I did not buy a return ticket!

21

The Theatre

Eventually, after frequent scanning of newspapers and visits to various theatrical agencies, I discovered the Royal Academy of Dramatic Art. It was called R A D A for short and was situated in Gower Street, near the British Museum. I wrote asking for an interview with the Principal and in due course I was given an appointment and found my way to Gower Street.

On arrival at the Academy I was shown into the office of the Principal. After a few moments he appeared, a tall, middle-aged man who, after shaking hands with me, began to ask questions.

'Your age?'

'Twenty-one,' I replied.

A look of doubt crossed his face. 'Rather old to start training for the stage,' he commented. 'Have you any theatrical background or connections?'

I shook my head.

'No connections with the theatre?'

I shook my head again.

'Pity,' he said.

'I – I've matriculated at school,' I said, trying to scratch up some assets. 'And I played the lead in *Tilly of Bloomsbury* . . . and it was rather a success . . . or so I was told.'

'Where?' he asked.

'India.'

'India!' He sounded as if he'd never heard of the place. Then the penny dropped. 'Oh, I suppose you mean with an amateur theatrical company,' he said with scorn, and dismissed the event as if of no importance whatsoever.

There was a silence. Then he asked, 'Well, if you've matriculated, is there anything in literature that you can still remember and would like to recite to me . . . poetry for preference?'

185

Without even answering him, I began to recite Hamlet's 'To be, or not to be – that is the question'. It was something that I had had to learn by heart at school and which I had frequently repeated to myself, not only for its poetry but because it seemed to be voicing the problems of the whole universe – which, of course, included me.

At the close of my performance the Principal rose to his feet. 'Splendid!' he said. 'You not only speak with a feeling for the meaning of the piece but you speak with clarity . . . you know how to project your voice.'

After that remark I decided to mention my lessons with Miss Fogarty.

'Oh yes, she is an excellent teacher,' he said. 'Wish we could get her here!' Then he patted me on the shoulder and said, 'I'll sign you in. The next term starts in a few weeks' time. All the details will be sent to you shortly.'

I walked out and down Gower Street as if in another world. The following week, back in the shop, I whispered the good news to Jeanne. When I told her where the Academy was, she remarked that the journey from Bayswater to Gower Street would be a long and expensive one. 'Why not come and stay with me?' she asked. 'I have a flat in Crawford Street. It's only ten minutes to Gower Street on a Number One bus.' And so it was arranged. My landladies and I parted as good friends, and I far preferred riding to and from Gower Street on a Number One bus to my previous journey by underground from Bayswater to Bond Street. I seemed to be sitting on the wide lap of good fortune, and I found it both comfortable and comforting.

At RADA we all worked very hard. We had our own little theatre, the Vanbrugh, and a highly gifted staff. We learned voice production, theatrical production, acting, physical training, how to walk on and off stage. We were taught every imaginable and unimaginable skill of the trade. But what I loved most was the stimulating company of young people, of both sexes, all of whom were as interested as I was in every single detail of theatrical accomplishment. We were all involved in something we loved; and many of my contemporaries – who included Celia Johnson, Robert Morley, Patricia Hayes and Eleanor Gielgud – were to become famous.

After some months I discovered that every second year, at the end of the spring term, RADA hired one of the London theatres for an afternoon's display of the senior students' talents. The event lasted for four hours, and four celebrated actors and actresses, two male and two female, sat in a box and were the judges of these theatrical performances. The scenes to be played were taken from both classical and contemporary playwrights.

So, towards the end of my two years' training, I was among the students eligible to take part in one of these acting displays, which was to be held at St James's Theatre. The only part that had not yet been cast was that of the charwoman in Galsworthy's *The Silver Box*, who had been falsely accused of stealing. It so happened that I and one other girl, Agnes, were rivals for this part; and Agnes had a theatrical background which I did not. I was at my wits' end: which one of us would be chosen to play the charwoman?

Mr Page, the man in charge of theatrical production, couldn't make up his mind between us. Then, finally, he decided in favour of Agnes. Sensing my overwhelming disappointment, he drew me aside and whispered, 'If anything goes wrong, I'll give the part to you, without doubt.'

But I knew that this was the sort of thing that people in the theatre said to each other, and which had earned them their reputation for being insincere. I also knew that as the performance was to take place the following afternoon there would be no chance whatsoever of my getting the part.

I returned to Jeanne's house and crept up to my bedroom, not wanting to speak to anyone but rather to rehearse my portrayal of the charwoman, because she had become almost like a part of myself. Of course, by now I was word-perfect in my part and also in my heart. The Cockney accent was no problem to me because since childhood I had been able to mimic. If the part should come to me, I knew exactly how I would play it: I would stand in the centre of the stage with my arms folded, and my hair screwed back, and I would remain completely motionless throughout the whole performance. I would answer every false accusation with the same deadpan voice of sheer despair; profound despair because all the forces of society were ranged against any belief in persons like me, a mere charwoman.

Yes, I had put everything I'd got into an imaginative concept of how to play this particular part. I had rehearsed it over and over again in my bedroom. I'd even dreamed about it. So it was small consolation to me that I had only missed it by a head.

Entering RADA the following day I was surprised to find Mr Page waiting for me in the front hall. He advanced with urgency. 'You've got to play the Galsworthy part,' he said at once. 'Agnes is in bed with influenza and her temperature is over a hundred. You must play it . . . there's no one else.'

'I'll play it,' I said calmly. I had already discovered that sometimes when the blood was racing in my veins I could remain very calm.

'We must go and rehearse . . . at once . . .' said Mr Page. He was much more agitated than I.

So we had a brief rehearsal. But, as I had anticipated, just the two of us alone in the Academy's little theatre was very different from standing at the centre of St James's enormous stage and facing a theatre packed with people. Also I had to hang about in the wings for most of the afternoon because the extracts from *The Silver Box* came at the very end of the performance and the charwoman did not appear until the final scene. So I made my long-awaited entrance when the four judges in the box – Sir Gerald du Maurier, Edith Evans, Frank Vosper and another famous actress whose name I forget – had already sat through nearly four hours of students' exhibitions, and the audience were doubtless feeling under the seats for their coats and pulling on their gloves.

On cue I made my entrance from the back and walked very slowly down the stage to stand centrally, innocent, yet accused of theft. With my arms crossed and an expression of resigned despair on my face, I replied to my accusers with flat (but audible) dissent. I was innocent; and as I began to speak I noticed a strange stillness fall upon the audience. Perhaps they were really interested? But I never changed my position of resigned despair; nor did I greatly vary the tone of my responses. I was a Cockney charwoman. I was falsely accused. I would be found guilty and sent to prison. My awareness of the audience came second to my awareness that I was this new person on the stage: a wronged woman who had no hope of justice. I only realised that I was released from this entity by the sudden and sustained clapping, and even the stamping of feet. It was what the critics would call 'a warm reception'.

Then it became noticeable to all of us that the judges in the box were huddled together conferring about the three awards that were to be given: the Gold, the Silver, and the Bronze Medal. Consequently the curtain did not drop and the clapping continued.

Suddenly the Principal of the Academy appeared on the stage. The audience fell silent. 'The three medals have been awarded to the following students . . .' He mentioned the names of the students who had gained the gold and silver medals and then he continued: 'And the Bronze Medal has been awarded to Miss Ingaret Giffard.' Tremendous applause broke out from the audience and I suddenly realised that I had to join the other two students on the stage to receive our medals for the best performances of the afternoon. Also we had to bow in response to the clapping and stamping of the audience. It was a staggering moment. Even my matriculation, however satisfying, had not carried with it the added bonus of public recognition. As I stood there facing the lighted and crowded auditorium I could scarcely believe my good fortune.

The following day, without wasting a moment, I wrote a note to Sir Gerald du Maurier, one of the actor judges, asking for an interview with him, which I was granted. And in two days' time I entered St James's Theatre by the stage door! I was wearing a new grey flannel dress and a huge red felt hat, and my heart was beating at a tremendous pace. As I walked into Sir Gerald's dressing-room he looked up and said, 'Heavens, I thought you were at least forty years old!'

I sat down and for a time we talked rather aimlessly about his daughters. Finally I screwed up my courage and asked him if I could have a part as an understudy in his currently rehearsing production.

'Of course!' he said. 'Of course! You gave a first-class performance. I'll run you into something.' He looked at his watch. 'Be here tomorrow at ten sharp. That's when we start our daily rehearsal.'

I walked out of the theatre as if I were walking on air!

I turned up punctually next morning and, as if by right, went in at the stage door. I saw that the cast, a very distinguished cast at that, for I could recognise Lady Beerbohm Tree among them, were sitting in a row on the stage with scripts in their hands talking. My entrance drew a few glances but no other response. So, greatly daring, I pulled up a chair and joined the group, seating myself at the far end. But, of course, there was nothing I could do because I was without a script.

So, for the next three hours of rehearsal, I just sat and stared blankly in front of me. Sir Gerald was sitting in the stalls down below and quite some distance away. Occasionally a member of the cast eyed me with curiosity, adding to my uneasy self-consciousness.

Some time around midday Sir Gerald arose from his seat in the stalls. 'We all meet here again at two o'clock,' he said, and then made his way out of the stalls to the back of the theatre and disappeared. Subsequently the whole cast drifted off the stage and no one spoke a word to me. I followed them, feeling extremely lost and confused.

Then a nice-looking woman came out of an adjoining office and saw me.

'What are you doing here?' she asked.

I told her about my interview with Sir Gerald.

'Oh, the naughty, naughty man!' she said. 'That naughty man simply cannot say no to anyone.'

'But he said he would give me something in this play . . . an understudy part or something,' I protested. 'He said he'd "run me into something".'

'Dear child,' this nice woman said. 'We've already been rehearsing for two weeks: all the understudies were fixed weeks ago. There's no possibility of anything for you in this play: no chance whatsoever.'

'But he said – '

'There's just one thing Sir Gerald can never say, and that is No. He's a naughty, naughty man. I'm his secretary so I should know,' the nice woman replied. She put her hand on my shoulder and we walked up the corridor, and again I left the theatre by the stage door – but this time presumably for ever.

It was on occasions like this that my deep need for David rose up, as it were, from the dead. For still deeply and darkly within me, as it would be for many years to come, his image lay buried as if in a deep grave. It was a grave that had no monument at its head and so, being nameless, it had no identity; yet this very anonymity seemed to add to its power. Sometimes the memory of David would rise up inside me with such force that it felt almost like a sickness. I had discovered that 'events' were the only means whereby I could combat these onslaughts. Events, therefore, were of enormous value to me. My winning of the Bronze Medal had been of assistance because it had added to my personal self-confidence. But now, as I made my way back to Jeanne's house in Crawford Street, I felt totally defeated. Nothing that one truly cared about was any good, ever. That was the obvious conclusion. So surely, it was better not to care about anything? My future seemed to hold an emptiness that was unparalleled even by the stifling meaningless days, or the dancing nights, of India.

Jeanne came back early that evening from the shop. It was one of the three weekly evenings when her professor spent the night at Crawford Street. He was a charming white-haired man, erudite and clearly entranced by Jeanne's warm-hearted foreign gaiety. I never questioned whether their relationship went beyond that of friendship. Curiosity, as such, had never greatly attracted me; it had always struck me as a rather vulgar exercise, and inaccurate as well. Interest in other people was a very different matter, however, and this had been second nature to me since childhood.

My doleful mood soon became apparent to both Jeanne and the Professor, so I told them the whole miserable story. There seemed nothing more to be done now but to return to Plymouth.

The Professor, however, was very helpful. 'Of course not,' he said. 'You have two years' training behind you and in public competition you have won one of only three medals.' He paused. 'I know little about the theatre,' he continued, 'but I do know that you must now find a good agency and ask them to put you on their books for a job . . . just as a writer, like me, finds a good agency to recommend his books to a publisher.'

Hope flared up in me. 'Is that what one does next?' I asked.

'Of course,' he replied, smiling.

And so, the following day, I made it my business to discover which were the best theatrical agencies in London. But when I came to give them my credentials I quickly discovered that everything was against me. The Bronze Medal was brushed aside as having no professional importance whatsoever. What theatrical experience did I have? None. What knowledge did I, or my relations, have of the theatre proper? None. More disadvantageous than anything, I discovered, was the fact that I was 'a lady'. I spoke like a lady. Presumably I looked like a lady. Possibly I behaved like a lady. And 'ladies', when it came to hard work, were just unreliable amateurs. Curiously enough I rather sympathised with this conclusion, but I was determined to prove them wrong.

So, for the whole of the next three months, I spent every morning, except Sunday, in the waiting-room of one of these famous agencies and every afternoon in the waiting-room of the other famous agency. There was just one occasion when I did miss a Saturday morning because I had been invited away for the weekend. As I walked into the agency's waiting-room on the following Monday morning the stagecaster looked up. 'Pity you weren't here on Saturday,' he said. 'You'd have got the job as understudy to Margaret Bannerman!' I was certainly learning the hard way.

22

Breakthrough

Going to stay with new friends, the Youngs, was a welcome diversion from the tedium of my week's uphill slog in the theatrical profession. They lived expansively, though not expensively, in Surrey, and I had been introduced to them through an extremely nice man called Edward Hale who held a senior position in the Treasury. Badly wounded in the First World War, he still walked with a limp, and I had instinctively felt him to be a lonely person, with his gentle manner and a face that carried within it the beauty of great suffering. I cannot remember exactly how he and I first met. He was very musical, so I may have sat next to him at some concert or opera, or I might have helped him on to a Number One bus! Anyway, we had become friends and I had told him of my theatrical ambitions. I had also mentioned that my parents were at present living in Plymouth, which was too far away and too expensive for me to get to at weekends. It was then that he had suggested that I should come with him one weekend to stay with some friends who kept 'open house' in Surrey. I had explained that I would have to get back to London on Sunday night. 'So will I,' he had smiled, and so I had accepted the invitation joyfully.

I had to make my first journey to Redhill alone because Edward was kept working at the Treasury for the whole of that particular Saturday. At the last minute I remembered that I had no weekend suitcase, for the lock was being repaired. So I bundled a nightgown, a sponge-bag, a comb and a powder puff into a large woven bag in which my mother used to keep her tapestry work, and then took a bus to Victoria Station to catch my train. I was met at the other end by a chauffeur-driven car and taken deep into the countryside, then down a long drive leading to a very large mansion. Automatically the chauffeur jumped out to open the car door and take my luggage . . . which, of course, I had not got! So he rang the front-door bell instead. Almost immediately the door was opened by a shortish woman, dressed in well-worn country clothes, with three dogs at her heels. She had a wrinkled, weather-beaten face, grey hair and very blue eyes. Had she been tall and thin instead of totally the reverse, she would have reminded me instantly of Aunt Magdalen. In any case they both had the same rather abrupt manner. She was my hostess, Mrs Young, known to her friends as 'Mip'.

'Are you Ingaret?' she said.

'Yes.'

'Where's your luggage?'

'Well, I haven't got a suitcase, so I've brought my night-things in this,' I replied, holding up the 'knitting-bag' and feeling no embarrassment whatsoever. 'Is that all right?'

Our eyes met and we both laughed. She herself did not care about etiquette any more than I did. We were to become great friends.

It was a strange but delightful household. Mr Young, a tall, good-looking man, was a prominent Lloyd's underwriter, and a bit of a loner. At weekends he spent much of his time in his shirtsleeves supervising the estate, the shooting, the stables and the kitchen gardens. And nearly every Saturday night the large house was as filled with intellectuals as India had been with soldiers! Of the three regular weekenders I think Edward Hale was Mrs Young's favourite, for she would walk round the golf course with him carrying his clubs. But the one who interested me most was Eric Farmer, who was head of a secret government department concerned with industrial psychology, perhaps because I immediately discovered that he had a sister who was a nun, and nuns had always fascinated me. The third 'regular' was a younger man called Aubrey Blackburn who, curiously enough, was employed by a booking agency which did business with both the theatrical and the film world. But he held such a senior position that he had probably never even heard of understudies . . .

The Youngs' 'open house' weekends gave me something to look forward to during the dreary and seemingly useless hours that I spent in the theatrical agencies in London. For I stuck to my routine with dogged persistence. I even refused an invitation from Princess S— to go as her guest by ship to New York, sharing a first-class cabin! I also refused an invitation from some very old friends of my mother's who offered to take me in their yacht to Norway. Hardest of all to turn down was a chance to visit France, a country I so longed to see that I had taken French lessons as an 'extra' at Bedford High School. Instead I just sat on, and on, and on, first at one theatrical agency, and then at the other, without even reading a book or a newspaper.

Then, unexpectedly, a woman producer appeared on the scene. She was trying to get a company together to go up to the repertory theatre in Huddersfield and perform plays by Shaw, Pinero and Galsworthy. I later heard rumours that she was inclined to drink too much, which, if true, perhaps explained why she had signed me on at sight! Anyway, at long last I had a real acting job, and consequently I began to enjoy every minute of every day as the three weeks of rehearsals got under way. Finally we were all ready to depart for Huddersfield, where I had arranged to share digs with another member of the company, Celia Johnson (who was one day to become a very famous actress). On the opening night the theatre was packed and the audience was both appreciative and perceptive, which I had somehow not expected from a northern industrial town.

Just as our tour was approaching its end, I received a letter from Mip Young, my new friend in Surrey, asking me to come and stay with them in Scotland where, apparently, the Youngs had another estate. 'After all, you're halfway to Scotland already,' she wrote in her blunt way. 'So I'm counting on your coming.'

I decided to go. I had done my stint in the theatrical agencies. I had got my acting career on the move. I had had good notices. At last I had acquired what was called 'experience'. Surely it could do no harm now for me to take a legitimate ten days' holiday? Besides, I'd never seen Scotland: it would be a great adventure, and also a great delight. So with the grease-paint barely rubbed off my face I rushed out of the stage door, mended suitcase in hand, to catch a train to Perth where I would be met by the same car and the same chauffeur as in Redhill. As we headed north, a great change was noticeable in the countryside, and once into the Highlands the landscape was truly amazing. In its sheer immensity it reminded me of my native Dartmoor, but the Highlands, in their grandeur, somehow seemed to possess one, whereas my Devonshire moors merely communicated with one. Was their power so much greater because they so forcibly reminded me of David? I could still remember how, in India, he had talked to me of his Scottish Highlands. Would his memory never set me free?

Being driven by the chauffeur along the lengthy, almost empty road between mountains, both orange with gorse and purple with heather, and rearing ever higher towards the empty sky, was a revelation to me. Then, unexpectedly, we reached a silent and motionless lake (or 'loch' as I learned to call it), seemingly sleeping in the shifting evening light. The Youngs' house was situated right by the water's edge, cradled in silence and surrounded by these same colourful mountains. It was an idyllic arrival in every respect. Mip was in the porch to greet me, wearing her oldest clothes and with the customary number of dogs gambolling around her.

'Like a walk?' she asked as we kissed. 'Stretch your legs?'

So after dumping my suitcase in the hall, we walked along the narrow path bordering the loch. I can remember it vividly: the breathtaking silence; the loch with its brow slightly furrowed with tiny wrinkles from the evening breeze; and the protective mountains flushed now with the rosy light of the fading sun.

I remember also that on our way back we met the postman on a bicycle concluding his evening round of the great waters. He dismounted politely.

'Good evening, Malcolm,' Mip said. Then she turned and stared at the far end of the loch where dimly, rising out of the water, I could see some mechanical constructions, above which strode the skeleton forms of two massive pylons. 'Isn't it terrible, what they're doing to our loch?' she asked angrily. (Apparently the loch was being dammed in order to raise the water level for some hydroelectric scheme which would bring electricity even to the more remote parts of the Highlands.)

Malcolm, the postman, turned and followed her gaze. Then in his broad Scottish accent he said very simply, 'Aye, Ma'am, oi loike to see nature and science go hand in hand,' and, mounting his bicycle, continued on his journey. I have never forgotten his words.

I had a wonderfully refreshing stay in Scotland with the Youngs. It was there that I met their youngest son, Jimmy, for the first time. Dark, with dancing brown eyes, a ready smile and a tallish, slender figure, he immediately reminded me of a faun. He was about three years younger than I and very different from the kind of people who came to the Youngs' weekend house-parties. He was a good shot, a patient fisherman, a splendid horseman, and also (as I was to discover later) a natural dancer. He was fun. But behind all these extravert activities I detected a certain wistfulness in his face when seen in repose. He was reputed to be leading a hectic social life at Oxford, so nobody expected him to pass his exams. Perhaps nobody had ever expected quite enough of him? And so he had not expected much of himself? It was a haphazard thought that passed idly through my mind.

To my great surprise, after about a week in Scotland I received a telegram from Aubrey Blackburn, the friend of the Youngs who worked for a film and theatrical agency. The telegram said: 'Suggest you return immediately. Two understudy parts and one small part available in play soon coming into rehearsal at the Fortune Theatre.' I was over the moon with delight and so were the Youngs. Again I packed my suitcase and Jimmy volunteered to drive me to Perth in order to catch the night train to London. I discovered that he was as good at driving a car as he was at shooting the game driven before him on the moors. He talked quite a bit about a girl he had liked very much at Oxford; but when I asked him what he was going to do when he left Oxford he seemed hazy. He laughed a lot and as he saw me into the train he said, 'You must come to the Leander Club with me in the spring to watch the boat race.' Then he looked with some amazement at the third-class carriage door. 'No sleeper?' he asked.

Leaning out of the window I said gaily, 'Too expensive!'

A look of slight incomprehension crossed his face. Then he pulled my head down and kissed me gently on the lips. 'Don't worry,' he said. 'My girlfriend and I have split up . . .' Then the engine gave a whistle, so Jimmy stepped back to watch my departure as the train slowly drew out of sight. I thought to myself what a really nice person he must be to have explained about his girlfriend just because he had kissed me!

On arrival in London I found that Jeanne had already let my room to someone else, but she said I could sleep on the sofa in the living-room. Then I rang up Aubrey.

'Come to the Fortune Theatre at ten tomorrow morning,' he said. 'If they take you on you'll be understudying both Edith Evans and Athene Seyler together, with a small part as the maid.'

I put down the phone almost gibbering with excitement. The next day I went to the Fortune Theatre on the top of an open bus and arrived half an hour too early. However, quite soon all the cast were gathered together on the stage, and I was surrounded by many famous people; and I was chosen to be the understudy of two of them and also given a small part of my own! Athene Seyler and I were of much the same proportions but Edith Evans was so much taller than me that smaller replicas of her stage clothes had to be ordered. On meeting Edith Evans one realised at once that she was a most impressive personality. Before making a public entrance in the theatre she would always stand in the wings repeating softly to herself, 'I am the most beautiful woman in the wo-orld.' She would say these words over and over again. Of course she was not the most beautiful woman in the world, and she knew it; yet when she made her entrance on stage, *she was*! Athene Seyler had a fantastic sense of wit and comedy and she was to become a dear and treasured friend.

The first night was a thrilling experience for me. To start with, there was my careful 'making-up' in my own dressing-room . . . and the smell of grease-paint became as dear to me as the scent of spring. Then there was the thick lowered curtain and behind it the invisible hum . . . hum . . . of human expectation. Finally, out went the lights, the hum died instantly, and then very slowly the curtain rose as if in deference to the brilliantly lighted stage. And it was at that moment that I had to make my first entrance in my tiny part. I had to cross the stage, draw back the curtains of the imitation window backstage, and then move downstage and off, disappearing in the opposite exit. But the bustling way in which I did this managed, somehow, to get a titter out of the expectant audience.

Of course I wrote to tell my mother all this exciting news. Almost every day there was something new to report. Her letters in return told me that they were still at Plymouth but shortly moving to their new house near Guildford. One included a postscript: 'Darling, I think that as you now seem to be settled in London you should have your own little flat. Would you like me to find one for you or would you prefer to find it yourself? I will pay the rent, and I could afford £100 p.a.'

My own flat! I almost collapsed with the sheer joy of being. If only David . . . always, always David stirred in the dark grave of my memory.

Now that the play was launched, of course, I had every day free, except the two afternoons on which there were matinees, to look for an unfurnished flat. I had a fancy for one in Chelsea and eventually found exactly what I wanted: two rooms, kitchen and bathroom, and situated at pavement level. It was on a corner close to the King's Road, and the trams from across the Thames stopped immediately outside.

The next thing I had to do was to find a 'daily', for the kitchen hated me as much as I hated it: whenever I approached the stove, something would fizz or flare or boil over in rage. Eventually I found a Miss Pile who would give me an hour five days a week, which I could pay for out of my earnings, and she proved to be a guardian angel. She bustled around the flat while I just sat and wrote my diary. So many things seemed to be happening in all directions, opening up aspects of life of which I had previously been quite unaware, that the diary soon took on the proportions of a book.

Once installed in my little flat, which was now filled inoffensively (or so I hoped) with secondhand furniture from the King's Road, the days passed very quickly. Piley whisked round in the mornings while I sat in the small sitting-room, so absorbed in my writing that I hardly noticed the trams unloading and loading just outside my window. In the evenings I would hastily swallow the cold food that Piley had left ready for me and then go and wait at the corner of the King's Road for the bus which would take me to the Fortune Theatre.

Dinner after the theatre was initially something of a problem since I couldn't afford to eat out, and I couldn't, or wouldn't, cook. Then Eric Farmer, a fellow guest at the Youngs' 'open house' weekends and happily now a close friend, came to the rescue. Twice a week he went hunting in the country, 'riding to hounds' as he called it, and on these days he would time his return to London to coincide roughly with the close of the evening's performance. After picking me up from the theatre he would drive me across the river to where he had digs in a large vicarage. There, sitting before a bright fire in his bed-sitting-room, we would have a late dinner, which he would prepare, and talk, ceaselessly, about everything under the sun. Eric told me many tales about his 'little ladies' in the hunting field; in fact, he talked about them so much that I sometimes wondered if they really existed! He was also deeply concerned about a young boy, a pageboy at his club, whom he was interested in trying to help. But mostly our evenings were spent discussing serious matters, in particular philosophy and religion, and the vistas that were opened up to me during this period of my life can never be forgotten. Gradually the two dinners a week became three as our friendship deepened, until finally dinner with Eric became a taken-for-granted nightly event which continued for several months; as did the run of the play.

Then, quite suddenly, one night as we were sitting by his fire after dinner Eric said very quietly, 'Are we mad not to get married?'

I was totally astonished. Slowly I got up, left the fire and went to look out of the window. Below us, hidden in darkness, was the large vicarage garden, crowded with trees and bushes, which reached down to the south side of the River Thames. There, invisibly, flowed the calm and invincible waters of that river. I stared across to where the pinprick lights of tall buildings combined with other intermediary illuminations to send a glow up to the distant sky, creating what seemed like a different world on the other side of the river. Then I turned round and went back to the fire.

'No, Eric,' I said. 'We are not mad "not to get married".' We remained silent for a while, then I suggested gently, 'Shall we take our clothes off and lie on your bed?'

So we sat on opposite sides of the large double bed and, wordlessly, we did exactly that. We undressed and I lay under the eiderdown on one side of the bed and he lay on the other for about ten minutes. Finally, silently, I put out my hand and held his, and we lay thus for a few minutes longer. Then, still without speaking, we got up and dressed again and nothing more was ever said on the subject. Eric drove me home and we continued our old relationship as if nothing unusual had occurred.

A few years later, when I was engaged to be married, my fiancé and I received a wonderful wedding present from Eric. It was a large and most beautiful painting of a young girl with long hair sitting under an umbrella and gazing wistfully into the distance. 'This is how I think of Ingaret as a young girl. Good luck to you both,' said the note, and it was signed, 'Eric'.

'Good God,' said my fiancé, almost bitterly. 'He tried to bugger me when I was at school.'

It was only then that the penny dropped: I suddenly saw a light on something that I had never before envisaged. Eric's 'young ladies' in the hunting field, his deep interest in the pageboy at the club . . . I sensed that the pageboy belonged in one half of Eric's life and that all he and I had shared belonged in the other . . . and, sadly, two halves do not always make a whole, as he himself must have long since discovered. Surely the gap between these two halves could be filled by nothing but a profound and persistent sense of loneliness? Or was I wrong? I couldn't know. All I do know is that I feel nothing but a deep tenderness for, and gratitude to, this brilliant man who opened my mind to a whole new world of intellectual and spiritual riches. And whenever I study his painting, which hangs in my bedroom, I see it not as a picture of myself as a young girl, but as an expression of a very deep side of Eric's being or, as I prefer to put it, of his soul. To me the painting depicts a part of him looking out wistfully under the 'cover' of the umbrella, and trying, perhaps in vain, to find a completely human resolution.

Some years ago I was sad to read Eric Farmer's obituary in *The Times*; and each time I look at the picture I wish him well and hope that, in some small measure, he may have received companionship from our strange but never strained relationship.

23

A 'Decent Sort'

For the next few months I continued my life in this very satisfactory way: writing most of the day, the theatre two afternoons a week and every evening, talking far into the night with Eric, and brief weekends in Surrey either with my family or with the Youngs. The only change was that Jimmy now came up to London nearly every weekend from Oxford, so we got to know each other better. Nobody was surprised when he failed to get his degree, least of all himself; and, as he often said, what would he have done with it anyway? Yet, although he excelled at any number of extravert activities, it was as if he were still seeking for something; or so I thought. But seeking for what? I had no idea. Neither, I think, did he. However, that did not prevent us from enjoying an occasional 'dance to dawn' evening in London.

By now I had become deeply immersed in the theatrical profession. I had been told that people in the theatre were 'catty', jealous of each other, and that you couldn't believe a word they said. I, on the contrary, found everybody helpful and amusing . . . with the attractive convention of calling each other 'darling', quite irrespective of sex or feeling. I found all aspects of working in the theatre both exciting and stimulating: the tense atmosphere, the silences and, equally, the applause; above all, 'pretending' to be another person by careful and imaginative interpretation. All this was, to me, like real life except for the fact that the theatre 'characters' were typed across our scripts instead of walking across the street.

Then, like a shooting star, came more good news. A theatrical company, headed by Nicholas ('Beau') Hannen and Athene Seyler, was going on tour to South Africa with three plays, and they wanted me to go with them. I think I was even more elated at being offered a real part in each play, not just understudies and 'walk-ons', than at the prospect of travelling to a place that I had always thought of as the other end of the world!

On the memorable day when I joined the rest of the company at Waterloo Station to catch a train to Southampton, from where we would board a ship bound for Cape Town, I saw a most beautiful woman leaning out of one of our 'reserved' carriages. Tears were streaming down her face as she waved and waved despairingly to someone hidden from me by the station pillars. She wore a grey fur coat with a bunch of violets pinned to the lapel. The violets, I thought, would never die if so plentifully watered by her tears!

'Who is that woman?' I asked.

'Oh, that is a friend of Miss Seyler's,' was the answer. 'I think she's a sculptress and rather famous, too, I'm told . . . and she's coming with us.'

We had quite a steady and hard-working voyage out to South Africa, during which time I came to know the sculptress, Hazel Armour, who was eventually to become one of my closest friends.

On arrival in Cape Town our attention was reluctantly drawn away from the mysterious, dominating aura of the famous Table Mountain towards the more mundane confusion of cabs, taxis, shops, boarding-houses and trams, and the differing colours of the myriad people roaming the streets – white, black, gold and brown.

Rooms had already been booked for all the cast in a hotel near the theatre, in the centre of Cape Town, but I had little sleep that first night owing to the unceasing noise of traffic and loud, high-pitched voices at the tram-stop right outside my window. The next day, our one 'recovery' day before starting work, I spent no time unpacking but went instead searching for the sea, which I soon found, and exploring its harbours, ships and beaches. And then, high on a green hill, quite isolated and overlooking the sea, I noticed a house which, on investigation, indicated 'Rooms Vacant' outside. I went in and booked a room, after being rather curiously examined by the owner, and took a taxi back to the hotel to fetch my case. I left my change of address for the stage producer and hoped for a more restful second night in this isolated and highly perched house, where with luck the calming voice of the sea might reach me. But I hardly slept that night either, for I was disturbed by the continual noise of doors banging, opening, shutting and banging again. It went on all through the night. Was there no peace to be had even at 'the other end of the world'?

When I arrived at the theatre to start rehearsing the next day I was met by the horrified face of the stage manager.

'Is this your new address?' he asked.

I nodded.

'But you can't possibly stay there,' he said. 'It calls itself a boarding-house,' he gave me a quick look, 'but it – it's a very suspect – a very low-grade affair.'

This explained all the door-banging that had gone on during the night. 'Do you mind if I'm half an hour late for rehearsal?' I asked him. 'I'll go and fetch my things now . . . and thank you for telling me.' So I returned to my rowdy room by the tram-stop, telling myself that trams, and possibly brothels, were just varying symbols of so-called civilisation.

From the second day after our arrival we all worked very hard. Athene Seyler, whom I now knew well, and Beau Hannen were in charge of the productions, and our plays, with such famous names attached to them, were received with enthusiasm. The tour in South Africa was both successful and pleasurable but it had been a working trip for all of us and we had only been able to scratch the surface of South Africa itself. I remember people asking me, 'What do you think of South Africa?', and all I could answer was that I felt it to be an Old Testament country.

What made the trip particularly memorable for me was the friendship I struck up with Hazel Armour, the sculptress. She was Scottish, with a wry wit and great talent. Apparently she was married to a very rich man and in love with a very poor one: hence the tears on Waterloo Station! But the greatest thing we shared was laughter.

Suddenly, at the end of three months as the tour was drawing to a close, Hazel came to me and said, 'Ingaret, supposing I decided to go back to England another way, up the east coast of Africa, across the Mediterranean and so home that way, would you come with me? Of course I'd have to change our tickets and my husband would pay for both of them.' Then her Scottish blood stirred. 'But we might have to go back second-class,' she added.

I was overjoyed. 'I don't mind what class we go back in. I'd love it.'

So after the last curtain call Hazel and I said goodbye to the company with kisses and hugs and even a few tears. And then, on our own, we began our return journey with a different steamship line, up a different coast, and across a different ocean. We had two single second-class cabins. And when we came up on deck, to start with we cast disdainful glances at the glittering and indulgent facilities of those going first-class.

For Hazel and I were extremely happy in the rear of the ship: we kept our two deck-chairs close to the rails and far from our fellow travellers, and shared reminiscences and jokes, and our friendship developed. The only person we really noticed was a young sailor who seemed continually to be scrubbing our decks. We noticed him because of his good looks: he was tall, graceful, blue-eyed and fair-haired, and had an air of great distinction. Our ship, in a German line, was called the *Ubena* and was returning to Hamburg. Yet this young man did not look German. One day when he was scrubbing the deck close to us I asked him his name. 'Hans Petroushka,' the young man replied, looking up.

'German?' I asked.

He shook his head. 'No, Russian . . . but I live in Germany.'

I was surprised that he spoke English at all and said so.

'I like spik all languages,' he said wistfully.

There was something very sad about him, even in the persistence of his concentrated scrubbing of the ship's decks.

The *Ubena*, on its journey north, stopped at various ports: Port Elizabeth, East London, Durban, Lourenço Marques, Dar es Salaam, Zanzibar, Mombasa, and on until we reached Port Said. Hazel and I went ashore at every opportunity, somewhat tentatively until it occurred to me that it would be nice to have a man to accompany us. So I asked Hans if he was allowed off the ship when we docked at these ports.

'Sometimes,' he shrugged.

'Then come with us,' I suggested, 'when you can.'

So we three had quite frequent walks along the beaches at our various ports of call, and in this way we came to know Hans well. His family had suffered badly in the First World War. His father had been killed; they had all been forced to come to Germany; and Hans, at the age of twenty, was the only wage-earner in the family. His one ambition was to learn English, for this, he felt, would open the world to him. As we strolled together on the sands looking for shells, we discovered these facts about Hans which he disclosed haltingly.

Then suddenly, one morning up on deck, I saw Hazel returning from the first-class part of the ship. 'Where've you been?' I asked curiously. We had always been very frank with each other.

'I've just put up a notice on the first-class board asking if anybody would like to have their head done,' she replied. She was by now well-known as a sculptress, her work having included the figures on the First World War Memorial in Edinburgh. She had also sculpted quite a few famous heads and so had a trail of celebrities as clients; and being professional, she always carried her 'cuttings' with her.

Even as she spoke, we saw a tall man approaching. He was a major in the US Army and he wanted to have his 'head done' as a birthday present for his wife. He was travelling with two friends, and if Miss

Armour would care to come along to his cabin for a drink they could discuss terms and times of sittings.

Hazel and I exchanged amused glances as we followed the American major back to his luxurious cabin, little realising what we were letting ourselves in for. One of the major's travelling companions, Fred, was a tall, lanky, dark-featured American in his thirties, who immediately set his sights on me; the other was a Danish Count who was married to a famous writer, so obviously experienced in the ways of women that he did not need to make a pass at either of us! But the American major was soon seen to be the directing spirit of us all, and suddenly, incredibly, for the first time in my life – which had always been so curbed by circumstances, lack of money and social mores – anything and everything seemed possible in this delightfully unconventional company.

For instance, at Ismailia the American major suddenly suggested that we should all leave the ship, hire a car and drive across the desert to Cairo: there we would explore the city, spend one night at Shepherd's Hotel and rejoin the ship at Suez! To me it sounded like a fairy tale. The men all cheered the idea and were eager to be on the trail. Hazel, whom I now discovered to be highly temperamental and filled with fears and fancies both rational and irrational, was deeply alarmed at the whole project. 'We don't really know these men, Ingaret,' she said, 'they could be up to anything. Or we might break down in the desert . . . and so lose our ship.' Her fears poured out one after the other when we were alone in her cabin. Listening to them was almost like going round a picture gallery in which every picture, or fear, seemed to need a different focus. However, we were both carried along by the slightly inebriated enthusiasm of these three men, and finally we each packed our night-things in one small suitcase, having agreed to join them.

By now we had docked at Ismailia and saw the endless desert of white sand stretching out all round and beyond us.

'Oh, just look at it!' whispered Hazel. 'It's terrifying, people always get lost in deserts.' Nevertheless the large taxi standing already hired, with a turbaned driver, meant that the expedition had really started. The American major helped Hazel into the back seat, with the Count and himself sitting on either side of her. I sat next to the driver with Fred, the rogue, on my other side, his hands persistently seeking my hand, or creeping up my bare legs. Then suddenly I heard stifled weeping. Looking round I saw that the sobs were coming from Hazel, whose face was covered by a black veil. She had brought the veil, of course, against the glare of the sun but it looked like a widow's weed! Whereas I had merely put on my dark glasses. I felt so hilarious that I couldn't help laughing immoderately at the difference between Hazel and myself. However we all tried to comfort her as we ploughed, drove, slithered or raced across the so-called desert road. The daytime heat was tremendous; but we just drove on and on into baking whiteness.

Arrival at Cairo was a change but scarcely a reassuring one for Hazel. We hooted our way through the colourful eastern crowds till finally we arrived at Shepherd's Hotel. Sweating and exhausted, we went into the large, cool, fan-ridden foyer for tea, then Hazel and I went up to our spacious double bedroom and bathroom. The two beds were heavily draped by mosquito nets; in fact, they looked rather like two brides at a double wedding. We had cold baths, re-dressed and then went down to the foyer where the men were still drinking.

'Planning what to do with this evening,' said the American major.

'A gambling den,' said Fred. His speech even then was slightly blurred.

I didn't know anything about gambling so I said, 'Dancing!'

Hazel, once again looking very beautiful, said feebly, 'Couldn't we just go to bed?'

'But who with?' Fred said, laughing uproariously at his own joke.

'I think dancing is a good idea,' said the American major quietly. Fred gave me a wink and despite myself I smiled. He was an outrageous person yet, despite his height and his dark glasses, there was something almost child-like about him.

After dinner we set off in another taxi, and as nobody spoke any of the native tongues the American major just said 'Dancing' and the taxi-driver (as he thought) obeyed his instructions. Finally we drew up at an enormous emporium: it looked like a football stadium except that it was entirely under canvas. Hazel had on a summer dress; but I had travelled across the desert in cotton shorts, so all I could think of to wear for the evening out was a silk-embroidered Chinese dressing-gown, knee-length and with no fastenings down the front. However, I put a leather belt round my waist and used a few safety-pins, hoping that the front would stay fastened. Fred of course spotted these at once. 'Open to invitation!' he cried, in a voice now distinctly blurred.

Finally we all tumbled out of the taxi and made for the emporium. 'Wait for us,' the American major told the taxi-driver. 'I'll pay you when you take us back.' Then, holding on to one another, we battled our way through an enormous crowd into the 'dance hall'. The place was packed with local people, all climbing the stairs to seemingly endless floors, and as we were swept by with them I tried to cling on to Fred with one hand and keep my dressing-gown together with the other. This was not easy because many of the veiled women were stroking my bare arms and trying to slip their arms round my waist: in my innocence I supposed they had never seen a European woman before. At last we clambered into our seats on the fourth floor of this enormous canvas erection. It was more like a bull-ring than a dance hall because the circular area below, which was completely empty save for a sort of gymnasium-like wooden structure in the centre, was covered in sand. Then a tall youngish man, clad only in a loincloth, entered the sandy arena and he was accompanied by a young boy of about twelve years old, similarly attired. The man now started to divest himself and the boy of their loincloths and then he climbed the wooden structure where he took up an inviting position. The boy followed him up and then climbed on to the man's back ... presumably with a view to having sexual intercourse in a variety of positions.

Instantly the American major realised that the forthcoming perform-ance was to be an exhibition of homosexual activities, and that the taxi-driver had misinterpreted the meaning of the word 'dancing'. He rose to leave, signalling for us all to follow, but we were so tightly wedged in that any attempt to escape would, I am sure, have provoked a very nasty and even dangerous reaction from the spellbound audience.

Then suddenly shrill whistles rang through the emporium, followed by the echoing cry, 'Police! Police!' The whistles grew more and more intense. And that, of course, meant that the audience began to panic. Everybody scrambled to their feet in a rush for the exits. For us, on the top tier, it was like watching the breaking of a dam as a flood of bodies poured out and down the stairs. We five Europeans tried to cling together and succeeded moderately well; but during our slow descent of the stairs, nothing would stop the women from stroking my arms and trying to bring their faces close to mine. At last we reached the exit where our taxi was thankfully still waiting for us. We tumbled into it. Hazel was badly shaken and I was practically in my underclothes as my dressing-gown had been pulled hither and thither by the predatory women. Even the American major was extremely upset. 'Shepherd's Hotel,' he said sharply to the taxi-driver.

It was nearly midnight by the time we all tumbled into the cool and unusually empty foyer. Hazel clung to my arm. 'Let's go up to bed,' she pleaded. There was no argument on that score. Fred, who on arrival had immediately gone to the bar for a neat whisky, now joined us. 'I'll see you up,' he said rather thickly. 'My room's on the same floor.' So, after the usual goodnights, the three of us went off together. But, instead of leaving Hazel and me at our door, Fred pushed his way into the room with us. 'Mush finish my whisky,' he said in a slurred voice, and sank into a chair.

Hazel made a dive under her mosquito net and there started to undress. 'I must get some rest, Ingaret,' she kept on whispering in a pleading voice. 'Get rid of him, Ingaret . . . get rid of him!'

But this was easier said than done. Fred was very drunk and he absolutely refused to move. So we two sat facing each other in so-called comfortable chairs, but I had never felt so uncomfortable in my life. For, despite all my pleading, with each gulp of neat whisky, Fred became more and more obdurate. 'Wanna sleep with you,' he said, over and over again. And every time he said it Hazel, beneath her mosquito net, burst into a fresh bout of inarticulate but very audible sobs. Suddenly I couldn't help laughing at the idiotic situation the three of us were in. But laughter was, of course, immediately mistaken by Fred for encouragement, and he probably attributed Hazel's increased sobs to my heartlessness.

This was the first time that I had ever been face to face with a drunken man, but instead of finding it alarming I found the whole situation hilariously funny. It was like a farce in the theatre: the pleading drunk, the demolished artist, and the sober virgin. But I realised that, to extricate myself, I had to become extremely practical. First I must try to stop laughing, as it was not only raising Fred's temperature, it was lowering Hazel's. So, with great difficulty, I managed to control my laughter and, trying hard to keep a straight face, I went and sat on Fred's knee. I had decided I must put on a very good act. Fred's hand, of course, immediately went up under my dressing-gown, but I had learned my part. 'No! No!' I said loudly (so that Hazel could hear). 'We can't do that here, Fred . . . we can't do anything here, Fred,' I repeated forcibly. I had noticed by now that Fred was trying not only to focus his eyes on my face but also his mind on what I was saying. His arm tightened round me: his hand ceased wandering. 'We can't do anything here, Fred,' I repeated emphatically. 'Not here . . . so let's go to your room.'

Fred remained motionless for a moment. Hazel's sobs under the mosquito net became increasingly desperate. I stood up. I pulled Fred up too: the empty whisky glass fell to the floor and broke. But that somehow helped me. At least it was the end of something.

'Come on,' I said, taking his arm. 'Come on.' Somehow I held him up and we managed to totter towards the door. Then I opened it and, with Fred, stepped outside. Then, like a flash, leaving him leaning against the wall, I nipped back into our bedroom and instantly locked the door. And as I did so, quite irrationally, I felt myself to be a cad. 'Cad' was a word

I had only ever heard used in relation to Dickie Bramble. But now I actually knew what it felt like to be one!

The following morning we all gathered in the foyer of the hotel and, taking the lead as usual from the American major, we decided to abandon the idea of going on to Suez. Due to our late retirement the previous night, the stifling heat, and the monotonous desert scenery, the return journey by hired car to Ismailia was carried out in a somewhat minor key, and we all rejoiced to see our ship again and ready at anchor.

As we crossed the gangway, carrying suitcases in our hands, a now sober Fred said quietly, 'Hey, kiddo, you stood me up last night.'

I looked at him. So he had not been so drunk that he had forgotten how the previous evening had ended. This tall, gangling American, his teeth as white as his clean silk shirt, his dark eyes dancing with – amusement, tolerance, intent . . . I didn't know which – was incomprehensible to me. 'I wanna have a word with you, kiddo,' he continued. 'See you later.'

To Hazel, and perhaps to me also, going back to our single cabins, hearing once more the ship's heart beating beneath us, was like coming home. Then came the first tremble of departure as our ship slowly pulled away from the quayside and moved out towards the challenging oceans. But the advancing waves were not to be the only challengers. Fred sought me out in my corner in the second-class (while Hazel was working on the American major's head in the first-class) and started to talk to me, as always on the same subject.

'Say, honey, you're a grand kid . . . but why did you stand me up in that hotel?'

'I didn't particularly want to . . . but I had to.'

'Why?'

I shrugged my shoulders.

'D'you shrug off all your chaps?' he asked.

I didn't know what to say to that because I had never before been in a similar position.

But Fred was sharp. 'Say, what about those other chaps? Haven't there been any?' he asked with sudden curiosity. 'Or am I the first?'

I said nothing, which, of course, implied to Fred that he was right.

'So in fact there haven't been any other chaps?'

I paused; and then nodded my head.

Fred stared at me in astonishment. 'Honey, how old are you?'

'Early twenties,' I said, feeling guilty.

There was a pause, then he leaned forward and took my hand. 'Say, honey, some day you've gotta take your foot off the brake and put it on the accelerator . . . and give some chap a joyride. So why not start now with me?'

I was quite speechless. There was no question of love; no question of marriage; no mention of my, perhaps, having a baby. Yet surely the first two things came before, yes, before, sleeping with a man?

As if reading my thoughts, Fred said quickly, 'I'll make sure you'd be in no sort of trouble afterwards, honey.'

Suddenly, when Fred spoke quietly and seriously like this, everything felt different. Abruptly I got to my feet. I felt stymied . . . as Roger would say on the golf course. 'I'll – I'll think about it,' I said quickly, and got up to leave him. But no such luck.

He rose too and took my arm. 'Look at me,' he said.

I looked up. Now he had a very gentle expression on his dark face. 'It – it'd be great for me, honey . . . a great honour . . . a great experience too. I'd never forget that.' He dropped my arm and so we parted.

During the three remaining days on the ship my thoughts revolved around our conversation. And the more I thought about it, the more I saw a certain sense in everything Fred had said; his very directness, too, held an attraction for me. It occurred to me that if I were seriously considering Fred's proposition, it had several points in its favour. First, it would be a valid and natural experience; and, as such, I did not feel it to be in any way 'wicked'. Secondly, Fred was an American and leaving England immediately after our arrival there in order to return to his own country, so, after the 'event', I need never see him again. In consequence, I would be able to live through a very important experience without having to pay for it emotionally. I did feel rather appalled at the relief that this thought brought to me, but even that did not mean it was a 'wicked' or irresponsible thing to do. After all, I was old enough now to be living my own independent life . . . and Fred, in his way, was a straightforward person.

So, as Fred and I were leaning over the side of the ship with only twenty-four hours between us and Southampton, I said quietly, 'All right, Fred. Tonight, cabin 33: I won't fasten my door.'

He turned and looked down at me with delight. 'Honey, you're great!' he said. 'Great!' He had an enormous smile on his face. 'And you won't regret it, kiddo, I promise.'

During our last day before reaching England I could think of nothing else. England seemed so remote that it could have been on the moon for all I cared. Then, in the evening when I was in my cabin changing for our last dinner, I suddenly heard myself saying aloud, almost casually, as I stared at my reflection in the mirror, 'Oh God, I don't feel I am about to do anything wrong . . . in fact, it seems quite sensible. But if it is wrong, please stop me from doing it . . . will You?'

When I went to bed that night I left my cabin door unlocked. I felt so untroubled that instantly I fell fast asleep.

Next morning I woke with a start. The door was still unlocked but nothing had happened! Nor could I feel any movement in the ship . . . so clearly we must have docked. I looked out of my porthole. I could see the sun still rosy from sleep, only just opening an inquiring eye beyond the horizon. Yet despite the early morning sun it was quite cold. I dressed hurriedly: I liked watching the dawn and so I ran quickly up on deck. There I saw the American major standing by himself by the rails of the ship and staring intently inland. I joined him.

He turned to me. 'Bad luck about poor old Fred, isn't it?'

'Fred?' I followed his gaze and saw that only one gangway was down, across which two men were very slowly carrying a covered body on a stretcher. Was he drunk? Or dead? The early morning scene looked utterly macabre.

'Yep.' The American major pointed. 'Emergency gangway. That's him. I've just got him sent off to hospital: temperature of a hundred and four degrees. Last night, poor chap, he got a sudden attack of malaria. Apparently he's subject to occasional relapses.'

I was unable to find a reply. The rain was now beginning to fall quite heavily against the faltering sunlight. From India, I did know something about malaria: I knew that a change in climate could bring it on very quickly. So, shivering slightly I said, 'I s'pose it was the cold and the damp.'

'Too right,' the American major replied. 'Bad luck really. Poor old Fred. He sure was a decent sort.'

I was silent for a moment, then I said quietly, 'Yes, sure, he was a decent sort.' What I did not add was that somehow I could not quite believe it was only 'the cold and the damp' that had so suddenly brought on Fred's attack of fever.

24

Professor Jung

After a brief farewell talk with the American major I went back to the second-class to have a quick breakfast with Hazel. Then we picked up our suitcases, labelled our trunks, and went to join the bustle for disembarkation. On the way I suddenly remembered Hans, the young Russian sailor, so Hazel and I went 'backstage', as I called it, to seek him out and say another goodbye. Hans looked so downcast at our departure that I said quickly, 'Let's exchange addresses, then we can keep in touch. If ever you come to England let me know and we can meet.' At the very mention of the word England his face brightened, so we swapped addresses, shook hands and parted.

As we stood in the queue for disembarkation, I thought again and again about Fred and all the things he had said to me, and their implications. I kept on telling myself that his acute attack of malaria on the very night that I had agreed to sleep with him (now, at least, I could admit that to myself in plain English) *must* have been an extraordinary coincidence. Yet the memory of that casual half-prayer I had projected into the mirror whilst doing my hair remained constantly with me. But surely it was beyond the realms of possibility that God could ever know, let alone be interested in, who slept with whom and for what reason? The ambiguity of the whole incident continued to perplex me.

Hazel's hand on my arm drew me back to the present and I saw that now no less than three gangways were down, and quite a crowd was gathered on the quayside awaiting the arrival of the passengers. Hazel and I stood clutching our suitcases and watching the blurred outlines of faces through the now persistent rain. The sun, as so often in England, had tired of the human day and gone back to rest.

Then suddenly, through the rain, I saw an arm lifted and waving . . . but to whom? I stared more closely. Now two arms were waving, fairly close to each other. Suddenly I heard Hazel by my side say, 'It's John!', and almost at the same moment I recognised that the other waving figure was Jimmy Young. We waved back, but I think we both felt a sense of estrangement, from everything and everybody, although for different reasons: a slight sense of anticlimax.

Eventually we got ashore. Jimmy and I were introduced to Hazel's husband, John Kennedy, who was a distinguished soldier and public figure in Scotland, and then she and I, with tears in our hearts if not in our eyes, parted company. Jimmy carried my suitcase, looking more like a faun than ever with his brown eyes twinkling as he walked beside me: tall, slim, and curiously elegant even in his plus-fours.

'Why did you come to meet me, Jimmy?' I asked.

'Why? Well, because we all missed you, of course,' he replied lightly. Then he added, 'Besides, I've something to tell you.'

I smiled to myself. More news about his latest girl . . . or was it girls? However, on reaching the car, I remembered that he was a fast and very competent driver; also that he did not like talking whilst he was driving. So that would give me a chance to think.

Once we had put my luggage into the boot of the car, we set off through the English countryside. It was now spring in England and the landscape, as it flashed by, was green, tranquil, and lushly prolific. I thought back to those dry deserts of Africa, so exposed to the sun as to be rendered impotent by its heat. What battles even nature herself had to wage in order to achieve some form of natural life! Then I noticed that the car was slowing down as we drove through a small village. I kept having to repeat the word 'England' to myself in order to remind myself where I really was. With its main street of small cottages, some with comfortably padded thatched roofs, it was all so familiar and yet, illogically, the sense of almost total unfamiliarity persisted within me. I wondered why. I was coming home; and in both childhood and adolescence the word 'home' had always underlined my sense of reality. People too, whether I had liked them or not, had seemed more real if linked with the word 'home'. Even nature, animals, the gallant spirit of life which had given the flowers their brilliant and varying colours, and the sky its changing moods of almost human variety, all of these had held for me a deeply felt and valued need when connected with the word 'home'. Religion, too, had been equally charged, but in a different way: at moments it still flared up inside me, so perhaps it had been preserved even though not actively pursued?

Jimmy's acceleration of the car's pace along the wide road suddenly distracted me. I listened to the steady sound of the engine making its rapid progress. I noticed as always Jimmy's deft yet steady handling of the wheel. Then suddenly I was struck by the similarity between Jimmy's concentration on his outer journey and mine on my inner one. The throb of the Daimler's engine took me back to the trembling movement of the ship's engines at sea. I thought back to those seas, to those vast oceans across which I had travelled, which carried within them a whole world of hidden life, and which, because of their immensity, stretched not only out of sight but also far beyond human imagining. These oceans ruled so indomitably and autocratically that even man himself, despite his scientific contrivances and inventions, was utterly subject to them. Yet, paradoxically, or so it seemed to me, these worldwide-rulers, the oceans, were themselves subject to the remote effects of a seemingly small and often invisible heavenly body, namely the moon. No matter what varying passions seized the oceans, passions that led both man and rock and land to be mere objects for disposal, no matter how separate were their areas of being, the moon still exercised its extraordinary power, even when it was totally invisible. I knew, of course, that 'gravity' was the technical word given to explain this strange phenomenon, and it suddenly struck me that it was also a most apt and expressive word. For, as I saw it, this interrelationship between the elements was a very grave issue.

I asked myself whether it was possible that man himself, like the oceans, attracted some 'remote control' from these very same heavens? After all, the differences in the manner and mode of man's being that were scattered across the universe were in a way similar to the varying aspects of the world's oceans, some ice-bound, some warmed by the sea, some made dangerous by the currents hidden deeply within them and always ready to exercise their submerged powers of destruction. And if man and the oceans shared certain basic similarities, perhaps they also shared the reality of a directing and omnipotent heavenly power, so that even personal events, as between man and man, could also be subject to the same 'remote control'?

I became aware that the car was slowing down, doing a turn and finally pulling up outside a pub.

Jimmy turned off the engine. 'I'd like a glass of beer,' he said. 'What about you?'

'A coffee perhaps,' I suggested.

We went into the bar. Jimmy ordered the drinks and we sat down together at a small table in the corner.

'You're looking well,' he said.

'Tanned from the sun!'

'But you're very quiet.'

'You like to concentrate when you're driving fast,' I smiled, 'I remembered that.'

He nodded. 'But what were you thinking about? I could almost hear it rumbling about inside you.'

His remark confirmed for me the fact that I had always felt him to be a sensitive and intuitive person. 'I was thinking about the moon,' I replied.

'But moons don't rumble!'

'All the same they're important.'

'You're telling me! The moon's quite a cocktail on a romantic occasion!' He gave me a spontaneous wink. I had always been his confidante in relation to his latest girlfriend.

'Which was why I asked you what you've been up to lately,' I replied. It was the sort of idiotic conversation in which we sometimes indulged.

Jimmy's smile vanished. 'I'll tell you later,' he said. 'But it's not at all what you think. Far from it!'

He rose rather abruptly, and we left the pub and went back to the car. 'Let's get to London, quick,' Jimmy said, 'and then I'll tell you.' Then suddenly he asked, 'Are you very tired?'

'No. I'm not a bit tired,' I replied.

'Then let's go and have dinner and dance at the Hungaria, shall we?'

'I'd love that,' I said.

During the rest of the journey I thought mainly about Jimmy. He was as attached to his family – father, mother, and elder brother – as they were attached to him. But they looked upon him as something of a lightweight, more keen on girls than on books and learning. And in relation to the successful intellectuals who frequented the Youngs' home at weekends, of course he was. But I had never been convinced that this was an accurate assessment of Jimmy. To me he had always appeared to be someone who had become confused in his inner searchings . . . as I, too, had been. And this had provided a kind of foundation-stone for our relationship, which was easy and carefree and full of shared adventures. So now what had Jimmy got to tell me? And why was he so hesitant about it?

My sense of dissociation from the reality of my homecoming persisted even when we arrived at my little flat in Chelsea. Jimmy brought in my trunk and suitcase and put them in the bedroom, and then went out to park the car. I could see at a glance that Piley had kept the place spotlessly clean in my absence; and there was a pile of letters on the table. I went to pick them up, then stopped. Jimmy would be back in a moment and

I had a hunch that somehow he would want my whole attention. The letters would keep.

I returned to the sitting-room and sat down in my shabby comfortable secondhand chair. I still felt strangely disorientated, even in my own flat. The trams, grinding to a halt outside, reminded me of Cape Town rather than of Chelsea. Then I heard the front door slam and Jimmy came in carrying a bottle of beer.

'Good!' I said. 'There's only milk in the fridge.'

Jimmy opened the bottle, took a glass out of the cupboard and sat down opposite me.

'It's not a "who", it's an "it",' he replied, but without a smile. Suddenly his face appeared to me to be almost pathetically serious. Then he blurted out, 'I've got a job!'

Instantly I felt reassured. Since coming down from Oxford I knew that Jimmy had had enormous difficulty in securing the offer of a job; in fact, not even his father had been prepared to find a place for him in his business at Lloyd's.

'So what sort of a job?' I asked.

'I'm going to the Sudan,' he said.

Momentarily I felt astonished. I knew vaguely where the Sudan was: south of Egypt and not far from the Red Sea. In fact, in our car trip into the desert we had possibly not been all that distant from the Sudan.

'What will you do there?' I asked.

'Grow cotton . . . it's a government enterprise.'

I remembered the aridity of the desert and the assault of the heat and I simply could not imagine anything growing there.

'And one's given one's own bungalow,' Jimmy went on with a touch of excitement. 'Apparently there are just thousands and thousands of acres of cotton irrigated by our canals, with local people to do the planting and the weeding.'

'And what will you do?' I inquired.

'Well, I'll just ride round daily on my horse and see that the men are doing their jobs.' He paused. 'And there's a club to go to,' he added.

I remembered the clubs in India and that gave me some relief. 'When do you go?' I asked.

'In about a month.'

'And for how long?'

He gave a half-smile. 'They give me six months' leave every two years,' he said. 'I should be back in a year's time – or before, if they sack me.'

'Of course they won't sack you. You're an out-of-door sort of person . . . you're a marvellous horseman . . . and if you're as good with the

215

Sudanese as you are with other people you'll get on fine.' Suddenly I remembered India. 'Of course there may not be a lot of girls around!' I added.

Jimmy grinned at me and the atmosphere lightened. 'I've thought of that too,' he said. 'But I've had a good innings, haven't I?'

There was a moment's silence. Then Jimmy looked at his watch and rose. 'Well, I'll be off to the club now, have a bath and change . . . then I'll come and fetch you and we'll celebrate at the Hungaria. All right?'

'Fine,' I said.

After he had left I sat motionless. My sense of remoteness from reality had completely vanished; instead I felt myself to be deeply involved with the present. How was it possible to send someone like Jimmy, gregarious, a fine sportsman, seemingly irresponsible in certain ways, yet gentle and true in all that mattered . . . how was it possible to send someone like him to somewhere as remote and soulless as an African desert? And, to make matters worse, I remembered that on my recent travels I had heard the Sudan called 'the white man's grave'; and the epithet had been used more than once. But of course I'd made no mention of that to Jimmy. Somewhat to my surprise, I realised that his news had made me profoundly uneasy. I had the sensation that I had had feelings of this sort before: yes, they corresponded in great measure to the protective instincts that since childhood I had had for my mother. Yet surely it was inappropriate to feel this way about Jimmy, a strong and healthy young man just starting out on his career? I must remember that, I told myself severely, and act accordingly.

So I tried to dismiss my fears, rose to my feet and in so doing I saw my unopened letters lying on the table. I crossed the room and picked them up, noticing that one was a telegram. I dropped the letters and tore open the telegram apprehensively: why did one always associate telegrams with bad news? It said, 'Your book accepted by Jarrolds.' It was signed by the woman literary agent (who was also a poet) to whom I had given the piles of exercise books which had served as my diary since I had been living in London . . . and now all those scribblings were to become a book! I sat down quietly for a few minutes because my legs felt shaky, and then I telephoned my mother to tell her the good news.

Even as she answered my call I could sense from her voice that things were not going well with her. So I arranged to go down to Surrey the following weekend to see the new house, and, hopefully, to be able to help her with her old inner fears. I wanted to thank her, too, for paying the rent of my flat, which had been the springboard for my new-found independence.

I took a bus down to Guildford and found my way to the house from a nearby stop. Although my mother called it 'dull', it was actually quite attractive, with five bedrooms and three sitting-rooms, and a good growth of trees and bushes between it and the main road; behind it was a tennis court, and alongside it a garage and stables with a small flat which could house a married couple. But the only links with nature were the trees which surrounded the house and the exotic plants in the conservatory in which my mother sat for long hours doing her tapestry work. It was a near-miss of suburbia.

I asked no questions and waited, as always, for my mother to confide in me when she was ready: direct questions always alarmed her into a defensive position. So I told her about South Africa, and about our expedition to Cairo, and I made the bedroom scene in Shepherd's Hotel sound so funny that finally the tension left her and we both rocked with laughter. It was at such moments that she seemed more like an intimate friend than a mother. Then gradually, as she relaxed, I asked her about Roger, and then about herself.

There was a pause. Then suddenly she burst into tears. 'They've all come back, darling . . .' she brought out the words with difficulty ' . . . those fears . . . those dreadful fears. John wanted us to go abroad and have a rest after moving house . . . but it wouldn't be a rest for me . . . it would be hell. Anything new is always hell . . . and yet I know that I need something new inside myself . . . to get away from this hell of fear.'

I took her in my arms and held her closely to me; and as I waited for the horrors to lessen, so my own thoughts became more active. During the past seven years, there had been plenty of movement in my life, some success, new inner vistas and wider outer horizons; but it was those evening talks with Eric Farmer that remained most deeply rooted within me. He had introduced me to new ideas, new words, new names, and a totally new approach to inner life which had teased me into making inquiries; into reading new kinds of books, too. In consequence I now knew that two great men at that very moment existed: one lived in Austria and was called Freud; the other lived in Switzerland and was called Jung. And they were both experts in something rather new (to me) that was called 'psychology'. These two great men had initially been partners in their intensive exploration of the inner world of man, then they had parted company because of a difference in emphasis: Freud believing that 'sex' held the key to most inner phobias or fears; and Jung believing that such disturbances came from the psyche or 'soul'.

So now I said gently to my mother, 'Why not get Major John to take you to Switzerland to see Professor Jung? He's the expert, you know. He could give you good advice.'

At this her tears broke out anew. 'How could I go, darling? I couldn't go alone. And even if John came with me we couldn't just leave this house empty. We've got a married couple but I don't really trust them . . . and this house is filled with such valuable things that your father collected – that screen in the hall, for instance, and all the antique furniture . . . it's worth thousands of pounds . . .' Her tears increased.

I gave her a hug. 'All right, darling . . . stupid of me. Of course you couldn't go. But listen to me – ' She lifted her beautiful face marred by tears. 'I'll tell you what we'll do. You write to Professor Jung, tell him fully about your feelings and your terrors . . . and ask him if *he* knows anyone in this country to whom you could go for advice. I'm sure there must be someone . . . and from what I've heard, I feel sure he's just the man who can help you. I've read a bit about him.' Then I added, 'And "psyche" is the Greek word for soul.'

My mother hesitated. Her tears finally jerked into silence. Then she muttered, 'I – I've seen so many doctors . . . I – I don't believe in them any more.' Then with another burst of agonised tears she said, 'I – I don't believe in anything any more . . . how can I?'

That my beautiful, courageous, devout and yet suffering mother had come to this crisis of faith so late in life moved me so profoundly that I had difficulty in checking my own tears. Then, taking her hand, clenched and sweating with her inner agony, I said firmly, 'You are going to write now, this very moment, to Professor Jung.'

Even that was a battle. 'You write to him, darling,' she pleaded with me. 'You know all about it. I don't.'

But I refused. 'No, sweetheart,' I said very gently. 'It is you who have to take this step. I've given you the meaning of the word "psyche"; that is as far as I can go. Now it has to be your decision. That will be part of its great value for you. And when you get a reply, it must be you also who answers it . . . though of course I'll come down and discuss it if you want me to.'

And so the letter to Professor Jung in Zurich was finally written and despatched by my mother.

Again, it had been thanks to my talks with Eric Farmer that I already knew something about the deeply hidden area in the soul of all human beings which Freud and Jung called 'the unconscious'. In my untutored way, I saw this as a kind of storeroom in which all the major and even minor experiences of life were retained, even those that were scarcely remembered or possibly completely forgotten. Indeed, it seemed to correspond with a dimly perceived area of awareness within myself: namely, the feeling that beneath everything that one did, and even the things that happened to one, there was another state of being; and not only of being but of power. This seemed to me to exist in the same sort of dimension as what, in my early years, I had called 'religion', and which, for a time, had provided a satisfactory explanation for it. Then, as I had grown older and been engaged in the normal pains and pleasures of growing up, and also in the pursuit of personal independence, some-how this sense of a deeply buried part of the self had assumed greater significance and reality for me than the daily practice of religion. Paradoxically, this very shift in approach had opened up in me new areas of imagination, belief, and also trust. The key word for me was 'psyche'. Religion, of course, maintained belief in the soul of man; as I did. But things apparently could go wrong even with the soul of good and great men. Surely, then, it was just as important to have doctors for the soul as it was for the body? Having lived since childhood with the constant illness of my mother, any new approach that might help the illness that was founded in the depths of her being aroused my hope and interest.

Within a few days my mother received an answer to her letter. It was written in Professor Jung's own hand and gave the name of a Dr Godwin Baynes who practised in Harley Street. He also gave my mother Dr Baynes's home address which, as it happened, was only about fifteen miles away from her new home. Somewhat doubtfully, my mother wrote and asked for an appointment and received an answer within a few days. I took her up to London, to Harley Street, and waited for her in the waiting-room. I caught just a glimpse of Dr Baynes as they came out: a tall, good-looking, strongly-featured man, with an open face and direct blue eyes.

Out in the street my mother took my arm.

'What is he like?' I asked.

'Well, he asked me questions . . . they always do . . . and I answered them. Then he talked to me a bit . . . and I told him that I hadn't understood a word he'd said.'

My heart sank. 'What did he say to that?'

'He simply smiled and said, "That doesn't matter. Your unconscious will have understood." '

We walked down Harley Street looking for a taxi. Once inside it I asked the pertinent question. 'Did you make another appointment?'

'Oh, he was very nice about that,' my mother replied. 'He suggested that I should go to his home once a week . . . you remember he lives quite near us? So John could drive me over. The doctor thought the journey up to London would be rather tiring for me; and very occasionally he does see people in his own home.'

I felt my heart give a jump of joy. However, I just said very calmly, 'Oh, that would be nice; much more personal.'

'Yes, that's exactly what he said,' my mother replied.

And so a weekly routine started that was to put down good and firm roots as my mother worked with Dr Baynes.

25

Cheffie

The acceptance of my book by Jarrolds had been more of a shock than an excitement. I had never seriously contemplated the possibility of its being published. However, it was to run to three editions! After a few weekends spent with my mother I decided to spend a weekend with the Youngs. It was to be a happy reunion after my departure on tour to South Africa.

Unfortunately it was the weekend immediately after the publication of my book. It was autumn, and there was a large wood fire burning brightly in the drawing-room; and round the fire sat the usual guests, together with the Youngs, each with a copy of the book in their hands. They had all bought one! But despite the warmth of the huge log fire I felt the atmosphere round me slowly beginning to freeze. Only then did I remember how frankly I had written about the Youngs' weekend house-parties and the people who attended them. Some of the details and incidents I had thought to be quite funny as I wrote them; but to the victims of my humour, sitting speechless and motionless around me, they were far from amusing. The only thing that broke the silence was the turning of a page, or a crackle from the fire. Unable to decide what to do I finally rose, in escape, and went for a long and solitary walk. It was the only way I could keep my nerve. Jimmy, who was not present at this weekend gathering, was the only person who had found the book funny. I waited for quite a while before I went to the Youngs again, to allow them time to forget all the comical, and possibly cruel, things that I had found to write about them in my book.

Jimmy still came up to London nearly every weekend, using my flat as his headquarters by day and his club at night. It seemed that he would have to wait quite a while before being signed on for the Sudan project. He had tropical kit to buy in London and a topee, about all of which I was able to advise him. So, with a not very happy heart, I helped him with his shopping and it was as if, through dealing with these practicalities, we got to know each other in a new way, a less light-hearted and a more trusting way. And whenever possible we danced at the Hungaria, although even there our conversation was mainly domestic.

'Shall I take out white flannels to the Sudan?'

'Shorts would be better, I think,' I answered.

'And what about my riding tackle?'

'I should leave that here in England . . . you might be needing it some day on leave.' I smiled, though I didn't feel like smiling. 'After all, in the Sudan you might have to ride a donkey through the plantations. Who knows! The Sudanese often ride donkeys: they like it.' I always tried to make him smile if I could. But I was not going to allow him to indulge in any blissful English images of 'riding to hounds'. 'These deserts are curious places, you know,' I added.

'You don't like them?' Jimmy sounded almost anxious.

'Not much. But you may. After all, you'll be doing your job.' Despite my own inner doubts I wanted to encourage him.

Then, in the middle of my uncharacteristically domestic London life, I suddenly received another call from the theatrical world. Beau Hannen and Athene Seyler were taking their acting company to Finland to put on a show during 'British Week' and they asked me to join them. Hazel Armour had also been invited, to help with the company and to bring out as much of her sculptural and painted work as it was possible to transport to Finland without damage. Hazel and I had by now made so many varied travels together and become so used to each other's idiosyncrasies that we both accepted with delight. I had agreed to write another book for Jarrolds, but without committing myself to a date for its completion, and Finland sounded too romantic to miss: no heat, just snow and ice and beautiful mountains . . . and it only took a few days by boat to get there . . . though, of course, crossing the North Sea would be very different from the southern oceans that I had enjoyed.

But when I told Jimmy of my plans his face clouded. 'You're always going away,' he said. 'Why can't you stay put?'

I was surprised. 'But it's only for a fortnight,' I said.

'Yes, but that's quite a long time – when I could be ordered out to the Sudan at any moment.'

I was both silenced and at a loss. I had not realised that his departure could be so very imminent. And Jimmy was grumpy, something he normally never was.

I took his hand. 'I'm sorry, Jimmy,' I said. 'But I can't cancel it now

222

. . , it's too late. They're relying on me for help with the theatrical side . . . and my ticket is already booked.'

Jimmy relented. 'Sorry,' he said. 'I'm being rather a cad. But I – I was a bit disappointed. I – I wanted to talk to you about something.'

About the Sudan job, I thought to myself. And there wasn't anybody else to hand who knew much about either the human or the practical aspects of those African deserts. 'We'll talk about it directly I get back,' I said, and took his hand.

Jimmy did not answer. He just pressed my hand, looked at me and forced a smile. 'You're rather sweet, you know,' he said.

And so I had my week's 'jaunt' in Finland for the celebration of 'British Week'. Beau Hannen's and Athene Seyler's small company, together with Hazel and me, set off in a ship which, to someone whose sole experience of sea travel was in P&O and British Indian liners, looked about as small as a tadpole must seem to a whale, and I was seasick for the whole of the voyage. Once we arrived in Helsinki Hazel and I left our luggage at the spotlessly clean hotel we were booked into and strolled out to get a breath of fresh air. Wherever we went, we saw Union Jacks flying, and all the shop windows seemed to be packed with mackintoshes – which, to the Finns, were emblems of British wear – each shop apparently vying with the others in variety and design. What with the Union Jacks flying all over the city, the theatre filled to capacity every night, our bedrooms comfortable and quiet, and mackintoshes filling all the shop windows, we had a much appreciated if uneventful week in Helsinki.

From the start of the return journey I lay flat on my bunk and that somewhat allayed the effects and assaults of the North Sea. But it was not a happy occasion. The sea and I, despite our affinities, were not good travelling companions.

I arrived back in London quite late on an autumn evening, still feeling a bit shaky.

No sooner had I put down my luggage than the telephone rang. It was Jimmy. 'How are you?'

'Fine – except for the crossing.'

'Can I come round?'

'Of course,' I said. 'There's nothing to eat or drink but there will be a lovely fire going.'

'Right,' Jimmy said. 'I'll have a snack at the club and come along later.'

So I built up a gorgeous coal fire and sat beside it eating the cold supper Piley had left me, waiting for the front-door bell to ring. When

Jimmy finally arrived and I opened the door to him with a smile on my face, I realised at once that something was wrong. He was the sort of person who normally took everything in his stride but tonight he looked subdued and unsure of himself.

We sat down in the sitting-room. 'How did it go?' he asked.

'Quite fun,' I said. Then I added, 'And how do you go?'

'Oh, all right, I suppose.' He paused, and then added, 'The Sudan people have given me my date for departure.'

I felt deep concern. 'When?'

'In a month's time.'

I thought quickly. October . . . that should be when the African deserts were coming to the end of the hot weather . . . or would have been if they were in India. So I said, 'It might not be too hot.'

'Oh, I don't mind about the heat,' Jimmy said, with a touch of impatience. 'I just don't really want to go all that far away now.' He hesitated. 'But of course I suppose I'm lucky to have a job at all.'

'I thought you liked the idea of going abroad?' I suggested.

'I do.' He looked at me across the room, and then burst out, 'But I don't want to leave you . . . I just don't, that's all.'

I was completely at a loss. 'Me?' I faltered.

'Of course. You're the only person I've ever met who understands everything, which I suppose means just me . . . but you do understand me, don't you?'

Suddenly he got to his feet. Crossed the room, and pulled me up into his arms. 'Oh, darling, my darling. Could you ever think of marrying me . . . could you?'

I looked up at him. His usually dancing brown eyes now looked at me with a kind of hesitant desperation.

'Yes . . . yes, Jimmy, dearest, of course I could,' I answered without even thinking.

In an instant his arms were around me. He lifted my face with his hand and stared down at me in disbelief. 'You could? You will . . . really?'

I nodded as best I could in his firm grasp. Then he kissed me gently on the lips. Instantly, the truant memory of David's kisses at our first meeting in India, which had left me responding in every area of my being like an electrically awakened mechanism, darted into my head, and even into my body. For just one moment an outburst of tears threatened me . . . but tears for what?

Instead I clung on to Jimmy. 'Yes, dearest Jimmy. Yes, I will marry you,' I said very quietly. 'I will . . . I will.'

In retrospect I can see that we were two very uncertain people stepping, hand in hand for safety, into ever deeper and more unfamiliar waters. At the time, of course, I was aware of nothing but the warmth of this common need which was igniting us – the need for companion-ship, for a recognisable purpose in life, and a certain mutuality in disposition.

We squashed ourselves on to the tiny settee and clung together and then began to talk. Only a month before Jimmy was due to leave for the East . . . should we tell people that we were engaged when it would be at least a year before we could get married?

I put my head on his shoulder. 'And what will you do until then?' he asked.

'Stay here and write, I suppose,' I said, adding, 'and keep in touch with your family, of course.' There was a sudden pause. 'But will they like this idea?' I asked uncertainly.

'They like you,' Jimmy replied. But we both realised that it was not exactly an answer.

'I'm three years older than you,' I said slowly.

'Then the family will think you'll be able to keep me in order!' Jimmy laughed.

He tilted up my face and kissed me again very gently. 'Actually it's going to be two-way traffic with us,' he said. 'Everything is going to be two-way traffic.' He paused, and then said suddenly, 'By the way, I ought to give you a ring, an engagement ring, oughtn't I?'

'I don't want one,' I said firmly.

'Why not?'

'Unnecessary,' I answered. 'We know what we're about, so let's leave it at that.'

'You are a strange one,' Jimmy said. 'All the girls I've known would have given their eyes to have a diamond or two to flash about!'

'Disappointed?' I asked.

'You bet,' he said, and hugged me.

I had been right in my forebodings. The Youngs, when we went down to see them that weekend, were taken aback by our news and in no way particularly helpful. Lack of money; an uncertain future; the three-year difference in our ages; Jimmy's previous unreliability in relation to the opposite sex; all these odds were stacked together like a pack of cards. However, we kept our own trumps strictly hidden and our tempers under careful control and, when we left on the Sunday night, comparative calm had returned to the household. But I sensed that the price I might have to pay would be my friendship with Mip Young. I wondered if she saw me as a successful 'fisher of men' who thought that I had landed a good catch in her younger son?

The following weekend we both went down to see my mother. She, of course, was quite different in her reaction to the news of our engagement. This was her first meeting with Jimmy and she liked him very much: perhaps she was glad that I had at last consented to marry someone – and someone *nice*. But she was an extraordinarily intuitive woman. Did she, or did she not, see our relationship working on a permanent basis?

Now that we had told both families of our engagement (even without a ring), that had given a certain authenticity to the whole situation. Jimmy's departure for the Sudan was now only three weeks away, so in the short time left we shopped together and planned for the future, and danced much less than usual. I was to discover that dancing at the Hungaria was expensive – and that the question of marriage was inextricably bound up with the issue of money. Jimmy and I were to be separated for a year: then he would return to England on leave and we would be married, have a honeymoon, and I would go back with him to the Sudan. Jimmy's salary would then have to support two people; and meanwhile my allowance from my mother would only just pay for my trousseau, both tropical and otherwise. Suddenly, preparing for marriage felt rather like keeping a storehouse where daily one checked the debits and credits and kept accurate accounts. Paradoxically, I felt as if life was closing in on me instead of opening out, no matter in which direction I looked. So why did I continue with this venture? On reflection, I think it had something to do with a protective instinct which, since early childhood, had been unwittingly developed in me through my relationship with my mother. And through that experience, uncon-sciously, I had found this attitude to be a creative one, just as creative as was my writing, or becoming some character in a difficult part in a play. The only difference was that the protective role with a human being must always be as invisible as possible; otherwise the effect on the other person would be negative.

Finally, at the end of our tireless month of budgeting and planning, the time came to say goodbye to Jimmy. He turned up at the flat with his leather trunks and, because he was wearing his topee instead of carrying it, and also wore dark glasses, he seemed like a stranger. We had decided against my going to the station with him, or to his port of departure, so, after our leave-taking, I went to the post office to send a telegram of love and good wishes to his ship. Then I returned to the flat, sat down, and started to write.

I had decided to try and write a play next. It was to be called *Because We Must*. 'Must what?' the audience were expected to ask themselves. And the answer was, 'Compromise'. Without quite knowing it, I think I had already learned that lesson.

The time passed quickly. Loving the theatre as I did, it was fascinating trying to write a play, even though, as an amateur, I realised that it would not be so much written as rewritten! At the weekends I could go to stay either with my mother and stepfather or with the Youngs. The announcement of our engagement had caused ripples in the placid pool of Young friendship; but somehow the ripples died away. And there were Jimmy's letters to look forward to, even though these were few and far between because, in his part of the Sudan, there were only two posts a week – one in-going and one out-going. He wrote that he could play polo at the Club but, as it was about a hundred miles away, a game of polo meant a journey of two hundred miles across the plantation tracks in very dusty conditions. He supposed there would be cooler weather some time, but he had not as yet found out when! At the moment it was nearly a hundred degrees in the shade – when you found it! He wasn't complaining, he said, just trying to give me the feel of the place.

Jimmy's letters to me, which I suspected were much more frank than those to his family, always seemed to bring with them the glaring heat and light of those African deserts. I did not feel that he was really happy, although he never admitted as much and just tried to make a joke of the whole thing. Yet this was to be our mutual life: this isolation; these yearly separations (for Jimmy wrote that all the women had to return home in the hot weather). Quite suddenly, I woke up one morning determined that before I committed myself to life with Jimmy in the Sudan I must see both him and the country. I wrote that I was coming out to stay with him for a month or so, to get the lie of the land. In time his reply came, saying, with a hint of alarm, that he would love to see me . . . but I'd have to bring a chaperone with me. In the sort of set-up in which he worked, it would do him no good if a young girl came out and dossed down with him, even if she did call herself his fiancée. It might even get him the sack!

I wrote back immediately to say that I would bring a chaperone and buy an imitation engagement ring. My impatience at the idiocy of it all I did not mention. But how to find a chaperone, and one who could pay her fare and who would have the time to come? I rang up nearly everybody that I had ever known: they all had either husbands or children or relations or jobs – none of which could possibly be left. I was in despair. Who could I find? Then suddenly, out of my childhood past, I remembered an erstwhile nun who, in retirement, had been living in a cottage quite near Folkestone with a woman friend. Once, when Roger and I were very young, we had stayed a few days with her by the sea. Even as a child she had impressed me; and the very word 'nun' had made me open wide my eyes. And now I remembered her name too: Cheffins.

I looked up the number in the telephone book and rang her up. Even after the passage of fifteen years her voice sounded exactly the same.

'Cheffie!' I said. 'It's me . . . Ingaret Giffard . . . do you remember?'

'Of course I remember,' the deep quiet voice replied.

'Well, Cheffie,' I said. 'I'm engaged to be married . . . and I want to go and visit my fiancé, who is in North Africa, to see what sort of place it is, so that I can take the right things when I go out there after marrying him . . . but I can only go if I have a chaperone. Would you come with me?'

Still in the same deep calm voice she replied simply, 'You'll have to give me three days to get some light clothes.'

I knew at once that the old Cheffie, whom I remembered from early youth, was unchanged: unruffled, very practical, and very brave. What I did not realise when I put this proposition to her was that she was seventy-two years old.

'Oh, Cheffie, how wonderful! I'll get two passages booked for us. You don't mind going second-class?'

'I couldn't afford anything else,' she said at once.

'Nor can I!' I laughed. 'But I'll get things on the move and let you know . . . and thank you. Oh, have you got a passport?'

'No. But I'll get one.'

After a great deal of time spent in travel agencies' offices, I eventually succeeded in booking a cabin, second-class, in an Australian immigrant ship. I did not question which route it was taking, I merely rejoiced that there was a spare double cabin and that the fares were abnormally low. And the sailing date gave us ten days to get ready!

We arrived at Tilbury to find a strange-looking vessel awaiting us: solid, low-decked, and without any of the trimmings that I was used to, such as deck-chairs and canvas blinds against the sun. And all the passengers were men, so far as I could see. Cheffie seemed quite unperturbed by this, and, although she had never been to sea before, proved to be a splendid sailor. I had my usual three days' 'acclimatisation' period (to put it politely) and when I tottered up on deck I found Cheffie seated on a canvas chair, well for'ard, watching the sea on either side of us as it curtsied low to allow us passage.

She turned her head slowly as I joined her. 'This is quite beautiful to me,' she said quietly, and turned back to the sea. 'It is unbelievably beautiful.'

I think the appearance of a young girl caused a slight tremor through the male passengers, who spent most of the day in the bar as well as much of the night. One man actually bothered to fetch a canvas chair for me as there did not appear to be any more on deck. I asked for it to be put next to Cheffie's, and there the two of us sat together, perched in the bows, backs to the world, for the entire voyage. We could spend a whole morning without speaking a single word to each other. And no explanation was needed. I had never before enjoyed such perfect companionship. After lunch perhaps we had a rest; but always the sea and the two canvas chairs recalled us. Only as it grew dusk did Cheffie and I begin to talk, and we did this generally in our cabin or during supper, which was early. But the jollity and joviality of the men in the bar seemed to go on right round the clock.

Of the many things that Cheffie told me about herself I remember one with particular clarity. In the very devout and somewhat isolated order to which she had belonged, prayers and contemplation and some social work occupied most of the day. Cheffie was always a very devout nun, but she was also a great admirer of Christabel Pankhurst and an ardent suffragette; not, of course, because she was politically minded, but because she believed women to be as rich as men in their contribution to a working humanity, both spiritually, intellectually and imaginatively. This presented Cheffie with a problem. She was a devout follower of Christ; and violence was forbidden by Christ: so how was she to be loyal both to human realities and to her spiritual beliefs? She told me that she suffered weeks of agony because of her blind indecision. Then, one day, as she awoke, she knew what she had to do. She picked up a hammer, tucked it under her black habit, and began to walk towards the church where she attended Mass. Passing Gorringes department store on the way, she pulled out the hammer and smashed three of the shop windows, tucked the hammer back under her habit and went on to Mass to confess her sin; and also the fact that she did not believe it to be a sin. So, during our voyage to Suez, we got to know each other very well, and our points of view seemed to coincide.

At Suez we had to catch a train south to Aswan, from where we would take a river steamer down the Nile to Wadi Halfa. From there we had to catch another train in order to reach Khartoum, where Jimmy would meet us in his car to drive us the hundred or more miles back to his bungalow. So, after disembarkation from the ship, we took a taxi to the station in Suez with our joint trunk and two light suitcases, second-class tickets and dwindling supply of money. On arrival we showed our tickets to a porter and then followed him to the train. There I received a tremendous shock. Of course I should have remembered from India that Europeans never travelled second-class. Due to my thoughtlessness, we were faced with spending a night and two days in circumstances which were truly horrific. Our porter peered and pointed and chattered unintelligibly (to us) while we walked the length of the train in search not of our booked seats (as I had supposed) but of two people prepared to squeeze themselves closely together in order to give us two women enough room to sit down. Finally two corners were made for us in an already baking and overfilled carriage; the windows were shut, and tiny children clambered all over the occupants, which now included us. The children were filthy, as were the other passengers: the bright-coloured saris could not conceal the dirt, the sores on the bodies and the skin rashes on the hands and feet, and the smell of betel-chewing and crowded humanity was overpowering.

As the train jerked forward I gave a desperate glance at Cheffie. In the corner opposite me she continued to sit upright, staring imperturbably out of the window. I knew she was inwardly both content and concentrated, for nothing else could have provided that calm detachment. She even occasionally touched the head of some small diseased child as it tried to pull at her habit. So I took my cue from her, thanking God that I had remembered, before departure, to have us both inoculated against every tropical disease imaginable. And there was yet another problem. As the hours wore on and darkness fell, the corridor of the train became stacked with sleeping, sprawling passengers, most of the men white-robed and white-turbaned, and a visit to the WC (which had to be used with such care that it was quite a skilled operation) entailed picking one's way between those prostrate bodies. After what seemed an interminably long night the sun rose, unwelcomed by me because it contributed to the strength of the smells and the heat. We stopped at occasional stations but the second-class section of the train never emptied: it merely got fuller. By late afternoon the name of the station at which we should get out came into view: Aswan. Cheffie and I, helped by a porter, scrambled thankfully out on to the platform. He picked up our trunk, looked at our tickets, and we clung to our suitcases and followed him.

I could see the beautiful steamship in which we were to sail down the

Nile. She sat on the calm waters like a comfortable white swan . . . waiting, just waiting, I thought with a jump of joy, for our arrival! But, to our dismay, the porter indicated that we had to join a long, long queue of people carrying braziers, children, and huge bags of food slung over their shoulders; some held on to a tethered donkey, or a goat, or even a pariah dog. Then, almost immediately, I realised why. The ship carried behind her an enormous open raft, and this raft was quickly filling up with passengers together with their cooking utensils, their animals and their young children. And, as we waited in the queue, Cheffie and I were also moving slowly towards this raft. We, too, were to travel on it! My heart and my courage seemed to fail me. Three days and three nights on that raft – with no protection from the sun and no food provided.

My legs began to shake as I drew ever nearer to the man in charge who, behind the desk, was checking off the passengers as they were despatched to the raft. At last it was our turn and I stepped in front of Cheffie to speak to the official.

'Please – ' I began. Hearing a European voice, the man looked up and saw Cheffie standing behind me. 'Please, can you tell me how many people the raft can take?' I stammered.

'Fifty,' he replied impassively.

'And supposing there are more than fifty passengers for the raft? What happens then?'

'They go steamer.'

I held my breath . . . and then brought out the words with difficulty: 'So please, could you – could you tell me how many people are already on that raft?'

The man hesitated and then, with his pencil, began to count a list of the names. I never took my eyes off that pencil as it worked slowly downwards, with him calling out the numbers in English . . . 45, 46, 47, 48, 49, 50, 51, 52.

'What good English you speak,' I interrupted ingratiatingly. 'So can you help me, please? This – this lady and I have only second-class tickets because no one in England told us about the raft.' (I was quick to blame the English both in my words and in my voice.) 'So, as there seem to be two people too many for the raft already, could you be very kind and perhaps see that we are sent on to the steamer?' I looked at him with what I hoped were large, helpless blue eyes.

He responded immediately. 'True, true, Missi-Sahib. English wrong, very wrong . . . but I make all right.' He ticked off our names in his book, endorsed our tickets, then looking up he pointed us in the direction of the steamer. After that appalling train journey of nearly twenty-four hours with no sleep, I almost burst into tears from sheer relief. However, remembering my stepfather's unfailing courtesy to our bearer in India, I held out my hand. 'May I shake your hand in thanks?' I asked him. He beamed as we shook hands, and then he turned to the next passenger.

Cheffie and I moved out into the glaring sun and followed our porter towards the first-class boarding steps of the steamer. As we approached, I saw four or five European men leaning over the side of the deck, waving to us and shouting. They seemed to be saying that they would have been prepared to rescue us if we had been directed to the raft! I waved back, took Cheffie's arm and we made our way on to the steamer where a tall and immaculately clothed steward gestured to us to follow him.

To our amazement and delight he led us to a first-class cabin which corresponded to the elegance of the ship itself. It was beautifully clean, with a hand-basin and two luxurious-looking bunks, and an electric fan overhead was busily stirring the hot air into a deceptive coolness. We unpacked our night-things and then wandered up on deck. Wherever we went there was the same spotlessly clean comfort, and thick canvases above to protect us from the sun. The engines started up and our beautiful river steamer trembled into movement. With scarcely a ripple of the Nile, we moved slowly southwards into even hotter climes. Occasionally on the banks of the river we saw the remains of temples to the gods and goddesses of antiquity. The Nile was deeply flooded, it was said, and these ancient monuments were to be removed to safety some distance inland. We stared at them from the deck as the steamer passed sedately by, causing little or no agitation in the water level, and then at the empty and seemingly inaccessible desert land that now lay on both sides of us, in open communion with the white, blazing sun.

Cheffie and I kept to ourselves, always on the shady side of the steamer, and comfortably stretched out in deck-chairs. I personally felt exhausted; not only by the exigencies of the journey, but also at the prospect of spending a further two days in the train that was to take us from Wadi Halfa to Khartoum. Each day seemed to grow hotter. Finally, late one afternoon, we reached Khartoum, which was to be our meeting-place with Jimmy. There we were able to get a conveyance, a trap with its half-starved pony, to take us to the Grand Hotel that Jimmy had chosen as our rendezvous.

On arrival at this cool and impressive hotel there was no sign of Jimmy, so we ordered tea and decided to sit on comfortable chairs, centrally placed, to await his arrival – and we had a very long wait indeed. There was, of course, no means of communication at that time in this part of the world and so we could not attempt to contact Jimmy or his employers. We just had to go on waiting and hoping . . . which, I decided, under the present circumstances, was one of the most exhausting exercises possible. As the hours slowly passed, my apprehensions rose. Suppose Jimmy were dead . . . had been killed in a car accident? We had barely enough money to pay for a plate of food and no one to turn to for help. We waited five long hours, indeed until evening had become night and it was pitch dark outside.

Then, suddenly, into the central hall of the hotel walked Jimmy. He looked pale and thin and, with scarcely a glance around him, he came straight over to us, took me in his arms and kissed me.

'Oh, my darling . . .' We were both nearly in tears. Only Cheffie remained (apparently) unmoved: as always she was just herself, yet always somehow so much more than herself.

'I'm terribly, terribly sorry,' Jimmy said. 'But I had a couple of punctures on the way up.' He turned to Cheffie. 'I'm afraid it's been a long wait for both of you.'

I introduced him to Cheffie; and then he asked, 'Had any food?'

I shook my head. So Jimmy ordered us a cold 'picnic' supper, as it was called, which we ate hurriedly and then followed him out to the car. By the lights from the hotel it looked the sort of car which could easily have two more punctures, very different from Jimmy's Daimler back in England. However, we settled Cheffie as comfortably as possible in the back seat and I sat in front beside Jimmy. As we left the well-worn streets of Khartoum we plunged into a dense blackness pierced only by the car's faltering headlights.

'How much further do we have to go?' I asked Jimmy at one point, to break the silence.

'About as far again.'

It was obviously not the moment for conversation or comment. We plunged, bumped, and occasionally skidded down a track leading southward: it was as furrowed as some ancient brow on the desert's expressionless face. The dim headlights dipped and danced as they did their best to show us the way, but the heavy, dusty air was lifeless and remained so to the journey's end.

At last we arrived at a small square building situated in the middle of nowhere. The car drew up. We helped Cheffie out of the back seat where, she told us, she 'had had a nap', then we all three struggled up the steps on to the verandah. There, in one corner, were two beds; and round another corner was a single bed which was Jimmy's. I could see by the light of one lantern standing at the top of the steps that all three were lavishly decorated with mosquito nets.

'Bed,' I said. So Cheffie and I, with our suitcases and helped by the dim light of the lantern, stumbled towards the two beds. Fishing out our nightdresses, we dropped our clothes on the floor and then, without even washing, we slipped under the mosquito nets and fell into a deep and immediate sleep. Jimmy, with consideration, had put a tin chamber-pot under our beds, and a bottle of iced soda water beside us; but we both slept straight through what was left of the night. One way or another we sweated all the moisture out of our bodies; and were only awakened by the burning finger of the rising sun touching our cheeks.

Slowly and silently I sat up (for Cheffie was still asleep). For as far as I could see, there was just one long uninterrupted expanse, and this flat land was covered by short green growth: the cotton plants, I presumed. Quietly I slid out of bed. Round the corner Jimmy's bed was already empty: presumably he had left even before the crack of dawn. So all that remained for me to do until Cheffie awoke was to contemplate this totally flat, totally empty, baking landscape. It appeared to hold no living life within it. Even the extended cotton fields looked like a false green wig that the earth had put on itself to hide its unnatural baldness. And the sky above was white with the malaise of the heat: it could as little be called 'the heavens' as could the crumpled white sheets on our beds. I stood and stared; then I crept round the corner to find that Cheffie was stirring. Then she too got out of bed and stood staring out at the surrounding countryside. At last she said, very quietly, 'I would never, under any conditions whatsoever, consider spending the rest of my life in this appalling country.' After that we both got dressed and the subject was never mentioned again.

Life in the Sudan, as I was quickly to discover, was not really life at all. With an effort it could be called living. During the first two weeks, the days were indistinguishable one from another because each was exactly the same as the one before and the one that came after. At crack of dawn Jimmy rode off on his horse to supervise the richly productive cotton growth that was all around us; the only other thing that was in purposeful activity was the sun. One day Jimmy suddenly announced that he was driving us to the Club as he was playing in a polo-match, but Cheffie firmly but politely refused to make the trip. It certainly was a long, long desert journey, and on arrival the Club had the appearance of a broken-down little shack with, of course, a bar. I watched the polo with a few other people and in the interval got into conversation with the Governor of somewhere . . . presumably of that province. We must have been talking about the discomforts of the Sudan's heat-laden climate because I remember him giving me a very personal and estimating look. 'Of course, the less women wear the better,' he remarked. 'A naked woman is very beautiful . . . but not a man . . . a man is always too untidy in his make-up for my liking.' Perhaps I was a prig, but I found this man really rather detestable.

Then, during what remained of the game, a member of the opposing team accidentally hit Jimmy with his polo-stick, cracking Jimmy's ankle rather badly. Somebody bound it up but he had to go to hospital to have it properly set. I was intensely surprised that there was a hospital in this outlandish spot. Someone else very kindly drove me back to our bungalow. But the next day I had a slight attack of dysentery and so was quickly rushed off to the same hospital. Consequently our dear and wonderful Cheffie was left alone in Jimmy's bungalow for two days and nights. But she seemed quite unmoved by such events. She had given her verdict on the country on arrival. The fact that I had joined Jimmy in hospital almost immediately after his admittance apparently caused quite a lot of gossip, if not scandal! It was that sort of society.

At the end of our month Cheffie and I returned to England. I remember little of the return journey, presumably because a lot of it was repetitive, but there was one big difference. Jimmy had seen to it that we both travelled first-class the whole way home. Once more he drove us to Khartoum, and as we left, he took me in his arms and said, 'Only six months now and I'll be back on leave with you in England. Leave to get married, too!' he added with a smile.

26

I Talk to a Priest

With all the wedding arrangements to be made, the period that followed our exploratory visit to the Sudan passed very quickly. I had looked upon getting married as a serious and important decision made by two people, but that seemed to be the least of it! There was my trousseau to be ordered and fitted and bought: underclothes, overclothes, and particularly the fittings for my white satin wedding-dress; all these had to be attended to at least twice a week. I spent nearly every weekend with my mother and stepfather in Surrey, making lists and lists of people to be invited to the wedding, which had now been fixed for the beginning of July. Friends of my mother's were lending their house in Grosvenor Street for the reception, so I decided on a nearby Anglican church, St George's in Hanover Square, which, although fashionable, was also rather beautiful. Then there were the bridesmaids' dresses to be designed and made, the caterers to be chosen and briefed, and letter after letter of congratulation to be answered in addition to the hundreds of invitations sent out.

Any hopes I had nurtured of finishing my play whilst waiting for Jimmy's return were still-born; the dialogue in the script got all mixed up with the dialogue of everyday pressures. It was like trying to speak two languages at the same time. So I put the play on one side and instead wrote daily to Jimmy, feeling none too sure that, across those endless miles of desert and with only one post a week, he would receive more than a handful of my letters. I also spent an occasional weekend with the Youngs, still happily entertaining their regular houseguests. We all avoided talk of the future for fear of causing constraint or argument. Mip and I even had a few of our customary walks together accompanied by the dogs; for, after all, she was going to be my mother-in-law.

Emotionally this was an extremely difficult period for me, in particular the moment when I had to give notice that I would be leaving my little flat in Chelsea – which I regarded as symbolic of a natural emancipation that had enriched the whole meaning of my life.

The ceaseless preparations, combined with the burdensome need to give up my precious flat, must have taken their toll on me, for one day my mother said rather anxiously, 'Darling, you look worn out. I think you should take a week's holiday before Jimmy gets back.'

I felt quite alarmed. Surely one should not look 'worn out' at the prospect of getting married? Nevertheless, the word 'holiday' prompted me to start scanning the Personal Column of *The Times*, and before long I saw an advertisement which caught my interest: there was a room to be let in a castle near Nice that had once belonged to the Royal Family of Yugoslavia. Now it was run as a private hotel but still standing in its own palatial grounds and only a short distance from the sea! I had always longed to go to France and now, at last, perhaps the moment had actually arrived to see, and smell, the country of my ancestors, and even perhaps to learn to speak in the French way. I was elated by the prospect. It would compensate in some way for the imminent loss of my little flat in Chelsea.

Plans were soon made, and I even remembered to search out my ancient and little-used bathing-costume. Then I set off for Nice in a state of high excitement, enjoying a smooth passage across the Channel before starting on the long train journey south from Calais. All day I sat up watching the green, open and sometimes extravagantly wooded countryside flash by. Rivers danced in the sunlight and, as the hours wore on, little mountains began to peer at me from the far distance. Paradoxically, as we drew further south, there was even an occasional glimpse of snow on a distant peak. With a picnic to refresh me, I continued staring out at this strange and beautiful land until, with the fall of darkness, I had a sense of the approaching Mediterranean as I sat dozing intermittently in my corner seat, propped against the window.

I awoke to a sunlit landscape: splashed in colour and untrammelled in outline; and later, between the hills, came quick glimpses of what just had to be the sea!

On arrival in Nice I looked out for a man with a flower in his buttonhole who was supposed to be meeting me. I saw him at once, tall, dark and sporting a red rose. He took my suitcase and led me to a minibus into which he helped me, and then we drove along the main road from Nice in the direction of the castle. The sea stretched out on my left, serene and completely untroubled, with tiny white waves looking as if they had been crocheted on to the bright blue hem of the vast expanse of water. The man who was driving did not talk much, for which I was grateful.

Then, finally, we turned in at an imposing gateway, and I could see a turreted country house standing at the end of a long tree-bordered drive. At the door a woman was waiting to meet us. She must have been about forty years old and, to my surprise, she was English; in fact, in appearance and manner she reminded me of a school-mistress. She took me up a grand, curving staircase to my bedroom. It was rather small, but it was papered with patterned satin on the walls and it had a large window overlooking the smooth lawns below, with truant trees dotted here and there on the closely cropped grass.

Downstairs, the same standard of affluence prevailed: the drawing-room was enormous, with a large grand piano and huge windows which allowed access to the luxuriant gardens.

'Lunch will be served between one and two,' said the school-mistress type formally.

'Oh, I'd like to stretch my legs first,' I replied, and was aware of an easing in her mood.

I strolled up the long drive and across the road to the sandy beach nearby. People lay stretched out sunbathing, so I did the same. It was wonderful to feel so free and to be able to enjoy the warmth of this astoundingly friendly sun and not to have to escape from it, as in the East. I must have slept for several hours in this atmosphere of total relaxation, for it was a coolness in the air which awakened me. I looked at my watch. No wonder I was feeling hungry. It would soon be dinner-time! I jumped up and quickly made my way back to the castle. As I walked up the drive I heard sounds of music coming from the drawing-room. Rather uncertainly I went in. It was filled with men, foreigners even to France, and they were all either singing or playing with abandon. I hesitated and then was approached by one of the men. He spoke broken English and explained that they were all Russian aristocrats. They had escaped from Russia after the war and found their way to France. They all lived in disused railway carriages which had been dumped in a field outside the town. Oh, there was plenty of work available here – reading gas meters, acting as attendants at the bathing centres, waiting in the restaurants – and in the evening, whenever possible, they all gathered in the castle to sing their Russian songs.

And sing they did. While I and a few other guests were sitting in the dining-room, all at separate tables, eating our evening meal, we could hear the bursts of laughter and song mingling together in the adjoining drawing-room.

There were even fewer guests at breakfast the following morning. No one spoke to me, nor to anyone else so far as I could see. Again I made my way to the sea, and spent the whole day stretched out on the sands in the sun, wearing my bathing-suit. I was very happy: I'd never had a long-term, full-blooded relationship with the sun before. On the third day I was glad to notice that I had acquired a tan. This gave me confidence to have a dip in the placid Mediterranean waters and afterwards I returned to the castle full of a sense of adventure. Then, while combing my long hair in the little bedroom before dinner, I heard bursts of singing come from the garden below. The Russians had spotted me and were singing romantic songs in Russian, all addressed to their 'princess'! Considering their abandoned and extradited situation, I nearly wept.

On the third day I bought myself some oil to rub on to my exposed body as I saw everybody else doing on the beach. But when I returned to the castle for lunch I was amazed to see four police cars, and a police van, drawn up in line in the drive. To my frightened imagination, police seemed to fill the whole drive.

I advanced to the front door expecting to be immediately arrested, for I saw a policeman standing in the doorway.

'*Vous restez ici, mademoiselle?*'

'*Oui,*' I answered shakily. '*En vacance.*'

'*Alors . . . vous devez partir avant ce soir . . . tout le monde doit partir . . . nous avons deux personnes dans notre charge.*'

Then, to my horror, I saw the English school-mistress type, together with the tall man who had met me at the station, being hurried past me down the front steps and into the police van. And both were handcuffed!

I wasted no time. I packed my suitcase, thanking heaven that I had bought a return ticket (as was my customary insurance against the uncertain future), and took a taxi to the station. And so, somewhat shaken and totally mystified, I managed to catch a night train back through France, crossed the Channel the following afternoon, and arrived in London late in the evening. There was a letter from Jimmy awaiting me, saying that he was arranging to start his leave from the middle of June – which brought me back down to earth.

Even Major John could hazard only a few vague guesses as to what had prompted the invasion of the castle by the police. Illicit drug transactions? Bankruptcy? Cheating at the gaming tables? Espionage? Improper behaviour of some sort must certainly have led to my hosts' arrest. In any event, although my visit had ended prematurely, and on a rather sinister note, nothing could take the welcome taste of France out of my being.

Answering the front-door bell one morning not long after my French adventure, I found Jimmy standing outside.

'Didn't call you,' he said, smiling. 'Wanted to give you a double surprise.' He looked thinner, even gaunt, and paler; but he was smiling.

We hugged each other. 'Give me all the news,' he said. 'I'm never certain whether all your letters reach me in that blasted place.'

So we sat side by side on the sofa. It felt rather strange, sitting closely together and planning our honeymoon. We had, after all, been separated for many months, and even longer if I omitted my brief visit to the Sudan with Cheffie. I gathered that Jimmy had left his luggage at the United University Club and proposed to go back to his family in Surrey that evening. 'Must try and break the ice somehow,' he said.

So our reunion was brief but Jimmy later reported that he had managed to put a brave face on the discomforts of the Sudan. I only hoped that the Youngs were not all so hale and hearty that they failed to notice the alteration in his appearance.

Jimmy came up to London with his father every day, and either came to see me or went to his tailor, or to his club. We managed one evening out at the Hungaria, and it was after this, when Jimmy had seen me back to my flat and was about to go to his club for the night, that I said to him suddenly, 'Don't you think it would be a good idea for us to sleep together before we get married, rather than after?'

He looked at me in surprise. Then he said quietly, 'No, darling. I don't think that is at all a good idea.'

I didn't argue the point. Then he took me in his arms and kissed me gently on the lips. We clung together as if my suggestion had stirred up new feelings in both of us; then, quietly, we disentangled ourselves. Jimmy gave me one more kiss and I shut the front door of the flat, undressed and got into bed. Absurd as it sounds, at this point I think my virginity had become something of an uneasy stronghold; in fact, it had almost become a matter of common sense that I should discontinue it. But this realisation didn't prevent me from falling fast asleep.

The following morning I woke quite suddenly to find myself filled with a great sense of haste. I dressed 'as if the Devil were after me', as one of our nannies used to say, then, after a hurried breakfast, I dashed outside and hailed a taxi. 'Hanover Square, please.'

I scrambled in and directed the taxi-driver to St George's Church where I was to be married. I jumped out, paid him and went inside. Only a churchwarden was there.

'I want to speak to the vicar, please,' I said rather breathlessly.

'Vicarage next door,' the elderly man said.

I spoke pleadingly. 'Then would you be so very kind as to ask him to come and see me? He is marrying me here in a fortnight's time and I have something very important to ask him.'

The man hesitated. Then he replied, 'All right, lady . . . to oblige.' He smiled at me and left.

Alone in the church I was aware that I was trembling. I hardly seemed to know what I was doing here. All I knew was that I had to be here.

Then I saw the vicar walking towards me up the aisle in his long cassock. 'Well, my child, you are in trouble?' he asked paternally as he stood by my side. 'How can I help?'

My words, which had not been properly thought out, tumbled from me as if of their own accord. 'Well, I – I'm being married here in two weeks' time . . . but I don't think you ought to marry me in your church.'

'Why not, my child?'

There was a pause. Then I blurted out, 'Because I believe in divorce.'

'Divorce!' The vicar stared at me in amazement. 'But surely, my child, this is not the moment to be thinking of divorce.'

'Oh, but it is!' I interrupted. The urgency of my feelings disregarded good manners.

'But you are coming here shortly, to be married presumably to someone whom you love?'

'Yes, of course I am,' I said with some impatience. 'I wouldn't have dreamed of getting married for any other reason.'

'Well, then – '

'But you must understand . . . there are two very important reasons why I really should not be married by you, or anyone else, in a church. First, in the Prayer Book I have to swear both to you and God "To have and to hold till death us do part", haven't I?'

'You do, you do, my child,' the vicar replied quietly. 'And you feel you cannot promise that?'

'Of course I can.' I drew a deep breath. 'But I shan't be meaning what you think I shall be meaning, so in a way I shall be deceiving you.'

'Can you explain a little more clearly?'

'Yes.' I paused, then said hesitatingly, 'Well, Christ didn't believe in bodily death, did He . . . I mean, surely the whole point of the Resurrection was that He transcended physical death? So when I swear "to have and to hold till death us do part" I shall not be meaning the death of the body when one or other of us is popped into a coffin and buried in a grave . . . I shall be alluding to what I consider can also be a very real death in a marriage, namely, the spiritual death of the marital bonds between husband and wife.'

The vicar remained silent, then he asked, 'And the second reason?'

241

'As I've told you, divorce – and I've looked it up in St Matthew's Gospel where Christ and His disciples were discussing just this point together. Christ is reported as saying to the disciples, "Whosoever putteth away his wife, save it be for fornication, committeth adultery." Whereupon the disciples say, with reason as I see it, "Then, Lord, it is not good to marry." To which Christ replied, "All men cannot receive this saying save he to whom it is given: but he that is able to receive it, let him receive it." ' I paused. 'But the one exception made by Christ, namely "except it be for fornication", seems to have been wholly ignored by the Church. And this, surely, is in complete contradiction not only of Christ's words, but also of His whole attitude to love and understanding of man's own human life?'

There was a long silence. Then the vicar said quietly, 'Nevertheless, young lady, I would very much like to marry you in my church.'

'Even after what I have told you?'

'Particularly after what you have told me, and my prayers will go with you. Never forget that.'

The vicar advanced and put his hand on my head. 'Bless you, my child,' he said. Then, making the sign of the Cross, he turned and left me in the church.

So I could be married in church after all. I sat down for a moment in a pew and listened to the silence all around me. It was a silence that was more reassuring than I could ever have imagined, so I sat on. Outside I could hear the distant rumble of traffic and rays of sunlight still filtered through the stained-glass windows, illuminating some of their brightly coloured pictures. Finally my wandering eyes settled on a window depicting Christ nailed to the Cross, His head sunk on His chest from the sheer agony of His endurance. For a few moments I remained with Him: but the anguish of His suffering finally shifted my gaze. Christ must greatly have loved mankind, otherwise He could never have taken upon Himself the agony of 'being', which as He knew, was to lead to His death. Then suddenly I remembered that last, desperate and abandoned cry, 'My God, my God; why hast Thou forsaken me?' And immediately this very cry seemed to me to imply an even deeper and more significant aspect of Christ's physical suffering. Then, it slowly came to me that perhaps, and again through His care for us, Christ had not only taken upon Himself to love, to live and to die for mankind, but also, the better to serve us, He had taken upon Himself something of man's human 'fallibility'; for how else were we to understand the deep agony of that last desperate cry of 'forsakenness' – by God, his own Heavenly Father? Then suddenly quite a new question popped into my mind as if of its own volition: if Christ really had taken upon Himself something of man's 'fallibility', how was it possible for any Christian to regard himself as 'infallible'? Even the jerks of the bus on the way home did not help me to find an answer to that question.

On returning to my flat, my mind was jerked into a very different area of being. I found a letter from my mother, posted the previous day, saying that Uncle Bernard had had a stroke. Aunt Magdalen, greatly distraught, had written to tell her and the details were gruesome. Uncle Bernard had been up at the altar taking the service of Holy Communion when he pitched to the ground, with blood pouring from his mouth and mingling with the 'Blood of Christ' which, of course, had spilled from the chalice with his fall. My mother's letter ended with the suggestion that we should both go down to Aunt Magdalen the following day to see if we could help. She and Uncle Bernard, with their faithful parlourmaid Winifred, had moved from the Vicarage to a small semi-detached house in Maidstone, the nearest town, so as to be close to a doctor and the hospital in the event of my uncle needing treatment.

After reading this letter several times I telephoned my mother and said that of course I would go with her. So the next day we left by train on the familiar holiday journey. We spoke little, pondering instead on the macabre import of Uncle Bernard's collapse. I could not help recalling the occasion when, as a child, I had been rescued from what could have been a dire and totally destructive experience in my uncle's study by the sound of the Voice saying, 'This is man: it has nothing whatsoever to do with God.' Now, jogging along in the train, I found this memory as reassuring as ever. I also wondered to myself whether perhaps the understanding I had of my mother's emotional entanglement with Uncle Bernard might not be more profound even than her own.

On arrival in Maidstone we took a taxi and soon found ourselves outside a little suburban house. Winifred, the parlourmaid, opened the door, her face blurred with recent tears. Then Aunt Magdalen hurried out, lean and lank, with a small dog at her heels as usual. She greeted us with evident relief and then started, without tears, to tell us the whole story while we all three sat in the sitting-room. She concluded by saying, 'And he can't speak a word . . . or won't. Even the doctor thinks he could if he tried.' Suddenly she turned to me. 'Perhaps he might speak to someone younger . . . would you go in and try, Ingaret? He is only next door. He can never leave that room, of course . . . but he might speak to you.'

I felt I had no choice, so I rose reluctantly, went out and quietly opened the door of the adjoining room. The sight of Uncle Bernard at

243

the far end, sitting in his pyjamas and dressing-gown on what looked like an enormous commode, gave me a tremendous shock. He had grown a long white straggling beard which hung down until it covered his crotch, and above it, his glassy blue eyes stared out unblinkingly, without movement, into nothing. They carried no feeling – if feeling was still possible for Uncle Bernard – or intelligence within them; they just kept on staring out blankly.

'Hello, Uncle Bernard,' I faltered. He made not the slightest movement. I tried again once or twice, but still there was no response. It was as if 'nothingness' occupied the whole room; until in the end I turned resolutely and left.

'Did he speak?' Aunt Magdalen asked immediately.

I shook my head. I felt shattered. Could there actually exist an area which was 'nothing'?

Perhaps my mother sensed my unease. 'Can we see over the rest of the house?' she asked.

So we went upstairs. 'Only two up and two down,' said Aunt Magdalen. 'And this is the only bedroom: the other room is filled with things that I brought from the Vicarage.'

Her bedroom had in it a large double bed and a dressing-table by the window. At the bottom of the double bed was a sofa, the kind which you could sit up in, lean your head against, and then stretch out both your legs, but without ever being able to lie flat. It was simply not large enough.

'Winifred sleeps on that,' Aunt Magdalen said airily, indicating the sofa. At the time it struck me that the devoted parlourmaid would have to endure an extremely uncomfortable night's rest. In retrospect, I feel sure that mistress and maid must have shared the same double bed.

After an early tea my mother and I left to go back to our separate homes. Again we hardly spoke to each other on the train. We were both thoroughly shaken by the whole experience, although at least my mother had been spared the experience of seeing Uncle Bernard. As for me, a rather odd question kept repeating itself in my mind: whom, I wondered, did Uncle Bernard hate the most – his wife, who apparently without difficulty had sarcastically condoned his sexual excesses; my mother, who herself had almost fatally and hypnotically become entangled in them; or me, who, as a child, had physically both overcome and evaded him? Because, as I saw it, only hate could turn one's world into a 'nothing'.

Back in London that night I was glad to go out dancing with Jimmy. It took a very nasty taste from the far past out of my mouth.

27

Escape

Early in July 1931, when I was in my late twenties, Jimmy and I were married. I did not find it a very exciting occasion although most of my contemporaries, whose overriding aim was 'to get married', had been ecstatic even when they became engaged. This made me wonder if I were somehow abnormal. Even the fact that it was a very smart wedding, with a reception in a beautiful private town house, failed to impress me. Now that I had had my talk with the vicar and had dispersed the religious lump on my conscience, I felt quite calm; and, of course, I felt happy to be with Jimmy. Our relationship had lasted for some years on and off, and I knew him to be a caring and sensitive person. When he heard about my abruptly curtailed holiday, he had insisted that we should go to France for our honeymoon. 'And I'll see that this time you don't run into the police,' he had said with one of his happy smiles.

So he borrowed one of the family cars and we motored to the South of France, which was in full season. The sandy beaches were filled with people, all sun-bathing and swimming in the contented sea. Jimmy and I joined them. I still could not swim but I splashed about and got tanned, while Jimmy swam around and watched the beautiful, scantily clad women all around us with such amused interest that I found myself wondering whether our marital intimacy had failed to satisfy him. Then I reproached myself for being unduly curious. I had always found the term 'idle curiosity' to be a well-matched phrase; and I disliked both the adjective and the noun.

Also, I had to come to terms with more immediate problems: Jimmy's leave was shorter than I had thought. We had to be back in the Sudan by early October – which was when the 'cool' weather was supposed to start.

'I thought you had longer leave every year?'

'So we do, normally.' Jimmy let the sand trickle through his long fingers back on to the beach, but his eyes were fixed on an almost naked brunette lying on the sand a few yards away from us. 'But for me this counted as compassionate leave.'

'Why compassionate?'

'In order to get married, of course.' He grinned.

I had heard of the phrase in India but it had always been in relation to illness. My stepfather, for instance, had had compassionate leave when he stayed on in Naini Tal to be with my mother when she had enteric.

'It's such a funny word to use in relation to a wedding.'

Jimmy made no reply, for his interest was elsewhere. So I had time to reflect on the thoughts which the word 'compassionate' had aroused in me. I was aware that something that could be called 'compassion' had always played a large role in my relationships with other people, including Jimmy. I had always felt that I understood the real Jimmy in a way that other people, including his own family, did not. But had this been presumption on my part? Or even a misjudgement? On consideration, I thought not. From our first meeting Jimmy had made no secret of his weakness for the opposite sex. And I myself was equally susceptible to men. During my four years in India I had been surrounded by them. I had had quite a few proposals of marriage; and I had always been gentle in my refusals, for I had realised that it was simply a question of demand exceeding supply. In consequence I had grown to understand men in a way that I had not yet found possible with women. And, of course, since childhood I had both known and lived out a most profound compassion for my mother. The thought suddenly occurred to me that perhaps our marriage was based too much on compassion and not enough on passion.

I was brought back to the present by Jimmy pulling me up from where I lay on the sand. 'Come on, darling,' he said. 'It's damned hot here. Let's take a walk along the prom and have a spot of exercise.'

We strode off along the seafront, keeping close to the placid waves which seemed almost to be dozing, so comforted and cradled were they by the brilliant evening sunset, and then made our way back to the hotel to freshen up before changing for dinner.

Our room was on the sixth floor of the hotel, facing directly towards the sea. There was a deep drop from our window to the ground below and, in the interests of safety, stout iron bars had been firmly fixed across it. On arriving back at the hotel, Jimmy went straight to the bathroom. 'Mind if I have the first bath?' he called out.

I told him to go ahead and strolled over to our enormous window.

The sky was still brilliant, blushing deeply as the sun, with shy delight, was preparing to drop slowly into the outstretched arms of the waiting sea. I wondered whether their unity was one of passion or compassion! I stood there for quite a long time considering this question and watching the sunset, which I loved both for its heavenly glory and also for its human acceptability.

Then, slowly, unwillingly, I turned back to our bedroom – but came to an abrupt halt. I was not in our bedroom at all! I was in some prison cell! I could see the black prison bars quite clearly, regularly spaced, straight in front of me. The evidence was right there, unmistakable, absolute: I was indeed a prisoner in a cell, and the horror of it seized hold of me. I burst into tears – tears of such violence that they had to be muffled by the pillows as I threw myself on to our bed. When at last I had mastered them and raised myself in the bed, I realised that the black bars on the white walls of our bedroom were merely the reflections in the brilliant sunset of the bars across our window. Even so, the experience itself had been totally authentic. But why? I could never find the answer. Equally I could never forget the deadly reality of those few moments of terrifying captivity. As time passed I was able to ask myself, was it hysteria? Was it hypochondria? Most terrifying of all, was it a premonition of some kind? I never mentioned this extraordinary and horrifying experience to anyone, not even to Jimmy.

We stretched out our honeymoon in France for as long as funds permitted and arrived back in England at the end of August. Almost immediately, or so it seemed, we were sucked into the fierce incoming tide of all the sundry details attached to our joint return to life in the Sudan. First, I had to arrange for my new, unpolished Gordon Russell oak furniture – a sideboard, dining-table and two chairs – to be crated out to the Sudan. I also had to search out my old Indian 'sola topee' to take with me: the very sight of it brought back my distaste for the voracious tropical sun. Gradually my trunks filled with easily disposable clothes, for the sweat and the heat did not give anything a very long life. We spent a final weekend with Jimmy's parents and the atmosphere was (or so I thought) idiotically cheerful. I put that down to the fact that Jimmy had not only got a job, but was keeping it. However, when we visited my mother for our last weekend before sailing she was very quiet although emotionally controlled. She had not forgotten my accounts of the Sudan after my first visit there with Cheffie, but she said nothing.

And so I embarked on my second journey to that desert land. By now the trip through the Mediterranean was no longer a novelty but the gently varying moods of any sea were always a delight to me. This time

Jimmy was in charge and on arrival he arranged all the details for our further travelling. We left the ship at Alexandria, caught a train for Shalal, and then boarded a riverboat and made passage down the Nile to Wadi Halfa, where we embarked on the long and slow train journey to Khartoum. And each day the monster sun glared down on us as if in triumph.

Before returning to England Jimmy had garaged his car – now a Model-T Ford Roadster with a canvas top – in Khartoum. He put it through various tests, all of which seemed to satisfy him, and off we started on the hundred-mile drive to the bungalow. As we jolted along the same route we had travelled with Cheffie asleep behind us only a matter of months before, my calm and stoical friend was uppermost in my thoughts . . . for, sadly, in the middle of my wedding preparations, I had heard that Cheffie was not only very ill but dying. I had gone at once to visit her in the nursing home. She recognised me immediately and managed to raise her hand to mine. 'I've often thought of our voyage,' she whispered. 'I'm so grateful to you. Do you know, that was the only time I've ever been away from England in my whole life.' And she sank back on to her pillows. It was not long afterwards that I heard she had died. I was thankful that I had stayed for quite a long time just holding her hand, for I knew that silence between us was as easily shared as words. She was a great and devout woman.

Stepping out of the car before the familiar bungalow, behind which the sun was only now beginning to set, I gave one glance round the everlastingly flat desert. The sight of it so depressed me that I turned blindly and went back to the car in a moment of panic.

Jimmy took my arm. 'Let's go in together,' he said. 'It begins to cool down about now.'

Our luggage was brought into the bungalow and I sat down in a canvas chair. So far as I can remember there was not even a *punkah* to disturb the hot, leaden air. But Jimmy was right, for after I had sat motionless for some time, the sun, with an affectation of good will, sank slowly in the white-faced sky and we were left alone.

We had arrived in mid-October, and even though we would be returning to England in the spring, when Jimmy had his first 'long leave', this was not much comfort to me because the sameness of the days gave one little sense of the passage of time. The only variation was in the temperature, which grew steadily hotter.

Just before dawn Jimmy would slip out of bed beside me on the verandah, dress, mount his horse and ride round miles and miles of cotton growth, supervising the poor, bony, Sudanese workers already bent over their varying, or perhaps unvarying, tasks. I would watch him until he became a mere exclamation mark silhouetted against the sky already rosy with birth, and then disappeared. That was my great morning activity. Very occasionally, a man on horseback would appear outside the bungalow. Without dismounting he and I would have perhaps ten minutes of conversation. He was a pleasant and intelligent man but I was always careful not to say anything derogatory about the Sudan and the existence within it which, with incredible exaggeration, was called 'life', for I knew that this man was in charge of the whole Sudan enterprise; he was therefore Jimmy's boss. He was also, I discovered later, a distant relation of Ramsay MacDonald, the then Prime Minister of England.

From him I learned that it was the British – the pioneers of successful irrigation schemes in India – who had been inspired to think up a similar scheme for the Sudan, which had previously been open desert country with no natural resources whatsoever. A great barrage had been built across the Nile in order to trap the floodwaters on which the agricultural life of Egypt depended. These floodwaters were then directed into a vast system of canals which created an island of productive soil. And with unimaginable patience and persistence this island had been turned into a vast cotton-growing area under the order and direction of young men from England. Jimmy arrived at a period when the Gezira, this island of intensive growth in the middle of the largest desert on earth, was at its most productive. And it had to be seen to be believed. But it also had to be endured, and demanded powers of endurance beyond the imagination and experience of ordinary English people. However, as I lived to learn, there were many Englishmen who were glad to be associated with this remarkable and imaginative Empire scheme. The Sudanese people also welcomed it, for hundreds of them were now employed in the cotton fields. So from every angle it was a success story.

What to do with my days? I told myself that, surely, these were the ideal conditions in which to write: total and absolute silence, with only one interruption in the day, namely, Jimmy's return for a brief lunch. But things did not work out like that. Somehow the hot lifeless desert without spawned a similar inactive desert within, which could not be artificially irrigated into fertility. My imagination was manacled by the extreme heat: sometimes even to lift a spoon and fork to my mouth at meal-times seemed too great an effort. I began to fear that I was going mad when such thoughts entered my head. Then, reassuringly, I remembered that I had had heatstroke in India immediately on arrival there. Perhaps that had weakened my resistance to these similar conditions?

So instead, I channelled my depleted energies into letter-writing. I wrote once a week to the Youngs, and daily to my mother. But the weekly post-bag carried two very different types of letter. The letters to my mother contained affection and deliberate reassurance as to my situation. The letters to the Youngs told of the meaninglessness of the passing days; and of the danger of sunstroke, dysentery and malaria. But even as I wrote I knew that the Youngs were so full of the radiance of outdoor health that these hazards would be looked upon by them merely as 'Ingaret's hysteria'. I wrote of Jimmy's simple qualities of application and endurance, and questioned whether this experience was to be either the betrayal, or the test, of them. I wrote of the open-mouthed hours in the daily clock of life from which came no nourishment and no related relevance to the passing time. Only the sun existed in strength; and it was without mercy. Was this the pattern, I wrote, on which Jimmy was to base not only his young life but also his whole existence? I never wrote about myself; and I never personally complained. I wrote to the Youngs every week for many months, but they never replied to my letters. Sometimes I wondered whether they even read them. Perhaps, seeing the same foreign stamp, they just destroyed them unopened?

Sometimes I also wondered how the other wives felt, but I do not remember meeting any of them. The Syndicate bungalows were situated with vast distances between each, the better to supervise the huge area of cotton growth, which stretched north, east, south and west. Despite the Youngs' lack of response, I continued to write to them in rebellion against this hazardous and sterile existence. On one occasion, I even wrote and asked my mother if she could convey to Jimmy's father the suggestion that, being a man of influence in the City, he might manage to find a small corner somewhere for his younger son which would destroy neither Jimmy nor his fond links with his family. I heard some months later that my mother had had an interview with Mr Young but that it had proved abortive.

And so the months passed into forgetfulness: they changed their names but nothing else. I did not even become pregnant. And it struck me that when, and if, I did, it would mean almost total separation between Jimmy and me for many years to come, for a child could not be brought up in the Sudan. Whereas in India there had been easy communications and splendid doctors and hospitals, both civil and military, as well as the 'hills' to which one could go for recuperation, none of these amenities were to be found in the endless miles of desolation in the Gezira. Sometimes I even wondered if the reason why I had not become pregnant could be due to our confined circumstances. Yet caged animals could mate and bring forth their young, surely? I did not really know, and after a time I became too listless to care.

Privately, I prayed that some chance event would occur which would prevent our ever coming back to the Sudan after our approaching leave. My pregnancy, of course, would be such an event. Sometimes I would trick myself into mental acceptance of the present by such words as loyalty, self-sacrifice, stoicism, but I soon saw through the pretence. Life was given one to live; and I was going to live it, no matter what the cost, and so was Jimmy. He was a cheerful person and made light of much, but he was thinner . . . and he had occasional stomach trouble . . . and his smile was not so ready.

At long last, towards the end of March, we started to prepare for our legitimate return to England. Then Jimmy had a brainwave. 'Why don't we motor back?' he asked suddenly.

'What in?' I asked.

'Our car, of course,' Jimmy answered.

I nearly laughed but then I recalled that the Model-T Ford Roadster had certainly dealt with the chunky, unmarked desert tracks like a professional. If we sank into desert holes its determined wheels, together with Jimmy's expert handling, would somehow manage to surmount the slippery, seductive sands even though there were no large rocks or stones to put behind the back wheels.

'How far would we have to drive before we reached the Red Sea?' I asked.

Jimmy shrugged his shoulders. 'A good bit more than a hundred miles,' he said.

I was somewhat taken aback. I could see us as castaways not on a desert island, but in an open desert with no possible communication with the outside world, and only our dear, battered old Ford as representing salvation. 'Where would we sleep?' I asked.

'Well, we could sleep in the car perhaps, or on the sand . . . and I believe there are a couple of District Commissioners in bungalows somewhere between us and the Red Sea,' Jimmy said airily. 'We could stop off at one of them and they could put us up for the night.'

I felt relieved. 'Can we warn the D Cs about our coming?' I asked.

Jimmy shook his head. 'Not easy,' he said. 'But nobody minds other people turning up unexpectedly out here . . . in fact they rather like it . . . makes a change.'

'And when we get to the sea, what about the car?' I asked.

'I've already booked a cabin for two, fourth-class, in an Italian ship, and I've said I'll be bringing a car aboard. I've bought a couple of new spare tyres, of course, which should see us through if we motor back through Europe. Then we'll take the car across the Channel . . . and drive home.'

He looked at me inquiringly.

Suddenly the whole idea became real and even exciting . . . although the last phrase rather chilled me. Where *was* home now that we were married?

'I think it sounds fun,' I said, and then I paused before adding, 'Have you mentioned it to anybody else?'

'Oh, yes,' Jimmy said. 'I've asked around.'

'And what do other people think?'

'Oh, they think I'm quite mad,' Jimmy said with a grin. 'You see, there is only one train a week which goes across the desert to the Red Sea. And once the rains start even that can't run. But going by car we can set off a bit earlier and I reckon we can get across in ample time to avoid the rains.'

I could see no flaws in the argument. The project sounded a bit risky but nevertheless I was thrilled. It really would be a tremendous adventure.

'Then let's do it, Jimmy,' I laughed. And so, rather earlier in March than was customary, we started off in our little car, with our two suitcases in the boot and the two new tyres enthroned on the back seat.

We spent the first night partly in the car and partly on the sand. How Jimmy ever found his way remained a mystery. But he had taken certain bearings, and somehow he knew how to keep on driving eastward; and we didn't talk at all, for I could see that he was totally concentrating on finding our individual passage through the impersonal desert. At the end of the second day, we spotted a sort of eruption in the far distance. And as we bumped and slid our way nearer to it we saw that it was indeed a bungalow . . . with the Union Jack flying, or rather flopping, upon the roof. Thankfully we drew up and were welcomed by the District Commissioner and his wife. We'd made it . . . or rather Jimmy had! For almost immediately on arrival I collapsed. I don't think I was completely unconscious, for I remember being put to bed with all the blinds drawn and a fan breathing lightly above my head. I even heard the word 'heatstroke' and tried to open my eyes. Someone noticed the effort, for a man's voice shouted, 'Ever had it before?'

I nodded, and then lost consciousness.

I came round a day or two later but only to find that Jimmy had vanished! Panic arose in me . . . but a kindly servant, who had obviously been put on watch, rose and fetched the D C's wife, who hurried in.

'It's all right, dear,' she said, taking my sweating hand. 'Quite, quite all right. Your husband has left in the car to make sure he reached the coast before the rains start.'

Seeing my look of alarm and horror she patted my hand. 'Don't worry, dear . . . we've arranged everything with your husband. We're going to take care of you for a further week or so and then you'll have got over this wretched heatstroke, which I understand you've had before?'

I nodded, my eyelids were drooping. 'India,' I muttered.

'Badly?'

I nodded. Then the darkness closed down again. Only the faint sound of the fan moving the air reached me. I lay with icepacks here and there, and was grateful for the gentle God-given movement of air on my cheeks.

After four or five days I felt better. I heard voices coming from the front verandah . . . and laughter. Heavens, could people still laugh in this ghastly country? The sound aroused me and feebly I began to sit up, get up . . .

My hostess hurried in. 'I heard you were moving,' she said. 'Clever girl! Would you like to join us?'

I shook my head. I pointed to the blessed fan whirling above my head and sending its moving air into the heavy heat. I felt I could never leave that boisterous but life-giving contraption.

My hostess understood. Then she said hesitatingly, 'Shall I tell you our plans?'

I nodded, feeling grateful, and even able to listen and to understand.

'In three days' time the weekly train passes quite close to us here, so we will take you in our car to the nearest halting place and put you on that train, which is going to the Red Sea. We'll start at about five o'clock in the morning . . . and then, about six hours later, your husband will meet the train at Port Sudan. He's been in touch with us. Your ship doesn't sail till about five o'clock that same evening, so that will give you plenty of time to arrive, meet him, and he will take you and settle you in your cabin before the ship sails.'

It all sounded feasible, possibly even wonderful. I smiled, only half taking in the plans. The main point was that I had only three days in which to get well. After that, cars and trains and Jimmy would take over. I got back into bed, closed my eyes, then put out my hand to my hostess, said 'Thank you', and again fell asleep.

I spent the remaining days sleeping or resting. Reading, of course, was quite impossible, but the welcome prospect of escaping from the Sudan occasionally penetrated the haze of my mental confusion. On the fourth morning, before sunrise, my kind host and hostess helped me into my cotton knickers and sleeveless cotton dress and gave me my dark glasses and my tiny suitcase, for Jimmy had taken all the other luggage. Thankfully, at five o'clock in the morning one could breathe. When we reached the railway halt we got out and stood in the shade of a hut until, eventually, puffing laboriously across the desert, we saw the idiosyncratic sight of a stout railway engine creaking and jerking its way towards us and pulling behind it a scatter of carriages! I was helped into a first-class compartment which was empty. It was still quite dark but now there was just a suggestion of sunrise across the distant sky.

'You're due at midday in Port Sudan,' called out my kind hostess as she waved me off.

I moved to the shady side of the carriage and looked at my watch. Only hours to go, then Jimmy and I would be off and away! I couldn't fill in the time reading because I knew this would give me a terrible headache, so, with nothing but the bleak and featureless desert outside, I turned my attention to the face of my watch and sat counting the minutes as they passed. I think I must have been the only European in that weekly train, for I had the carriage to myself and I saw no other passengers during the entire journey.

Suddenly, after about an hour of clock-watching, there was an enormous jolt . . . and the train came to a juddering halt. Pushing down the window and daring the heat of the sun, I looked along the railway line and saw that the wheels of the engine were standing in water which had flooded not only the track but parts of the surrounding desert as well. I sank back on to my seat with my knees shaking. The rains! The rains had overtaken us, or rather me, and I knew that that meant we might be trapped for days in this ghastly morass.

At that moment my carriage door was abruptly opened and the Sudanese guard stood before me. Not speaking much English, he flung his arms apart in a gesture of despair.

'What's happened?' I cried futilely. 'Has the train broken down?'

He understood the word 'train'. He shook his head. Then he came to my window and pointed to the sky. 'Water,' he said.

My fears confirmed, I began to think about the predicament Jimmy and I were in. Would the rains cause us to miss our ship after all? How would Jimmy find out what had happened to me? And even if he did find out, what could he do about it? Then it struck me that if the rains could stop a train, a car would not have any chance whatsoever. Or had Jimmy perhaps managed to get across the desert before the rains started?

I stood up and held out my wristwatch to the guard, and pointed to the figure 12 (our official time of arrival). Then I pointed to 1, 2, 3, 4, 5, 6 . . . and with an expressive gesture asked, 'When?'

The guard understood. But he shrugged his shoulders. Then he went and leaned out of the window and looked down the waterlogged line towards the engine. Then he turned, shrugged his shoulders again and pointed hesitantly to the figure five on my wristwatch. What did that mean? Five hours' delay? Or that five o'clock would be our time of arrival – in which case there would only be an hour before our ship left Port Sudan? Just then the train gave a sudden jerk forward. Haltingly we were on the move again.

The guard bowed and departed. I went to my suitcase and took out the bananas and one of the iced water bottles which my kind hostess had provided. I spent the next four hours concentrating on the movement of the hands of my watch and somehow the discipline of this helped to steady my nerves. Finally dusk fell and began to turn to darkness, and I could now see a few faint, distant spots of light. Port Sudan? When the guard came along to collect my suitcase I knew that it must be so! I jumped to my feet – and nearly fell. I sat down again. The lights grew brighter . . . and they turned out to be lamp-posts along a road. And then on that same road I saw two bright moving lights, getting closer, the headlights of a car. I prayed that it might be Jimmy in our old Ford. And it was! When the train drew into Port Sudan, Jimmy was there on the platform to meet me and, clutching my suitcase, we hurried off. And Jimmy didn't even forget to tip the guard; he was that sort of person.

'Quick,' he said, taking my arm. 'They're holding the ship for us for the next half-hour.'

I didn't ask any questions. I just sat dumbly beside him as we shot through the darkness. Then he took my arm and the suitcases and we tottered up the gangway.

'I've changed our cabin from fourth-class to third-class,' he said gently. 'Fourth-class we'd have had to cook our own food.' He settled me down in a bunk in a cabin. 'Stay here till I get back,' he said. 'I've got to get the car aboard.'

I remember little of that sea journey to Genoa except the chugging of the ship's engines . . . or was it the train's? I didn't really know. I think I must have slept for most of the short voyage, for I can recall nothing else besides meals on a tray which were brought to my cabin, the whirring of the fan, and the slight movement and sound of the sea . . . which soothed me beyond belief. Jimmy was in constant attendance and made no effort at conversation, which I think would have exhausted me. He merely repeated now and again, 'Well, we've made it.' And that, together with the murmur of the sea, was all I needed to be told.

We reached Genoa in the middle of April. We had neither of us discussed the European aspect of our 'long leave', I think because, without admitting it to ourselves, we both rather dreaded our arrival in England. We both sensed the difficulties that might arise with Jimmy's homecoming. Or was it only my letters that his parents had resented and so ignored? However, my apprehensions evaporated as soon as we started our slow and delightful dawdle northwards from Genoa. Our beloved Model-T Ford Roadster, now washed and polished, looked as good as new. But Jimmy examined the canvas top with a certain anxiety. 'A crack or two,' he said. 'Must be the sun that's rotted it.'

But I felt hilarious. 'What does it matter?' I laughed. 'I can't think of anything better than sitting in the front seat beside you with the rain pattering down on my face!'

Jimmy grinned. 'I can,' he said. Then he took me in his arms and kissed me . . . and so we set off. I found the whole casual journey through Europe fantastically beautiful. Then suddenly I had a brainwave.

'Jimmy!' I said. 'We may be short of cash when we get home.' I knew that Jimmy earned a good wage as an 'Empire-builder', but I also knew that money had a conjuror's capacity for simply vanishing. 'Yes, it really could be a brainwave. Suppose every day I make continual notes and you take photographs of all the marvellous mountains, and rivers, and things we see. Then, on arrival, I'll write my notes into an article and send it to the Ford Motor Company and they might decide to use it as a sort of advertisement for their car! And it would give us something to keep as a reminder of the journey!'

Even after the ship docked in Dover, we put off answering the question that I am sure had been uppermost in both our minds as we journeyed north through Europe: whose family did we visit first? Then I noticed that the road we would have had to take if we had been going to Jimmy's home had been bypassed; but it was only some miles later that he said quietly, 'I think we'll go and call on your mother first: she may be worrying.'

It was the sort of thing that Jimmy would think of, and I was greatly relieved to be able at once to alleviate my mother's fears.

So finally our heroic little Ford turned in at the familiar drive gates. I could see my mother sitting in the garden waiting for us, still doing her tapestry work! As Jimmy drew up by the front door, we both ran and embraced my mother with laughter that was close to tears. She told me afterwards that, despite her joy at our arrival, momentarily her heart sank at the sight of the Ford-T Roadster.

'The last time I saw you in a motorcar was in a Rolls-Royce driving away from your wedding reception. Seeing you both in that battered little two-seater with the holes in the canvas roof was a strange contrast!'

But as she kissed us both she was laughing gaily. Then Jimmy asked if he could ring up his family. I didn't envy him.

28

I Did Not Know the Answer

The return home was a test for both Jimmy and me. With only five months before we were due to return to the Sudan at the end of September, I told myself that there wasn't much time to waste. After we had left my mother we spent an uneasy few days with Jimmy's family, then we went up to London, ostensibly to see friends, but actually to look for jobs for both of us. I sent off to Ford Motors the article written about our journey home from the Sudan, for which they paid me quite well; and daily Jimmy hovered round the offices of friends that he had made at Oxford, or at his parents' home, hoping to be offered a job, but without much success. He got an occasional bite which, after tasting, he finally spat out. One of such offers had been that of working in a West End restaurant as a trainee chef!

Then my old friend Eric Farmer rang up and asked me out to lunch at his club. I was delighted and counted on finding understanding and alliance with him. But this was not to be.

'Ingaret, my dear, you're taking a very serious step in influencing Jimmy to give up his job,' he said gravely, as we started the first course.

'I'm not influencing him. We are merely supporting each other,' I replied.

'But you are the stronger character,' he persisted.

'Strength of character is not expressed merely by trying to get one's own way,' I answered.

It was quite like the old days, when conversation between us had been both free and open.

'But Jimmy has got a good job,' Eric continued.

I interrupted. 'Jimmy has got one hell of a job,' I said. 'He has certainly got a job that pays him a good wage, but that doesn't mean he has a good job in relation to life. In fact, in the Sudan, there is no life.

There is just desolate existence, which also will mean countless lengthy separations between us during the hot weather each year.'

'But if you had children – ' Eric suggested tentatively.

'Then life together would be quite impossible,' I replied. 'No baby, and no child, could ever be taken out to that climate. So if I did have a child it would mean almost total separation between Jimmy and me.' I paused. 'But, happily, as yet that event has not occurred.'

'But you want children, presumably?'

'Actually, I don't really mind either way. But if I did find myself pregnant I could never return to the Sudan.' I paused. 'So, as you must see, the Sudan is just a short-term project . . . and the sooner the two of us can get out of it the better . . . while Jimmy is still young and can lay claim to work-experience and can also produce and use good references.'

Eric sat silent. Without ever mentioning the matter, we had dealt with the question of contraception to his satisfaction. He then said thoughtfully, 'It is interesting that there are certain tribes in the East where, when a drought descends upon them, the women all become infertile: consequently they have to wait for the rains to come before they can become pregnant again.'

'I congratulate them,' I said dryly. And then we both laughed.

We parted after this, to me, somewhat disappointing meeting. Eric seemed incapable of understanding that the Sudan simply could not be viewed as a long-term project and that consequently the sooner Jimmy found another job the better. Only my mother seemed to appreciate our predicament. But she, unfortunately, had no influence in the business world in which Jimmy was concentrating his searches.

During the following week or two, while Jimmy was doing the rounds of his friends in London, I remained in our room in the Kensington boarding-house where we were staying, scanning the columns of the newspapers which advertised jobs and stumbling over the outline of the play that I had started writing before my marriage. On fine days I sat out in Stanhope Gardens writing on my knee, and the hours seemed to fly by. It would be an exaggeration to say that I was happy. The shadow of our uncertain future fell across each page as I wrote it. But no shadow could really obscure the fascination of each new situation as it arose seemingly from the very nib of my pen. I was so absorbed in *Because We Must* that when Jimmy returned in the evenings, his face shrunken with gloom, I never asked him any questions. The look on his face gave me the negative news: no job had been offered.

At the weekends, almost gratefully, we spent the time either with

Jimmy's family or with mine. My mother, with her infinite understanding, tried her best to be encouraging, but during the weekends we spent with the Youngs the one sensitive subject was our future, and I was very aware that it was I, not Jimmy, who was looked upon as the culprit . . . perhaps because I was three years older than he and 'should have known better'. All I could do was hold my tongue, go for long walks in the countryside, and let Jimmy try to wheedle his way round the problem.

Inexorably, the day we were due to return to the Sudan drew nearer and nearer. We had booked a cabin in the ship that was to take us east; we had booked seats in the train that was to take us to Southampton; we had even booked a double room in a small hotel near Victoria Station, where we would be starting our journey. Our trunks were packed and labelled. We had asked no one to see us off from Victoria, not even my mother. I felt the strain for all of us would be too much. Instead we visited our respective families to make our brave farewells and, at the Youngs', had to contend with such infuriating parting remarks as, 'Lucky you, going back to the sunshine!' . . . 'We envy you that outdoor life!' We both kept our cool and held our tongues.

On arrival at our hotel we silently settled in for the night. Neither of us had much to say. The horrid fact was that I now felt myself to be an outsider from both Jimmy's worlds: that of the Sudan and also that of his family. There was a time when we would have gone dancing at the Hungaria to lighten our spirits, but those days were over. Instead we went to bed very early because Jimmy said he was tired. Then, next morning, when I drew back the curtains, I saw that he was looking very flushed and yet had a strange, haggard look that was new to me and alien to him.

'D'you feel all right, darling?' I asked anxiously.

'Feel a bit sick,' he said uncertainly.

I searched for my thermometer – since going to India I had always carried one in my sponge-bag, no matter where I was going – and at once I took Jimmy's temperature: it was 103 degrees! Suddenly I was very frightened, but I knew what to do: ever since childhood there had been various kinds of illness, both visible and invisible, with which I had had to deal. In consequence, when living in London, I had always had the name of a really good GP written in my notebook.

I rang him at once. 'Dr Wood . . . sorry to disturb you so early . . . it's Ingaret calling . . . Ingaret Giffard that was . . . now I'm married, I'm Mrs Young, staying at the Little Green Hotel near Victoria Station. My husband has a very high temperature . . . 103 degrees . . . and we're due to leave for the East in a few hours. Could you be a dear and come along and tell me what is wrong with him?'

Dr Wood and I had always been friends, quite apart from our medical relationship, so within the hour he had arrived and was attending to Jimmy. When he came out of our bedroom he looked very grave.

'No question of his travelling,' he told me outside the bedroom door. 'I think he's got amoebic dysentery . . . but he must certainly go to the Hospital for Tropical Diseases for a thorough diagnosis. Even if it is only bacterial dysentery he would have to go to hospital with that high temperature.' He paused. 'Because of it I would prefer him to go in an ambulance. Don't want him to get any complications . . . so I'll ring the hospital from here, now, if I may.'

I was dumbfounded. Jimmy, who was never unwell, was now seriously ill. While Dr Wood was telephoning the hospital, I went back to reassure Jimmy. 'Dr Wood thinks you may have dysentery, darling,' I said, playing it down. 'He wants you not to bother to dress and he's sending an ambulance to take you to hospital. He says that's best for everybody concerned because there you can have a thorough diagnosis.' I saw how white Jimmy now looked, and his natural (or unnatural) thinness made him look like a skeleton.

'What – what about – ?' he began feebly.

I knew what he was trying to say. 'Don't bother about anything,' I said, lying boldly. 'I've already sent a cable to the Sudan explaining that your delay in returning is due to sickness . . . and I've cancelled our berth in the ship . . . and when we get the final diagnosis from the hospital, I'll ring your family.'

Jimmy closed his eyes, partly from relief and partly from sheer exhaustion, so I withdrew quietly from the room. From the telephone on the landing I made all the necessary calls and sent a cable to the Gezira headquarters. I hesitated, and then decided that I would wait till Jimmy was in hospital before letting his family know that he was ill. They lived in such a vigorous state of natural health that they might consider an 'eastern' sickness to be an affectation rather than a serious affliction!

I went with Jimmy in the ambulance to the Hospital for Tropical Diseases and waited there with him for as long as possible. Then Dr Wood told me that his diagnosis of amoebic dysentery was correct, and he added, 'Lucky we caught it in time . . . very, very lucky we caught it in time.'

So I went back to our hotel and changed our double room for a single room into which I moved our trunks and travelling gear. Then I rang my mother and told her the news. She wanted me to go and stay with her but I said that until the bug had been dealt with I would remain in London, because I was the only person allowed to visit Jimmy daily. Also, he was new to illness in a way that I was not and I hoped my continual presence would be reassuring to him.

Jimmy's condition was expertly treated; and the bug, presumably, was killed. But then, with the start of the English autumn, a complication arose: Jimmy developed pneumonia.

I was amazed. I had had pneumonia as a child, but whereas we had been living through the winter in our little home with no other heating than the kitchen stove and a paraffin heater that had to be carried from room to room, Jimmy had been in a warm, comfortable hospital ward.

I asked Dr Wood how this could possibly have happened.

'Well, your husband was in a pretty low state of health anyway,' Dr Wood told me, 'and he's suffered a quite drastic change of climate.' He spoke as if that explained everything. Then he repeated slowly, 'We are very, very lucky to have caught it in time.'

In the weeks that followed, I had quite a number of long-drawn-out hours to fill. I thought continually, and wrote spasmodically, and, during this time of waiting, something was working deep within me. It was a repetition of Dr Wood's twice-repeated phrase: 'lucky we caught it in time'.

'Lucky' indeed, and at the very last moment, too. Until now there had been too much to do for me to be able to go into the fortuitous timing of Jimmy's illness in any depth. Now I asked myself, was 'lucky' the right word? Was it not possible that the timing of the whole experience had also been meaningful? 'Luck' was not meaningful, nor was it logical; in fact it almost implied the reverse. Could one, and should one, believe in something that one did not understand? People talked about one's fate, but what did Fate mean? I myself did not believe that the course of one's life was determined by the star under which one was born. Yet nor could I refuse to believe that there was some commitment between us, as individuals, and some other force or power that I found difficult to name. So the question continued to baffle me . . . until, quite suddenly, the word 'trust' took the place of the word 'believe'. Yes, perhaps both 'mind' and 'spirit' could be motivated into consciousness. Compromise could easily be the illegitimate child of 'belief', but 'trust' surely must be the love-child? Yet I sensed that the whole drama of life was played out in the vast theatre of our awareness and unawareness; and that each facet of reality had its own part to play. Then suddenly, when I stopped trying so hard to make sense of our miraculous rescue, an odd idea flashed into my mind: 'God and man have to be separate, otherwise communications between them would be impossible.'

The day finally came when Jimmy was allowed to leave hospital. Consequently I rang his parents and told them that I would be bringing him down shortly, but they insisted on sending a chauffeur-driven car to collect us. I had made a point of asking Dr Wood to give me a detailed list of written instructions regarding Jimmy's convalescence because I sensed that my own knowledge of either good or bad health would immediately be discounted in that hale-and-hearty household – and how right I was!

It was by now well into October and beginning to get chilly, but when Jimmy and I went to our large bedroom I was concerned to find that, while there was a bunch of flowers on the dressing-table, there was no fire in the grate. I produced Dr Wood's letter which said: 'Room temperature to remain at 67° day and night.' There could be no argument about that, so piles of wood were brought upstairs and stacked by the fireside. Mip seemed surprised that Jimmy immediately had to go to bed – though this had been his first day up. Once again I had the detailed written instructions of Dr Wood to back us up.

'Who is this doctor?' Mip asked abruptly.

'One of the best GPs in London,' I replied. 'Would you like to ring him? I've got his number.'

Mip frowned and turned away. And she and I had been such friends until I became her daughter-in-law!

'Perhaps when Jimmy's in bed . . . he'll probably go to sleep at once,' I said, 'you and I could go for one of our long walks with the dogs. I can't tell you how sick I am of being shut up in London.'

It was a true statement, but calculated to find favour.

'All right,' Mip replied. 'I'll go and get the dogs . . . don't be long.'

And on these terms we manoeuvred our way through the next few weeks. The Sudan was rarely mentioned and even the feel of it had almost faded in my own mind. Jimmy's recovery was everybody's most pressing concern. I continued to obey Dr Wood's instructions to the letter. When Mip, in her bluff way, came into the bedroom to inquire about Jimmy's progress, she would automatically throw open the window beside our bed, muttering something about 'more fresh air'. On her departure I immediately shut it, leaving just a few inches open at the top in order to maintain the recommended room temperature. For the same reason, throughout the night I stacked the fire from the piles of logs lying beside the grate. This brought back memories of sleeping in my mother's room in the little 'pebbled' house when I, too, had had pneumonia . . . but looking back it felt like another life.

After what seemed a very long period of time Jimmy recovered sufficiently to get up and dress; then he was able to come downstairs. Although a local doctor said he was completely in the clear, I insisted that Jimmy and I were driven up to London to get a final decision from Dr Wood; and he confirmed this opinion. But, addressing Jimmy, he added a warning: 'It's autumn now and beginning to get cold. If you can spare the time, you ought to go to the South of France, or some such place, for a month or even six weeks. It's still very sunny and warm down there.'

On our return to the Youngs' I passed this recommendation on with some trepidation. Mip, of course, pooh-poohed the whole idea. 'If you want warmth,' she said, 'what's wrong with the Sudan?' But Jimmy's father saw the difference – with the result that the Youngs sent their son to the South of France for six weeks. They paid his fare and hotel bills and gave him some ready cash to take with him. In fact, they paid for everything – except for me to accompany him!

At the time I paid no regard to this because I was so thankful to see Jimmy beginning to look himself again. So, the chauffeur having driven us up to London, I waved him off in the boat-train, calling out, 'Make good use of the French food, darling. Put on a stone or two if you can!'

'You too, please!' Jimmy called out of the window. And I saw that there were tears in his eyes as he left. He was a very sensitive and feeling person, but he knew that he had to go.

I left immediately to spend a week with my own family. As always, I told my mother everything.

'All the same, I'm afraid there's no hope of the Youngs ever agreeing to your leaving the Sudan,' she said.

'And now there's no hope or fear of our ever going back,' I replied at once.

These were brave, bold words, for the future was so frightening that I scarcely dared to contemplate it.

But once again Fate stepped in to help. During the last years I had always kept in touch with my friend Hazel Armour, the sculptress. Suddenly one night, while I was still staying with my mother and trying not to worry about the future, I got a telephone call from Hazel in Scotland.

'Ingaret,' she said, 'John has been very ill . . . he's had an operation. But now we've got two good nurses . . . and the doctor says I must have a rest and, if possible, a holiday. Could you possibly come with me?'

'Oh darling,' I cried into the phone. 'I'd simply love it!' I told her briefly the coincidental facts of my own present position.

'Oh, darling, how spiffing – '

'But when – ?'

'John'll pay for everything – '

We kept on interrupting each other in our excitement.

'Oh, how dear of him.'

'What shall we do?'

Without hesitation I said, 'Ski!'

There was a pause.

'But I've never – '

'Neither have I,' I burst out laughing. 'But it couldn't be worse than that brothel in Cairo, could it? We'd never even been to one of those before, had we?'

We were both so convulsed with laughter that neither of us noticed how long we had been on the telephone. Then I heard Hazel say faintly, 'All right . . . you find a good place . . . and we'll both go – and ski.'

'When?'

'As soon as possible.'

'For how long?'

'It doesn't matter. About a month . . . John'll pay for everything.'

'We'll both be champions by then,' I said. And we burst into laughter again at the idiotic way in which we were behaving.

So, the following day, I went up to London to make inquiries at the Austrian Skiing Agency.

'I want to book two single rooms at a skiing resort,' I said.

From behind the counter the assistant looked at me. 'Where?'

'Where would you suggest?'

'You've got to go somewhere pretty high to get snow now,' the Austrian replied.

'Yes . . . but where?' I asked helplessly. The Himalayas were the only mountains I had ever seen.

'Well, many places,' the man shrugged. Perhaps he smelled an amateur and was not interested.

'Well, let's start at the end of the alphabet and work forwards,' I suggested. I reckoned that would hasten our choice, and indeed it did. For the man immediately said, 'Zürs.'

'Is there really a place called Zürs?' I asked.

He nodded. 'And high enough too to ski.'

So I booked two single rooms at an hotel, and rang and told Hazel the news . . . and also the manner of the choosing!

Again we rocked with laughter over the phone, but not until we had decided on an immediate date for departure.

A week or two later we set off for Zürs. We had bought skiing clothes (my mother had given me mine as a present) and I had been told by the agency that on arrival we could hire skis, sticks and boots.

The journey was accomplished without strain; and the excitement began when we arrived in Calais and boarded the train that was to carry us across a great slice of Europe. We had sleepers but were aware of everything, even in our sleep – or so it felt. Then daylight came and brought with it a sense of the presence of approaching mountains. Snow soon seemed to cover almost everything: in the valleys little chalets and farms snuggled up into it as if in the warmth of friendliness. As the hills came of age and turned into mountains, equally a whole new area of awareness seemed to open up in me. The Himalayas had been a far-distanced, mystical experience: a communication with the unknowable. With the pure living water of their melted snow-caps they had administered the sacred ritual of christening on the dry, open, empty plains beneath them. But here, in this deep European valley, I became aware of a new understanding of the individuality in nature. These mountains, so closely in touch with the nestling humanities, had themselves somehow become human through the contact. I was to learn later that they all had their own names, their own recognisable profiles, and their own individual idiosyncrasies both in formation and disposition.

As our train puffed and chugged its way through the valleys, Hazel and I both sat silent. That was one of the great attractions of our friendship: we shared a sense of silence as well as of laughter.

Eventually, staring out at each station in order to read its name as we progressed haltingly along yet another beautiful valley, at last we came to the platform with the name for which we had been looking. As we climbed out of the train two men, with the name of our hotel written in brass letters on their caps, hurried forward to take our suitcases. I had expected a car to be waiting outside the station; instead there were two horse-drawn sledges, one for our luggage and one for us. Hazel and I were bundled into our sledge and for about two hours we were drawn by the sturdy mountain ponies up the steep, snow-covered slopes. The track was knife-edged, with a deep fall on one side, dropping down to where in the far distance below us was a thick formation of fir trees, gathered like troops to catch any one of us who came accidentally slipping down those terrific slopes. On the other side of us was an equally tall wall of snow-covered mountains reaching up apparently to the sky. And the only thing to break the silence was the crack of the driver's whip, and the crunch of the ponies' feet on the narrow snowy pathway.

Suddenly the driver pointed out something sitting like a blob of black in the middle of the whiteness. It was our hotel! From a distance it looked like a lone outpost, but on arrival we found it to be both warm and welcoming, with a large fire burning in the main reception room which, we were to discover, also served as bar, dining-room, sitting-room and dance-room. Subsequently Hazel and I were shown to two nice though small bedrooms at different ends of the hotel.

During dinner on our first evening I noticed that a 'tall, dark and handsome' man (as the saying of the times went) had changed his position at the table which he was sharing with another man and had scarcely taken his eyes off me during the whole meal. After dinner, the dining-tables and chairs were pushed to the back of the room, the floor was polished and candles were lit. Then the gramophone started playing a dance tune and the dark man immediately rose, crossed the room and, in Italian, asked me to dance. Hazel, meanwhile, had met a French Count and was busy discussing art and architecture with him. So I accepted the invitation from this extraordinarily good-looking man whose name, I discovered, was Helio Frisio (or, as I called him later to Hazel, the 'Hell of a Barber'). He was a magnificent dancer and in this I could match him. It did not matter that I could scarcely speak a word of Italian, nor he of English, for he was interested in a language that was neither Italian nor English, and the manner of his dancing bore this out. Once his arm was round my waist he kept my body closely pressed against him; his cheek too was frequently pressed against mine; and occasionally when we were in a dark corner he would give my ear an unexpected nip with his teeth, which sent a quiver of surprise and also of excitement right through me.

This behaviour continued evening after evening. Before the gramophone needle had done even a single turn, the 'Hell of a Barber' was advancing across the room to claim me as his dancing partner. He danced beautifully and the room was lit only by the fire and by flickering candlelight, so Helio Frisio had everything going for him; and he knew it. He would whirl me round, suddenly press his cheek or his lips against mine . . . and then just as suddenly, in the middle of some whirling turn, he would release me. Scarcely had I drawn breath than he was up to some other skilful trick of physical delight. I told myself that, as he was a foreigner, and seemed to take all this for granted, perhaps it was all right. So I gave up . . . and I gave in: in other words, I continued to dance with him.

Every evening, for me, the fascination of this man increased. I would stand at my bedroom window in the morning watching him as he skied off down the steep, snowy slopes; and even the movements of that tall, elegant figure as it gracefully performed a sideslip, or a crouching swift descent to the bottom, could hold my breathless attention and kindle my physical desires in anticipation of the evening to come. Sometimes he held me so tightly that I could feel the whole urgency of his own desire . . . then the tricks would start. In some dark corner of the room his tongue would suddenly thrust itself between my parted lips – parted in order to help my gasping breath – or his wandering hand would caress my nipples and continue to do so as if he knew that this aroused ripples of desire through my whole body. Looking back, I can see that he was an expert in the skill of arousing passion. He prepared my body with the skill of a first-class chef who was getting a tasty dish ready for consumption.

At last, after nearly two weeks of this secret initiation rite, the dreaded, yet longed-for, words were spoken.

'Questa notte . . .' He held me closer. 'Nella sua camera . . . prego . . . prego.'

Already it was nearly midnight, so I couldn't . . . not so quickly . . . or could I?

'Numero dieci. Non è vero?' he was whispering. Apparently he even knew the number of my room.

I nodded my head if for no other reason than because I had no breath with which to speak.

'Domani,' I whispered back, just audible above the seductive tones of the music. 'Domani.'

He hesitated. Should the dish be taken directly from the oven . . . or given a little more time in which to bake?

'Promesso?'

'Promesso,' I whispered. Speech was too articulate for my aroused emotions. So I nodded my head.

Suddenly he released me, kissed my hand, and left me. I waved goodnight to Hazel and went to my room and sat on the bed. I tried to collect my thoughts but, unusually for me, I could not even think. I could only remember, over and over again, this man's whole repertoire of physical conquest. Finally I undid my clothes, letting them drop around me, and managed to pull myself out of my obsessive memories of this Italian. But I could not manage to sleep; my mind was lost, as was my body, in lively yet aching desires.

Then suddenly, as if from habit, I stumbled out of bed and knelt by the bedside. 'Oh God,' I prayed, 'You know what I want to do and what I'm going to do . . . but if it's wrong, please stop me.'

After that I clambered back into bed with a certain relief and after a time I fell asleep.

I was awakened early by an urgent knocking on my door. Surely not the Italian? I jumped out of bed and opened the door. The chambermaid was standing there.

'*Telefon, signora.*'

Telephone! Telephone up here in the skies! What on earth could have happened? My mother – ?

I pulled on a dressing-gown over my nightdress and followed the girl along the corridor. Yes, round a curve in the passageway there really was a telephone up here in the skies! I picked up the receiver.

'It's me, Jimmy!' The voice sounded clearly.

I was staggered. 'Where are you?'

'At the bottom of your mountain . . . I'll be up by lunchtime.'

My heart dropped. I stumbled for words. 'How – how – how lovely.'

'See you soon . . . no more change . . . see you soon. Lunchtime.' The conversation ended.

I went back to my room and sat on the bed just staring at the wall, not even bothering to put on my skiing kit. Jimmy would arrive in a few hours, and my tempting assignation with this devastatingly attractive Italian was off . . . and off for ever. I stared blankly at the bedroom wall, feeling quite horrified at my profound sense of disappointment and deprivation. What really had been the fascination of this encounter? It wasn't the man himself . . . for I knew nothing about him except his nationality. It was his obsessive physical expertise that had captured me; and I was not used to being 'captured'. A sense of emancipation had been as natural to me as was reading: even as a young girl this had been in harmony with the behaviour of my childhood. Yet even I, who so fervently believed in personal freedom, could get caught in an entanglement of the senses as easily as a fish could be lured by a tempting bait. It was both a pleasant and also a terrifying revelation.

So what of Jimmy, my husband? I had always known him to be as attracted by women as he was attractive to them and I would never have dreamt of asking him if he had been 'unfaithful' to me; and, strangely, I felt no curiosity in regard to this. We both had our own lives to lead: and surely, loving a person, as I did Jimmy, meant allowing that person to have responsibility for his own conscience? But what of me? It was much, much more difficult for me to accept my own physical vulnerability.

Very slowly I got to my feet, dressed, pulled on my skiing trousers and my socks, and finally my skiing boots. I had taken to skiing in a big way, but now, suddenly, tottering down a steep slope, stemming, then trying to bring off a turn and probably falling in making the effort, held little attraction for me. Normally Hazel and I both laughed when we came a cropper and, still rocking with laughter, we would help each other to our feet. But now, somehow, I seemed to have had enough of falling.

Jimmy arrived, as expected, in his sledge in time for lunch. And I changed my place at our table so that I would not be sitting facing the Italian; instead I had my back to him. When he saw that, and also saw a strange man seated at my table, I hoped he would take the hint. And, in fact, I knew that he would. The 'Hell of a Barber' would never be prepared to share a woman, not even on the dance floor. I was even confused enough to be glad that Jimmy danced as well as did the Italian!

Then, after Hazel had left us in the middle of lunch, I suddenly remembered a question that I had to ask Jimmy . . . who, I was glad to see, was looking his old self again, not so thin, and very tanned by the sun.

I waited and then looked at him. 'Jimmy, when did you decide to come and join us?'

'Oh, I decided quite suddenly,' Jimmy answered. 'I got my train ticket through the hotel and then rang you.'

'It was early morning here – ' I began.

'Oh, I decided at about ten o'clock last night,' Jimmy replied.

After dinner . . . just when, after a struggle, I had decided to give in to the Italian . . . and had breathed out a little prayer to support me?

'But why did you decide to come so suddenly?' I asked.

Jimmy looked rather surprised. 'Well, somehow I felt you needed me.'

The twin sisters of Ignorance suddenly raised their heads inside my mind and asked simultaneously, 'Do you believe?' and 'Do you not believe?' I could not meet their wide, open-fixed gaze, for I did not know the answer.

When Jimmy, Hazel and I were preparing to make the journey back to England a few days later, Jimmy suddenly had one of his brain waves. 'Listen, you two,' he said, 'I've got to leave tomorrow for an appointment in London.' He paused. 'But why don't you both stay on here for an extra week?'

I thought of the Italian and shook my head.

'But it's a good idea,' Jimmy persisted. 'Up here you haven't had much chance of skiing at all, perched in the middle of a high mountain and with no ski school at hand to help.' He paused again and then said reflectively, 'I remember, as children, we all went in a family party to Gstaad in Switzerland . . . and there we hired a skiing guide . . . and he not only taught us how to stand up on our skis but also took us places on them. I remember it was absolutely spellbinding!' He paused. 'So, seriously, why don't you both take an extra week's holiday . . . not here, but in Gstaad? I could go now and book rooms for you at our old hotel. Why not?'

Hazel and I were speechless. Then I said feebly, 'Isn't Switzerland terribly expensive?'

'I can manage a week for you,' Jimmy said.

'And, of course, John would pay for me,' Hazel said tentatively; so tentatively that I wondered whether she really wanted to stay on. I think we both felt rather stunned at the thought of yet another experience.

Jimmy went at once and booked us rooms at his long-remembered hotel, and at the end of the week we all travelled together to Zurich. There Jimmy put us on the right train for Gstaad. Bidding us farewell, he told me he had engaged a proper skiing guide to help us learn the rudiments of skiing. 'You're a marvellous dancer, Tiny,' he said to me. 'You ought to be able to ski quite easily.' And as he stood on the platform waving to us, he cried, 'It's a good idea, it really is!' Then he rushed off to catch his connection from Zurich home to England . . . if England really was home.

Arriving in Gstaad several hours later Hazel and I, clutching our suitcases, descended on to a neat and open little platform. A uniformed chauffeur hurried towards us and took our bags, and we were driven in the hotel bus through the thriving little village. Then we went up a slight hill, turned in at the gate of a long drive and arrived at our so-called hotel. As we entered, our immediate impression was of a private house rather than a hotel: I knew at a glance that all the furniture in the entrance hall was antique, just as Hazel knew that the pictures on the walls were valuable.

The lift, however, was modern and with Swiss efficiency took us quickly up to the top floor. There we had two single rooms on the same landing. My room faced straight along a deep, yet open, valley on either side of which mountains rose high in snow-covered sublimity. I was to discover that the top of one particular mountain on the west side of the valley was tall enough to be the first to catch the rays of the rising sun, so I would wake very early in the mornings to watch this mountain-tip put on the golden crown of dawn. I also insisted on having breakfast in bed just to be able to watch with fascination the whole exchange in nature which foretold the future of the coming day.

Jimmy was as good as his word and, on our first morning, a very nice *Skilehrer* called Arthur came to the hotel to see me. The fact that he was the head of Gstaad's ski school rather daunted me at first, but he turned out to be a wonderful teacher. His patience and dedication to his job were impressive, and almost every day he took me to the top of a different mountain. Hazel did not always join us, preferring instead to capture some particular aspect of the beauty that surrounded us, either in paint or pencil, or even clay. I used to joke with Arthur that if he didn't teach me how to ski, at least he taught me how to fall down properly! In fact, each day I was able to follow him more and more easily, and by the end of the week I was reasonably steady on my skis if no great demands were made on me. In this short space of time Arthur had become a friend, and, unbelievably to me, so also had the mountains. Those ecstatic days of 'serious' skiing around Gstaad passed all too quickly, and soon it was time to go back to England. But even though we were homeless and jobless, I decided that was a much more welcome prospect than returning to the Sudan.

29

The Tarot Cards

Once back in London I sorely missed the silence, the majesty and strength and beauty of the snow-covered mountains, and the capacity to 'be' that I had experienced among them. Here in London one was chipped into little bits by noise, dirt and the grind of daily financial reckonings. We soon realised that, cheap though it was, we could not afford to go on living in our boarding-house in Stanhope Gardens . . . so what next? Every day I studied the lists of accommodation 'To Let' just as eagerly as Jimmy studied the 'Situations Vacant' columns.

Finally, one day, it seemed that I had found what I was looking for: a mews flat to let in the West End for only two pounds a week! I knew, of course, that Jimmy would be greatly helped in his search for a decent job by having a 'posh' address, so, in high spirits, I went by bus to view the flat which was in Devonshire Mews, close to Regent's Park. It was tiny but charming, consisting of two rooms, kitchen and bathroom, over a garage (which we would let, in order to help pay the rent). I also liked the owner, who was to become a well-known writer, and his wife very much. We agreed on a rent which was very reasonable and I went back to the boarding-house walking on air. But early that evening I received a telephone call. It was from our prospective landlord. Would it be convenient for me to come and see him the following morning, he asked. 'What about a cup of coffee?'

I was delighted. It sounded friendly; and I felt in need of friends. So at eleven sharp I arrived at the flat.

I was drinking my coffee when my host said, half turning to his wife, 'Since yesterday we've received another offer for this flat, which is a considerably better one than the terms we agreed with you.' He paused. 'In fact, we've been offered double.'

My heart sank into my boots, but the expression on my face never changed. 'Then of course you must take it,' I said instantly. 'You're under no legal obligation to us: and we couldn't possibly afford that amount of rent . . . much as we'd love to take the flat.'

There was a silence.

I rose. 'I'm very sorry to lose it,' I said courteously, 'but I quite understand that we've been outbid. I wish we could afford to pay more but I'm afraid we can't.'

I held out my hand to shake both of theirs. Only the day before we had had quite an interesting conversation. Now the promise of friendship, and of an attractive home of our own with a good address, had vanished. With a slightly forced smile I said goodbye and left.

Going home on the top of a bus, I asked myself whether, in the end, Jimmy and I would have to return to that death-trap, the Sudan. Or would we have to turn to the Youngs for financial help? I found the latter alternative almost as distasteful as the former. From the Sudan I had sent Jimmy's parents a detailed and precise budget which showed that we could, together, live on £400 a year, with an undertaking to keep a daily record of expenses and send them a monthly account of our outgoings. But Eric had subsequently told me that this letter had been looked upon as poppycock by the Youngs, so I was not inclined to appeal to them again for help. I felt quite beaten.

That evening the phone rang again. It was the owner of the mews flat. 'We've reconsidered the question of the flat,' he said. 'We should both like you and your husband to have it. You can move in any time and we will leave you an inventory to sign.'

I cannot remember how I thanked him for accepting our offer, but I do know that I could scarcely keep back my tears of gratitude and relief.

The flat in Devonshire Mews was perfect for our needs: only four rooms to keep clean and tidy, and an anthracite stove which was far less trouble than a temperamental open coal fire. In the mornings, after tidying the flat, I wrote and rewrote my three-act play *Because We Must*, and after a cold lunch I went out to buy what Jimmy had decided we would have for dinner. Then, in the evening, he returned to cook our meal, which he enjoyed doing, although these days I could not help noticing a look of grey despair on his face when he came home. I knew that his father had shuffled him into a so-called job somewhere in Lloyd's, but I had never dared to ask exactly what he did.

About a month after starting work at Lloyd's, Jimmy returned early one evening, sat down in the single armchair, and put his head in his hands.

'Tiny,' he said, and looked up. 'D'you know that I do absolutely nothing . . . all day long . . . absolutely nothing.'

I was horrified. That was my idea of hell; worse even than having to do the housework and cooking.

'But why?' I asked.

He shrugged his shoulders. 'I've no idea,' he said flatly. 'As far as the office is concerned I don't exist . . . though, of course, I do occasionally open a few important envelopes and put them in the right pigeonholes.'

A kind of rage possessed me. 'Then don't stay in the office all day, Jimmy,' I replied, pacing up and down our tiny sitting-room. 'If the office doesn't want you, just walk straight out of it.' I turned to him. 'After lunch, why not go to the club and play a game of squash with your friends . . . there's sure to be someone there who'd like a game.'

We had both agreed that a continued membership of the United Universities Club would be worthwhile as it would enable Jimmy to keep in touch with old friends, and perhaps make new friends, who might come up with a possible job for him.

Jimmy lifted a woebegone face. 'Good idea,' he said. He was a first-class squash player. 'I'll give it till the end of the month . . . not hanging about the office, I mean.'

Then, about a week later, Jimmy came home with a beaming face. He stood in the doorway and said quietly, 'Tiny, how much do you think I've earned this week?'

I shrugged my shoulders, whether from despair or hope I did not know.

'Thirty-seven pounds,' Jimmy replied.

I jumped to my feet with joy. 'Oh, Jimmy! How?'

'Something called a conversion loan,' he replied.

I had no idea what that was, although I imagined it was some kind of commission Jimmy received from buying or selling shares, but it greatly changed our mode of life. Somehow Jimmy had made his entry into the City. He belonged.

After this breakthrough we decided that, as well as a good address, we needed a larger flat in order to be able to entertain the sort of people who could be useful to Jimmy. Since childhood I had absorbed all the priorities of social life; they had never meant anything to me in themselves, yet I knew the procedures as naturally as I knew the alphabet. So, with glorious ambition, I gave a month's notice to our landlord and searched for somewhere else to live. It so happened that a block of flats had just been completed round the corner in Devonshire Street and I found, on inquiring, that there was one flat still vacant on the fifth floor. It had three bedrooms, two large and one tiny, a sitting-room and dining-room, both facing south, a kitchen, a bathroom, and central heating! I asked for 'first refusal' on this flat, giving the name of one of my 'handled' relatives as a referee, then I took Jimmy to see it. He was horrified.

'But we can't possibly afford it!' he said.

'Oh yes, we can!' I laughed. 'Because I'll let the big front bedroom to a doctor for bed and breakfast . . . excluding the weekends. And what I'll charge him will pay half the rent. And the tiny room at the back next to the kitchen we'll let to somebody young who can't pay much but wants a base in London for use during the week.'

Looking back, I can see that my experience of being hard-up in early life was invaluable to us during this time of 'getting by'. It had taught me that, somehow or other, one had to learn how to wheedle poverty into compliance, and so get round it and see it off. In consequence, we moved into Devonshire Court having already let the big bedroom to a specialist in Harley Street for a large rent which included breakfast, and the tiny room off the kitchen to a friend's brother for a nominal sum, on the understanding that he would make his own breakfast.

A routine was soon established. Once our lodgers had left for work, and Jimmy for the City, I would simply 'tidy up' and leave the real cleaning until the weekend, when Jimmy and I would do it together. That way I had most of the morning to get on with my writing. My lovely Gordon Russell dining-room furniture had by now arrived back from the Sudan, and as I sat in my dressing-gown at the unstained oak dining-table, the still almost unbelievable truth that we were never going back there seemed to be imprinted into my being and to colour the very words I wrote. At about midday I gathered up my papers and had a cold lunch in our miniature kitchen, after which I got properly dressed. Then, if the shopping were quickly done, I would perhaps go for a long walk which, even with the roar of the traffic, left my mind an open space in which I could think about my play. I always returned just in time to make the beds and do the washing-up before Jimmy came back from work. It was, I supposed, a very mundane way of leading London life; but it left my imagination free during the greater part of the day.

An extraordinary event happened shortly after we had settled in at Devonshire Court. Jimmy and I were asked to a somewhat grand cocktail party in a private house overlooking Piccadilly and there must have been about two hundred guests. Suddenly our hostess, whose name I have forgotten, appeared by my side.

'Ingaret,' she said, rather breathlessly, 'there's someone over there who wants to meet you. Her name is Lady Cartwright. Would you come over and let me introduce you?'

I was puzzled but I followed my hostess willingly across the room. Lady Cartwright was in middle life, fair, with a quiet, gentle manner. After we had been introduced she drew me into a corner, near one of the large windows, and spoke above the noise of the chattering crowd.

'I wonder if you would come and have lunch with me one day, and allow me to tell your fortune? I do this sometimes, and I use tarot cards.'

I had never heard of tarot cards but her suggestion sounded intriguing, so I accepted the invitation readily. When I went to lunch with Lady Cartwright the following week, it turned out to be an easy and informal affair. Then, when lunch was over, my hostess pulled out her tarot cards and started laying them out on an adjacent card table. There was obviously some meaning in the way she arranged the cards, for she did it very slowly and deliberately, and in rather a tense silence. When she had finished, she said simply, 'I see three things. I see your husband, surrounded by important business papers. I see that you are going to have an illness which in itself is not serious but the after-effects will be.' She paused, and then she said, 'And I see that you are going to meet the man of your life.'

After that there was quite a long silence while she gathered up the cards. Then she smiled at me. 'That is all I can see,' she concluded gently.

I rose and thanked her profusely for the delicious lunch and all the trouble she had taken. For some reason I was reluctant to ask her why she had singled me out from that huge, chattering mob of people. I think I felt that if I did ask her I might be trespassing on professional ground. So I said nothing, and returned, both amused and interested, to Devonshire Court.

When Jimmy came back from the office late that evening the first thing he said was, 'Well, how did the lunch go?'

'She's a very nice person,' I said, 'but the fortune-telling part was absolute rot! She even said she saw you surrounded by important business papers!'

As Jimmy had such a very makeshift and unimportant job at Lloyd's we both roared with laughter at the thought of him in some conspicuous and responsible position. Then I went on to tell him the other two predictions made by Lady Cartwright, namely that I was going to be ill, and that I was going to meet 'the man of my life'. These sounded equally far-fetched, so we dismissed the whole affair as nothing more than a pleasant lunch party and I soon forgot all about Lady Cartwright and her tarot cards, so absorbed was I with my writing during what remained of the winter and the following spring when, finally, I finished my play.

Not quite knowing what to do next, I rang up Aubrey Blackburn (who was still professionally involved in the film and theatrical world) and asked him if he could recommend an agency to which I could send my play. Aubrey replied that, not fully trusting the post, he would be happy to drop in one morning and pick up the typescript.

So, in a few days' time, the front-door bell rang early in the morning and Aubrey stood outside. I hugged him, brought him in, and handed him the manuscript.

He glanced through it. 'You've got thirteen characters and two sets,' he said.

I nodded. I knew that made it an expensive production. Also, was not thirteen supposed to be an unlucky number? But there was no time for that sort of thinking . . .

So I hugged Aubrey again, thanked him, and told him not to feel pressed because I already had a second play in my head that I wanted to write; and then we parted. And I got started on my second play.

About a month later, while I was scribbling away on the dining-room table, the front-door bell rang again. I rose unwillingly from my writing and opened the door. Aubrey was standing outside, and he carried my easily recognisable manuscript in his hand. My heart sank. Obviously he was going to return the play to me with the usual apologies.

'Come in and have some coffee,' I said flatly, shutting the door behind us.

'I've just seen Bronson Albery,' he said, taking off his hat and throwing it on the hall chair before following me into the sitting-room. 'He's read your play and he's very keen on it. In fact, he wants to put it on.'

I sat and stared at him. 'My play . . . you mean . . . put it on in London? My play . . . *Because We Must*?'

'Yes,' he said. 'And Bronnie owns no less than four theatres, so you shouldn't even have to wait long. You'd better come along and meet him. He wants to start casting straight away.'

I don't think I have ever felt so deliriously fulfilled and almost crazily happy as I did at that moment. I, a perfectly ordinary person, really had something to give to life . . . I could scarcely believe it. My joy remained with me over the next few weeks. I went to see Bronson Albery at Wyndham's Theatre and the casting proceeded in the traditional manner. We had only one difficulty: the casting of one of the four young girls who were the backbone of the main structure of the play. Neither Bernard, the producer, nor I, could get it right. Then one morning Bernard said to me: 'I've found her! The girl to play Pamela!'

I waited, overjoyed, for him to continue.

The name he produced was quite unknown to me: 'Vivien Leigh.'

And he added, 'She's got the most beautiful neck I've ever seen.'

As the author of the play I found this announcement rather disconcerting. A beautiful neck sounded a paltry credential for one of my most important characters! Fortunately I said nothing about my misgivings for, of course, Vivien Leigh proved to be a superlative choice.

At length rehearsals began and I went to them all. Not that I had anything particular to say or do (unless called upon by the producer); I merely sat at the very back of the pit, as was the custom in those days, in order to make sure that all the voices were audible that far away from the stage.

During the weeks of rehearsals, publicity announcements regarding the cast appeared occasionally in the newspapers. Costumes had to be chosen, rejected, and chosen again; and understudies engaged. Finally came the public announcement giving the date of the play's opening performance. For the author this was all heady stuff but I was so absorbed in every minute detail of the production that I did not allow it to go to my head.

On the first night, Wyndham's Theatre was packed. Only people who love the theatre as I do will be able to imagine the emotions that were aroused in me when the anticipatory hum of the audience suddenly died down and, very slowly, the curtain rose to allow my personal statement to present itself, full-face, for judgment by complete strangers.

I sat, motionless, in our box, with Jimmy, my mother and my stepfather. The box was so filled with flowers that they almost hid me from the audience, which was exactly what I wanted. I wanted an impartial judgment on this one occasion, so when, after the final curtain call, there were cries of 'Author! Author!', my only response was to dodge round the flowers and blow a few kisses and give a few bows to the audience below. The critics were all that really mattered to me now: they were the doctors who would determine the lifespan of the patient! It was not until long afterwards that I realised that the 'success' of the play had meant little to me. What did matter was that I had been able, obliquely, to convey to other people an aspect of life that was highly meaningful to me, namely that of 'compromise'. Suddenly I found myself wondering whether the emphasis that I had put upon 'compromise' was partly because I myself found it so difficult.

The applause finally died down and the curtain dropped for the last time. The audience slowly made its way out of the crowded theatre. My mother and my stepfather motored back to the country, and after many hugs and kisses behind the scenes, Jimmy and I left the theatre and went to our familiar haunt, the Hungaria.

After supper we danced endlessly and Jimmy remarked, 'We are dancing here till morning!'

'Why?' I asked, laughing.

'In order to buy the first editions of the newspapers,' Jimmy replied. 'See what the critics have to say!' He looked down at me. 'If necessary, we'll have breakfast here.'

So, very early in the morning, Jimmy and I went out and bought all the newspapers that carried coverage of *Because We Must* and took them home to read and reread. One of the theatre critics mentioned 'Chekhov'; another spoke of the play's 'Chekhovian flavour'. That was enough for me! 'Compromise' – I reflected in the taxi on the way home – as I had experienced it and expressed it in the play, operated on two levels. At a conscious level it was both valid and useful; but at a more profound level it was a form of personal betrayal . . . I didn't know whether I was thinking these words, or just dreaming them.

The play ran right through the winter and on into the spring. Then a momentous tragedy occurred: Jimmy's elder brother was killed in a car accident. It was a devastating blow for Mip, for he was her first-born child. He was married and had children but had never really been part of the Youngs' weekend parties, so I had not known him well. He was his father's partner at Lloyd's, and would, of course, have succeeded his father on his retirement. So the death of the Youngs' eldest son created havoc, not only emotionally but also in very practical terms. I felt so desperately sorry for Mip that I went to spend a few days with her in Surrey, leaving Jimmy and our PGs to look after themselves. And somehow, through this shared experience of grief, Mip and I were able to pick up and piece together the fragments of our friendship.

Ironically the death of Jimmy's brother transformed our financial circumstances and, therefore, our lives. For, in consequence, Jimmy was suddenly needed to carry on the Young connection in preparation for his father's retirement. The tables indeed had been turned; but at a terrible price. With Jimmy now a junior partner at Lloyd's I immediately dispensed with the lodger who had rented the tiny room behind the kitchen. After all, one day, who knew, perhaps a maid might occupy it? By now, my second play was well on the way to being finished and we divided the weekends between our two families; and by now, even with the Youngs, the very word 'Sudan' had faded into nothing.

The weekends spent with my mother, of course, were always easy. There was a new deep contentment in her life. She still went every so often to see her psychiatrist, Dr Godwin Baynes, who had been a friend of Professor Jung's in Zurich, and who, together with his family, had been of enormous assistance to her. She was still very beautiful, and despite her inner tensions and confusions, she always remained astute and also youthful. It was during one of these weekends that my mother suggested that we should all three go to a local race-meeting. She, like Jimmy, rather enjoyed an occasional gamble, either playing bridge, or putting a little money on a horse which I'm sure was selected just because she liked its name! On arrival at the small local race-course, separated from the public by a strong rope, we left our car in the car-park and, having placed our bets, joined the rest of the crowd as close to the rope as possible. It was a friendly country gathering without much official constraint, and with much cheering and enthusiasm.

So we, too, leaned over the rope to watch and shout as our chosen horses came galloping round a bend in the course, ears back, jockeys almost flat in their seats and applying their whips with zest. We could hear the thud of the galloping horses coming ever nearer and nearer. Then, quite suddenly, as we were all leaning forward to watch their furious approach, one of the horses, without warning, threw his rider and bolted straight towards us. It hit me first, then Jimmy, and then my mother: we were all three knocked unconscious.

I remember that I came to very slowly, but without any memory of what had happened. I heard a roar in the distance which I thought was the sea, but which, of course, was the clamour of the crowds. Then I realised two things: I was in a tent; and I was in terrible pain in my head and neck; but I still had no idea what had happened. Then I was aware that there was a nurse by my side.

'Your family is all right,' she said gently.

I couldn't even remember who my family was. But I opened my mouth and whispered, with an enormous effort, 'Will this affect my work?' . . . and again I lost consciousness.

In fact, this accident turned out to have very serious consequences for me. Jimmy and my mother and I, with the nurse, were taken in an ambulance to our respective homes; but I remained unconscious all the time. I was the one who had taken the first violent impact from the bolting horse, and I lay for days in the spare room of my mother's house in a state of semi-consciousness. When I began to come round I had another agonising experience to contend with. I was tormented by noise, which seemed to hurt my head so much that I could hardly bear it. Nor could I do anything to escape from it. So I cried from the sheer agony that this noise caused me. I tried to explain my suffering to my mother's sister Stella who had come down from London to help look after us.

'Oh, nonsense,' she replied, 'they are only filling the stove in the kitchen for the central heating . . . that's all it is.'

But to me it was a hell of pain, both in my head and all through my nerves. True, it only happened three or four times during the day, but I spent the hours in between on the verge of tears, dreading the onset of the noise which sent this pain through the whole of my shocked and stricken being.

Fortunately, what I had said to my aunt was repeated to my mother. She too, of course, had suffered some shock; just as Jimmy had had his cheek cut open, presumably by a loose, hanging stirrup. But I was the one who was most seriously injured. When my mother heard my aunt's somewhat irritated account of what I had said, she immediately went down to the kichen and instructed the resident married couple in future to fill up the stove not by pouring anthracite into it but as noiselessly as possible, shovelful by shovelful. She was clever enough, in my defence, to add that it was doctor's orders!

Gradually I struggled back to so-called health, and it took not weeks but months. First I sat up in bed; later I was helped to dress; and then I was taken downstairs to lie on the sofa. Curiously enough I could still scarcely think. Finally the local doctor said I should not go back to London until I had had a long rest, and that I was not to be left alone.

It so happened that my mother had some friends who lived in Aldeburgh. She suggested taking me there for a recuperative period, and her friends found rooms for the two of us in a small boarding-house which looked over the sea. (Jimmy, of course, was unable to join us as he could not be spared from the key role he now played in the family business.) The boarding-house was not only comfortable but it had a large open verandah on the third floor. As it was now early summer, my mother and I sat there, out in the fresh air, with the silence broken only by the moods of the waves. It was a heaven-sent semi-recovery period. As I was unable to read during my convalescence, the relaxing murmur of the sea filled an empty and uneasy gap.

Later, on my mother's arm, I could take short walks along the village street and one day I felt well enough to go with my mother to have tea with her local friends. They talked and I listened with as much concentration as was available to me. Then I heard mention of a cottage for sale for only two hundred pounds. I remembered the six hundred pounds that Mip had promised us for the purchase of some sort of weekend retreat when Jimmy assumed his new responsibilities at Lloyd's, so I tottered round to view Halfcrown Cottage, as it was called.

The place, which was occupied by one old lady sitting in a deck-chair with a paraffin stove beside her, was damp, dark and dirty, but it had two rooms upstairs and two down. And it had its back close to the sea, even though it looked on to a small street. So, after consultation with Jimmy, I bought it, aware that what was left over from Mip's gift would cover the necessary alterations: a stove that gave hot water, and some secondhand furniture. We were in the country, so nothing went wrong. The local builder was efficient and honest. I grew to know the electricity man, the gas man and the postman, and they all became friends. And Halfcrown Cottage was soon transformed. At last I understood what it felt like to have a home that actually belonged to one, just as one belonged to it; a home that was not rented, or leased, or maintained with the income from paying guests.

The extravert activities that were an integral part of this new mode of life suited my very shaky condition at that time. I had tried on more than one occasion to write, or rewrite, certain scenes in what was to have been my second play. But I could not even get to the end of a page. It was as if the power of my mind had suddenly been switched off and pain had taken the place of thought; and this happened over and over again, to be followed by a despair which totally smashed my powers of concentration. However, the task of choosing and buying cretonne curtains, secondhand furniture and new mattresses for Halfcrown Cottage never had this effect on me. These exercises demanded a different response from my mind. I never really had to think.

Finally it was possible to return to London. I struggled with my writing but the pain brought on by this struggle robbed me not only of hope, but even of the desire to write. Jimmy was busily engaged at Lloyd's and he came home late and tired. Weekends, of course, were spent away from the noise and the seeming futility of life in London.

It was during one of these weekends, when Jimmy had gone to stay with his parents, that I went to visit my mother and learned that my naval brother Roger had been transferred. His ship was now stationed near Cape Town.

I was rather dismayed by this news at first. I had seen so little of Roger in recent years, and had only briefly met his wife, Phyllis, for they had been married during one of his foreign postings. I, too, had been to South Africa and had loved it; and I, too, had been working when I went there. Suddenly the enjoyment of life during my theatrical tour in South Africa seemed to belong to another era.

'Why didn't you tell me before?' I asked.

'Thought it might be rather a shock to you,' my mother replied.

'Well, it is . . . in a way,' I answered. 'I haven't seen Roger for ages . . . or so it seems.'

'That's the Navy,' my mother replied quietly. And I knew that she, too, had missed him. Then she looked up at me and smiled.

'And you haven't been exactly stationary yourself, have you?' she said.

I let this remark pass and continued, 'Seriously, I think I might give myself a holiday. I still can't concentrate and write . . . and I must learn how to get back to my work . . . so perhaps a good long holiday might be the right way to start? Besides, I'd like to get to know Phyllis.'

My mother's subsequent remark surprised me. 'Well, if you do decide to go abroad for two or three months,' she said, looking up from her tapestry work, 'I think that will be the end of your marriage. It's never really had a chance to put down roots.'

I was amazed, and I had no real answer to give her, except the rather lame reply that I felt I had to have a holiday if I were ever to write again.

On returning to London after the weekend I decided to tell Jimmy about my idea of visiting Roger in South Africa.

'It's quite a good moment to go,' Jimmy said, 'if you feel that way. Because, you see, I shall be very late home from the office from now on. Being a partner in a syndicate at Lloyd's is one heck of a job . . . I'm at it all day long.'

'If I went I could get you a good daily,' I suggested, 'just to tidy up in the morning and do the shopping for your evening meal.'

'Fine,' said Jimmy. Then he paused. 'And of course I may not be back every evening for a meal . . . but I could always let her know . . . the daily, I mean,' he added hurriedly. And then he concluded, 'Let's think about it.'

Which we both did, with the result that I booked a passage on a German ship, the *Watussi*, going to Cape Town. And I simply longed for a breath of the sea and the murmur of the sea (though perhaps not for the movement of the sea!). And it was years since I had seen my younger brother.

PART IV

Laurens, Ile de Porquerolles, early 1930s, just before our first meeting.

30

The Full Moon

And so I set sail anew. For a change the Bay of Biscay was almost calm, and I spent only one day in my cabin before going up on deck. I had by now acquired a technique in sea travel. Once on deck I put my deck-chair under one of the elevated lifeboats. In that position there was no room for another deck-chair to be pulled up alongside mine but there was space enough for me, alone, to sit, watch and size up the rest of the first-class passengers. Jimmy had insisted that I should travel first-class.

So, spreading myself out comfortably in my deck-chair beneath the lifeboat, I prepared both to write to my mother and also to observe my fellow passengers. In my first letter to her I wrote: 'There is only one person in this ship worth talking to and he is a fair-haired young man who walks about by himself with two or three books tucked under his arm.' I had noticed that this fair-haired young man also spent quite a lot of time in the bar with an American couple who had become friendly with him. From time to time all three would emerge from the bar and sit as a trio on the deck opposite me. The Americans were man and wife, voluble and seemingly light-hearted. The fair-haired young man, who was, I guessed, about thirty years old, seemed glad of their company; yet at the same time he remained somewhat aloof from them.

After several days in my secluded corner, reading a little and writing occasional letters to my mother and Jimmy, I found that I could engage in these brief moments of concentration without arousing the aching pain in my head. So perhaps I was getting better? Then, one morning, I heard someone playing the piano in the lounge, playing classical music and playing it beautifully. I got up, walked past the Americans, and crept very quietly into a corner of the empty lounge where I settled down to listen. I loved music, and the piano in particular, and vague childhood memories of listening to the Reverend Haywell playing Bach in the Vicarage drawing-room, with his tongue hanging out from sheer concentration, returned to me. Then a movement in a far corner of the lounge brought me back to the present: there sat the fair-haired young man who was also listening to the music. I felt a moment of confusion. Had he followed me in there? Or had he, too, come in because of the music? Listening to this superb rendering of Mozart and Beethoven, I realised that music was exactly what I needed. Extraversion had been sucking me dry for what seemed like years. Now I yearned for some introverted experience which would, I hoped, help me in my writing – if I was ever going to be able to write again.

When the pianist rose and left the lounge I felt so lost that I crept back to my quiet corner under the lifeboat with the music still playing inside my head. The fair-haired young man had also disappeared, perhaps to join the Americans in the bar? I lay back with my eyes closed, listening to the murmur of the stirring ocean and still hearing snatches of the magical harmonies of Mozart. Solitude, in natural surroundings, seemed to be the only way in which to contain my inner tensions of pain.

The following day, after the fair-haired young man and I, at opposite corners of the lounge, had listened again to the unknown pianist's music, I found that he had followed me to my corner on the deck. There, with me sitting in my deck-chair and him sitting cross-legged on the deck by my side, we discussed first the music and then ourselves. He was a writer and journalist, whose first book had just been published in England, and he was returning temporarily to his native South Africa to do research for another book. I, less interestingly, was going out to visit my naval brother now temporarily stationed in South Africa.

'In Cape Town?'

I nodded. 'He lives somewhere outside Cape Town.'

'Fishoek?' he ventured.

I nodded again. Then I asked him the name of his book which, somewhat hesitantly, he gave me. 'Publishers pull one's work to pieces,' he said with a touch of bitterness. 'They've taken out one character whom they see as being irrelevant. One day I'll rewrite the book and put that character back in.'

'What was he . . . in the book?' I asked.

'A priest,' he replied shortly.

I was surprised. Already we seemed to share as interests many of the more serious aspects of life.

From then on the trio became a foursome as I was asked to join Laurens (for that was his name) and the two Americans at their table on deck. The Americans were high-spirited, in more senses than one, yet, despite all that they drank, they proved to be generous and amusing company. They found the fact that I never touched alcohol a matter for great hilarity.

'Alcoholic?' they asked, with customary American frankness.

I laughed, and shook my head. 'I just don't like it,' I replied. 'It always depresses me. The only really funny thing about it is that I've got such a good palate that I was once offered a job as a wine-taster!'

This nearly brought the house down . . . or, more accurately, the deck-side table. But I noticed that Laurens did not join in the laughter. I discovered, as the days passed, that he rarely laughed. He could be dry in humour, and also witty; but laughter seemed remote to him.

Then one evening, as we were all four sitting on deck after dinner, a simple, but to me highly significant, incident occurred. I was sitting facing the sea, and the sky was scattered with stars. Laurens sat opposite me with his back to the sea, and the two Americans were on either side of me. Compatibility and drinks became partners and produced volubility. Then suddenly, above Laurens's head and clearly outlined against the evening sky, I saw the full moon gradually come into view. Despite the trembling movement of the ship it rose slowly, slowly, as though right out of the dark shape of Laurens's head, finally achieving total visibility as if through some miraculous happening. Even the stars twinkled as if in recognition of a miracle. Transfixed by the sight I fell silent . . . just staring, staring.

'Say, honey, what's eating you?' queried the American man.

As if in a trance I replied, 'Nothing . . . I'm — I'm just watching the full moon rise out of Laurens's head.'

This idiosyncrasy, or idiocy, appealed to the Americans, who rocked with laughter. But Laurens neither laughed nor made comment of any kind.

Later on that evening he suggested, diffidently, that we should dance, for the band on deck was playing dance music. So we moved off. He was not a good dancer but it didn't matter. It was good to be together, and close, and without the need for continual talk. It was very good.

A few days later, after a game of deck tennis (which he played extremely well), Laurens came and squatted down beside me in my deck-chair. From that position he hesitated, and then he looked up at me. 'There's something I want to show you,' he said. He put his hand in his pocket and pulled out a number of snapshots which he passed to me. He had already told me that, as well as writing books, he farmed in Somerset, so I had imagined that they would be pictures of his farm and the surrounding countryside. However, the snapshots before me were of a young woman and two children, and this came as a surprise to me.

'My wife and children,' he said quietly.

To this day I can remember the leaden drop of my heart. I knew instantly that this was his way of telling me that he was a married man. Laurens already knew that I was married because I was a 'Mrs', but that he, too, should be so deeply committed temporarily robbed me of words.

'Thank you,' I said and handed back the snapshots. We sat on in rather a long silence.

As our ship ploughed through the water I listened to the wash of waves against her prow, but now I could only hear them as protests. It seemed incredible that this quiet, introverted young man should be married and have two children. But, as I told myself, at least he had not tried to deceive me.

After the first shock of surprise it seemed that nothing had changed, or perhaps could change, in our enigmatic relationship. Even to myself I found Laurens difficult to describe. His profundity of spirit seemed to be on such friendly terms with his undeniable acuteness of mind and the width of his knowledge. Surely these three attributes did not usually walk hand in hand . . . or did they? Equally his broad forehead, and beneath it his large blue eyes, bore the stamp both of strength and also of great gentleness. We continued to sit in comfortable silence under the lifeboat, and when we talked it was not as if we had only just met but as though we had never been parted. Then one day Laurens said, 'I've dozens of snapshots of the farm in my cabin. Would you like to come down and see them?'

It was afternoon, a time when most people were taking a nap either in their cabins or on chairs dotted about the deck. Momentarily I hesitated, then I rose and followed him down to his cabin. We sat on the edge of his bunk and he handed me a book full of snapshots. I began slowly to turn the pages . . . until, quietly, Laurens took the book from me and together we lay down, rather wearily, on the bunk; I, with my head on his shoulder, had the comfort of his strong arms around me. We lay thus for some time, at one both with ourselves and with each other.

It had not been an erotic indulgence; it had not been an expression of physical attraction. It was a human experience; but it was also something beyond human understanding. As I lay there in Laurens's arms I felt that somehow we had both put our personal signature at the bottom of one of the more closely-written pages of life itself. When at last we rose I knew that although I was the same person, there was one profound difference. I was no longer alone: in fact I could never be alone again. Things would go wrong, of course, but when they did, and I could totally share the experience with another human being, that would change the texture of the calamity because it could be contained in the rightness of our consummated communion. These were poor words, I knew, with which to express the feeling of life's inevitability, brought into being by our common self-recognition.

And so the voyage, both inner and outer, continued with neither pressure nor discomfort. Our relationship conformed in some curious way with the steady beat of the ship's heart and her obedient curtseying movement as she magically made her way through the glittering seas. Everything seemed to belong together and so to be in unison.

After I had seen the snapshots I asked no more questions. In outline I knew the truth: Laurens was a dedicated writer and journalist as well as a farmer. For financial reasons he was finding this double life extremely difficult, and both his writing and his farming and, I supposed, his family, were suffering in consequence.

On arrival in Cape Town we had to part. While Laurens was collecting our luggage, the first thing I did on landing was to go and buy a copy of his book from a nearby bookstall. Laurens then escorted me to the railway station, from which I was to catch a train to Fishoek. When we were standing on the platform waiting for my train, Laurens saw the package I was carrying and asked, 'What have you got there?'

'Your book,' I answered simply. 'I'm longing to read it.'

For the first time I saw his face light up with delight, almost as if he knew that he, himself, was being recognised.

As the train drew out of the station the expression on Laurens's face moved me very much. I could sense the struggle he was having to maintain his outer responsibilities and, at the same time, to keep his undoubted creative talent alive. In my own small way I, too, had known the inner exhaustion brought on by the tug-of-war between domestic duties and attempted creative expression. But I, at least, had no family to maintain.

Roger and Phyllis lived in a bungalow halfway up a very steep hill which overlooked the sea. My reunion with Roger was warm and loving. Although he was now a married man and a Commander with three gold stripes on his uniform, our relationship was as it had always been, except that, meeting him on his own professional ground, I sometimes felt more like his younger than his older sister. Roger's wife Phyllis was a capable and generous person who welcomed me with genuine affection. They appeared to be a very devoted couple.

And so the days passed happily and without strain. Domestic chores, at which my sister-in-law was expert, were quickly completed. Then we would scramble up one of the steep hills behind the house, or we would go on expeditions to the sea which, far below, stretched its long limbs round the erratic coastline as if to embrace the whole concept of Africa itself. There were also numerous cocktail parties, and even a dance or two, on board various ships, and trips in Roger's car to visit South African beauty spots.

Then came a day when I got a telephone call from Cape Town. Laurens told me that he had a free day and asked if he could come and visit us. My brother and his wife were both open-hearted and sociable people, so Laurens was made very welcome, and he and I went for a long scrambling walk in the hills. He told me, quite simply, that he would come over whenever he was free – which would not be very often.

I moved through the rituals of these extravert days as if in a dream and only came fully alive when Laurens telephoned to arrange one of his rare visits. Sometimes I wondered whether the reality of our compatibility was as meaningful for him as it was for me.

The six weeks ashore passed quickly, adding up to a sort of mixture of life in India and life in Malta, both so very far behind me. Only when Roger and Phyllis took me for a drive in the car to see the surrounding countryside did I get to know the real South Africa more intimately; if that is the correct word for such a brief encounter.

The day for my departure finally arrived. Having bidden Roger an early-morning goodbye, Phyllis drove me into Cape Town to board my ship. The ship, as if eager to put out to sea, lay lazily by the quayside; the decks were very busy and the gangways were down and full of movement, reminding me poignantly of my first visit to South Africa, when I had drunk so liberally of the heady wine of personal emancipation. Was it really only five years ago?

Suddenly a figure detached itself from the crowd on the quayside and approached me. It was Laurens.

'I've come to see you off,' he said quietly to both Phyllis and me.

My heart jumped. But words were not at my command. As if to help me, the ship's siren suddenly boomed out and we all three moved slowly towards the gangway. Table Mountain towered over us as sombre and magical as life itself. And, as was its custom, the sun shone and the sea shimmered in response. The colourful sights and the foreign sounds on the quayside made their own unique contribution to so-called civilisation and introduced me anew to what, in everyday life, posed as reality.

Then the moment for embarkation arrived. I kissed Phyllis warmly, then I shook hands with Laurens who was standing beside me.

'I'll be back in England one day, you know,' he explained. But what did that mean? Indeed, what did anything mean?

I went aboard reluctantly. Finally the hooters shrilled out the warning for departure. The ship shuddered. Then, very slowly, the harbour and the indistinguishable bunch of human figures grew smaller and smaller. Only one solitary figure stood apart and so was perhaps recognisable. I comforted myself with the thought that out of the very head of that same figure I had seen the full moon rise slowly from the dark heavens, illuminating all about it. So surely the motivations of both heaven and earth would determine its reappearance in another place and at another moment in time? My heart so longed for this happening that I felt the slow tears trickling down my cheeks. Finally, even Table Mountain faded from my vision; and all around the sea lay flat, seemingly from the very heaviness of light.

31

Laurens

Arrival in England turned out to be better than anticipated. Jimmy met me not at Southampton but at Victoria Station. He looked fit and well. After he had kissed me he said, 'Couldn't come down and meet the ship, darling. I was too busy in the office.' Our life, it seemed, like a piece of music, had been transposed from a minor into a major key. And on arrival at the flat in Devonshire Court I found that Jimmy had got rid of our remaining paying-guest.

'I gave him fair notice,' he said gaily. 'It was a bit of a bore, breakfast and all that.' He paused. 'Besides, now we don't really need the money.' He went on to explain that, as the only family partner in his father's business, he was doing extremely well. 'I've got to work hard,' he said, 'but it's worth it.'

To celebrate my return we went to dine and dance at the Hungaria that night. Our table was already reserved and laid for two, and the waiters made it clear that Jimmy was by no means a new customer.

'This is the table you always like, sir,' was one of the first things that was said.

'Thanks, Thomas,' said Jimmy with his ready smile, and I was to discover that he knew all the waiters by name. As we sat down, he said to me, 'I've been here quite a bit since you left. Without you the flat was a bit gloomy.'

I refrained from asking him who he had brought with him.

I had been away less than three months, yet in that short time our whole world seemed to have changed: a cocktail before dinner and wine with the meal (neither of which I touched), together with a lavish tip for the waiters and a taxi home! There was also an invitation for us both to go down to Jimmy's family for the weekend.

'I'd rather make it the following weekend, if that's all right,' I said.

'I'd like to go to my mother this coming weekend.' And that, too, was arranged. I spent the first weekend with my mother and gave her all the latest news of Roger and Phyllis, and their way of life. 'Very devoted and very domestic,' was my summing-up. 'And, of course, enjoying naval life.' But I never mentioned Laurens.

When Jimmy and I went to visit his family I was given a warm welcome. As was customary, Mip and I went for long walks with the dogs; and it obviously helped her to talk to me about her eldest son, whose tragic death she was still trying to come to terms with.

On one of our expeditions she suddenly stopped walking, turned to me and said: 'I don't want you to go on flogging yourselves with those PGs . . . I want you to have a home of your own in London.'

'There aren't any PGs now.' I laughed. 'And we've already got Half-crown Cottage entirely due to your generosity. It's going to make a huge difference being able to spend weekends by the sea instead of in London . . .' Then I had a sudden idea. 'Perhaps we could have a small house in London on a mortgage?' I suggested. 'Somebody told me the other day that that was a good way to buy property.'

'Of course I can help you with that,' Mip replied. 'And if you're as clever with the house as you were with the cottage you'll make a fortune. But I would like you to buy it outright rather than on a mortgage. Then it will really be an investment.'

Very gratefully I agreed. This was partly because I was still quite unable to write in the real sense of the word. I could write a letter or a note, but I could no longer write with concentration from my own imagination; nor could I type, which in some ways was even more physically painful than writing. I had hoped that my holiday in South Africa would have helped, but on my return I found that, in fact, it had made no difference at all. Now, thanks to Mip's generosity, I could allow property to become my pastime until these two major obstacles were somehow surmounted.

In the weeks that followed I scanned property notices and viewed many houses in the Chelsea area. Having been so happy in my tiny flat off the King's Road, with the trams stopping in a friendly way outside my windows, I felt I must live in Chelsea, if only because these old associations were so positive. At last I found exactly the right small house, facing south, in a quiet street, with three-storeyed eyes staring down at me, seemingly in warm welcome. And the house had two essentials: central heating and a tiny garden at the rear, with a forsythia tree which at that particular moment was in full bloom! And so Jimmy and I finally acquired our own 'freehold' property in London. I even found the word 'freehold' attractive and hoped it would somehow have a beneficial influence on us!

To begin with, the practicalities of moving into our new house were a welcome diversion but then, quite suddenly, either from the strain of choosing cheap but likeable curtains, carpets and furniture, or over-seeing various other domestic arrangements, I suffered a return of the agonising pain in the back of my head and neck. I was advised by the doctor to 'take things easy' which, at a time like this, was the most difficult thing imaginable to do. Happily I had found myself a won-derful 'daily', Mrs Pearce, who looked after the house and particularly the kitchen, and we could talk together as human beings. The only really concentrated work that I could do was in my tiny back garden. If I took it slowly, pulling up weeds and buying and bedding-down new plants did not cause any of the shooting pains in my head and neck.

One morning soon after we had moved in, the telephone rang: rather an unusual event in my somewhat quiet life. I picked up the receiver. It was Laurens . . . and he was in London! I nearly collapsed from sheer joyful surprise.

'Laurens!' My heart was now beating far more strongly than was my head. 'How long have you been here?'

'I arrived early this morning . . . when can we meet?'

As far as I was concerned we could meet anywhere and at any time; but because I was so confused with joy I said, 'Could you perhaps come here and have tea?'

Laurens's voice came back very calmly down the phone. 'Can't wait that long, I'm afraid.' There was a pause, and then he said, 'Why not come and have lunch with me here in the City?'

So I went by bus to the City and to the address that Laurens had given me. He met me at the door of the restaurant. 'How is the writing going?' he asked.

I nearly burst into tears. He was the only person in my world who would have asked me that question. There was a pause and then I replied, 'There's something I want to tell you.'

So we sat in a quiet corner of the restaurant and during lunch I told Laurens about the racing accident and how near to despair I was at times at having lost my ability to write. Laurens was also the only person I knew who would truly understand my predicament.

'Have you had an X-ray?' he asked quietly.

'No,' I said. 'They all say this is just the result of the shock.' Then I remembered something else. 'Although a doctor did tell me I should not try to type. He said the position could be harmful to me . . . but I want to hear about you,' I finished hurriedly.

There was quite a long pause, then Laurens said, 'Well, here I am. I go back to my farm this evening; and then I'll be commuting up to London daily.'

'From Somerset?' I asked in dismay. 'Surely it'll be dreadfully tiring going up and down each day, won't it?'

Laurens did not answer, and the silence was intolerable.

Suddenly I had a bright idea. 'If you want a room during the week Jimmy and I can give you one. The house is in a bit of a mess because we've only just moved in . . . but if you'd like to use it there is a spare room, and bathroom too.'

There was another long pause. Then, very slowly, Laurens said, 'Yes, but could I?'

We neither of us needed to explain further. And of course the real question was 'Could we?'

'Perhaps we could try it out,' he said finally, 'while I look round for somewhere else.'

I felt overjoyed: whatever it cost we would not be parted. 'So when can you come?' I asked.

'Well, any time,' Laurens replied. 'I've only got one trunk and a holdall.'

My heart sank. 'So you won't be based in London for long?'

'Oh, yes . . . I hope so,' Laurens replied, adding, rather ominously, 'It rather depends on what's going to happen to us all.'

I rang up Jimmy and told him that I had run into a friend I had made in South Africa: could we put him up for a few nights while he looked round for a room? Jimmy agreed at once, for he was a very easy and hospitable person. Also, since his partnership at Lloyd's, I sometimes got the feeling that he had quite an active and even interesting life outside our home, to which he often did not return until late in the evening.

So Laurens moved temporarily into our house in Cadogan Street. He and Jimmy met for the first time that very evening. It all seemed to work quite well on a practical level. For a start, Jimmy, knowing I was not alone, came back from the office even later than usual. Laurens, whose hours as a journalist were even more erratic, often came home very late indeed. On one such occasion he had left his front-door key behind and the next morning he told me so very apologetically.

'Did I wake you up?'

'No, why?'

Laurens explained that, rather than disturb us, he had climbed up the drainpipe from the basement to the third floor and let himself in through the tiny bathroom window in the roof. I was quite amazed. Who was this man who could quote T. S. Eliot, Gerard Manley Hopkins, and Shakespeare by the yard, and yet also would shin up a drainpipe rather than take advantage of the hospitality offered to him by his friends? Did I laugh? Or did I cry? With a remarkable person like Laurens, such questions were forever arising.

After staying with us for two or three weeks he came back from the office early one evening and said quietly: 'I think I ought to be pushing off now. Don't want to outstay my welcome. I'll find a room somewhere or other in this area.'

'I – I think I've found you one already,' I said. We did not need to explain things to each other, so I refrained from telling him that the nights he had spent with us had been extremely painful for me. As I lay beside Jimmy in our huge double bed the tears would sometimes roll down my cheeks . . . and I had to let them roll, for I feared that by sobbing I would have shaken the bed and woken Jimmy. The torment of unfulfilled unity had become almost unbearable. 'It's rather a nice room,' I added, 'and only a few minutes' walk from here.'

And so this new arrangement was carried out. Whether it worked or not I did not really know. I seemed unable to find any pattern in my life. At the weekends, of course, Laurens went back to his family in Somerset. During the week, our communications were mainly by telephone; and the brief meetings we managed to arrange seemed somehow pointless – and poignant.

And then Fate took a strange hand in our affairs. I was suddenly rushed into University College Hospital with appendicitis, and an operation was performed with as much speed and skill as possible. I was 'allergic to anaesthetics', I was told when, eventually, I had come round sufficiently to be able to understand what was being said. I was also told that I should never forget this vital fact in the future. But for me the future was out of sight . . . so I fell asleep again. I learned later that Laurens had visited me every day when I had been unconscious. He had stood quietly at the end of my bed, watching me, and then left without disturbance; although sometimes he had touched my hand at parting.

The after-effects of the operation were long-drawn-out and complicated, so I made a very slow recovery. Gradually, in a hazy way, I became able to think again; or perhaps just to remember. And the very first thing that I remembered was Lady Cartwright and her tarot cards! It was quite two years since our lunch together. My memory for dates was imprecise but her words came back with crystal clarity. First, she had said, 'Your husband will be surrounded by important business papers.' Then she had told me that I would have an illness which was not serious, but that the consequences would be. And thirdly she had said, 'You are going to meet the man of your life.' And all three things, which Jimmy and I had laughed off as impossible at the time, had actually happened! I think the realisation of this somehow helped my recovery.

In time, I came out of hospital and was back in my Chelsea home. Yet 'home' was a strange word now, for everything seemed to be such a long way off. Mrs Pearce, who came in every day, looked after me as carefully as she did her own husband. Physically she was a small woman, yet her inner stature was great, and my devotion to her is continuous.

Eventually I was able to walk about again, but it was as if I was pacing up and down the same inner 'impasse'. I was healthy and yet I was trapped. I felt myself to be bound, hand and foot; or, more accurately, by heart and head. Jimmy was now both hard-working and successful, so in the outer world there was little that I could not command. But in my inner world I was lost. Laurens was my only symbol of reality . . . but what was reality? I had totally lost my bearings.

Then one day I decided that I could bear the pull and tug of this strain no longer. As things were, I did not even want to write . . . perhaps partly because I knew that I couldn't?

So very quietly, without saying a word to anyone, I took out a map of Europe and studied it. How far away could I get? It had to be a long way, for I needed to prepare myself for a new start in life – a completely new start. And for that I needed distance from all associations, both negative and positive.

I stared indifferently at the map. Portugal was the place furthest south, and it was a country about which I knew nothing; that would be helpful. I would go to Portugal. Perhaps in some unknown country, with everyone speaking a completely unknown language, I would be helped to see my life objectively . . . and so get my priorities right . . . and so be able to do something . . . instead of just drifting . . . drifting painfully into nowhere.

32

The Open Question

So I went again to a travel agency and booked a sleeper in a train which would take me to the very southernmost point in Portugal. This place was, in consequence, by the sea and its name was Praia da Rocha. It had only one hotel which was called the Grand Hotel. The money to cover this enterprise was now, of course, not a problem. I left my address, and a promise to the three people closest to me – my mother, Jimmy and Laurens – that if anything went badly wrong I would let them know immediately.

Looking back on my life, I can see that my repeated attempts to seek refuge in unknown and foreign countries were, in some measure, just a projection of my longing to be able to come to terms with my inner confusions; and, consequently, to find some permanent resolutions regarding them. Up until this point, frequently recurring 'events' had been the order of my days and, as in the maintenance of a fire, shovelful after shovelful of these had been needed to keep life burning brightly within me . . . or so it felt. But I now needed something more than 'events' to keep the fire of life alight. Events did not lead me to my longed-for goal. I suddenly saw a parallel between my own situation and the cards my mother held in her hand at the bridge table. They had only two colours: the blackness of ignorance, or red signifying danger. And it was the minds and the hands of the players that determined their playing. And the area of activity was always the same . . . just a card table. So, if the parallel were correct, how did one leave the area of 'events' and reach the inner world of the inevitabilities of Fate? I needed a sense of that inevitability. I was tired of choosing. All the more so because, quite frequently, I had been proved to be right. Now I wanted more than anything else in the world for life to choose me, and I felt that the only way to achieve this was to distance myself for a time from my own areas of unidentifiable confusions.

I knew that something was, or had been, physically wrong with me. Shortly after Jimmy's fateful illness, I had been forced to follow him into the Hospital for Tropical Diseases for treatment of what had finally been diagnosed as a milder form of amoebic dysentery, and on leaving the hospital I had been given a stringent diet consisting mainly of boiled fish and milk pudding. As food itself had never greatly interested me (except perhaps in terms of taste) I had continued this diet up to the present time, along with the other disciplines imposed upon me following my accident at the race-course. Inevitably these physical strictures had led me to question myself constantly about my ability, or inability, to recognise and so to accept and digest the truth of my own inner life. If, as I suspected, this had become an area of strained confusions, then could not these be contributing to the slow recovery of my physical strength? As I set out on my voyage of discovery – a voyage to transcend the ordinary facts of life and find the illuminosity of certain inner truths – it came to me, and with some enlightenment, that presumably this was the way nuns felt when they first entered nunneries; not that that was something I had ever wished to do.

After a long journey right across Europe and down to its most southerly point, I arrived late one afternoon at Portimao. The words 'Grand Hotel, Praia da Rocha' were intelligible to the porters at the station, so I hired a sort of buggy, pulled with indifference by a thin donkey with a nonchalant driver, smoking and loosely holding the reins. After travelling a mile or more along an uneven track through a barren and baked landscape burnt brown by the sun, I glimpsed the sea, and was even able to hear its murmur as we pulled up at a sort of shanty hotel bordering the main track which appeared to be the general roadway. By now it was early evening and the sky was flushed with the warm tenderness of a departing day. I felt hopeful as I descended from the buggy and made my way into the so-called 'Grand Hotel'. I was shown a room that looked out towards the distant sea beyond high cliffs that fell steeply to the beach. The hotel seemed clean: it had a bar (which I was to discover was generally empty), and a small dining-room with only two tables laid – one of which was mine!

As I sat down and ate my first Portuguese meal, I thought with amusement that my notion of comparing myself with a nun taking refuge in a nunnery was not too far off the mark. The Portuguese food was delicious, but it was quite unlike my diet of boiled fish and chocolate blancmange. Consequently I spent most of the first night either being sick or retching noisily. I simply couldn't eat breakfast, which, as in many European countries, was brought to me in bed the following

301

morning, so I just lay there, judging the rest and starvation to be the best way to recovery.

Then came a knock at the door, and after a pause the door opened slowly and a very beautiful woman entered uncertainly. 'I heard there was another Englishwoman staying here who was rather unwell,' she began.

'Well, not exactly – ' I replied. 'Just stupid really. I'm supposed to be on a strict diet . . . but somehow in the excitement of arriving here I forgot all about it!' I explained to her about the amoebic dysentery and then I added, 'Would you be awfully kind and explain my diet to the hotel manager because I can't speak a word of Portuguese!'

And so started a long friendship. Norah was married to an Australian and they had made their home, and given birth to two sons, in Praia da Rocha. They and another family were the only British inhabitants in the village, although of course, in the summer, a horde of tourists arrived. Norah was not only beautiful, she was also a poet! I could not believe my good fortune. And, as a long-term inhabitant, she knew all the dietary dangers and local hazards, and was equipped with all the necessary medicines. She told me that, sadly, sea-bathing was dangerous here; that the assault of the ocean as it strained to smash against the cliff-face, only to fall back, exhausted, was directed by powerful undercurrents in these invading oceans.

One evening shortly after my arrival, passing the normally deserted bar, I was surprised to hear a man's voice speaking a mixture of English and Portuguese. I looked in. A tall man, and obviously English, was talking to the bartender. At that moment the bartender noticed me and immediately said something in Portuguese to the Englishman, who turned towards me.

'I hear you've just arrived,' he said.

'Nearly a week ago.'

'Like it?'

'It's too soon to say . . . but I think I shall.'

'Like a drink?'

'A Vichy water, perhaps,' I answered, with Norah's warnings still in my mind. The man ordered my drink and his whisky and we drifted to a nearby table. I learned that he lived not in Praia da Rocha, but in his own yacht moored down at Portimao. Conversation proved easy. He had both humour and good manners.

'You must come and see my yacht one day,' he said, 'and meet the crew.'

The next day a note arrived for me. It was all in verse and was signed

'James'. It was also very amusing. So, just for the fun of it and also to pass the time, I wrote a reply, also in verse, and gave it to the bartender to deliver to James. To my delight, I noticed that the writing of these couplets did not bring on one of my splitting headaches.

Quite quickly my new life fell into a kind of pattern. Every morning, on waking, I thought of Laurens; and the pain and the happiness that this brought me just had to be lived with. Norah and her family occupied most of my mornings; and our congenial conversations brought such relaxation and pleasure that my need to write seemed less pressing. After midday it grew extremely hot, so a rest, with the voice of the sea in my ears, was enjoyable. Then sometimes, during the late afternoon or evening, I would spend time with James, writing and rewriting idiotic verses in competition with him. Sundays came and Sundays went; but of course there was no intelligible church service to which I could go. So my love of Laurens and my love of the sea had to fill the empty gaps. Mysteriously, once a week, I received a copy of *The Times* by post from England. I soon guessed that it was sent by Laurens as his way of communicating without personal intrusion.

The uncertainties in the outside world seemed to correspond with my own inner confusions. A man called Hitler was making a nuisance of himself, indeed proving a menace. Country after country was under threat from, or occupation by, Germany. Austria had been occupied before I left England; Czechoslovakia too had succumbed. Now it looked as if Italy could be suborned into submission; and Poland might also be occupied. There was huge confusion in home politics, too. The Prime Minister, Neville Chamberlain, had lied about Britain's capacity to defend herself in case of war. War? I remembered from childhood the lasting emotional reactions that the war-wounded heroes staggering through the streets of Folkestone had aroused in me. Surely, in a single lifetime, one would not be called upon to endure two world wars? The weekly newspaper that Laurens sent me was invaluable not only in providing a link between us, but in keeping me up-to-date with contemporary affairs. My personal uncertainties were somewhat diminished by the terrifying manoeuvres in the international scene, but my absence from Laurens now brought me more pain than happiness as the weeks went by. What was going to happen to us all?

Suddenly one day I made the discovery that saddled ponies could be hired in Portimao. So I hired one of these ponies for a day and, by myself, went on an expedition of discovery into the mountainous, bush-covered hills far behind Praia da Rocha. Both the pony and I drew in our breaths as we made our way up the steep, winding and little-used tracks, the

303

pony gasping in the struggle to make the ascent, and I from fear of the deadly drop on either side of us. When we finally reached the top we were rewarded with a breathtaking view. On one side was what looked like the whole of Spain; and on the other, far beneath us, was Portugal, with its even more distant sea. Looking in the Spanish direction I wondered whether a small clutch of civilisation lying way, way below us and beyond, could possibly be Seville? The pony and I browsed in both senses of the word before we finally turned to make our precarious way down the uncertain and at times precipitous track.

Late that evening, tired but jubilant, I told James of my adventure and, to my amazement, he looked at me very gravely indeed.

'Did you really do that?'

'Yes.'

'You must never go there again.'

'Why not?'

He paused. 'We have no Don Juans here . . . but we can rustle up a brigand or two.'

'Brigands!'

'Yes. And if they got hold of you, you'd just disappear.'

I can still remember the icy grip of horror that seized me at his use of the word 'disappear', and the memories it revived of my narrow escape from kidnap in Port Said. To disappear would mean that I would never see Laurens again . . . never, ever again. I began to shake with the terror of it. Rape, murder, torture didn't enter my mind; only the agonising realisation that life would be of no importance to me whatsoever without Laurens's presence.

'You've gone very white,' James said anxiously. 'I didn't mean to frighten you.'

'You haven't,' I replied shakily. 'You just flung a door wide open in my mind . . . that's all.'

There was a long silence, then James said, 'You know, I've got to go back to England quite soon, for about five weeks, but I've a suggestion to make to you.'

'Yes?'

'Would you like to spend that time down in Portimao on my yacht? Pedro would bring you up to the hotel whenever you wanted to come . . . and fetch you again in the evening after dinner . . . or whenever you wanted him to. It would be perfectly safe for you to sleep there, with Pedro in charge.'

I was thrilled at the thought of sleeping on the yacht, which was moored quite a long way from the harbour quayside. I would hear the slap of the wavelets against the side of the yacht, and the gentle cradling motion of the empty and tranquil waters; and I would be in the care of the yacht's crew. Pedro was aged about twenty-four and the two junior crew members were in their late teens.

'I'd love it,' I replied. 'But wouldn't they mind, the extra work and all that?'

'They have a good life and a good wage,' James replied quietly. 'They see the world . . . and they do as they're told. If they didn't they'd be off at short notice. We've never had any complications at all.'

So when James went away for several weeks I moved in and spent the nights and most of the mornings on the yacht. My early 'breakfast' was brought to my cabin by Pedro; and as I sat up in my bunk eating it, listening to the footfalls of the crew on the deck above and the gentle wash of the waves against our hull, I could almost imagine that I was sailing away to the end of the world . . . but the depressing fact remained that I was getting absolutely nowhere. Only in my talks with Norah was there any real interchange at a deeper level. One day, quite by chance, the story of the racing accident cropped up – which prompted me to tell her of Lady Cartwright's predictions, although I left out the bit about 'meeting the man of my life'. I could never mention Laurens to anyone. If I did, I felt sure I would be given advice; and words and ideas were not applicable to the situation as I experienced it. It was a state of being, and of belonging, that was not in the world of ordinary affairs. Its inevitability frightened me; yet, at the same time, it was the one thing that sustained me.

After I had told Norah about the bolting horse, she said, very earnestly and quietly, 'Ingaret, there is one man that you must go and see, and as soon as you get back to London. His name is Streeter. He is an American and an osteopath.' She went on to tell me that, after the First World War, her husband had been, as she put it, 'shot to pieces'. He had been practically immobilised, and in constant pain which was often almost unendurable. His injuries were so extensive, and the hospitals so crowded, that no one had known how to go about 'putting him together again', as Norah put it. Then, by chance, they had heard of this man called Streeter; and out of desperation they had gone to see him in Park Lane where he practised. It had taken time and money, both of which fortunately they had . . . 'and look at him now!' Norah concluded as her husband ran up the verandah steps, his golf-clubs slung over his shoulder.

'We were just talking about Mr Streeter,' she said to her husband.

Norah's husband flung down his clubs and said, smiling at me, 'The miracle man!'

Norah, who was a woman of great intuitive understanding, pressed the matter no further, but hearing about 'the miracle man' had given me new hope for the future. I had now been in Portugal for about six months: I had avoided returning home because of the agonising conflict implicit in Laurens's and my relationship. On the one hand I felt this was something to which, as a family man, he should perhaps not commit himself; on the other hand I knew that our common need of each other was a profound and mutual reality, far, far removed from the physical world, and that it was impossible to turn one's back on such a God-given gift of fulfilment. This talk with Norah somehow helped me to see things in a different light. Suppose Mr Streeter really was a 'miracle man'? Suppose I really could return to lead an active and creative life? I made up my mind at that moment to return to England and, having done so, there were letters to be written and answered; and it was particularly important to make an appointment with Mr Streeter.

Then one evening I told James of my decision.

'I shall miss you,' he said quietly.

'We can always exchange a verse or two!' I replied lightly.

He shook his head. 'Things don't work out that way,' he answered slowly.

About three weeks later I said goodbye to my dear friends, Norah and her family, then I carefully put the appointment card I had received from Mr Streeter into my travelling handbag and took a buggy to the station. My luggage was light, for I had not expected to stay so long. I found my sleeper and climbed into the train. Then, to my amazement, I heard a tap on the window and saw James looking in. I was overjoyed, and let down the window with a bang. We exchanged a few words . . . but somehow words seemed difficult for him. So I told him I would write and say all the things that one finds it so hard to put into words at the moment of parting from a friend. Finally the engine gave its shrill foreign whistle.

James put up both his hands and held my face between them. Then, very gently, he kissed me on the lips. 'It's been a miracle,' he said quietly.

The engine gave another squeal and jerked us apart. I leaned out of the window, waving. James stood to attention until I was out of sight. Then I sat down, bewildered. A miracle . . . but how? It took me quite a long time to figure out what James must have meant. Slowly the pieces of the puzzle came together: crew of three young men of different ages; his life, spent solitarily and apart from his family . . . which, in England, would have had to have been lived at a high social level . . . and into which a *woman* had suddenly appeared who was also suffering an inner

306

loneliness but who shared his sense of fun and had an independence that freed her from conventional judgments. Yes, that could have appeared to James as a miracle. Suddenly I did not doubt it. Whatever the outcome of my return, I could at least feel happy at the caring relationship that James and I had so briefly and so easily shared. But that small happiness could not alleviate the deep sense of anxiety that invaded my whole being in relation to the world at large.

33

The Miracle Man

After such a long absence from London it seemed strange to walk once again up the three steps leading to my front door, and then to let myself into my own home with my own doorkey. Mrs Pearce, whom I hugged with warmth and relief, gave me a scribbled note from Jimmy, saying, 'Welcome home! Shall try to get back early this evening. Love, Jimmy.'

I screwed up the note, opened the drawing-room door and heard the familiar tick of my beautiful ormulu clock. Then I dropped Jimmy's note into the wastepaper basket . . . and listened to the clock again. This clock had been a friend since childhood, so what was it saying to me now? It sounded so wise. Yet I stared round the room as if I was seeing it for the first time. Only one question occupied my mind. Would Laurens ring me? Or should I ring him? As if in answer to that very question the telephone suddenly rang. Sometimes such synchronicities could happen between us. Trembling, I picked up the receiver. Wrong number. I put the receiver down, then picked it up again. No, I must leave it to Laurens to ring me. Before my departure we had both decided not to write to each other: letters would, and could, confuse the issue . . . whatever that issue was. For a while I wandered about like a stranger in my own home, then I changed my travelling clothes up in the bedroom and stared out into my little back garden where the leaves of the Virginia creeper were already dressed in autumnal colours. Somehow, although colourful, that did not seem like a good sign.

The telephone rang again. It was Laurens!

'Darling!' I kept my voice low.

'When can we meet?'

'You say – '

'Tea-time? Same place?'

Tea-time felt like next year. 'Yes,' I whispered.

'You all right?'

'Yes . . . I am now.'

'*Au revoir* then.'

I knew he was speaking from a busy office but just that brief exchange rebuilt my world. I relaxed and looked at my watch; I had only four hours to wait. There was time for me to take a walk before Laurens and I met at our customary café, which was midway between my house and Laurens's bedsitter; and there were a few things I wanted to buy in the nearby shops. I would have to make a list or I would never remember them. Oh, Laurens –

So I made a list; and I made myself take a walk; and then I made myself go and buy my few unimportant purchases. It was outside Peter Jones's back entrance that I suddenly recognised a tall and familiar figure.

We both stopped, amazed.

'Mr Haywell!'

'Ingaret!'

Yes, it really was Mr Haywell, the young curate from the Vicarage in Kent, who had spent his leisure-time playing Bach with his tongue hanging out from the efforts demanded of him by the musical scores; and to my shame I used to mimic him! But all that was years and years ago!

'What are you doing here?' I asked.

'Looking for you,' he said. 'I got your address from your aunt.'

I looked at my watch. I had time to spare. 'Let's go and have a cup of tea,' I said.

And so together we walked into Peter Jones and up to the restaurant, and I found a table by a window. We sat opposite each other comfortably, and I remembered the hours and hours I had spent as a child perched on his windowsill, talking . . . talking . . . in quiet voices . . . because possibly, just possibly, he should have been writing his sermon!

Remembering all this I smiled across at him. But his face looked grey and drawn. 'What is it?' I asked gently. 'Can you tell me?'

'Only you . . .' He stumbled over the words. And then suddenly the whole thing came out in a rush. 'I'm married,' he said. 'But they didn't tell me – ' his voice broke. 'They didn't tell me – '

I waited; and then the words came again. 'There was insanity in the family . . . but they never told me. And now she . . . she's in a lunatic asylum. My wife is in a lunatic asylum . . . and they say she'll never come out . . . never. I can't even see her . . . not that she'd know me . . . the way she is now. But they never told me – ' His voice broke again and there were tears in his eyes and rolling down his cheeks. He had his back to the main body of the restaurant, and I was grateful that our privacy was safeguarded by the clatter of the china and the chatter of the clientele.

I put my hand on his. Mr Haywell, the innocent, the saint-like innocent of my childhood, Mr Haywell, deceived and duped. 'Mr Haywell, surely you can do something about it . . . to release you?' I paused. 'You're a victim . . . you've been deceived. Surely, somehow, the marriage could be annulled . . . under such circumstances? And, as you say, your wife need never even know.'

'She knows nothing now . . . she is quite, quite insane.'

'Then it wouldn't hurt her, if the marriage were annulled?'

Mr Haywell looked at me and I have never forgotten the agony in his face. He leaned forward.

'But it would break me,' he said. 'I should have to leave the Church. And I love my Church.'

It is difficult to explain the horror that went through me at those words. Mr Haywell's Church was also my Church: and it was supposed to be the Church of Christ Himself . . . the Loving Son of a Loving God. Nothing made sense.

'But surely — ' I began.

Mr Haywell shook his head. 'No,' he said. 'I've inquired. A divorce on any grounds whatsoever would mean that I must leave my Church.'

I felt it would be less than helpful to move into the field of differing opinions, so I just kept my hand on his; and we sat together for a long time saying nothing. Yet the accord between us was complete, as it always had been. I could even stroke his hand quietly and say to him: 'You know, you proposed to me once, when I was only twelve . . . so let's just say "Third time lucky" — if it is God's will.'

Bravely he managed to give me one of those long-remembered gentle smiles. And I felt a certain release in him. I didn't look at my watch but I knew that shortly I was due to meet Laurens. So we sipped our tea in a united silence. Then I picked up my gloves, showed the waitress my account card, signed the bill and slowly we moved out of the restaurant, down in the lift, and out into the street. We stood for a few moments in the fresh air, saying little. There appeared to be nothing to recommend, except endurance. Then the thought came swiftly to me, like a flash of lightning, that at least he would have his belief in his Church. He would follow the martyrs of old. He would not have to become a martyr, he was one already, a saintly martyr; and down the ages martyrs had died for their Faith.

I turned and faced him. 'Mr Haywell, you have your Faith,' I said very gently. 'And that is the one invaluable treasure.'

As he stood looking down at me his expression changed back to the old, gentle, caring look that I remembered so well. Then he took my face in his hands and said, very quietly:

> 'Time cannot change, nor custom stale
> Her infinite variety.'

Then slowly yet resolutely he turned and left me. I never heard of him again; and somehow I could not, or rather I dared not, inquire. Faith was his only solution.

I looked at my watch and started walking in the direction of the café where I was to meet Laurens. I was well ahead of time, but was grateful for a period of recovery. I had only been back in London a matter of hours but already I could feel the dangerous national disturbances in the air. I bought a newspaper and ordered a cup of coffee as I skimmed over the alarming headlines: 'War inevitable' . . . 'Churchill stands firm' . . . 'Our Navy's strength is below standard' . . . 'Inadequacy of our Air Force' . . . 'Chamberlain's weakness'. I think that if I had not been about to be reunited with Laurens I might have burst into tears. Instead I ordered a second cup of coffee and at that moment Laurens walked in.

At first glance I could see that he looked strained and tired, but his expression lit up when he saw me. He sat down beside me and took my hand. I was so moved that I scarcely dared look at him; so for a few moments, awaiting our coffee, we sat in silence.

Then he said to me, with great gravity: 'I've a few things to tell you.'

My heart sank. Why did I always expect to hear the worst?

'The first is the least important, so I'll tell you now. I've sent my wife and both the children back to South Africa . . . and I've sold my farm in Somerset.'

I was astonished. 'But why?' I asked.

'You've been away a long time,' Laurens answered, 'and things have changed in your absence.' He paused. 'I think a war seems highly likely . . . that's why I've sent my family back to South Africa. They'll be safe there with a bit of luck, and they wanted to go. My wife has lived there, and she prefers it to England . . . and the children will get an excellent education. I have property there, so I can afford to support them from South African currency . . . if the worst comes to the worst.'

'You mean – ?'

'A war, of course.'

Suddenly memories of Portugal swept over me: a fairytale country,

with brigands in the mountains and surrounded by invading oceans . . .
and yet seemingly so remote as to be free of international threats and
entanglements. I even remembered daydreaming that perhaps one day
Laurens and I could go and live there together. But now –

'If there is a war,' I asked slowly, 'what would you do?'

Laurens looked surprised. 'Join up, of course,' he said. 'I was just
coming to that.'

'Where?'

'Why, here, of course.'

'But why didn't you go to South Africa with your family?' I asked
tensely. For me, any separation would be better than the thought of
Laurens at war, in danger, day and night. 'That's where you were born,
isn't it? That's your homeland.'

'Yes,' he replied. 'It is, in a way . . . at least, that's where I was born.'

'Then why did you leave it?'

'Apartheid,' he said simply. 'I just can't take it.'

We sat in silence for a moment; and then I said with sudden bitterness,
'How can that drive you away from your country? All over the world
people are practising "apartheid" in one way or another.' Suddenly
I remembered Mr Haywell. 'And even in the churches. Look at the
"apartheid" practised between people who call themselves Christians.
They get split into little pieces regarding their rules and regulations, and
all in the name of religion. I think that's much worse than discriminating
against people just because of the colour of their skin. Yes, Laurens,
you – you ought to go back to South Africa.' (At that moment any fate
in the world seemed to me better than that Laurens should be in danger
of his life.) 'And even if there is a war,' I asked urgently, 'why should
you have to join up?'

'Because if there is a world war I would join up to fight for something
I believe in. There's nothing anyone can do in South Africa about
"apartheid". Only disaster can solve that problem . . . and disaster will
choose its own moment,' he replied quietly.

I think he sensed the turmoil of my feelings, for adroitly he changed
the subject which was obsessing me. 'But I want to hear about you, my
dear one. Tell me about yourself . . . and Portugal. Done any writing?'

I shook my head. 'I didn't dare to try. All that way away and nobody
understanding anything about it . . . my neck, I mean.' Then I suddenly
remembered something. 'But one really important thing happened in
Portugal that I must tell you about,' I said slowly. 'I made a great friend
while I was there . . . a poet, with an Australian husband who was "shot
to pieces" in the last war.' I told Laurens about the 'miracle man' who

had cured Norah's husband, after being incapacitated for so many years. 'She kept on telling me that I must see this Mr Streeter. He has a practice in Park Lane,' I added.

'And certainly you must . . . at once,' Laurens said. 'I'm going to make you an appointment now.'

'It's all right. I've already done it . . . by post,' I explained.

'Good . . . and I hope you didn't forget to mention your friend's name? You see, my love, there may not be much time to waste. That's why I'm so eager for you to see him as soon as possible.'

Laurens was a strange person: more than profound in his understandings, yet immediately practical in his reactions.

Later that week I went to Mr Streeter's address in Park Lane and was shown into his consulting-room. He was quite an elderly man, not very tall, but with a feeling of great efficiency about him. I was terrified of being touched by this unknown, so-called doctor; but I kept on reminding myself of Norah's husband.

Mr Streeter told me to stretch out on the long flat couch that dominated his consulting-room. Then, without saying a word, and without jerks or pain, his gentle fingers probed the whole of my spine, and then concentrated almost solely on the area of pain which was at the back of my neck. Finally, after what seemed a long time, he helped me up, and also taught me how best to stand up on my own.

'Say, Candy-pull,' he said, with a broad American accent. 'I wanna see you perhaps two, or even three, hours every week . . . okay by you?'

'Yes,' I said weakly. I would have nodded but after the inspection I had received I was almost afraid to turn my head.

'Take it easy, Candy-pull,' said Mr Streeter. 'Relax. And follow the instructions I've given you down to the last detail.'

And so we made the next appointment and I continued to see Mr Streeter regularly for several weeks. I never asked him any questions; and he never gave me any information. It was just a matter of mutual confidence – and the ability to pay the monthly bills, for which I thanked both Jimmy and Heaven.

Then came the great day when Mr Streeter's clever, probing fingers ceased their search.

'That's done it, Candy-pull,' he said. 'You can go and write your head off now, or try to.'

Slowly, and sideways, I got up off the couch, as he had taught me to do.

I stared at him. 'But the diagnosis . . . what was wrong?'

'Wanna know?' He smiled and came very close to me. Then he said in a voice that was almost a whisper: 'Candy-pull, the tremendous smash of that bolting horse against your head, and catching you sideways, very nearly broke your neck . . . and you know what that means.'

A shudder ran through me; but it was easy to believe.

'But now it's all back in place again, and the bones have settled in, and your neck's firmly in position. In fact, Candy-pull, it's as good as new. So now you can go and write. But take it easy: only very short periods for a start . . . half an hour or so . . . and you mustn't touch the typing yet awhile. The most important thing for you to do is swim . . . but only breaststroke, and take it very slowly. That should help.'

I asked around and discovered that there was a magnificent swimming-pool at the Grosvenor House Hotel in Park Lane, together with a most helpful instructor. So I bought a new bathing-costume, went to the hotel and introduced myself to the instructor, Mr Hines, in the enormous basement swimming-pool, and told him that I wanted to learn how to swim. He told me to go and change and when I emerged, feeling extremely nervous, he took me right up to the deep end of the almost empty pool. I found this rather alarming, for I had imagined that I would be jumping around in the shallow end. However Mr Hines, who carried a long pole in his hand, was adamant that we should go to the deep end. He then told me, very nicely, to go down the steps and start to swim.

I looked at the seemingly bottomless water in front of me and said, 'But I don't know how to swim. That's why I'm here!' At that moment I felt quite terrified.

'All I want from you is that you give an imitation of some of the people that you must have seen swimming.'

It was the word 'imitation' that did it. After all, I had been 'imitating' people for years on the stage. So I made my way tentatively down the steps, thinking only of the people I had seen swimming in the sea. I kept my head up and my eyes open, and the pole was always within reach of my hand as I splashed forward in a determined struggle. And somehow I managed to 'swim', or rather splash, my way the whole length of that enormous pool. When I climbed out I could tell that Mr Hines was pleased with my efforts. He was such a nice man and, as I was to discover from my daily swimming lessons, utterly committed to his job.

Then one day I arrived to find the pool closed.

'Where is Mr Hines?' I asked.

'Dead,' came the sober reply.

'Dead! But how?'

'Overwork,' was the simple answer. 'He was here every day from dawn till dusk, just teaching people.'

I could have wept. I had lost a friend. At the same time I knew it was the way that a dedicated swimming teacher would have chosen to die. In gratitude to Mr Hines I continued to go swimming daily.

And so Mr Streeter had lived up to his reputation of being a 'miracle man'. Unlike Norah's husband, I did not take up my golf-clubs, but I did very occasionally take up my pen and start to write. And I did learn how to enjoy swimming.

During the next few weeks I made every effort to lead a so-called normal life, but psychologically this proved difficult. The clouds of the future were very black indeed. Even Jimmy felt them gathering in the office.

'The financial world is standing on its head,' he said.

But despite, or perhaps because of, what I had witnessed as a child, I found it difficult to believe that the growing disproportions of the world situation would escalate into a second world war . . . brought about not by rivalry in territorial or national rights, but by a typical 'closed shop' attitude to life itself. Surely people must now see through this subterfuge and its corresponding uselessness? I could get so far in generalities . . . and feel a possible sense of reassurance . . . but my individual response to the prospect of another war got no further than Laurens. If he were to lose his life defending his adopted country, I knew I would no longer have any desire to live. I also knew I would never commit suicide . . . but only because I felt that that would cut me off from him in any future spiritual life, in which I believed. I knew, too, that Laurens's father had been a Dutch nobleman and his mother had come from a French Huguenot family, and that together they had fled to South Africa in order to escape 'the corruption of Europe'. What a cruel paradox, therefore, that Laurens, their child, should be prepared to defend, with his life if necessary, that very same 'corrupted Europe'. I preferred the irony to the agony of the thought.

34

The Theatre of Life

I had come back to London in the late summer of 1939 feeling rather like a nun emerging from a long retreat, dazed by the talk of war, doom and disaster that I found wherever I turned. After all, I had left England with Neville Chamberlain's words 'Peace in our time' still ringing in my ears, and I, like many others, had believed him. Consequently I could not fully understand how dangerously misguided he had been. Yet intuitively I sensed that there was more than just newspaper propaganda fanning the flames of public alarm all round me.

My first overt acknowledgment of threat was my bitter reaction to Hitler's treatment of the Jews. Seeing an appeal in the Personal Column of *The Times* for homes for Jewish refugees I replied to the advertisement, offering to take two, and was put in touch with a Jewish lady who begged me to have her nieces from Germany; she herself could do no more for them because she was helping some sixty refugees to escape to America and India. I said that I would willingly do so, and was given a date for the arrival of Sophie and Gertrud Dann. I expected to be confronted by two woebegone figures, perhaps clutching a single suit-case, so I was astonished to see a Rolls-Royce draw up outside the house and two very nicely dressed, obviously Jewish girls come up the steps and ring my front-door bell. I greeted them warmly and was thankful that I was doing something to help these two broken young women. They could not speak a word of English but were overjoyed at the thought of 'looking after my house'. They did their best with my shopping lists but would occasionally arrive home with the strangest foods, which meant that Jimmy and I sat down to some very unusual meals! Having Sophie and Gertrud was a wonderful experience, partly ironic, partly comic, and greatly tragic. To this day, twice a year, I get cards and letters from these two women, who are still in England. They were the forerunners of the tragic events which were to befall us all.

One evening, Laurens, Jimmy and I were sitting reminiscing in the little back garden in Cadogan Street when Jimmy, giving vent to the tension we were all feeling now that England was unquestionably on the brink of war, suddenly said, 'Let's get out of this country for a few days. Why don't we go over to France?'

There was a long silence. Then Laurens said quietly, 'If we did that, we would take the risk of never being able to get back to England.'

I was stunned. Surely Laurens must be exaggerating? Yet he was the last sort of person to make an emotionally invalid statement.

Again there was silence. Then I said, 'What about my caravan? We haven't seen it for nearly a year. Let's go down to Devon and see if it is still there; and if it is, perhaps we can stay for a night or two and get a breather?'

I think I used the term 'get a breather' not only because the atmosphere around us was dark and stifling but also because I felt a deep, instinctive need to return to my natural beginnings which had been in Devonshire. The previous year, I had seen the caravan for sale at a Salvation Army gathering for five pounds! I had looked inside and seen that it was spotlessly clean and had a top surround of stained-glass windows such as one might find in a chapel. This, for me, had given the caravan a special kind of individuality, so I had bought it and Jimmy and I had towed it down to Devonshire and parked it in a remote spot on Dartmoor.

There was a moment's silence after this suggestion. Then Laurens said, 'As a matter of fact we have been working day and night in the newspaper world and I have actually been given the weekend off . . . so I could manage it.'

Jimmy said, 'I could drive us down there; but I would have to be able to keep in touch with the office by phone.'

My spirits soared. 'The caravan is only a couple of miles or so from that little village with the pub, Jimmy,' I said. 'You could telephone from there, couldn't you?'

Without further discussion we left early the next morning for the West Country. Jimmy was a splendid driver, so we travelled fast. At times it seemed that the country around was paralysed into inaction and that we were the only human beings in movement. Finally we arrived at the remote village with its pub, and from there, in the distance, through Jimmy's binoculars, we could see the small white spot that was, or might be, my caravan. So we bumped our way over the moors towards it.

When I unlocked the caravan I was thankful to find that it was neither damp nor dirty, merely dusty. I had brought a rug for the bunk, and Laurens had brought a tent. Sophie and Gertrud had put together a cold supper for the three of us, tidily packed into a cellophane bag, but before we ate, Laurens drove Jimmy to the village to make his telephone call to London. They returned with the news that Jimmy was urgently needed back in London and, in order to be in the office at crack of dawn the following day, he decided to take a fast train to London that very night. This sense of urgency in Jimmy surprised me; normally he was so easy-going. So, having driven back to Exeter to put him on the train, Laurens and I had our supper alone, sitting on the rug amongst the heather and watching the sinking sun add a new brilliance to the rich purples, greens and oranges of the far-flung moorland. The only sound to be heard was the gentle tinkle of an adjoining stream making courageous passage across the miles and miles of empty country. I told myself that this was nature and we belonged to it; and it to us. Thankfully Laurens and I were united in experiencing this very special feeling. Then, finally, very slowly, the sun sank, and in sinking lit up the sky with a wider and darker light. Speaking little, we sat and watched it, each with our own thoughts.

Then Laurens put up his tent, rolled up his coat for a pillow, and took a rug for a mattress. I, too, finally undressed, lit a candle, and lay down in my bunk. There was an immense silence without, which seemed to join hands with the almost consecrated atmosphere inside the caravan created by the stained-glass, and it felt wonderful to be living in the present instead of in trembling anticipation of the future. For, I told myself, life could not always be lived through meaning; but it did always have to be lived in trust.

I lay very still, staring up at the stained-glass windows illuminated by the candlelight. They told no story, as in a church, but their flickering colours merging together somehow gave me a sense of deep commitment. But commitment to what? Presumably the only commitment of real value was that given to life itself? But in what strange disguises 'life' could present itself. Did one therefore have to learn how to see through these disguises until one reached reality? Despite the queer remoteness of the silence about me, I fell asleep with this question still unanswered.

The next morning I woke early with a sense of being at one with the absorbed stillness that surrounded us, and slowly putting on my clothes I felt glad that I belonged to Devonshire. I pulled back the curtain at the caravan window and stared out at the brilliant light of the early morning already holding out its arms to embrace both me and the dark presence of the widely scattered moors. And then the thought flashed into my mind that never before had I really felt that I belonged anywhere, or to anyone; not even to my mother. Our very close relationship was based on a mutual acceptance, and also a valued understanding and love, of our basic differences. But here, under my very eyes, was somewhere that really did feel like home. Then I suddenly thought of my father; and I remembered how transfixed I had been by the photograph of him that had hung over my bed until, advisably, it had been removed. I also remembered that my father had requested in his will that he should be buried in Devonshire, at a place called Chittlehampton. So he must have felt this same sense of belonging. So far as I knew, nobody had ever been to visit his grave: I felt rather shaken by this realisation as I went out of the caravan to have breakfast with Laurens, who was busy buttering scones and making coffee.

I sat down on the rug and somewhat diffidently told Laurens about my thoughts regarding my father's grave. After a pause he looked at me rather absently, almost as if he were not seeing me. Then he looked at his watch and said uncertainly, 'Well, we may be able to fit in a visit to Chittlehampton . . . if it's not too far away.' Looking at his watch again he added, 'But first I must go and telephone Jimmy to see if he – he has got home all right . . . and find out how things are in London.'

He seemed in such a hurry that I said at once, 'All right, you go and telephone and I will do the washing-up, pack up and lock up, and be ready to leave when you get back.'

Laurens looked relieved and went off in the car; and I got busy. On his return I appeared to be ready for immediate departure but inwardly I felt far from ready to leave.

Laurens got out of the car slowly, and he also spoke very slowly. 'I got through on the phone to Cadogan Street,' he said. 'Jimmy says we must return at once and he suggests that we go back via Guildford to see your mother. He can easily join us there – if necessary.'

Instantly I was alarmed. 'But why? Is my mother all right?' I asked anxiously. 'Is she able to cope with all of us at such short notice?'

'Oh, Jimmy says she's very well: in fact, it was her suggestion that we should drop in and that you should perhaps spend the night there,' Laurens replied quietly, adding, 'I think we should leave as soon as possible, to allow time to visit Chittlehampton churchyard.'

So we packed our belongings into the car, locked the caravan and bumped our way back across the moors towards the road that would take us to Chittlehampton. The church was easily located but when we got out of the car to search for the grave it took us a long time, reading every headstone, before we finally found a small, simple cross inscribed with my father's name and his date of birth and death. The grave was thick with weeds, and the cross itself was covered with mildew which made the lettering barely legible. This, together with the dark shadows from a nearby hedge, was all that was left to my father, or of him. Suddenly I was greatly disturbed. Tears, either of fear or sorrow, threatened me. Then Laurens, perhaps sensing my feelings, took my arm and we walked slowly back to the car where we drank coffee from the Thermos flask we had brought with us before starting on the long drive to my mother's home in Surrey. As Laurens reversed the car, a sense of loss regarding my father assailed me, which was something that I had never felt in my life before. Perhaps in consequence of this, I pulled down the car window so that the air could blow in and somehow refresh me; which it did.

'It's quite cold for August,' I said.

There was a pause and then Laurens said quietly, 'But it isn't August. In fact, it is the third day of September.'

I was amazed. 'Is it?' I had been avoiding the newspapers in recent days, so had lost track of the date. But I did know that I needed that breath of fresh air, for I was leaving behind me a great entanglement of feelings; and the future facing me was so angular in its construction that I could not even visualise the outline. I stared up at the glowing sky which, in my imagination, seemed to be warming to my very thoughts. I turned to ask Laurens his views on this but he was determinedly concentrating on getting to my mother's as quickly as possible. Clearly this was not a moment for the voicing of inner thoughts.

It was Laurens who finally broke the silence. 'We must be there by eleven,' he said. 'The PM is speaking on the radio at 11.15 sharp.'

We made it to Guildford with a few minutes to spare, and as we drew up at the front door of my mother's home it was opened abruptly, not by the staff, but by my mother herself. After a quick kiss on my cheek she took Laurens's arm and led him aside and started questioning him. I had often wondered what she thought of our relationship but now, in some curious way, 'relationships' seemed to have vanished out of the window. All that was left was love, and terror, and unending and eroding uncertainty regarding the future. Was my mother talking to Laurens about 'current affairs'? Or was she talking to him about what could be called our personal affair?

'You will both stay the night, won't you?' I heard her ask anxiously, and I realised at once that instinctively, despite everything, she trusted Laurens and needed his quiet sense of authority, knowledge and support, as did I.

Laurens hesitated, then he looked at his watch and said, 'I should love to stay but I fear I must leave for London soon after lunch because I am on night duty in the office.'

'Then I'll come with you,' I said at once. 'Jimmy will be home later, and although Sophie and Gertrud are supposed to be looking after him, it is more likely that he is looking after them!'

Neither Laurens nor my mother tried to change my mind.

On that momentous morning of Sunday 3rd September all of us, including the staff, gathered in the morning-room. We sat there in silence for several moments. Then, at 11.15 am precisely, the Prime Minister, Neville Chamberlain, made the dire and solemn pronouncement that 'since eleven o'clock this morning this country has been in a state of war with Germany'.

The silence continued in the morning-room . . . then suddenly my mother burst into tears. I took her outside and together we walked up and down the lawn in the early autumn sunshine, down and up, up and down, until, from sheer exhaustion, her tears stopped. Then we returned to the house. The dismay and disarray in our small family unit was no doubt similar to that being experienced in millions of other households across the country that Sunday lunchtime.

After lunch, the staff having disappeared to the kitchen quarters, Laurens was filling up the car with petrol in preparation for our departure when Major John, joining us in the drive, drew me aside. 'Don't worry about your mother,' he said quietly. 'I am having an air-raid shelter made in the garden, not too far from the house and not too near it either . . . so no need to worry about us.'

His words of reassurance were unnecessary as I knew beyond any question of doubt that my stepfather would take care of my mother, no matter what the circumstances.

The last lap of our journey felt quite unreal and the world's present peril seemed to obliterate speech as a means of communication. Again memories of childhood seized me and I remembered waking to the sound of soldiers marching, marching, in the early hours of the morning . . . and hearing the erratic footfalls of wounded men, crippled or blinded or without limbs, as they began to fill the streets of Folkestone. Fear lay deeply within me but, strangely, it was not fear for myself. I feared only for Laurens. If he were wounded and became one of those blue-clad figures, then I could look after him and be with him for ever. But my real terror was that he might be killed. So completely did this agony of fear for Laurens possess me that I could scarcely envisage the world situation, or even consider the vulnerability of my own family.

As we drove through the outskirts of London I noticed that, high up, the sky seemed to be filled with what looked like balloons. They looked so delicate and beautiful floating about in the dark heavens that I almost smiled.

'Oh, how lovely!' I said. 'What are those things doing up there?'

There was a pause, then Laurens answered, 'They are barrage balloons.'

'But what are they there for?' I asked, puzzled.

'They are for our defence,' Laurens answered quietly.

'Our defence?' I was momentarily confused; and it was as if a curtain came down swiftly on that moment, leaving me, the only spectator, in complete darkness in the theatre of life itself. I sat very still, speechless, just staring ahead as the unlit streets of central London came slowly into view. All the houses seemed to be shrouded in darkness as if they were wearing widows' weeds. Was it possible that there was still time for the human spirit to discover its old, selfless values? I did not know: I just knew that, apparently, all that had been discovered under duress could still be lost through blindness of heart or greed of being.

Finally we reached Cadogan Street. My house was blacked out, as were all the others, so that we could not even see a glimmer of light. Laurens followed me up the front steps and then took me in his arms: we clung together. Above us, the balloons with their light movements were now heedless partners in the dance of death which was all about us.

Blindly I took the doorkey out of my bag and put it in the lock . . . then Laurens turned and went down to the pavement. I stood there in the deepening twilight, waiting as his footsteps faded. Finally, as he turned to wave to me, even the comforting glow from his cigarette was no longer visible.

PART V

Jung, taken four years after I first met him and as I best remember him, because he told me this was his favourite post-war snapshot.

35

The Blackout

As I opened the front door my hand, conditioned by many years of habit, reached out to switch on the passage light, and almost at once drew back. For an instant I had forgotten that at eleven o'clock that morning, when we had listened to Chamberlain's declaration of a state of war, everything had changed, and even so simple and natural an action as switching on a light had been strictly forbidden until all the blinds and curtains were drawn. It was a trifle, and yet it went deep and filled me with dismay, because it meant that any chink of the illumination which had for so long made home a bastion against the dark was now impossible.

I groped my way along the corridor to the cloakroom where I always kept a torch and, shielding it carefully, went about the house checking that the 'blackout' was being observed. All the while I was doing this I felt as though I were moving on two different levels of reality. There was the me who had just come up from the country on a glorious September evening and who had watched London announce itself on the limpid early autumn horizon, not with the treetops and spires which normally graced the skyline but with vast arrangements of silver anti-aircraft balloons floating in the honey-coloured twilight, imparting a sense of menace all the more sinister because of the beauty reflected on their surfaces. After this first glimpse of London prepared for war, driving through the strangely hushed and darkened streets, and my brief goodbye to Laurens, I had been invaded by an acute sense of ambivalent reality, until now, in my shuttered drawing-room, I was not only enclosed in the sombre present but was also back in my childhood, listening, with fear in my unschooled heart, to the tramp, tramp, tramp of soldiers marching by in the dark.

I remembered, too, another September when a light, as still and tender and precise as that of the day behind me, had trembled for days with the thunder just on the frontier between silence and sound to the barrage of thousands of great guns announcing another of the bloodiest onslaughts of the war. I thought of how it had all begun and how, young as I was, I had been shaken by the ominous warning which Grey of Fallodon had given us all in words that, like my mood, had a meaning on two levels: 'The lamps are going out all over Europe.' And I was struck with the feeling that what we were facing now was something more dangerous, more insidious and lethal because not only had all the lamps gone out in Europe, they were going out for an unforeseen duration in the cities, villages, hamlets and lonely farms of England, leaving a greater darkness in which not just a part but all of humanity was involved. The blackout, I felt, was reaching beyond the streets into the mind and spirit of man.

I dwell on my initial reaction to the blackout because it became, increasingly, the predominant element in the climate of heart and mind with which I confronted the Second World War. It seemed ever clearer to me that this blackout in the minds of men was responsible for the horror that now awaited us. It was a blackout which had shadowed the generations which preceded me and in all sorts of small ways had perplexed and haunted, in some basement of the human mind, the lives of people like my mother. It was the disguised and undiscovered agent of the unhappiness she had so bravely endured and which I had instinctively shared. And it was the specific and individual intrusion of this blackout into my own life that had led me to my first experience of what I have called 'the Voice', which spoke to me in a moment of extreme anguish with an authority that instantly convinced me: 'This is man: it has nothing whatsoever to do with God.'

Comforted for the moment that what the experience of 'the Voice' had so often symbolised and expressed for me in the past would not fail me now, I went to bed, and in the morning found myself ready to face whatever the future was to bring to my door, and all the implications which war would henceforth have for my personal relationships.

I knew already what the three men who mattered most in my life were going to do. My brother Roger, of course, was already with his ship *The Repulse* preparing for war. Jimmy, who had had some naval training at Osborne and who loved ships and the sea, was even now, after a hurried breakfast, on his way to the Admiralty to offer himself for enlistment. And Laurens, who was an officer in the forces of his native South Africa, but who felt doubtful that his country would come into the war, had decided to try and join up as a private in the British Army. By the end of the day both he and Jimmy came home to say that they had succeeded and would be receiving their call-up papers soon.

But what was I to do? Some weeks before, staying with friends in the country, a fellow guest of considerable influence who, in his youth, had been a protégé of Cecil Rhodes and who, unlike the rest of us, was certain that war was imminent, had seemed interested in the fact that I spoke French and knew some Italian and German. He took me aside and told me he was organising the censoring services for the war and that, if it should come about, he would very much like me to join his department. As soon as Laurens and Jimmy were out of the house the following day, I decided to telephone and make an appointment to see him. To my amazement he saw me straight away, and when we all three met up at home that evening, I was able to tell them that I had just accepted the post of Assistant Deputy Chief Censor and would take up my duties immediately. I remember how, far from resenting that I should have joined them in the rush to do war service, the three of us spent one of our last few happy evenings together celebrating our new roles with a bottle of champagne.

The office in which I worked was in a large building in Holborn. I shared it with an Edwardian short-story writer who is probably forgotten today but had a certain fashionable following in the pre-First World War days and the years immediately afterwards. In an age of magazines, he had been a regular contributor to one of the most prestigious of all, *The Pall Mall Magazine*. His name was Cosmo Hamilton, and he not only wrote Edwardian but looked and behaved it too. He had a flat in the Albany, dressed impeccably and possessed beautiful, chivalrous manners, and I often thought how lucky I was to have him as a colleague. At least once a week he insisted, almost as if it were a religious ritual, on taking me to lunch at the Savoy Restaurant where he had a corner table overlooking the trees between the hotel and the Embankment. There in this remarkably beautiful September, while the sun sparkled, the barges glided by and the water streamed peacefully past outside, it was impossible to believe that the Poles were being slaughtered in their thousands, Warsaw gutted by German bombs, and even the Russians, in one of the most perfidious and cynical of acts, were joining their professed enemies to take advantage of a country whose repeated partitioning between great powers has been one of the great scandals of European history. Yet there we were, enjoying the comforts of the Savoy and looking into a day as of a 'World charged with the grandeur of God'. And with that thought came the memory that I owed the line to Laurens who had introduced me to Gerard Manley Hopkins on the deck of the *Watussi* somewhere in the South Atlantic. No wonder the phrase 'a phoney war', which was to endure for another seven months, was already creeping into popular speech.

But, to do Cosmo and myself some justice, in the course of many a happy lunch we would suddenly fall silent and look around the restaurant full of people eating an abundance of things in an atmosphere of unrivalled luxury, both of us reflecting on an experience embedded for good in our memories. Cosmo would exclaim: 'I would never have thought, after the last war, that the world would ever be so stupid as to come to this again!' Then he would pause and, as if talking to an invisible audience, and with an emotion which he seldom showed in his normal behaviour, continue: 'Yes! A million of the finest and best of young men were not enough. If only they had lived, it might not have come to this!' And I would return with him to our office in Holborn with the reality of war reinforcing my fear that, like the million or more young people who had been killed in the First World War, my brother, Jimmy and Laurens were now in danger of being killed likewise.

From my office window I could just see the dome of St Paul's and, although I had lived in London for many years, I used to have the feeling that I was seeing it truly for the first time. I remembered a poem of Walter de la Mare's in which he said that we must always look on all things lovely as though for the last time, but it seemed to me that this wonderful dome, with the beauty of the day gathering around it, had its full impact on me then, in the face of the unknown. I kept remembering how it had risen out of the ashes of the Great Fire of London and was glad that it dominated my vision of the world through those hours of work. To me, it was evidence of some pattern in the human spirit which ensured that the aspirations which had sent this cathedral soaring out of fire would transcend all other fires to come as well.

More troubling to me than my own apprehension was the feeling that I was not doing enough to help. I even began to feel disillusioned with the people who ran the branch of the censorship organisation in which I was working. Our head was a retired Indian Army general who was well-known in his day not only as a soldier but as a writer of sorts; his name does not really matter because his attitude to our work was not altogether unusual in the early days of the war, so that I remember him more as a symbol than as an individual. There was the occasion, for example, one afternoon towards the end of September when I was busy clearing my desk so that I could get home before the blackout. The general's daughter, who also worked for him, as did his wife, came into my office and said reprovingly: 'Daddy won't be at all pleased to see you working like this.'

'Why not?'

'Because,' she said, 'he told us only this morning not to worry about work today. We are being inspected tomorrow by the Heads of Department and he wants them to find us all hard at work then.'

From that moment all my vague but urgent feelings of discontent came to the surface, and not long afterwards I resigned from Censorship. My immediate priority, I decided, was to concentrate on the two people closest to me, who would both be leaving for the war before long; only after that would I seek my own personal call to duty.

In the event, they both departed sooner than I had expected. Jimmy was called away to Portsmouth for a course of training, and Laurens went off to Shoreham as a private in the British Army, before being selected for a Wartime Officers' Course at Aldershot and Camberley. Happily, when Laurens had leave, I was able to spend most of my weekends with my mother and stepfather in nearby Guildford, and during the week be free to go to Portsmouth where I took a room in a hotel and tried to make a home for Jimmy. In this way I felt that human relationships, which were always my first concern, were best served. With the heightened perceptions which, alas, only war and danger seem to bring us, I felt singularly fulfilled during this period when my mother – who perhaps suffered most of all – Jimmy, Laurens and I were drawn closer than ever before.

More important still, during these months when I confronted the menace without by turning inwards towards what mattered to me most, I seemed, paradoxically, to be strengthening myself for confronting disaster in the outside world. I remember telling Laurens, 'We have to learn now to be outward bound the inward way and homeward bound the outward way.' Tentative as this inclination to move inwards still was, it was leading me away from the dimension of floating things and appearances, as the Zen Buddhists – according to Laurens – would put it, and towards a search for greater meaning in my inner world.

As October merged into November and the blackout became even denser with some of the worst fogs in London that I can remember, followed by the frost and ice and snow which made 1939 such a bitter winter, even the world of appearances seemed to be gripped by ice at heart and brought to a strange and ominous standstill. It was a standstill dominated by a sense of waiting for the worst – whatever that might be. I found myself longing for spring as I had never longed for it before, even though Hitler was generally thought to be waiting only for the end of winter before doing to us what he had already done to the Poles and the East Europeans. When spring finally arrived, it came, as it does so miraculously in England, with the violence of a volcanic eruption and a suddenness that made the months of waiting vanish like snow in a morning full of sun.

And then the real war broke loose. As it increased in scope and intensity, and the bombing of Britain began, all that was phoney not only in the war but in people seemed to fall away, and one began to see a new meaning in life with greater clarity than before.

I remember, during one of my weekends in Guildford towards the end of Laurens's course, that we spoke of war as a terrible healer called in by life when all natural methods to make man serve it creatively, and renew the outworn patterns of themselves, had failed. Other strange premonitions began to move into one's awareness, and intimations of the future appeared in what many saw as a moment of utter annihilation. For instance, we talked of the work that had been done at Cambridge on the nature of the atom and its possible significance for the course of the war and for life thereafter. Laurens told me of a remark one of his training officers had made: that he was convinced that the war, in a manner he could not possibly foresee, would be decided by something that would come out of the forces released in the splitting of the atom. I remember my own intuition which made me retort that, just as the atom was the smallest unit of matter which we could visualise in the here-and-now, it did not frighten me nearly so much as the split in the heart of man which had precipitated the war. What energies could not come out of such a divide in the soul? My response was indicative of the fact that this movement towards the world within me was gathering pace and direction.

All too soon these strangely happy days divided between Laurens and Jimmy came to an end. Laurens was commissioned and, having passed out at the head of his battalion with a report stating that he had proved exceptional in every way, he went straight on to Staff College in Camberley where he was suddenly given a week's pre-embarkation leave. At the end of his leave I accompanied him to London and saw him off at Liverpool Street Station in the blackest of blackouts. Laurens's only instructions were to report to the Transport Officer in Liverpool and, perhaps in an effort to lighten the gloom which enveloped us both, he remarked: 'I expect the War Office have discovered that I was born in Africa and so are posting me as some sort of military attaché somewhere in South America.'

He had hardly finished speaking when the air-raid sirens sounded an alarm, one in a series that had already become a nightly occurrence in London. Our goodbye was more like an amputation than a farewell in the darkened station, for the train too was blacked out and there was no point in exchanging even the flutter of a handkerchief to lessen the increasing distance between us and soften the bleakness of our separation which, although I did not know it then, was to be endured for years. I walked back along the platform like some kind of fly struggling through a stream of black treacle and, when I got home, found that I no longer automatically reached for the light switch just inside the front door as I had continued to do despite the blackout.

After a sleepless night, the morning newspapers were filled with the horror of the bombing of Coventry, and the real war, which had to be fought in the heartland of what resistance to Nazism remained in the world, by every man, woman and child in Britain, had begun. Within a fortnight Jimmy was ordered to his ship, and I was alone within myself as I had never been before.

The only clarity in my personal darkness at this time was an instinct, from now on, to fight what had become for me a two-dimensional war – the war without and the war within – from my own home. I was continually hearing people describing something that had happened to them and capping it with the remark: 'It really brought the war home to me.' Well, I decided not to wait for an 'it' to bring the war home to me. I was *taking* it home with me and I would fight it through what was nearest and most immediate, however trivial or big. I would fight on my own doorstep.

The moment I decided to do this I was relieved of one dark element in my spirit. Fear for my personal safety suddenly fell from me as a leaf from a tree in the glorious autumn just past, and until the end of the war, I never experienced it again. I also had no fear that, isolated though Britain was now that France had fallen, we would lose out to the evil confronting us across the Channel. All my fear was concentrated in one overwhelming dread: that anything should happen to Jimmy, Laurens or my brother.

Within a few weeks I had enrolled as an air-raid warden, helping to cope with the fires at night in the streets of London. By day, our housekeeper, Mrs Pearce, and I went to a small factory in a Thames-side warehouse, making fuses and priming cases for bombs; it had been started, I am proud to say, by a well-known actress I had once worked with. These two occupations satisfied the longing I felt to do something immediate and practical for the cause of war, but they gave me something even more important: a knowledge, understanding and love of the extraordinary, ordinary people of Britain. Examples of their humanity and courage will stay with me for ever, for not a day passed in our little bomb factory by the river, or on the streets that I patrolled at night, without some act of kindness or bravery to inspire and reassure me.

I remember a night of bombs, fire and flame when one of the people who worked with me in the factory by day and was an air-raid warden by night – and who in peacetime had been my chimney-sweep – went again and again into buildings crumbling and ablaze to rescue people from the rubble, even though burnt and wounded himself, and so became one of the first people to earn a George Cross. I remember Mrs Pearce's fury when those supervising the evacuation of children in their thousands to homes in the country, or to America, wanted to evacuate her baby daughter. She rounded on them as a lioness might in defence of her cub, exclaiming: 'Get away with you! I am not going to have that there Hitler separate me from my daughter and break up my family. What sort of person do you think I am?'

It seemed to me, who already had a keen sense of the significance of coincidences, that Churchill might have heard her speaking because, that very night on the radio, we heard him defy our enemies with the words: 'What sort of people do they think we are?' And I realised that he was the only person who could see us through, because he alone knew the inexhaustible reserves of courage, endurance, humour and compassion which the British people had invested in their history, so creating out of their past a present that was immensely rich in spiritual resources.

Uplifted, I watched this vast process of rediscovery of an historical identity reinforcing the value of the individual and eliminating all social differences and class distinction. Not only did we all seem to walk more equal and with a new kind of dignity in one another's sight, but we viewed each other with a heightening of perception and a new respect for individual differences, so that, despite the everyday horrors, our lives were enriched by this rediscovered dimension of unity of spirit. It came to a point where this trend seemed so precious that I almost felt that the war would have been justified if it taught us nothing else, and I prayed that the ultimate peace would not endanger it. At first I was startled, if not shocked, that the prospect of peace should give me any cause for misgivings, but as the war ground cruelly and painfully on, my conviction grew that it had been brought about by an accumulation of all the tiny consequences of some failure of awareness and lack of knowledge in our personal lives. It seemed to me that the war was trying to tell us something, not about nations or even civilisations or history but about our deepest and greater, but imprisoned, selves. I remembered a conversation I had had with Laurens on board the *Watussi* which had ended with his remarking that he believed profoundly that there was a personal and specific meaning in everything that happened to one in life, and that this meaning had to be lived, however painfully, before it could be known; and, until one accepted that, one's own life was in danger of becoming meaningless.

More and more it seemed to me that, if one could only unlock the secret of the origin and causes of this war, when it was a mere seed concealed in the deepest recesses of our spirit, meaning would once again defeat meaninglessness. I realised that I would have to start searching within myself before I would be able to understand what was happening so blindly to the world outside. And once I began to accept the possibility that there was no suffering so great that it could not be endured, if one saw a meaning in it, a kind of peace came to me, as if I had arrived at last at the still centre of the storm.

From there, for a time, it seemed significant how the pattern of the lives of the people around me lost all anonymity, and each acquired a shape that seemed specifically designed to fit the individual nature of the person concerned. It was as if their beings combined unknowingly with these hidden selves to make them into a kind of magnet which drew to itself, from all the immense variety of happenings, only those for which the energies at their disposal had been polarised and that they needed for self-expression.

There was, for example, someone whom we had always regarded as a gifted dilettante, a lovable and generous person but a reckless spend-thrift. He came of an ancient and distinguished family, with one ancestor who had been painted by Holbein and others who were trusted advisers to kings and queens. Instead of being accepted for war service he found himself in hospital, where he was told that he had terminal cancer and only a few months to live. He accepted the verdict, as he had done both good and bad in the past, as if it were of no great consequence, and yet both history and its significance for him in our bitter here-and-now helped him to come to terms with the nature of his illness. All of us who saw him during his last months were impressed by the way that an unsuspected paradox had transformed this man into a happy person from the merry-go-lucky person he had been before. One night he took his own life, leaving behind a brief note of explanation which redeemed all his yesterdays and was the greatest comfort to those who cared for him. The note simply said: 'I think there are many more useful to England than I who need this bed.'

There was also the story of David Davidson, whom I had known in those far-off golden days in India and to whom I had been so deeply attached and, very briefly, engaged. When war broke out he emerged from retirement and returned to his Highland regiment. Once, on a military exercise in the Midlands during the Battle of Britain, the company he commanded recovered some parachutes from German pilots who had been shot down almost overhead. Parachutes were still made of the best and strongest silk, and were therefore extremely valuable, but this did not deter David from purloining one to have made into a dress for his current girlfriend. This was discovered by the Military Police and David was ordered to report to London for court-martial.

He was making his way to the court after dark during a massed German attack when, in a narrow street not far from St Paul's Cathedral, a building collapsed in flames across the street, covering him not only with rubble but a burning beam which pinned him by the leg to the ground so that he could not move. The situation must have seemed hopeless, with the fire advancing along the beam towards him. Yet something in David, perhaps the influence of the ancient Highland spirit of his people, refused to give up. He moved and wriggled, despite acute pain, and eventually found a way in which he could steer his imprisoned leg closer to the fire until, at last, he was able to push it into the heart of the flames and hold it there until the fire consumed it from halfway below the knee downwards. Only then was he able to pull himself clear along the ground into the safety of the far side of the street.

Telling me about this incident in hospital afterwards, David said that at the moment when the fire released his leg, all the pain and horror of his plight were transformed into the most unutterable sweetness, and for the first time he realised consciously how great a gift, no matter how awful the circumstances, was the gift of life. This, to me, became almost a parable, because the human spirit is prodigal, and only when it has utterly spent itself, as David's had, is it forgiven by the Father of all, the suffering eliminated and the soul reinvested with the greatest of treasures: the meaning of which neither moth nor rust can corrupt.

Another example of how the war brought friends of mine into contact with aspects of themselves of which, previously, they had been unaware remains especially dear to me because it concerned the world of the theatre that, at one time, had been so much a part of my emerging life. Busy though I was making bombs by day and being an air-raid warden by night, I had never lost touch with Athene Seyler and Beau Hannen, with whom I had been on those memorable trips to South Africa and Finland in the carefree days of the early thirties before the shadow of Hitler fell over Europe. As Athene's understudy in many productions over the years I had got to know her professionally as few people do:

she was a great comedy actress with perhaps the most formidable intellectual capacity of her generation in the theatre. It was this quality, above all, that had led to her becoming a friend and correspondent of George Bernard Shaw during his most demanding, provocative, and productive period as a playwright.

Most of all, beyond and beneath Athene's intellectual stature and gifts as an actress which I observed so clearly, I was impressed by a natural warmth, immediacy, magnanimity, generosity and integrity. She had qualities of heart which exceeded even those of mind, and although she was a good deal older than I, it was this balance of conscious and instinctive qualities which particularly drew me to her. If there were one aspect of her character which perhaps saddened me – and I use the word 'saddened' deliberately, to imply neither criticism nor reservation on my part – it was that she proclaimed herself to be an atheist. We never discussed this or argued about it, largely because I knew I must not intrude where her own mind refused to go. Yet, for all her anti-religious avowals, I knew that she was, unbeknown to herself, living a truly religious life. This fact was borne out by the quality of her relationship with Beau Hannen. He was one of the most feeling men I have ever known – non-rational where Athene was perhaps over-rational, instinctive and intuitive where she was measured and reasoned – yet they were devoted to each other, not just because of this compensatory balance of qualities but because of the respect and love each felt for the differences in the other.

Athene and Beau truly exemplified all that their friends thought that a marriage should be. Legally and religiously they were not married, however, but had lived together for a generation or more in such a way that most people could not believe, when told, that the couple were 'living in sin'. This was not due to Athene's professed atheism and lack of respect for religion but because, in the Edwardian era, when Beau Hannen had tried to break free of a disastrous marriage, the King's Proctor intervened, making divorce forever impossible for him. This hurt me almost as much as it hurt Athene. It hurt me not just because I was her friend, but because the attitude of the Church towards the matter of divorce seemed to me totally unchristian and a violation of the very love which it purported to uphold.

On one of my rare afternoons at home, after a prolonged air-raid warning and while I was thinking of Athene and Beau and the hurt I knew they were feeling even more acutely at this time when their lives seemed so precarious, there was a knock at my door which was repeated three times. In the silence which always followed late-afternoon raids, these knocks sounded more like the summons of Fate than the postman's rap on the door. I went to open it and was handed not just a modest bundle of letters but a package too large for my letterbox. I opened the parcel first, to find that it contained a book about religion. I do not remember the title or the name of the author or who had sent the book, but as I turned the pages with quickening interest because of the area of spirit in which my mind had become engaged, I realised that it was not intended for me. The book seemed, even on that brief appraisal, to have been sent by Providence and to be singularly meant for Athene. I immediately put on my coat and walked, book in hand, over to Chelsea Manor Street where Athene lived, only a quarter of a mile away from my home. Neither she nor Beau was at home, so I scribbled a note on a page of my diary: 'Athene dearest, I have a feeling that this book is meant for you not me. Love, Ingaret', and left it outside their front door.

As a result of reading this book, Athene's atheism vanished like a bat in the twilight and she decided, after much turmoil of heart and mind, to become an Anglican. The difficulties she had to overcome before she could be baptised and confirmed in the Anglican Church would make a story in itself. On the appointed day, accompanied by Beau, and Sybil Thorndike and myself whom Athene had asked to be her godmothers, she went to Westminster Abbey where she was privately baptised in the chapel. Perhaps the most moving part of the ceremony for me was the moment when the baptismal service ended and Beau, who stood nearby, stepped forward. In a knightly gesture he took Athene's hand, raised it and kissed it in a way that said all. Sybil and I went home on the top of a Number Eleven bus rejoicing, whatever doubts we had about our Church removed and our faith reaffirmed.

Soon after this experience, which I believe I needed for my own illumination, an event occurred that not only shattered my new-found calm and conviction but snuffed out the light I had sought in my own home and in my spirit, and seemed to make my heart and mind part of the great blackout in the streets and cities of England.

Through the front door of my little house in Cadogan Street one lovely morning came one of those communications from the War Office of which we all lived in dread. I was alone in the house after a night of unusually heavy bombing and not properly awake, and yet the moment I saw the brown envelope I began to shake as if I already knew what it contained. The message was brief and to the point: Laurens was reported missing, believed dead.

I have never been able to visualise Hell. None of the traditional concepts of it had ever made any impression on me, even as a child.

Even the imagery of poets like Dante left me cold, and so brimstone and lava and everlasting fire had never held any terrors for me. Even today Hell remains a great indescribable, but from the moment I read that War Office communication I believe I experienced it: not flames, or fire, or brimstone, but an absence of light which seemed absolute and immovable. The old mystics recorded what I believe was an experience of utterly objective light – a light so great that it not only eliminated the darkness of the night but dimmed the sun and abolished all grace of shade and blessing of shadow until, within and without, one was all radiance and the congregation in the temples of the human heart was all song, rising to a vast 'Hallelujah'. All I can say of this moment when the brown envelope arrived is that, faster than any flash of lightning, illumination was transformed into total darkness and, as this happened, all sense of time deserted me.

For days on end this feeling of timelessness enveloped me, and something beyond darkness and despair, or even conscious annihilation of one's deepest self, took over. I would look at my watch and close my eyes and then, after what felt like an eternity, look at my watch again to find that only a few seconds had passed: at such moments the horror of facing a lifetime of incarceration in what Kipling has called the 'unforgiving seconds', and I now recognised as Hell, was brought home to me.

In so far as my condition could be eased, my mother, who was herself all too familiar with the frozen state of utter despair, and whom I had been able to help, even as a little girl, in a way that I could not now help myself, hastened to my aid. She went to the War Office, armed with this brief but devastating communication, and knocked on doors, and in between the knocking sat patiently on uncomfortable chairs in cool, marble and utterly impersonal corridors. She did this day after day until, at last, one authoritative door was opened to her and she was told that such a message was not intended to be final or even accurate. The rapid advance of the Japanese armies throughout South-East Asia, and the total collapse of communications in the final hours of the British pockets of resistance, had compelled the Government to send out provisional messages to next-of-kin that could prove wrong, hence the insertion of the word 'believed'. There was, they stressed, hope in that word, and this ray of hope helped my mother, and ultimately me, to find an uneasy peace in the years ahead.

It was nourished in me by something Laurens had said in the blackout on Liverpool Street Station, just before he had left for his unknown destination. He had always been a great person for talking about his

hunches and it was, indeed, extraordinary how accurate they had sometimes proved to be, so much so that a very distinguished psychologist
who had befriended and helped my mother had said they ought to be
elevated to the realm of 'intuitions'. I remembered Laurens laughing as
he replied that his 'hunches' were fundamentally home-made visitations
and did not deserve to be incorporated into the august realms of psychology. At the moment of our parting, as Laurens was about to board
the train, he had put his hands on my shoulders, shaken me gently and
said, almost playfully, as one would to someone who had refused to
listen before: 'I have a hunch that you, your mama, your brother, Jimmy
and I will come through all this. No matter what happens, please
remember this because we shall all have a lot of surviving to do.'

There finally came a day, the memory of which still flushes me like
wine, when to my great surprise I woke up to find that the night behind
me and the day which had preceded it seemed to have moved and left
a sense of something akin to speed. After so many motionless months,
I knew then that I was out of the great standstill which was Hell to me.
I had rejoined the procession of life, and my soul and heart and mind
were reincorporated into the rhythms of the seasons. I was determined
to live with life, whatever the cost. I found from now on that, though I
continued to suffer, my suffering had been stripped of its superhuman
elements and restored to its lawful and bearable human proportion.

The extent of my recovery can best be measured by the fact that the
feeling of surprise I experienced on waking was accompanied by an urge
to look for an immediate and specific cause to explain it. This blacked-out
world outside time in which I had recently been existing was so far
removed from the cause-and-effect attitudes which regulate our everyday lives that I would have been incapable, even the day before, of
questioning anything that happened to me. Now, having regained a
certain health of spirit, I was not content until I had found the catalyst
which had precipitated this sense of surprise into consciousness.

I finally traced it back to a chance meeting which had taken place a
few days earlier and which had seemed to confirm the instinct that had
impelled me, at the start of the war, to focus on the blackout in my heart
and home rather than in the streets of our towns and cities. I had felt
intuitively that if I persevered in my search not only for the causes and
meaning of the war, but also for a healing darkness within, the light of
the future would one day shine like the morning star to awaken me to
a new dawn. The memory of the Voice, which in my girlhood had
exhorted me to distinguish between what was God's and what was
man's, had, of course, played a supporting role in this search; and, even

more so, the certainty of direction which had accumulated around this experience and enabled me to help my mother through her lonely years of suffering and, finally, to put her in touch with Jung.

The same instinct which had made me insist that my mother should write to Jung herself, made me hold back when Jung, finding that it was impossible for my mother to travel to Zurich, had recommended her to seek help from Dr Godwin Baynes. I had felt in my bones that the decision must be entirely her own and that, once she was committed to working with Dr Baynes, I must not intrude on their private world; it was a world wherein one must 'tread softly', as Yeats put it in one of my favourite poems, because one would be treading on my mother's dreams.

So, since the brief glimpse I had caught of Dr Baynes at my mother's first interview with him some five years earlier, I had taken care not to encounter him again. However, the impression he had made on me had been both vivid and lasting: his physical presence immediately suggested a great, warm, lovable man. My mother had told me that he had rowed for his university as a student and was full of energy and an abundance of outgoing thought and activity and, at the same time, was intensely human and humanly fallible. I had often wondered if it was this combination of fallibility and physical strength which was responsible for people calling him 'Peter' because, in the world of Jung, he was a rock on which great work was founded.

By the time war broke out, Dr Baynes had worked with my mother so successfully that she had found a sense of personal meaning and identity through her suffering which kept her, however painfully, on course for the rest of her life, so that even Baynes's untimely death in the late forties did not unbalance her. In 1939, at my mother's request, Laurens and I had worked together to create an atmosphere of welcome among the writers and newspaper people we knew for the 'great book' – as she had described it – which Peter Baynes had written about his own experience of Jungian psychology, *Mythology of the Soul*. Unfortunately it was published only a few days before war broke out and sought the light in a world which had no mind for anything but war. Despite the fact that *Mythology of the Soul* was a book of great pioneering consequence in the English-speaking world, it would have been left to make its mark without the help of the press if Laurens had not persuaded the editor of one of the most prestigious pre-war weeklies, *The Nation & Atheneum*, to review it at length, which encouraged others to follow.

It was, I now realised, no coincidence that my 'surprised awakening' had occurred only a matter of days after I had had a second encounter with Peter Baynes. Arriving unannounced at my mother's home, I had been somewhat taken aback to find him there but on this occasion I decided that my intrusion had in a sense been earned. I was excited to learn that he was already engaged on another book, to be called *Germany Possessed*. The title he had chosen supplied me with the word for which I realised I had been searching to describe the condition of war to the bitter end in which we were all involved. But even more significantly, Baynes told my mother and me a story about Jung which was like a reference on a vast map of the area in which this world war was so grimly unfolding, indicating the precise point where I myself stood: the point of departure for my own private and personal voyage into the future. He told us that Jung, throughout 1913 and during the first seven months of 1914, was haunted by a vision of Europe drowned in a thick crimson tide of blood. The tide would swell until it lapped the summits of the highest ranges of the Alps and he would see this sea of blood full of floating corpses, headless bodies and torn-off limbs. Even though he applied to this vision all his skill of interpreting dreams and his long experience of unconscious manifestations in the consciousness of his time, he could make no sense of it and derived no inkling of what it demanded of him. He became so profoundly troubled by this that he thought he was assailed by madness, which he had already defined as an invasion of a partial, conscious state of mind by unconscious impulses. So much did Jung fear that he was no longer a normal being that he felt he should not lecture or speak in public in case he contaminated others with this unanalysable psychological affliction. He came near to calling off a lecture he had agreed to give at a British medical conference in Aberdeen in July 1914 but was finally persuaded to keep to his plans.

Returning home the following day, Jung bought a newspaper on landing in Holland and was confronted with the news of the outbreak of the First World War. Instantly, he understood what his dreams and visions had been trying to tell him. So great was his relief at this realisation that he was shocked to find himself almost welcoming the war. Once back in Zurich, he knew that his task from that moment on was to work on both the imperviousness in himself which had denied him the meaning of this vision, as well as the dimension in which this dreaming activity arose. Until he had done all he could to understand the process in himself that, long before the outbreak of war, had involved a dynamic part of his mind and soul in the horrors to come, he would not be able to continue his life's work of making mankind conscious of the need for wholeness, both individually and collectively, which he came to regard as the deepest urge of Creator and creation.

Somehow, in the course of the night which preceded the morning when I woke with a sense of time restored to me, I had realised that in my own small way I now had to follow Jung's example. But how? Unlike Jung, I knew that I had gone as far as I possibly could by myself. As I was to realise later, with hindsight, by proxy of my mother I had begun the process of making myself whole by helping her to find transformation and wholeness in herself. But I had now reached the point when I needed help myself, expert help, in the sense that I needed a guide who had been in this dark world where I knew I had to go.

I had a great friend who always teased me about possessing something he called a 'penetrating immediacy'. I am certain this immediacy was not always penetrating but it was there in normal times, although it seemed to have abandoned me in recent months. I was overjoyed to find that it had returned to me and that, before the new day had passed, I had the answer. I knew, from friends my mother had made through Peter Baynes, of another close friend of Jung's, Eddie Bennett, who was working in London but was about to go on war service to South-East Asia. I telephoned him that evening and, through him, was led to a remarkable doctor and psychiatrist called Alan McGlashan, whom I went to see almost immediately and worked with until the end of the war.

36

Point of Total Return

Whenever I think back on my time with Alan McGlashan I think of him as a healer. He told me how for years he had been content to maintain a large and successful practice as a general physician, but how he came to be more and more haunted by the feeling that he was doing only half his work. This feeling became so strong that he sold his practice and submitted himself to the burning process of rediscovery and exploration that is called analysis. When he emerged from this to continue his work as a doctor he was relieved to find that, at last, he was equipped to carry out his full vocation of healing.

The fact that Alan McGlashan's adult life had not been confined to his medical training and practice increased my confidence in him. As a youth he had joined the Flying Corps in the First World War and had nearly fifty fighting sorties to his credit, including a confrontation with Baron Manfred von Richthofen, 'the Red Baron', which had ended with their ammunition exhausted and a chivalrous wave of hands before each returned to base to recharge their planes. He had won awards for gallantry from both the British and the French and, after the war, had studied medicine at Cambridge. In addition, he was passionately interested in the theatre which had claimed so large a part of my own being and imagination; indeed, he had been a drama critic for some years. He was also a born writer and the author of a book on a mythological subject. His whole life, in fact, had not only been a dream of ultimate totality but an exercise in what Jung called individuation – the search for a lucid and rounded self – and I could not have been luckier in finding such a navigator on what I have come to call my night sea journey.

It would obviously take a book in itself to write a full account of this voyage to the end of night which I accomplished with Alan McGlashan, but an extract from a letter I wrote to Laurens, who had miraculously emerged alive in South-East Asia after the Japanese surrender, perhaps conveys the essence of it. By the fateful pattern of coincidence which Jung came to call 'synchronicity', the news that Laurens was alive coincided almost to the day with the time when Alan McGlashan and I concluded that he had taken me as far as he could on my journey, and that I was now as qualified a deep-sea navigator as he could make me. I will not attempt to describe my feelings on learning of Laurens's survival because any words here would diminish the light that this brought back to me. Suffice it to say that we were happily in touch again and I had come to the point where I could write to him, among other things: 'It seems to me that people's private and personal lives have never mattered as they do now. For me the whole of the future depends on the way people live their personal rather than their collective lives. It is a matter of extreme urgency. When we have lived out our private and personal problems we can consider the next collective step. Then it will be easy, but until then it will not even be possible.'

Strengthened by this meaningful synchronicity and a feeling of having been confirmed in the temple of life itself, I turned to my first love, writing, and at great speed wrote a semi-autobiographical book called *The Return Journey* – a book in which the central character reviews her life and, as a result of this reappraisal, goes on an immense journey to India and the high Himalayas which she had first seen as a young woman and whose snows had haunted her ever since. Unconsciously I was acting out in my imagination what T. S. Eliot expresses in a few ultimate lines in 'Little Gidding':

> We shall not cease from exploration
> And the end of all our exploring
> Will be to arrive where we started
> And know the place for the first time.

But, unlike the books and plays I had previously written, when I had finished *The Return Journey* I made no attempt to find a publisher, in spite of the fact that I was urged to do so by the friend who had credited me with 'penetrating immediacy' and whose career was teaching comparative literature. Something much more urgent had come alive in me. I wanted with all my heart and mind, of course, to speed to Laurens and, since that was not possible, I decided to spend some time in France, studying its literature and perfecting the French which had been part of my education. My friends all thought this a capricious whim and uncharacteristically wasteful of my time after so many years of war. There were times when the urge to live in France appeared to make no rational sense even to me, and puzzled and worried me intensely. But these reservations were no match for the intuition which had given birth to the idea and which would not be denied. Alan McGlashan viewed my decision as part of a seasonal movement of a spirit coming to maturity and demanding to be fulfilled, no matter how impractical or unimportant it seemed in rational terms. It was, he said, what the ancient Chinese sages had all preached; that before a human being could be totally in Tao — in complete harmony with the abiding laws of creation — he had to return to the spirit of his ancestors. That settled the matter for me. My father's ancestor, Walther, Comte de Longueville, had fought with William the Conqueror at the Battle of Hastings, and he and all his family had been intensely aware of their French origins. I had a cousin who had written, for private distribution, the history of the de Longueville family since 1066, based not on legend and fraternal myth and specu-lation but on authentic records in public archives and museums in Britain and France. This ancestral awareness now flared like a flame within me, so I went off to Grenoble and enrolled as a student at the university, where I studied for over a year until this debt, this obeisance to the land and the spirit of my ancestors, appeared to be discharged.

On returning to England I expected to be able to resume my career as writer and playwright, which the war had interrupted, but found that I had yet more work to do in this new dimension to which analytical psychology had brought me. At this point in my life I felt that I had to go to its source in Zurich and, if possible, work with a woman analyst, after working so fruitfully with a man throughout the war. I was convinced that there was a submerged and long rejected feminine element in life, which was just as important as the masculine one which had dominated our history and society and which I had to fulfil in myself as well. Again I was amazed at the resistance I encountered from my closest friends and relations; even Alan McGlashan seemed to consider my latest idea an unnecessary, if not rather indulgent exercise.

My mind was already made up by the time Laurens returned from his war, which had lasted nearly three years longer than it had for the rest of us. I marvelled at the precision of the timing of his return, painful as our separation had been, when it could have ended with the surrender of the Japanese in 1945. I could see now how the pattern of growth implanted in the quintessential earth of my being demanded that I should have that time for myself, that I should be alone with a newly discovered, lone self, take it by the hand and learn to walk with it, undisturbed even by what seemed like the fulfilment of a dream of happiness, before I would be ready for any real return to life. I thought of the words of Hamlet: 'There is a special providence in the fall of a sparrow. If it be now, it is not to come; if it be not to come, it will be now; if it be not now, yet it will come: the readiness is all.' At the time of Laurens's return my whole being was invaded by a spirit of readiness such as I had never known before, and which spread into every aspect of my life.

I could never again doubt that there was a special providence in charge of the pattern of my life and to which I could surrender myself without fear, however improbable its promptings. One of the first things this readiness demanded of me was to deal with all that was inadequate on my own doorstep. Close though Jimmy and I were to each other, we had both known intuitively that it was not the kind of closeness that justified continuing with our marriage. We faced up to this fact in the most understanding and affectionate of ways, becoming the first couple to be divorced under a new law that had been passed immediately after the war to make this painful process easier. Not long afterwards, Laurens and I – who had been tested as few people had, and emerged from the test with our attachment not diminished but intact and enriched – were married, and together we set off for Zurich. There too we found ourselves, from the beginning, encompassed within the sphere of this overmastering readiness.

We arrived in Zurich, I believe, at a golden moment in the small but dynamic, inspired and inspiring world of Jung. Not long before, the people who believed in Jung's teaching and had made their homes in Zurich to be near him, had persuaded him to let them found an Institute for the advancement of his work. Jung had agreed to this, somewhat reluctantly, and was to tell me later that he had warned his advocates that they would be lucky if it survived their generation. Yet the Institute had started well and by the time of our arrival it had attracted some fifty people from all over the world to study there and, after a process of analysis, to return to their homelands and continue the work they had begun in Zurich.

We had arranged to stay at an old-fashioned Swiss hotel on the Dolder, overlooking the city, with the lake and the foothills of the lower Alps beyond, and after an overnight rail journey from Calais expected to have a quiet day to settle into our rooms and call in at the Jung Institute and complete all the necessary entrance formalities. However, on arrival at the hotel I found a note waiting for me from Dr Jung, asking me to visit him at his home that very afternoon. It was a small thing but it somehow had a special personal significance for me, giving me confidence for a meeting which I had looked forward to with as much awe, and even foreboding, as eagerness. I regarded Jung's note almost as a 'sign of confirmation', such as the ancient Chinese looked for when going into unknown territory, because there was a sort of poetic logic about the fact that I was to see and meet Jung before I entered the Institute. After all, many years had passed since I had first heard of him and intuition had prompted me to persuade my mother to turn to him for help. During that long stretch of time, even though only by proxy of Peter Baynes, Jung had become a part of my mother's life and, therefore, of mine. My own work with Alan McGlashan, and the enigmatic, heart-searching journeys my mother and I had both made into the labyrinths of our undiscovered selves, had increased Jung's significance for us over the years. I realised that such a meeting would have been easier if it had been in the company of others, and in the formal setting in which all those who came to work in the Institute were normally introduced to Jung; but having travelled in time and space so far and for so long towards Jung and his place of work, I felt I had earned the right to meet him before I was let loose among his followers.

I was therefore in high spirits when I set out for his home at Küsnacht, not far from Zurich. It was a lovely afternoon, charged to the full with the tender, valedictory light of autumn whose mood of farewell to an abundant summer drew a sparkle, glimmer, sheen and shine from everything capable of reflection and was particularly active on the Zürichberg behind me. But as I entered the gates of the garden and began walking towards the house, I was overcome by nervousness, and by the time I was shown to a chair in the hall where I was to wait for Jung, I was almost alarmed that I could be so fearful of a meeting which I had anticipated with such eagerness. My attack of nerves was at its most acute when I noticed a pile of books that had been left on a small table beside me. As I read the titles I nearly collapsed into a fit of giggles because they were all the latest thrillers, including the most recent novel by Dorothy Sayers, who had become a wartime friend of mine. Immediately my nervousness vanished and was replaced by an immense feeling of contentment and confidence that I had come to the right place. At this very moment the door opened and a tall, broad-shouldered, loose-limbed man with a pipe in his hand and the smell of fresh tobacco about him stood in the doorway and said in a deep, resonant voice, 'Miss Giffard? I am sorry I have had to keep you waiting.'

I rose to my feet at once and, as I turned to face him, gave one last look at the pile of thrillers on the table. 'Ah, I see you are a thriller addict too, aren't you?' And he laughed with himself and me as if we were joined in some conspiracy, perhaps against what Chesterton called 'that sad and solemn thing, the intellect'.

'Yes, I am, on and off,' I said, 'and I was particularly interested to see that you had a Dorothy Sayers there, because she is a friend of mine.'

'Then I must be careful what I say,' he answered; 'but much as I admire and enjoy the lady, I am not certain she isn't a little bit above my ceiling. I am more on the Agatha Christie, if not the Edgar Wallace, level.'

The thought of anything being above Jung's 'ceiling' seemed so ludicrous that I nearly started giggling again, but was able to control the impulse as he showed me into a room with books lining three walls, and on the far side a window giving on to the lake and the hills beyond. Outwardly I hope I greeted him properly, but inwardly an excited schoolgirl self was saying 'Crikey!' What a splendid advertisement for his psychology.

I had, of course, heard about Jung's illness and heart attack during the war, and how he had been as near to dying as it was possible to be and yet still live. I had imagined that some element of frailness would have rubbed off on to his person from so close an encounter with death, but there was no hint of frailty in the man who confronted me. There was nothing but a great sense of physical and spiritual well-being that emanated from him so strongly that I would not have been surprised if it had manifested itself as some sort of ectoplasmic glow about his person. Everything about him was generous and well made, as if to accommodate a large, deep, expansive and expanding spirit. He even seemed to be dressed for a demanding outward and physical role: he wore a woollen shirt and woollen tie, a rough homespun tweed jacket of the kind that Oxford and Cambridge undergraduates favoured before the war, as well as a pair of grey flannel trousers and English brogues, and looked as if he had just come from some squirearchy in the Midlands after an inspection of the cattle and crops on his estate instead of from browsing in the dimension which those tiers of heavy volumes on the towering shelves around him suggested was his natural habitat.

When he spoke, too, his voice matched his physical presence and style of dress; it was not in a precise, cultivated, academic tone but deep and round and of the earth. It filled one with its own sense of well-being and welcome, and I was never again to feel nervous or afraid in his presence. At the same time his approach was sensitive and considerate and conveyed an immediate recognition of the identity of his visitor and a desire to respect it.

One of Jung's most outstanding gifts was that he seemed to know what whoever came to him, known or unknown, needed most, and I myself was very moved when, before I had even settled in my chair, he asked: 'And how is your mother?' As a result, we spent almost half an hour talking about my mother and her problems, the work she had done with Peter Baynes, and how she was facing up to life now that Baynes was dead, all of which I found both heartwarming and reassuring, particularly as at the end of our meeting it was clear that Jung had talked to me not only out of concern for my mother but even more so on my own account. After ending his final question about my mother with the exclamation, 'What a remarkable, brave lady she is! I wish that I myself could have done more to help her', he turned his attention to me and said, 'You know, I no longer take on regular patients myself. I have gone beyond the point of caring which Jack gets into bed with which Jill.' He had an expression of schoolboy mischief in his alert eyes and his face shone with such fun that we both burst out laughing, and for the second time I heard that wonderful laugh of his which, the more I heard it, fed my own laughter until I was quite helpless with it. I controlled myself with difficulty to hear him say, 'But I shall always like to see you from time to time, and would only add today that I think your instincts to work with a woman could not be more precise. I do hope that you will go and see my colleague Frau Wolff, and, if you agree, do your main analysis with her.'

By the time we had finished the sun was setting and the level light of evening shone straight through the windows, lighting up the volumes of books which filled one wall and in particular a copy of Holbein's *Portrait of Erasmus*. I recognised it instantly and my eyes held to it for a moment as I thought how it would please Laurens, whose Renaissance heroes were Thomas More and Erasmus. Jung knew instantly what had drawn my attention, for he said: 'You know, you are looking at someone to whom I owe much. Even as a student I was so drawn to him that I remember, at the age of nineteen, buying a copy of his essays in Latin and it is still one of my bedside books. It's his translation into Latin of the Delphic Oracles: "*Vocatus atque non vocatus deus aderit* – Called or not called, God shall be there" which is carved over the entrance to my house. I will show it to you on the way out.' But I hardly heard the last words because his quoting of the Latin resounded like a roll on drums to me, a sort of ancient call to battle, his voice so deep and far away. I noticed too that the sunset was like stained glass on the windows and the light had dwindled to a medieval glow; all around me the atmosphere seemed to have become strongly ecumenical, so that I would not have been surprised if it had been joined at that moment by the scent and smoke of incense. If there was one quality which dominated all other impressions of my first meeting with Jung, it was the profound and all-pervasive sense of reverence for all things which emanated from this great man.

On the way out we paused for a moment in front of the porch where, as good as his word, he pointed out the Delphic carving over the door, and again repeated its Latin rendering. I was to hear him do this a number of times for others and was always impressed that he never failed to utter these words as if he had just heard them for the first time on the steps of a Delphic temple overlooking a hillside covered with Epidauran pines. Then he insisted on walking with me to the little gate at the far end of the garden and letting me out into the street. After saying, with the relish he always had for Anglo-American slang, 'I'll be seeing you', he stood for a while in the twilight waving his hand in a strangely youthful gesture of farewell.

I had not been with Jung for much more than an hour, but I went away feeling as if it had been a much longer meeting and one in a series of others, as if a new chapter was about to start in my life because of the absolute sense of what I can only call 'confirmation' with which I left his house. I felt confirmed in the rightness of my decision to come and work in Zurich; confirmed in my surrender at all critical moments of my life to the intuition which had ultimately brought me to the meeting that had just taken place; confirmed most profoundly in my being and in a sense of a special, not egotistical but objective, identity; confirmed in my right to be alive in my own special time and in this special place in the universe. I think all of us who knew Jung at that time felt we had received a kind of blessing, a royal seal of confirmation, both private and personal, which we were taking back to life.

I thought back to my confirmation in Folkestone Parish Church and how full I was of an unshakable anticipation of change awaiting me after receiving the Bishop's blessing. As I sat in my pew and looked around me, I remembered how shocked I had been that nothing had outwardly changed despite the inner eventfulness which had surged through me during the whole ecumenical process. But now, walking in the rainbow light of an immaculate evening down a leafy Swiss lane with the lake water lapping on my left, it seemed that the real confirmation I needed had come to me, at a time when I had neither consciously sought it nor been prepared to receive it. I was confirmed through the sense of authenticity in my seeking which Jung instantly gave me, as I could never have been confirmed in any church or cathedral, and the proof of it was that I already felt a ferment of change begin to bubble within me. As a result, early the next day I went forth into the world of the Institute with more confidence than I could ever have thought possible.

The head of the Institute was Jung's senior and oldest male collaborator, Dr C. A. 'Fredy' Meier. Another influential figure was Jung's secretary, Aniela Jaffé, who was to help him write his greatest work, *Memories, Dreams, Reflections*, an autobiographical record not of external events which we all share and hold in common, but of a process of inner exploration and discovery, and more profound, I believe, than any work ever undertaken before in the history of man.

Aniela Jaffé made a deep impression on me right from the start. Although I was never to work with her professionally, Laurens and I got to know her well, and during our time in Zurich she added a great deal to the meaning of life for us. Physically she was a most attractive person, almost frail in appearance, with a beautiful face and eyes, and a delicate bone-structure which seemed to have been carved to match the delicacy and profundity, as well as the strength of spirit, within her. But profound a person though she was, she had a ready laugh and smile, and always radiated a sense of fun and inner happiness; she was also exceedingly sensitive without being touchy; imperturbable, and incapable of being personally offended. From the start I thought her one of the few truly resolved persons at the Institute.

The fact that Aniela Jaffé had come to Zurich as a result of a skiing accident instantly endeared her to me, all the more so when, talking to her about it one day, she remarked: 'Of course, at the time I thought and spoke of it as my skiing accident. Now I know better and realise it was no accident at all.' So intuitive and in a sense unconscious was the instinct that took her to Jung, following her accident, that she had no idea of why she had sought help from him. As a result, she said, in her sessions with Jung during the initial months of her 'analysis', she would sit in his presence almost speechless, while Jung, who had already recognised the power as well as the clarity of her intuition, would talk to her for hours on end, out of his own rich spirit and experience, of history, life, psychology and time. Looking back, she was horrified by her lack of response and understanding and her fear that Jung would 'give her up as a bad job', as she put it. But he never wavered in his support, and suddenly, after about six months, all the doors and windows within her imagination flew open and the inrush of light and understanding was almost more than she could bear.

I always loved this story, not only because of what it revealed about Aniela and about Jung himself but because it proved once more, if further proof were needed, that Jung followed no prescribed 'system' or methodology: his analytical approach was entirely determined by the needs of the analysand. From that moment Aniela never left Zurich again, helped Fredy Meier to build up the Institute, contributed enormously to its spirit and went on to become one of the most creative and productive among Jung's host of heirs and successors.

There are many who wrote much more extensively about Jung and are far better known than Aniela Jaffé but, due to Aniela's unique balance of heart and mind, her writings – many of which are yet to be published – will have more and more to offer with the passage of time; her book *The Myth of Meaning* will, I am certain, become a classic. Now, almost totally blind, Aniela can no longer write, but she continues her work as one of the most creative Jungian analysts in Switzerland and, in her being and writing, transcends the intellectual schisms and animosities that haunt all group activities.

Also in Jung's inner circle was young Marie-Louise ('Marlus') von Franz, completing her work on fairy tales and already working with Jung on a reappraisal of alchemy. There was Barbara Hannah, who had come to Zurich almost straight from a cathedral close and found the experience so meaningful that she remained there, to serve analytical psychology in the place where it originated, until the end of her days. There was the remarkable Linda Fierz-David, who had already significantly extended Jung's concept of the role of the feminine in man through her rediscovery of the dream of Poliphilo, and who brought a fierceness of passion and energy to all that she did. There was Cornelia Brunner, who had achieved something similar in her research on, and reinterpretation of, the work and life of Rider Haggard. There was Yolande Jacobi, who was invaluable in the Jungian community because she was an unashamed and gifted extravert in a world that was almost exclusively introverted: 'the cat among the psychological pigeons', as one bigoted Freudian once described her to me. There were a number of rich and gifted American ladies who had chosen to make their homes in Zurich out of love for, and belief in, Jung and his work and who, in providing places where the students could meet after work and talk and be well fed and entertained, were a profoundly important ingredient in the Jungian community. And there were millionaires whose pursuit and acquisition of wealth had somehow deprived their lives of meaning but who, through Jung and his work, had discovered a 'salt' which had regained its savour for them.

In the remote wings, at Ascona where Jung often spent the coldest part of the winter, there was Olga Fröbe-Kapteyn at her Casa Gabriella, where she organised her annual Eranos Conferences and where Laurens and I would go for weekends. Our friendship with Olga gave me much and ended only with her death. In addition, there were scores of outstanding men and women scholars, doctors, historians, poets, like Herbert Read, Aramaic experts like Gilles Quispel, ambassadors like von Fischer who, in their service in ancient countries like the Levant and Egypt, had acquired a love and knowledge of the mythological past and came to bear witness to the universality of Jung's work. Then there were those who followed in the footsteps of the great and incomparable Richard Wilhelm, the translator of *The Book of the Golden Flower* and *I Ching* (or *The Book of Changes*) which is to the Chinese spirit what the Bible is to Western man, and who initiated Jung into the great period of Chinese civilisation. This was to prove to be full of parallels and insights which not only confirmed Jung's own findings but enlarged the range and circumference of his seeking.

Last and of course not least, since they were also first, were Emma Jung and Toni Wolff. Jung left a final tribute to Emma carved on stone, in Chinese, at Bollingen: 'She was the pillar of my house'; and to Toni, also in Chinese: 'She was the fragrance' – in other words, the intuition – 'of my house'. I did not, alas, work with Emma Jung but Laurens and I often had tea and occasionally lunch with her in the Jungs' home at Küsnacht, and, of course, we saw a great deal of Emma every year during the Eranos Conferences at Ascona. At this time she was completing her great work on the Holy Grail, and we both went to her lectures on the Quest at the Institute. Through what she was, and what she gave, she enriched my life and made me aware of an element of the feminine that I had never experienced in such an illuminated fashion before.

Jung, who was an inspired host in his own home, made me wish that everybody in the world could see him as we saw him then, note the zest for life that surged through him, experience his sense of humour, and hear that elemental laugh of his, because it was such an immediate and incontrovertible testimony to the validity, impregnable sanity and totality of his psychological approach to life. He had by now ceased to practise psychiatry and was deeply engaged on what was the real work of his life: the rediscovery, exploration and restoration of the soul that modern man had lost, thus depriving himself of direction and meaning. Hardly a day passed when we did not seem to receive news of the unlocking of a door in another cell, from which some nuance of meaning essential to the increase of consciousness was released to contribute to the creation of a truly contemporary awareness. And it was in this profound work of liberation and emancipation that Toni Wolff performed for Jung, and for all of us in Zurich, a service which no one else could have rendered.

Perhaps the most important part of my experience in Zurich was my work with Toni Wolff, to whom Jung himself had directed me. I could not honestly say that I ever really knew her as a friend, but, through our work together, I came to know her in a way which surpassed straightforward and externalised friendship. My knowledge went deeper because it was knowledge as experience, knowledge in action, knowledge that transfigures and transforms, the knowledge one can only acquire when one has submitted oneself to a profound process of analysis with the sort of inspired analyst that Toni Wolff was. She had been helped in this through her own suffering and years of analysis with Jung himself, and their subsequent collaboration during the most critical – and one could almost say dangerous – years of his exploration of the last great unknown area of the mind: the collective unconscious.

In addition, she was a woman of great culture: a psychologist and, in a sense, a philosopher in her own right, who made a unique contribution to Jung's view of life and ultimate meaning. When he himself entered his own 'dark night of the soul', she was an assistant navigator because this was a world into which she herself had already been, both during her analysis with Jung and through the awareness she had gained from him of the suffering and alienated minds and spirit of the many other human beings, particularly women, who were his patients. She had come to know this night world so well that she added to one of Jung's greatest achievements – the mapping-out of the pattern and role of type in human beings – the nuances of a special feminine typology, so enabling him to complete his generic hypothesis. The written record of this discovery, entitled *Psychological Types*, makes difficult and exacting reading but is, I think, one of the most significant clarifications of the human enigma and a compass in man's search for a soul of his own.

My debt to Toni Wolff is enormous because, in addition to my work with her, she and Laurens formed a special friendship and almost every Sunday night while we were in Zurich we would dine with her. She, like Jung, was a generous and exceptional host. In addition she had what perhaps pleased me most, an aristocracy of mind and spirit, and that indefinable quality we called 'style' – style not in the snobbish sense, but which comes from the kind of grace life bestows on those who have, as it were, become harmonised to its laws.

Through our friendship with Toni Wolff, I could not help being aware of the problem that she had become not only for Jung and his family but for all those in, and on the fringes of, his circle. This was largely due to a natural envy that she was, within the act and meaning of life, almost as married to Jung as was his wife Emma. As one of Jung's greatest friends put it not long ago, Jung had two wives. None of the three made any concessions to a world of inflexible convention, and they conducted their three-way relationship quite openly. Emma Jung, great woman that she was, accepted Toni Wolff, and all the difficulties she created, with immense grace and generosity, so that she could say without reservation at the end of her days: 'I shall always be grateful to Toni because, at a time when I was bringing up my children and could not be a whole-time companion to my husband on the great journey on which he had embarked, she performed for him a service I could never have rendered.'

But I was painfully aware of how sharply divided and critical was the outside world which, in its feebler human ingredients, would gossip, snigger and even sneer at their relationship, invariably focusing and projecting their own enviousness and resentments on Toni. In the lectures that I attended something of this was apparent. As we entered a small lecture room in the modest building which houses the Institute and its library, in a street I thought significantly called 'Gemeindestrasse' – *Gemeinde* meaning community – a large bowl of red roses would be waiting to greet Emma Jung when she entered to give the first lecture of the day. After her lecture there would be a half-hour interval and she would be followed by Toni Wolff. To my amazement, I noticed on the first morning that the bowl of roses had vanished by the time Toni Wolff appeared. At first I thought this was merely an oversight, but when it happened morning after morning I realised that the removal of the roses was a deliberate act, intended to convey a kind of judgment and disapproval of Toni which I did not understand until I knew the whole story. Even Barbara Hannah, when tackled by Laurens many years later about the unconscious conspiracy of silence which followed Toni's death, replied to his suggestion that, in behaving and talking as if Toni Wolff had never existed, her colleagues were murdering her: 'You're right. We were, and still are, just plain jealous. I shall for my part put it right as soon as possible.' And she did so, handsomely.

As the days passed, I realised how right had been the intuition which took me to Zurich in search of increased awareness of my feminine self. I had already known that Jung was a great liberator and emancipator of the human spirit, someone who had opened up for the future a potential for freedom of spirit and expression that had never existed before. It soon became clear to me that, by following his own dreams and visions, Jung was serving not only the feminine in man but the long denied, creative, masculine element in the soul of woman. The issue over which Freud had ostensibly broken with Jung was the latter's analysis of the fantasies of an alienated woman patient, and it is clear, looking back on the whole range of Jung's work, as we can now, that his guide had been the estranged, the forgotten woman in the human spirit, the Ariadne in life who, though it provided the golden thread which led the human spirit out of the labyrinthine depths of itself, had been abandoned on a rock in a sea of her own tears and denied her return to a place in the city and citadel of the human spirit, which was symbolised by Athens.

This, I think, was the essence of Jung's startling originality. It is easy enough for men to follow a beautiful feminine face, as Dante had done in his great journey down into Hell and up to the heights of Heaven, accomplishing as an artist very much what Jung was to achieve as a scientist and healer. But the face that Jung chose to follow was the averted, the rejected, face of woman which man, by his one-sided rejection, had deformed and made ugly.

I could not, of course, have reached these conclusions, or been transformed by them, as I felt I had been in a small way, were it not for the work done first with Alan McGlashan in London and subsequently with Toni Wolff, who amplified and completed it for me in Zurich.

In addition to directing me to Toni Wolff, Jung had advised me to work along parallel lines with the head of the Institute, Fredy Meier, who gave me much, including a friendship that lasts to this day. Fredy Meier was also my teacher, especially in dream analysis which was the part of my training that interested me most. Again, the timing could not have been more right because, due to the years of preparation through my analysis with Alan McGlashan, in which dreams played a highly significant role, the dreaming process in myself seemed to have been both enlarged and accelerated. I dreamt more and had dreams that were outside the normal pattern of my dreaming and seemed to branch out almost into the paranormal. For some weeks before starting work with Fredy Meier, for instance, my old love, David Davidson, had reappeared in my dreams in an increasingly urgent way that left me apprehensive and shaken when I recollected what I had dreamt in the morning. I had not heard from David for such a long time that I no longer knew his address, nor had I given him much thought in the years that had elapsed since our last meeting. In all my dreams at this time – and, towards the end, I had them almost nightly – David was desperately trying to get in touch with me and his attempts always failed just when we were about to talk to each other. I finally mentioned this to Laurens and he offered to trace David through the War Office. In due course a rather mysterious reply came back, suggesting that I should get in touch with David's brother at an address in Kent. I wrote a very tentative letter to him, and received a reply by return of post. The brother said that David had recently died and had been desperately anxious to make contact with me before his death; he admitted feeling considerably relieved that he had been able to tell me this.

From that moment, the dreams vanished as suddenly as they had appeared and I have not dreamt about David since. It was as if he had told me all that he wanted me to know and had given me the address where, one day, I would be able to find him again.

I was still very moved by, and raw from, this experience when I started my study of dream analysis with Fredy Meier, but almost from the first day it had a healing effect on me. I already knew from working on my dreams with Alan McGlashan that the dream process was not just the key to unlocking the door into our collective unconscious but the sort of guide that Beatrice was to Dante through the unknown territory which one entered. Above all, I knew that the language of dreams was the language of truth, of the great unknown truth which creation was designed to unfold. There could never be a trace of falsehood in a dream and if it was held to be guilty of error, the error was not in the dream, but in our interpretation of it. I could think of nothing more exciting than learning and relearning how to read the vocabulary and idiom of this ancient, forgotten language of the spirit of man – which speaks to us through our dreams – so that I would never again get it wrong.

I remember in particular the series of dreams with which Fredy Meier began our introduction to dream analysis. I had learned from Alan McGlashan that, to the Jungian school, unlike that of Freud, the dream spoke not in images of a fixed and absolute content but in metaphors that were dependent for their translation on the dreamer's associations with the imagery. In this dream series we were confronted with the dreams of a man whose personal associations were unknown to us. They were the dreams of a man of great wealth plunged into a profound gloom which rendered him incapable of communication and cut him off from his fellow human beings. Almost the only person he ever spoke to was his wife who, hearing of Jung and almost at her wits' end, had brought him to Professor Meier in Zurich for help. The husband had resolutely refused to see or even write to Professor Meier, so every morning he would recount his dreams to his wife who would then go and tell them to Professor Meier; and so clear, archetypal and universal was their content that any personal associations seemed unnecessary. Fredy Meier did not hesitate to interpret them accordingly to the wife, who then went home and relayed the interpretation to her husband. After some months of this treatment the husband came out of his depression and was able to go back into the world with a sense of purpose and meaning fully restored to him.

I cannot begin to describe the exhilaration with which I followed this series of dreams. When I went over the dreams in my mind every evening after our analysis and discussion of them, it was almost as if I were watching the enactment of a play in my beloved theatre, because it was not long before I noticed a distinct pattern beginning to emerge, not unlike that of a classical drama: an opening act in which the human problem was presented; a central act in which the problem produced a crisis of meaning for the dreamer, of life and death proportions; and a third act in which the crisis was finally resolved. I never met the man or his wife who, between them, presented us with this dream series but I remember two striking photographs of the man himself: one taken when he arrived in Zurich, a portrait of despair made flesh and blood, and one taken not long before he left, a portrait of joy and meaning rediscovered.

During this study and process of dream exegesis through which Fredy Meier conducted us so superbly, I found that I had a gift for dream analysis, a gift that frightened me at times with the implications it held for the future and which I was not yet ready to put to use. This private sense of being gifted in such a way, and fear of the consequences of my gift, came to a head when, at the end of my time in Zurich, an essay I had written on dream analysis was presented to my class as an almost perfect example of what dream analysis should be. Professor Meier and even Dr Jung himself let it be known that they had nothing to add to it.

When I went to say goodbye to Dr Jung and his wife Emma just before leaving Zurich, I mentioned the problem that this feeling of being gifted presented me with. I told Jung that, more than anything else, consciously I wanted to resume my work as a writer and playwright which had been so rudely interrupted by the war. I had no desire, I said, to put up a brass plate on my door and start life as a lay analyst, although I was now sufficiently qualified to be able to do so. I shall never forget the smile of benediction on Jung's face, the hand of reassurance on my shoulder and his deep, prophetic voice, as it always sounded to me, saying 'Do not be anxious; when you are ready, people will come to you.' And so there it was again, at the end as at the beginning, the readiness that was all.

There is much more, of course, that I could say about the time I spent in Jung's world which, for me, was a microcosm of a macrocosmic temple of learning. All I will say is that I left Zurich more than ever convinced that Jung's great importance to our time was the religious significance of his psychology. From the age of three until the end of his days, Jung dedicated himself to the service of the soul in man; to enabling modern man to recover his capacity for religious experience which he had lost, and, by renewing his relationship with his Creator, to renew himself and his societies. In his famous television interview with John Freeman in 1959, Jung had startled the English-speaking world when, asked if he believed in God, he had declared: 'I do not believe . . .' He had then paused; and as he paused I can remember the sense of night pressing in at the windows, not only my own but those of millions of other people, as if his statement would shatter the glass and extinguish all light left on earth; when the silence became almost too agonising to endure, he added in a voice that had, as it were, the depth and authority of a far-off mutter of thunder: 'I do not believe; I know.'

Four years earlier, when I was asked to speak about Jung on television and radio on his eightieth birthday, I made a tape-recording in which he declared the same thing in another way: 'I cannot tell you what God is. There are no words that can describe him. But what I can tell you is that all my work has proved that the pattern of God exists in every man.' I still guard this recording as my most precious possession, not least because it also records Jung's great gift of laughter, a laughter that would have been impossible had it not been rooted in an innate sense of certainty about creation and its Creator. But though we laughed a lot together during that interview, it ended with me in tears, not because of any profound statements made but more from the indescribable sense of hope for life that was in the whole atmosphere of Jung's being.

All this and more I took back with me from Zurich, the 'more' including something which I knew would bring great joy and comfort to my mother. After one of their discussions about the war and the meaning of the Nazi invasion of the German spirit, Laurens, who had become a close friend of Jung's, returned with a story that might have been designed for her. Jung had told Laurens how, in May 1945, the night before the Second World War ended, he had had a dream. In this dream he was in the courtyard of a great prison when suddenly, outside, he heard the tread and, as it came nearer, the reverberation of the tread in the earth and walls of the prison, of millions of marching feet. Then the gates of the prison were flung wide and a voice declared: 'The armies of liberation have arrived!' And at the head of the army of liberation Jung saw an officer in British uniform, waving his hat frantically at him, and when he came nearer he recognised that it was Peter Baynes. The language of the dream was telling Jung clearly how he had created an army of liberation in the spirit of man that nothing could ever arrest or defeat. When Jung opened his paper the following morning he read the news of the capitulation of Germany.

It had taken a world war in 1914 to make Jung realise the overwhelming importance of the imagery and vision that rose of its own accord within himself and compelled him to accept it as the material on which he had to base his life's work. It took the end of the Second World War to confirm to Jung, through this dream, how right he had been to do so. And, as a by-product of that dream, the recognition, in Jung's unconscious, of the role Baynes had played in his work brought great solace to my mother.

The importance of the baggage I took back with me to London was confirmed when I opened the door of my house in Chelsea. As I put the key in the lock, there was a flicker of black at the back of my mind and, as if watching the re-run of an antiquated film, I saw myself turning the same key in the same lock, but in very different circumstances, on the first night of the war. This time I opened the door with Laurens by my side, the sun of early summer in the sky and birdsong coming from the garden at the back of the house. And lying just inside the door there was a letter which can only just have been delivered. I picked it up. It was from a friend, who wrote: 'Ingaret, I know how much you have worked at psychology. I am in a desperate jam with myself. Could you please let me come and see you, because I know you could help me.'

And so the first of what was to become a stream of people who turned to me for help over the next three decades had arrived at my door. Obviously, in the sense that Jung foresaw, I was now ready.

This readiness, it seemed to me, was emphasised by total success with my desperate friend. She had a profound inner problem not only in a pragmatic psychological sense but also one of natural conscience and morality. This manifested itself in a severe skin affliction which none of the eminent specialists whom she had consulted could cure. At our first meeting she informed me that she never dreamt and was a 'dead loss' in that way. But the next day she brought me a dream and from that moment the battle was won. I never imposed my views about her dreams upon her because it was not what *I* thought about them that mattered, but what *she* thought. I merely stood behind the dream and followed it, intruding only as a kind of dictionary in which she could find a word to explain the imagery that was incomprehensible to her, and within a few months this dreaming process saw her completely cured. The word 'cured' has to be qualified but, before I do so, I feel bound to mention a parallel process, within myself, that accompanied the progression of our work, and the importance of which I did not fully appreciate until it ended.

I remember Jung once saying to us that it was only in bringing the totality of ourselves to work on the problems of analysands that we could really help them, and that we should always take to heart an ancient Greek saying that 'only the wounded physician heals'. As my friend and I embarked on the final stage of our work on her dreams, I realised that something in me was being enriched and strangely enlarged, and that an inadequate part of myself – presumably what was symbolically meant by the 'wound' in the physician, which also needed to be healed – had all along been my ally and given me access to energies of renewal which I could not have reached in any other way. In this there was no egotistical sense of triumph, but an unsought comfort and reassurance that, by treating dreams – not only my own, but those of others – as the most intimate, private and precious possession of the dreamer, I had acquired a humility which in a sense opened the doors of my imagination and spirit to what was creative in my own objective within. More than ever, as the 'I' in me was diminished in the process, the sense of being in the greater keeping of what I was in time to realise was the 'thou' of the self, was quickened and has companioned me to this day.

It is significant that through my work the judgmental side of myself was gradually replaced by something which, in the beginning, I called 'evaluation': a desire to know the person who came to me for help in his totality; good or bad, light or dark, without condemnation or praise, and just for the sake of the sense of wholeness it gave them and me. And this sense of evaluation ultimately led to a total commitment to the mystery of objective understanding. Something of this was, of course, already deeply rooted in me through having had to understand from an early age my mother's suffering and her apparently insoluble problem and condition in life, but in the course of my work with other people, understanding flared almost as a state of being, a flame which in the Middle Ages the seekers after truth would have called a passion. I found a process of understanding that was one of the most exciting and rewarding urges I had ever encountered. I realised that this understanding could never be total, and that the worst thing that could happen to oneself and one's analysands was to believe, and to make them feel, that it could be. I could think of nothing more damning or paralytic than making someone feel that they were completely understood. No, it was just the feeling that one was on the way to understanding; that understanding was one's ultimate goal, and one sought it not only for one's patient but also for the light it shed on the lack of understanding of one's own self hiding in the shadows of one's awareness.

It was amazing how rewarding life became, even in its most dramatic representations, when one approached it humbly, seeking only to understand, without judgment or righteousness; how richly in the end life rewarded one's spirit and allowed one to see in the heart of it a grace and a generosity which caused it to give back with both hands what it had once taken away with one. Having achieved this degree of illumination, one wondered how one could have been so blind as not to see that this generosity was witness to the fact of the overall command, in light and dark, in pain and happiness, in birth and death, of the great inscrutable power which ruled the universe and all its creation and which, at the end of their journeyings, the great threesome – St Paul, Dante and Jung – were at one in calling 'love'.

All this and more I owed to the road which I followed after my first 'cure'. As I have intimated, my use of the word 'cure' is not intended to suggest that the problems which afflicted my first patient had disappeared. They were, however, out in the daylight, and she had recovered through her dreams the necessary moral energies to deal with them in the dimension in which they belonged: she had, in other words, recovered some of her capacity for religious experience. As I realised this I remembered Jung telling us that he had never effected what is so lamely called 'a cure' without enabling the sufferer to achieve this in some measure.

After such a beginning I could not turn back, and for some thirty years I have been compelled to forget my love of the theatre and of writing in order to concentrate on helping the increasing numbers of people who have come to my door. I was fortunate enough not to have to earn a living as the lay analyst I had become. I merely confined my work to all those who came to me of their own unsolicited accord, and that they did so both humbled me and made me fear because it showed how healing, and religion which is its master, were failing in the functions which justified their existence, and how desperate was the need for both to reappraise and renew themselves. This realisation strengthened me enormously during this new phase of my life because, as with Jung, religion and the Church into which I was born had always been the deepest concern of my spirit and imagination. This concern had increased during the long, random and directionless years before I went to Zurich, and had crystallised into a total commitment to do something for the healing, the closing of the split I had come to call 'infinite' in modern

361

man, the making whole which in the beginning was synonymous with being 'holy'.

This 'split' in man, that was 'infinite', had a special meaning for me. Deeply committed as I was to my analytical work, I could not suppress the writer and the playwright in myself indefinitely, and during one of my rare holidays with Laurens I had written a novel called *Split Infinitive*. It was inspired by a journey we had made through South Africa during which, in trying to understand the horror of the division between black and white, I had suddenly realised that this was an externalisation of a split in the heart and mind of modern man. In this novel, which had a South African setting, I dealt with the split between a man and a woman, in their marriage, and in the woman herself. At the end of the novel, during a vast riot of blacks, whites and Indians, the woman bridges the split in herself when she suddenly realises that the dark glasses which she had worn as a defence against the light of day are a symbolic shield against an inner refusal to see the horror of the division between what 'black' and 'white' symbolise in herself. She tramples on the glasses and, in the midst of fires, murder and automatic rifle-fire, her vision becomes whole and so does her marriage.

Laurens liked the book so much that he persuaded me to adapt it into a play, but on our return to London I did no more than send it to a producer I knew well. When he responded that neither he nor anybody whom he knew in the theatre was particularly interested in 'neurotic women', I took this as a sign to dedicate myself to healing the split infinitive in the real, suffering human beings who came to me for help.

On and off, at other times of leisure, I wrote other books – *Marriage Between the Lines*, for instance, which was accepted for publication provided I made some minor revisions; but so much more urgent did my work with real men and women seem that I never made the required changes and forgot about the book for twelve long years. I also wrote some short stories which, like my play *Because We Must*, were compared with Chekhov by those who read them, but again I did nothing about their publication. I wrote another, rather psychological novel called *Department Store*, and a play that seemed to me to go deeper than all the rest, *The No Place*, but that too is lying in an old cabin trunk with my other unpublished writings.

An important link with my writing self, and, I feel, also a creative element in what I was able to do analytically, was the editing I did for Laurens and a number of other well-known writers. It created in what I tried to do an atmosphere, I believe, of art in the broadest sense and protected me from making my work purely clinical and repetitive.

One task of editing was of profound personal significance to me because it made me realise how important the experience of India had been to me and how, despite the long years in between, all unseen it had kept me company and bonded me to a sense of human fellowship I do not think I would have ever been able to find in a similar measure without it. It came about because Laurens, on a visit to India, had met Nirad Chaudhuri who had started his writing career with that remarkable book *Autobiography of an Unknown Indian*. Laurens not only liked him but admired him for his courage and integrity both as an artist and a man. Accordingly he had helped to bring Chaudhuri to England and ultimately to establish him in Britain, where he still lives and works to this day near Oxford, more at home in every way than ever he was either in Bengal or New Delhi. He had written a life of one of the greatest Sanskrit scholars, Max Müller, which was published by Chatto & Windus under the title *Scholar Extraordinary*. Both he and the publishers had decided that the book, which ran to close on 600,000 words, was too long for the purpose it was intended to serve and wanted to reduce it by more than half and asked me to undertake the task. I do not think I have ever enjoyed editing more, and was overjoyed to find the following in his Acknowledgements:

As the author of the book I would say that the omissions have been made and the editing done with extraordinary skill. There is nothing more delicate and difficult than to deal with another man's writing. Ingaret Giffard's handling of this tricky task was such that when I read the results of her editing in the proofs – not having looked into the edited typescript – I could not be sure where the cuts had been made, and I discovered them by an effort of the memory. I think no author could say more about the editing of his work.

But what mattered most was that suddenly the years I had spent in India were evoked and spread out before me like a new and brilliantly lit landscape after the breaking of the rains. Since then I have continued to live with that experience and to find it a source of human enrichment which had actually passed me by at the time when I encountered it in all its immensity as a young girl. That girlhood experience I have tried to deal with in the pages behind me, but this other meaning of the ancient and rich civilisation of India which had entered, soft-footed, by a back door in my imagination, while I was enjoying myself as a young girl in its forefront, added nuances of human values I had not perceived before. Perhaps the greatest of these was a conclusion to which I turned as somebody in need of a compass, that however deprived of material possessions, comfort and physical security, and poor in a way that no European is ever poor, the human spirit can still be maintained, rich and triumphant. The constant remembrance of the immense dignity, the honour and the self-respect of the ordinary people of India, despite their poverty and their hardship, from then on put to flight all the behaviouristic presumption and dialectical materialistic bias which infects the West everywhere to some degree, not just in the shape of some Marxist ideology but, even more dangerously, psychologically, and its most profound by-product for me therefore was to confirm the importance of what I was trying to do for the people who came to me for psychological help.

The clearest illustration of the complex of things I found hard to express is perhaps exemplified by the measure in which one particular person from the past became a source of constant preoccupation. He was my stepfather's bearer who, with his wife, had done so much for us all during our years in India. Not a day seemed to pass now in which I did not begin to recollect the imagination, the selfless service, the devotion and love that this infinitely serving, infinitely caring old man gave to us. Often at night I would wake up and feel that even here in England he was still sitting not far from my bed, as he used to sit on the edge of the verandah where I slept on hot nights on the far Northern Frontier, so that no harm from man, reptile or insect should come to me. I have only to recall him in the many ways in which he went about his service to feel immeasurably humbled and human again. I know that two of the greatest sources of corruption of the human spirit come either from power or from suffering. I also know that our bearer was one of millions who suffered deprivation in a way that no European today can imagine but that, far from being corrupted by it, he turned it into a source of enrichment and love. I know that the memory of the brilliant young officers who became distinguished generals, the gifted members of that remarkable platonic body, the Indian Civil Service, the Maharajahs and the Maharanis and all that dazzling vice-regal world in which we moved, has dimmed and will soon vanish, but our bearer's memory shines brighter than ever.

I know that in the last roll-call I shall have in my imagination of all the people I have loved and who have influenced me profoundly in my life, he will be right in front.

During my long 'analytical' years I tended to forget about the books and plays I had written but my mother never forgot them and always wanted to know when I was going to do more about them. Over and over again she would say to me: 'Oh, Ingaret, I wish you could do less psychologically and go back to your writing. You were born a writer, you were meant to be a writer and you must never forget it.' Yet no one understood better than she did the unsought urge which had led me to Jung, and she realised, I think even more profoundly than I did, how the help I had been able to give her intuitively was enlarged by this with an awareness and conscious understanding that it had lacked in the beginning.

Her own need of help was still there. Alan McGlashan realised, as she did, that the problem which had so cruelly assaulted her as a young bride would never be resolved, and that although the work she had done on her own inner self with Jung's great English collaborator, Peter Baynes, had released energies in her indomitable spirit to contain the problem, the problem itself would be there to the end of her days. She was, in this regard, always a most moving kind of model of what life is really about. The more I had accompanied my mother on this inner journey, the more I had gone along the road towards discovery of her real self to which Jung had pointed me, the more I saw of the people who over the years came six days a week to me for help, the more did I realise that the value and meaning of life was deeply rooted in the fact that life itself was irrevocably problematical and committed utterly to the resolution of a problem implicit in creation itself. Life was, indeed, creation's answer to a problem posed to it by the conversion of chaos and darkness into light and order, and I felt that once the problem was resolved, inconceivable as it is rationally, something else would move in to take its place and that, too, would be problematical in a totally new dimension of creation. Problems were, could we but understand, our most precious possessions. They were the raw material of what was once called redemption. Without our problems there would be no redemption of being and no fulfilment of creation's seeking. Somewhere, therefore, there was a love of even our problems to be discovered and to serve in their transformation. We were all, through life, engaged, however minutely, in a problem of cosmic significance.

This was clear to me in my mother's love of what she felt was most creative in me, despite her own struggle with the shadow of the victim of creation that she was. She never lost sight of the potential of the creative in herself of which she had been deprived, and through that cared passionately for promoting my own creativity in me. That care focused essentially on my writing. As she drew near to her end, her concern for me did not diminish but grew more acute, and whenever I thought back on this increase of care on my own behalf, I realised how, in a sense, she and all who are the victims of a love which they may not experience subjectively, could achieve it objectively for others more

365

profoundly than they could have done if some act of grace had given it to themselves too.

When her end came, it came to her not through any specific illness but gently, as it does to those who have to move on because their journey in the here-and-now has reached its provisional destination. She had already been prepared for it by the way my stepfather had died, unafraid after his fashion, over a period of a year or so, not painfully, but, as it were, step by step down a ladder, a slight stroke being followed by others of increasing severity until, one lunchtime, he said he felt tired and had to go to bed. Once there he settled down peacefully, and his last words, important to me because they summed up my relationship with the 'Major John' he had always been to Roger and me, were: 'Don't forget to call me at four because Ingaret is on the radio.' I had hurried back from Italy to hold his hand as he died, a week later, but too late to hear him speak again.

Happily, when my mother's end came I was there to spend the last fortnight of her life constantly with her. I shall always be grateful that I was allowed this final privilege. I have never been able to follow the exhortation, hoary with age and centuries of repetition, that one must ready oneself by some sustained, conscious preparation for death. I have always felt that when the moment came, a moment of which we ourselves have had no personal and subjective experience, the answer would come out of life within us. The way my mother died was a tremendous vindication of my belief that whatever life hurls at us, no matter how cruel, how abrupt, how painful, it accompanies the assault with something which will not only overcome the hurt inflicted but also make it more worthwhile.

As I sat through those last hours with my mother, knowing that she was dying, I had no sense of the unexpected which comes to most of us when death overtakes somebody within our own circle of affections. Although, intellectually, all the world knows that just as they have been born so they will have to die, when death does strike in their vicinity they are emotionally always surprised and behave as if it were something which they had never expected. In my mother's end there was not only no element of surprise but a strange kind of logic of fulfilment and a sense of continuation. Death, I realised, seen from without, might appear sudden, brutal and final, but to someone in the process of dying, seen from within, it was another form of growth and expectation accompanied by a majesty that ennobled all its subjects impartially and left the seal of its order enmarbled in the still of their faces.

I remember taking an hour or two off at this time to go and see

Benjamin Britten, who had had a serious and ultimately ineffective heart operation within days of finishing his last opera, *Death in Venice*, and was still in hospital in London. He was devoted to my mother, who had been a most enthusiastic and ardent supporter of the games of tennis we played regularly over the years at the Red House in Aldeburgh in the ample summer afternoons, so full of light that even the generous sweep of sky in which East Anglia specialises could hardly contain it. He knew that my mother's end was approaching and asked after her most tenderly. I remember telling him that it was curious, the nearer the end came, how much less of an end it appeared to me and how daily I felt increasingly that I was witness to another form of growth and re-creation. He understood at once and just said: 'How like her to pass on such a feeling.'

On the last day of all she had a vision, a vision of Christ sitting at the end of her bed, and had a dialogue with the reality she personified in her vision. Of course I could only hear her side of it, but each step in the dialogue implied the invisible rung in the ladder which it provided for her. She would say something to the effect that she really could no longer carry the burden of the world in which she lived. There would be a pause in which she heard the answer, and she would reply: 'You really mean that? I can hand it all over to You?' And the answer was not only in the affirmative but added an ingredient that enabled her to say: 'It is really so much that you feel we should both now surrender it to God?' Again there was a pause and she gave a great sigh of relief and said: 'How wonderful. God – it is all over to You now.'

Great calm came over her. I had never seen her face more serene. She did not speak again and died in the early hours of the night that followed this afternoon. But in this feeling of her having been throughout involved in another process of growth, she rendered me perhaps the greatest of all her many services because it not only transcended the pain which her death caused me; it induced a kind of meaning which is greater than either happiness or unhappiness and which has enabled me to continue as if I am travelling on with her even more closely than when she was still living. Through it I came to realise how little of ourselves is limited to the here-and-now, how the greater part of ourselves is not contained or rationed in space and time, and that our greatest meaning lies in living the little as an all, beyond space and time, which, brief and brittle as it appears to be, makes now into forever.

Myself, at home in Aldeburgh, 1978.

37

Letting Things Happen

When I finally felt that I had earned the right to express myself once again through my writing, I found it quite impossible to return to the themes I had written about in the past. What now seemed to me most urgent was to reappraise my life as lucidly and simply as I could to show how the sequence of ordinary events that had befallen me had led me to devote nearly half of it, as a gifted amateur, to the care of human souls the Jungian way.

In the process of this reappraisal I realised that in working as a lay analyst I was not only justifying the terrible suffering which life had inflicted on my mother but was transforming this into an instrument, like some Geiger counter of the spirit, to uncover a vast field of magnetic and often angry new meaning massing in the human soul. I was responding to the Voice that has called to me at all sorts of intervals and moments over the years, and never more clearly than on that day when, at the age of twelve, I had stumbled out of the Vicarage study in a state of shock, bitterness and utter disillusionment. Without realising it at the time, this was the signpost pointing in the direction of the road along which I could learn precisely how to distinguish between what was God's and what was man's, and also discover how what was God's could also be rendered to man. Over the greatest of all temples to Apollo in ancient Greece there is written in large letters of gold: 'Man, know thyself', and to this command from the world of Apollo was joined my own experience of the Voice: 'Called or not called, God shall be there'.

These three elements formed one immense trinity of meaning for me that matured steadily through the post-war years leaving me, finally, at the point where I started this account not just of my life but of the life of the age which has shaped my own, knowing that the most urgent task of our time is to know ourselves in the human way; to realise that although the Lord's Prayer begins with the words 'Thy will be done',

God's will cannot be done on earth as it should be done until we know ourselves as He knows us. It is in the hope that I might perhaps have assisted in the cause of promoting self-knowledge and, through it, the wholeness of the individual, that I have found something in life for which not only I, but my mother, and all those who preceded us, had been born. I have found the freedom and ease of spirit that is, at the end of the night and beginning of the day, an allotment according to my need of the peace that passes human understanding.

If this sounds too large and complacent a claim, I would hasten to add that it is a sense of peace which does not eliminate regret but is heightened by my acknowledgment of failures and my own share of human fallibilities. I often wish, for instance, that I could have started sooner on the road and travelled further, but I could not because the waymarks depended on what happened to me in life. Without the happenings I have recorded here, first to my mother and then to myself and to all the other people who made up the vanished world of my childhood and youth, often anonymous and with a quality unrecognised by the world, I would have had no hint of ultimate direction and insufficient resources for the sort of transformation and transfiguration of events which gives one's life its meaning. In the end I could only do what life spontaneously, out of itself, put in my way and the power invested in me made possible. There were no wilful contrivances or substitutes or carefully cultivated experiences that could have taken their place. In that respect I am comforted that I have never resisted what came spontaneously to me out of life and time. However bitter and however great my resentments at certain points along the way, on balance I have always trusted in whatever happened to me, and through that trust I have found the signposts I needed.

Almost an infinity of happenings inspired me to follow, and try to get others to follow, a way that would lead to the totality and the wholeness which Jung called individuation. Significantly, the highest forms of courage I encountered on my journey were not to be found in some wartime spectacular but were enacted by ordinary people such as the indomitable chimneysweep whom I often accompanied in my air-raid-warden duties during the worst bombing of London. When I think of him, my faith in human kind is kindled into a burst of flame, as well as anger that he and millions of others, with all this and more in their being, have so little asked of them in so-called times of peace. I remember with shame how I had to watch this man drinking himself to death after the war because he was not allowed to give of his own individual worth in the way he knew best. The origin of war did not, I decided then, lie in some special compartment of the human spirit marked 'masculine aggression', but in the general failure and cowardice of civilian life to release the totality of our specific natures, unbridled and free, to express themselves as life had intended.

Through the years of my lay practice I saw some hundreds of unknown, ordinary people who, caught in a peace-time routine of arid repetition, were brave enough to shave, wash and dress to face another empty and meaningless day. It is the courage and endurance of such people on which, ultimately, human survival depends, and it is they who are the reason for my abiding regret that I did not start my analytical work sooner and so achieve more.

And finally, there is an unfulfilled aspect of my own life with which I have had to deal as a woman and which can still return to haunt me on calm summer evenings when the voice of the day has already vanished over the rim, like some kind of phosphorescent question-mark in the dark: should I not have done better if I had had children of my own? I have been married twice and yet I have had no children. Was that not a contradiction of my faith and all that I have said about totality and wholeness and letting nature have its spontaneous way with us all? I do not even now know how to answer this question, except to say that I intuitively anticipated the answer and left life the task of answering it for me. I never tried *not* to have children, and I am therefore inclined to feel that whatever was in charge of this finely woven pattern of my life would have seen to it that I had done so if children had been necessary for what I was called upon to do. I often think of one of the last conversations I had with Toni Wolff, Jung's closest collaborator, when we discussed the special typology of women with which she added to the general typology of man outlined by Jung in his book *Psychological Types*.

Toni Wolff held the view that women were also subject in their individuality to the laws of typology which Jung had sketched for men, and that they tended to be born of four different kinds. First, there was the woman born to be a wife and mother, charged with the upbringing of children and the care of her husband. Secondly, there was what Toni Wolff called the 'Amazonian' type, using the term not in the archaic sense but to describe a woman who was born to play a role in the world once reserved uniquely for men, and who has a place and a career of her own even though it puts her in competition with them. The third type was a woman who, although of a sex generally endowed with greater intuition than men, was far more intuitive than was normal even for women, and so, being filled with a sense of the infinite potential of

371

the future, served the 'not yet' in the 'here-and-now'. The fourth type of woman in Toni Wolff's thesis was born to be a companion and enable her partner/s to renew themselves and be more productive and creative than they could ever have been without her. She said that one had to be careful not to use these two forms of typology dogmatically but rather to view them as signposts, and she wondered whether the signs did not point to myself as falling into the fourth category.

Reflecting on her words today, I find it significant that, in all my years of working with people, I never had a sense of personal achievement when my analytical efforts were rewarded with success. I always felt as if something else, working through me, had effected what we all in the beginning, before we know better, call 'the cure'. Far from feeling exultant in those moments of breakthrough, I found myself humbled and overawed and deeply moved. It was as if life, by working through me, had been given to others who until then had seemed of the living, individual dead, buried in the increasingly collective existence of our time. Similarly, in helping my patients to understand the significance of their dreams, I was never tempted to lead, or direct them, but wanted, with a strange passion, only to produce the dream and its meaning whole in them. When, finally, they arrived through the dreaming process at the moment of illumination on their own inner road to Damascus, and I was possessed by a sense of having delivered, in terms of my contract with life, it is possible that I came near to experiencing what a woman feels when she has given birth to a child.

Through such feelings and intimations I have found consolation for my own state of childlessness, and the conviction has grown in me that, in life, there is provision for the mother in woman to fulfil itself in more ways than one; that whatever the prime importance of having children the straightforward, physical way, there is need and room for this instinct to reach out into many invisible areas of the human spirit on which creation and the renewal of societies depend, in order to help the future to be delivered and born in a greater way than all our yesterdays combined. Over the years I have come to believe that, if I had had children of my own, I would not have been able to help in this process of the birth of increasing creation. Indeed, in not having children perhaps I have been singularly blessed, and through that perhaps, too, something has been added to the measure of peace with which I have come to face the future: all regret vanquished and hope moving into the place of fear of tomorrow, secure in the certainty that this way of letting things happen, which has brought me so far, will not fail me with the appropriate happening at the end.

Index